MORTAL DOUBT

MORTAL DOUBT

TRANSNATIONAL GANGS AND
SOCIAL ORDER IN GUATEMALA CITY

Anthony W. Fontes

 UNIVERSITY OF CALIFORNIA PRESS

University of California Press, one of the most distinguished
university presses in the United States, enriches lives around
the world by advancing scholarship in the humanities, social
sciences, and natural sciences. Its activities are supported by
the UC Press Foundation and by philanthropic contributions
from individuals and institutions. For more information, visit
www.ucpress.edu.

University of California Press
Oakland, California

Library of Congress Cataloging-in-Publication Data

Names: Fontes, Anthony W., author.
Title: Mortal doubt : transnational gangs and social order in
    Guatemala City / Anthony W. Fontes.
Description: Oakland, California : University of California
    Press, [2018] | Series: Atelier: ethnographic inquiry in the
    twenty-first century ; 1 | Includes bibliographical references
    and index. |
Identifiers: LCCN 2018014806 (print) | LCCN 2018018645
    (ebook) | ISBN 9780520969599 (ebook) |
    ISBN 9780520297081 (cloth : alk. paper) |
    ISBN 9780520297098 (pbk. : alk. paper)
Subjects: LCSH: Gangs—Guatemala—Guatemala. |
    Violence—Guatemala—Guatemala. | Guatemala
    (Guatemala)—Social conditions.
Classification: LCC HV6439.G92 (ebook) | LCC HV6439.G92 F66
    2018 (print) | DDC 364.106/60972811—dc23
LC record available at https://lccn.loc.gov/2018014806

Manufactured in the United States of America

26   25   24   23   22   21   20   19   18
10   9   8   7   6   5   4   3   2   1

For Gwendolyn, Norah, and Audrey Alabama

They think they can burn the devil out, but wouldn't that mean setting fire to the whole world?

—Juande, former member of the Mara Salvatrucha, Pavón prison, Guatemala

CONTENTS

ILLUSTRATIONS

MAPS

Introduction

Conocereis la verdad y la verdad os hara libres.
(You will know the truth, and the truth will set you free.)
—graffiti, isolation block, Pavón prison, Guatemala City

Maras, transnational gangs, took root in Central America in the early 1990s, just as the region's Cold War conflicts were ending. At the time they were little more than disorganized groups of youths imitating Latino gangs born in Los Angeles, vying for turf in cities struggling to recover from authoritarian rule. Over the years, however, they have evolved into brutal organizations engaged in extortion, contract killings, and the drug trade. Feuds between Barrio18 and the Mara Salvatrucha (MS), the two most powerful maras in Central America, have helped to turn the region into the deadliest noncombat zone in the world.[1] At the same time, maras and *mareros* (gangsters), with their penchant for conspicuous tattoos and audacious violence, have become archetypal symbols of all that has gone wrong in Central America.

I arrived in Guatemala City in 2010 to begin field research that I hoped would penetrate the haze of fear and fantasy swirling about the maras.[2] Along with other cities in the Northern Triangle (Guatemala, El Salvador, and Honduras), this metropolis of some seven million citizens has suffered from the gang phenomenon, in its poor neighborhoods and sprawling suburbs, as well as in the nation's overcrowded prison system.[3] And in this city—as in other cities across the region—the rise of the maras has been concomitant with the onset of a new kind of insecurity. This is not the overtly political and ethnic violence of prior epochs. Today, Guatemala City is a time and place dominated by both the fact and the fear of out-of-control crime.[4]

Following the signing of peace accords in 1996, the nation's homicide rate climbed to 40 per 100,000, the fifth highest in the world, and between 2000 and 2008 Guatemala City's homicide rate doubled, with the numbers climbing to as high as 60 per 100,000.[5] In the city's "red zones"—poor, insecure neighborhoods often dominated by gangs or other criminal groups—security officials claim that homicide rates have shot up to over 190 per 100,000.

But in a sense, such body counts obscure more than they reveal. As hard and fast as these numbers may seem, what makes this violence so terrifying for so many is its profound uncertainty. Fewer than 5 percent of violent crimes ever make it to trial, making Guatemala a great place to commit murder.[6] Forces of order and disorder often make distorted reflections of each other.[7] At best the law appears helpless and at worst complicit, making the list of usual suspects in every murder, extortion, and robbery long and poorly defined. Police regularly exchange places with the narco-traffickers, kidnapping rings, gangs, and other criminal groups they are meant to arrest. Massacre, torture, and dismemberment are also popular techniques to make murder register far and wide. The cacophony of public reaction—sensationalist media reporting, politicians' grandstanding, the rumors coursing through violence-stricken communities—warps the fear into every realm of public life.

With so many murders left unsolved and unpunished, overwhelming doubt haunts collective perceptions of danger and mires every avenue of investigation.[8] As a veteran homicide investigator with the National Civil Police told me, "A death may occur for a failure to pay extortion. A death, well, may occur because of a drug-related settling of accounts and have nothing to do with the gangs. And that's all one can say." From behind his cluttered desk, he fixed me with an incongruous grin. "You might die because your brother got caught up with the maras. Who can say with more specificity? There are many acts that have such consequences."

Such extreme levels of violence, arising from such inscrutable sources, cast long shadows over Guatemala City. Violence and its terror dictate how city residents think and live. People cast about for ways of understanding what has become a "war without sense."[9] These struggles to make sense of senselessness, to draw meaning and certainty out of cycles of violence that refuse to be fixed in time and place, converge upon the figure of the marero. Actors of all kinds draw on him to make meaning in political discourse, newspaper and TV headlines, casual conversation and rumors, and daydreams and nightmares. For Guatemalans from all walks of life, this figure has come to personify all the wounds and illnesses of the struggling social body. Thrust into the public imagination, the symbolic power of the marero fuses everyday violence taking place in gang territories and other insecure spaces to the making of social and political perspectives dictating life across the city, the nation, and beyond.[10]

These brash vehicles of violence and emissaries of peacetime chaos have become absolutely essential to the making of a certain kind of order. Maras form a vital node, a flashpoint, in which overwhelming violence and fear circulating throughout the social body come into stark relief.[11] They are, in a sense, a way for people to know violence and its terror, or at least a way of providing a discernible form to the endless unknowns that make life under such conditions so terrifying. They have become a means of rendering the illegible legible, of imposing a sense of finitude and control on out-of-control insecurity. They have become the answer when no answers are enough. In a world that always appears to be coming undone, the maras play a pivotal role in holding it together. What's more, such meaning making is by no means isolated from the ongoing destruction of bodies, lives, and communities it is meant to keep at bay.[12] Efforts to explain and make sense of this kind of violence have knock-on effects that are absolutely pivotal to its perpetual cycles.

Tracing the maras' footsteps, this book tracks the deadly play among out-of-control predation, overwhelming uncertainty, and desperate struggles to carve a sense of certainty back into the world. Through stories and perspectives collected from Guatemalan gangsters and ex-gangsters, police and prisoners, journalists and taxi drivers, judges, human rights activists, and narco-traffickers, among many others, this book explores the histories, spaces, businesses, and violent spectacles through which the mara phenomenon has evolved. Of course the maras are not the problem, and the problem does not begin or end with them. They have been forged through relationships of exchange that collapse the deceptive divides between the local and the global, the state and its underworld, the innocent and the guilty, and so forth. By tracing the endless enmeshing of the imagining and the making of the world, I show how the maras' flesh and blood violence is indissoluble from their symbolic power in social imaginaries and how they provide cover for a host of actors feeding and feeding off peacetime insecurity.[13] To this end, the marero who walks the streets and the marero infesting strung-out imaginations blend and merge in ways that cannot be drawn apart. This doubled figure, in turn, provides a lens through which to witness the making and mooring of collective terror in Guatemala City and beyond.

ORDERS OF VIOLENCE, PAST AND PRESENT

How deep must one dig to uncover the roots of Guatemala's extreme peacetime violence, or for that matter, the roots of any contemporary catastrophe? The question begs an answer of infinite breadth and complexity far beyond the scope of any single book. But a story has to start somewhere, and in understanding how the maras were made and what they mean, the legacies of Cold War atrocities are both crucial and inescapable.[14] This history is particularly visible in the historic zone of Guatemala City, where activists continue to struggle to keep memories of the military's atrocities alive. They have posted images of the civil war dead and disappeared everywhere. These black-and-white portraits are plastered on car park walls, facades of buildings, and above the bars of certain cantinas. Many of them are Mayan villagers—men, women, and children—massacred in the highlands during military scorched-earth campaigns. Today they are called victims of genocide.[15] They are also trade unionists, students, journalists, and other "subversives" disappeared by the police, tortured by the military, and executed without ceremony.[16] A few are celebrated as martyrs, their memory sanctified in museums and scattered rituals of public mourning.

These faces are, without exception, solemn. They are reproduced from national ID cards, or in many cases from the archives of the police who kidnapped them. Their suffering, inflicted with considerable support from the United States, and the bitter disappointments of postwar progress, imbue these images with powerful emotional and political valence. They accuse, they plead, they condemn. Most of the bodies of massacre victims remain in mass graves in the mountains, bones woven and swirled together, picked apart by families and forensic anthropologists still searching for justice.[17]

As for the disappeared, some ended up interred in secret on military bases and in anonymous graves in city cemeteries.[18] State security forces discarded others like trash. At the height of the conflict, hundreds of bodies a month were dumped in the *barrancos*, steep ravines that cut through Guatemala City. Few were recovered by loved ones. Openly mourning these dead would only attract government suspicion. Public reaction to the government's campaign of urban terror remained quiet, muted by an "existential uncertainty."[19] There were few public venues within Guatemala where accusations or even inquiries could safely be made. There were plenty of rumors whispered fearfully among friends and loved ones, but nowhere for them to register in the public sphere.

FIGURE 1. Portraits of the disappeared plastered around zone 1 of Guatemala City.

In 1984 human rights organizations and victims' families finally confronted Defense Minister Mejia Victores, demanding to be told the whereabouts of the disappeared. Mejia Victores is said to have responded, "Disappeared? There are no disappeared—those people probably migrated to the United States to find work, or died in the 1976 earthquake."[20]

More than thirty years later, of the roughly forty-five-thousand men and women disappeared during the civil war, the bones of only a few have been identified and returned to their people.[21] For the rest, it is the car park wall, the bar bathroom, the stained sidewalk, and empty reliquaries in the homes of their families.

The legions of *desaparecidos* haunt the postwar order.[22] Lingering uncertainty over their fate steals the possibility of peace for those they left behind. "Disappearance is even more cruel than public assassination," writes Edelberto Torres Rivas, "since it raises the perception of danger by placing it in an imaginary world, unsure but probable, created by the possibility that the disappeared person is alive. While one suspects that the disappeared person may be dead, nobody knows the truth. Doubt, prolonged over time, is a highly productive way of sowing fear."[23] During the Cold War, counterinsurgent terror provoked and preserved collective doubt through the "sacred currency" of silence.[24] Such strategies proved highly effective.[25] With political, logistical, and sometimes financial support from the United States, military-backed dictatorships across Latin America destroyed progressive social movements and armed groups struggling to reform their societies from below, virtually ensuring that the causes for which they fought would remain pipe dreams in the era of so-called peace.[26]

Today, doubt about violence is still a basic fact of everyday life in Guatemala City. However, something has changed radically. Violence and its suffering move through the social body in ways altogether different from civil war atrocities. The most obvious distinction is this: in place of silence, a dissonant chorus greets peacetime brutality, screaming accusation, seeking to blame, determined to name the source of so much murder and suffering. Each act of violence that infiltrates the public sphere is immediately embroiled in the chaos of postwar political maneuvering for power and influence. Guatemalan politicians from across the spectrum blame their adversaries' policies for creating the conditions giving rise to so much murder. Researchers, activists, analysts, and journalists seek to describe, often in minute detail, how and why this violence is happening. International donors and organizations—the United States, the United Nations—make endless prescriptions for diminishing it.[27] The litany of voices rising up in response to contemporary violence creates a distinct kind of confusion. But these voices are no less paralyzing than was the past's profuse silence.

Such intense and fearful uncertainties about criminal violence help to push concerns over past injustices, no matter how grievous, into the background. In Guatemala City, the collective experience of living with violent crime has given rise to widespread nostalgia for what is remembered as the ordered violence of civil war. This nostalgia is certainly not universal. "Things are certainly better now," said Mario Polanco, longtime human rights activist and executive director of Grupo de Apoyo Mutuo (GAM), when I asked him to compare the terror of the past with that of the present. "Back then, you could be disappeared simply for owning a copy of Gabriel García Márquez's *100 Years of Solitude*. I had a copy that I would have to cover with newspaper so it wouldn't be seen on the bus. Now you have the freedom to think and say what you want."[28]

For most residents of Guatemala City, however, the freedom of thought and expression they have gained does not appear as important as the sense of security they sense they have lost. Today, among urban residents the dominant sentiment regarding the wartime past is that "in those days at least you knew if you stayed out of politics you could avoid trouble." Without the ideological, class, and ethnic categories defining who might be a likely target of counter-insurgent state brutality, the logic goes, the violence of Guatemalan society has become unhinged. Even if nostalgia for wartime terror is driven by distorted reckonings of the ever-receding golden past (as so much nostalgia is), such longing still exposes how unstable the present has become.[29] Peacetime violence has been freed from the narrow constraints of revolution and counterrevolution, making potential prey out of those who once imagined themselves safe, and every new murder becomes a hotbed for rumor and supposition, another reason to feel vulnerable.

What Maras Mean

The institutional and existential chaos of Guatemala's postwar order requires a standard-bearer capable of containing the collective confusion, rage, and despair. In their brash celebrations of brutality and the place they have come to occupy in the public imagination, the maras fit the bill.[30] Over the last thirty years, across the Northern Triangle of Central America they have become public enemy number 1, emerging as packed and contradictory symbols of violence driven by seemingly new faces and forces, yet still haunted by the ghosts of Cold War and even colonial atrocities.[31] This role is spectacularly overdetermined. Playing so perfectly to such a wide array of collective fears, the maras have come to represent "an almost incomprehensibly dark reality," emerging as the erstwhile emissaries of all the failures of peacetime progress to heal the wounds of war and find a path toward collective prosperity.[32] And so, investigating the making of the maras is a means of probing the spaces, circuits, and discourses—the worlds—out of which they emerge and which they cannot help but forge.[33]

The maras have come to represent a world unhinged by fear and violence, both past and present. The gangs are symbolic figures through which politicians, scholars, and others link the revolutionary past with the insecure present, and their violence becomes coded as a legacy and inheritance of civil war. In this sense, the MS and Barrio18 replace the Marxist guerrillas of another age as foot soldiers of the "new urban insurgency"[34] fighting in the "slum wars of the 21st century."[35] This rendering is dangerous in its own right, because it imputes a coherent politics to gang violence that it simply does not have, while opening the door to right-wing politicians' calls to remilitarize society in defense against the insurgent threat.[36] In El Salvador, Elana Zilberg highlights this confused play between past and present, showing how a veritable "hall of mirrors" turns contemporary conceptions of the maras into "double faced" reflections of a host of Cold War killers.[37]

Some scholars have tied the rapid spread of gang culture to deep socioeconomic inequalities.[38] While absolute levels of urban poverty are not significantly greater than in prior epochs, widespread access to globalized media has made poor youths keenly aware of their position on the proverbial totem pole. Gang membership can provide a "pathway to manhood" for ambitious youths with few options of finding dignified, licit employment.[39] Children growing up in poor urban neighborhoods have plenty of other reasons to join gangs: for self-protection, for revenge, to make money, to become desirable, to gain a sense of belonging, to survive.[40]

Likewise, the circulation of symbols, language, and imagery traveling via migrant bodies, Hollywood films, and the internet has also contributed to the gangs' allure for poor youth. Gangs are said to be products of a globalized consumer society and its inherent brand name fetishism. As Donna Decesare writes of gangs in El Salvador, "[K]ids desperate for 'real' Nike kicks will spend a family's whole remittance check, sell crack, or steal to buy them. Acquiring style is costly and requires some effort. Clearly, poverty is not the only thing drawing . . . youth into gangs."[41]

Popular opinions of what maras are and why they do what they do both interweave with and diverge from scholarly analyses, running the gamut of psychological, spiritual, social, and historical explanations. The notion that gangs are the inheritance of civil war, for one, is widely shared, prompting a taxi driver to tell me, "These gangs do the same thing to poor people as the guerrilla once did!" We spoke as he maneuvered his beat-up taxi through the early morning Guatemala City traffic. "All they do is extort and brainwash the people for their own destruction."

Or, as a truck driver who had served in the military toward the end of the civil war declared, "I know exactly how to take care of these maras. The same way we took care of the guerrilla. Give me 10 platoons of *kaibiles* armed to the teeth, and we'll clean them all out street by street, neighborhood by neighborhood."[42]

I asked him how he and his platoons would identify the enemy. "Just ask the people," he yelled over the grinding engine. "Everyone knows. Just ask someone who is not afraid to say."

Indeed, "everyone" knows, or pretends to. Experts and laypeople, politicians and pundits all seem to have an explanation of the why and wherefore of the maras.[43] Gangs are a deep-throated articulation of profound *odia y envidia*—hatred and envy—coursing through Guatemalan society.[44] Gang members are "like sex addicts, but addicted to killing," as a Salvadoran crime reporter declared at a meeting of police and nongovernmental organizations (NGOs) to discuss peaceful crime prevention. Another taxi driver repeated the common refrain that mareros "worship the devil and the Santa Muerte—they have given their souls to the Beast (*La Bestia*)."[45] An evangelical gang pastor ministering to a violent suburb of Guatemala City put it slightly more subtly. "The nights are worse," he said as he excused himself from our interview to return to his neighborhood. He laughed bitterly. "This is like Alcoholics Anonymous. They need a twelve-step program to stop from killing. Constant supervision, constant intervention, because killing is all they know."

The maras are also an *answer* to the conundrums facing vulnerable urban youth in search of protection. "When a drunken father comes home and beats a kid's mom and molests the kid's sister," said longtime youth advocate Emilio Goubaud, "and the boy tries to fight back and gets kicked in the stomach, the gangster is across the street. He offers the child a toke of his joint, and smiles at him. 'The whole world is shit,' he says. 'The only thing to do about it is to have more power. You want to fight your father? Here, take this gun. Fuck that bitch. He deserves to die. Welcome to *la vida loca*.'"[46]

For some, the maras' willingness to kill and die has made them useful mercenaries following the orders of higher powers—doing the dirty work of corrupt police, who in turn take orders from politicians, organized crime, and the rich elite intent on maintaining the status quo. For others, gangs are simply an ugly expression of a collective fall from grace and loss of traditional values. I asked Walter Villatoro, a well-respected criminal circuit court judge, why maras had become so violent. "Aha," he thundered, pounding his desk. "I will tell you! We have become rotten from the beginning. It starts with Caesarean sections, the separation of child from mother, feeding newborns animal milk, and leaving them alone in their cribs. The gangs are the vomit of a sick society."[47]

Like savage "Others" raised up through history and across cultures, the maras' image enshrouds and eclipses the complex structural and historical forces that make the catastrophic present so deeply uncertain. They have become another justification for savagery in the name of the law and order

FIGURE 2. Marero in isolation lockdown, Canada prison, Escuintla, Guatemala.

promised by so-called civilization.[48] They are foot soldiers in a vague and dystopian civil war. They are inhuman and unfeeling killers who do not fear death. They are youth trying to protect themselves, or maybe just to get some style. They are boys struggling to become men, parasites feeding off collective fear, by-products of consumer capitalism, and souls lost along a path blazing into an ungodly future.[49] In twenty-first-century Guatemala City, the incessant meanings made of the maras and "their" violence are as contradictory and contingent as the disordered order they represent. And taken together, the countless interpretations of what the maras are and what they mean make them into something else entirely: a kaleidoscopic looking glass through which the catastrophic present forms and dissolves and reforms in infinite, inscrutable patterns. Once again, it is "through a glass, darkly."[50]

EXPLAINING VIOLENCE IN THE NORTHERN TRIANGLE

Postwar Guatemala City is not alone in being dominated by what Hannah Arendt would call the "all-pervading unpredictability" of violence.[51] In the

MAP I. Northern Triangle of Central America. Source: Based on a United Nations map of Guatemala, https://commons.wikimedia.org/wiki/File:Guatemala_location_map.svg.

contemporary world, such spaces are legion.[52] Since the end of the Cold War the "democratic wave" and the triumph of market fundamentalism have been accompanied by a "gradual erasure of received lines between the informal and the illegal, regulation and irregularity, order and organized lawlessness."[53] In this era marked by renewed ambiguity and increased uncertainty, Latin

American societies in particular have witnessed an unprecedented increase in criminal violence carried out by a revolving cast of shadowy actors.[54]

Nowhere are such ambiguities of power and legitimacy more pronounced than in the Northern Triangle of Central America.[55] The array of local, national, and regional factors creating the conditions for out-of-control violence in Central America today is dizzying in its variety. It includes, to quote just one World Bank study, "rapid urbanization, persistent poverty and inequality, social exclusion, political violence, organized crime, post-conflict cultures, the emergence of illegal drug use and trafficking, and authoritarian family structures."[56] Likewise, the causes and conditions giving rise to peacetime crime across the region are virtually endless.[57] However, for those who must live and die with the brutal specters haunting urban life, such explanations do not explain much. In fact, the act of pinning down this violence to a discrete set of causes and conditions imposes a false sense of certainty that is itself another kind of violence. It offers a sense of assurance that can only be upheld by the security of distance. When we close that distance, the utility of such easy answers evaporates.

Perhaps this is why the most nuanced scholarship on the region's struggle with insecurity has long been riddled with doubt. In neighboring El Salvador, Ellen Moodie uses the term *unknowing* to capture how those living in the midst of postwar violence struggle with the uncertainties of everyday crime and insecurity and recall the ordered violence of war with fitful nostalgia.[58] For Honduras, Jon Horne Carter flags how silence and elision—leaving the violent realities of everyday life "unsaid"—has become a collective survival strategy for residents of insecure zones of Tegucigalpa.[59] For postconflict Guatemala, Linda Green demonstrates how fearful silence surrounds survivors' memories of civil war atrocity,[60] and Diane Nelson hones in on how life for the poor and marginalized is a struggle with duplicity—a sense of being repeatedly "duped"—by the failed promises of a failed revolution, by two-faced politicians in the present, and by the postwar order itself.[61] These analyses focus on the production of and struggle with uncertainty through discourse, anchored in what Michael Taussig might call the "epistemic murk"[62] of life in the midst of extreme violence and precarity.[63]

By honing in on the synthesis of symbolic meanings and their expressions in the physical world, I go through and beyond the discursive and epistemic to draw out the destabilizing psychological, emotional, and visceral impacts of living with the specter of extreme peacetime violence. My approach begins with the observation that the doubt at work here is not merely cognitive, but a structure of feeling that is woven into the built environment and etched upon the body.[64] It is as concrete as the prison walls that fail to quarantine criminals, as sharp as the razor wire slicing through city space, and as visceral as a palpitating heart. And since death is a daily risk, the doubt I am talking about cuts to the quick. This is *mortal* doubt. I mean mortal in two distinct senses. First, it is corporeal and embedded in the flesh; second, it holds within it questions that run the gamut between life and death and thus open onto crises of existential proportions. Such doubt sets the conditions for the confused traffic between terror and the array of reactions people employ to metabolize, confront, and make sense of it. Living with relentless encounters, both real and imagined, with the specter of violent pain and death means engaging in constant calculations and using vague variables to assess the risks of walking out one's door each day. The stakes are ultimately life itself, but they are also the existential and ethical foundations we use to order, make sense of, and live with what counts as reality. These foundations are physical and psychological: the sanctity of the human body, for example, or the perception of certain spaces as safe and others as unsafe. They are institutional: the state and its underworld, the prison walls that separate the incarcerated from the free. And they are ethical and existential, organizing how we think and act: truth and fiction, good and evil, structure and agency, guilt and innocence, life and death. Even under the most secure circumstances, such distinctions are far less clear-cut than common sense would have them be. After all, order and certainty are always built on shaky foundations, always falling apart and being built back up again. And life lived with profound doubt over the terms of everyday survival exposes just how false and fading these apparent foundations can be.

Given these circumstances, one is tempted to deride the certainties derived through the marero as fraudulent and deceitful, mere symptoms of "false consciousness" obscuring the relations of domination and exploitation defining contemporary social orders.[65] Indeed, one of the reasons I wrote this book was to expose the clumsy charades that hide the physical and structural violence of Guatemalan (and global) society behind the tattooed mask of the marero.[66] The point, however, is *not* to label the ways people make sense of violence and insecurity as either true or false, accurate or mistaken. The point is that in this never-ending search for certainty, truth and falsehood matter far less than how the meanings made of the maras induce individuals, communities, and institutions to act in certain ways. That is, symbolic renderings of the marero have material effects that impact the making of the world, which in turn feed into how people imagine the maras and the violence they represent, and so forth. Caught up in the loops and feedback effects that synthesize the material and symbolic in the messy construction of reality, this meaning making weaves through the social fabric, becomes embedded in the urban landscape, and is pressed into the struggle for power and profit in myriad ways.[67] In this sense, the maras form a key site upon which competing projects to control, order, and dominate Guatemalan society are exposed in all their violent contradictions.

The structure of the book reflects how the promiscuous play between the material and symbolic shapes the struggle for certainty at multiple scales and in divers spaces. Part 1, "Truths and Fictions," maps the synthesis of material and symbolic histories in shaping mareros' lives and collective history. Part 2, "Worlds and Underworlds," expands out from the maras into the prison system and the city to show how myriad actors—the state, private businesses, and military men, among others—feed and feed off the struggle to impose order on peacetime violence. Finally, part 3, "Spectacle, Structure, and Agency," explores how the spectacle of gang violence is produced and consumed on national and global scales, making accomplices of distant bystanders and undermining the very possibility of innocence for any of us.

I have written the helter-skelter chains of meaning and material effects into the arc of each chapter. Fantasy and reality weave together in ways that cannot always be pulled apart. However, since giving up on explanation altogether would only lead to losing the thread, I have tried to strike a precarious balance. The chapters conscientiously frame key aspects of the mara phenomenon and peacetime violence in order to guide readers along. These are the bones of the book. In between are the sinews and ligaments. These are short narrative fragments that offer neither analytical frameworks nor attempts at explanation. These narratives perform the entanglement of truths and fictions that is so integral to how meaning is made from and by the maras. They are meant to draw readers directly into the spaces, relationships, and acts of meaning making upon which this book is based.[68] One cannot carry out such research and expect to get out clean, so they also expose the destabilizing ethical encounters that define ethnographic research in the midst of so much violent uncertainty. Altogether, this structure is meant to guide readers into the confused struggle to draw order out of chaos, wherein readers are free to get lost.

In 2010, when I first landed in Guatemala City, I thought I had come to seek out the "real" marero. That is, I was determined to get as deep as I could into gang networks and tell "authentic" stories from the perspective of gang-involved youth.[69] I dreamed of embedding myself in a gang, as the anthropologist Dennis Rodgers had done in Managua, Nicaragua, a decade earlier.[70] In retrospect, my naïveté and oh-so-gringo hubris were breathtaking. I did, however, manage to make inroads toward my initial goal by linking up with evangelical and secular gang rehabilitation programs based around Guatemala City. Through these groups I became acquainted with a coterie of ex-gang peace workers—former gang members and gang associates cum social workers and pastors—who leveraged their experience in the streets into efforts at "rescuing" gang youth. My relationships with these men and women gave me access to prisons and a few neighborhoods where gangs operated.

Very quickly, however, I gave up on the fantasy of becoming embedded in a gang clique. The situation on the street was far more volatile than I had expected. One tell-tale sign was the failure of gang rehab programs to "save" more than a tiny fraction of the youth they served. For example, in one job-skills training program, funded partly by the US Agency for International Development (USAID), nine out of ten participants dropped out or disappeared before completion, many of them killed by police, rivals, or even their old gangs.

What's more, while I could gain permission from gang leaders to enter this or that neighborhood on an ad hoc basis, establishing a working relationship with an active gang clique seemed riskier than was worthwhile. The year before I arrived in Guatemala, Christian Poveda, a French filmmaker who had made a documentary about Barrio18 in El Salvador, was gunned down under mysterious circumstances.[71] He had lived and worked with a Barrio18 clique in San Salvador for more than a year and clearly believed he had earned the trust of the very mareros blamed for his murder. His death made international headlines, but typically, no firm explanation ever surfaced. There were plenty of rumors, however.

My friend Gato, a former gang member and social worker in Guatemala City, had worked with Poveda. He told me the filmmaker was murdered for

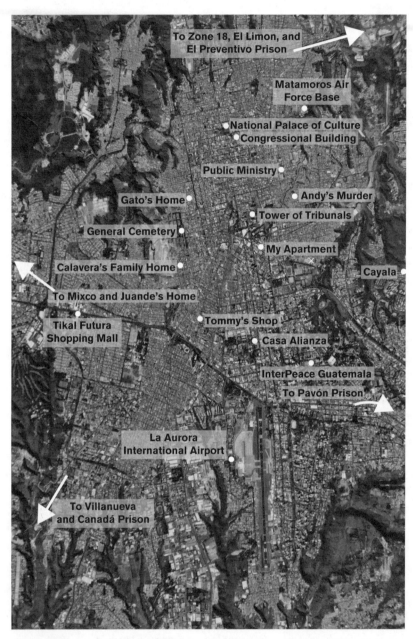

MAP 2. Guatemala City. Image courtesy of the Earth Science and Remote Sensing Unit, NASA Johnson Space Center. NASA photo ID: ISS022-E-86851. http://eol.jsc.nasa.gov.

having betrayed the gang by failing to follow through on promises to provide a portion of the proceeds garnered from the film. "You don't make promises to the mara that you're not sure you can keep," he said. A Salvadoran journalist claimed that pirated copies of the film had made it to El Salvador, exposing the clique to police scrutiny, and that was why they killed Poveda. Others were convinced it was in fact Salvadoran security forces that killed the filmmaker, in order to further demonize the maras.

Whatever the truth, it was rumors such as these swirling about the maras—and about so much of the violence taking place in Guatemala and across the region—that helped to instill in me an inescapable fear. Each time I walked out my door into my relatively tranquil neighborhood in Guatemala City, I would scan the street for anyone "suspicious." Coming home late at night, every figure silhouetted by the streetlights was a potential thief, murderer, or kidnapper. Of course the real predators would never stand beneath street lamps. And so in vain I stared into the shadows too, and saw things there that were not. I made constant calculations using variables of my own invention to judge which route was "safer" than another, which corner store (*tiendita*) less likely to be marked by thieves, which taxi driver more trustworthy than the next. It was an absurd game of probability without any rules or hard numbers at all, upon which I daily staked my well-being, and perhaps my life.

I was certainly not alone in this charade of creeping paranoia and false assurances. Politicians, the press, law enforcement, and the general populace all feed and feed upon such fearful doubt, and this helps to make any study of criminal violence an exploration of half-truths, unverifiable data, and rumors floating in and out of focus. While homicide counts are easy to come by, the kind of information that really matters—who is being killed and why, for example—is not.[72] "It has become impossible to know who is killing and why because it is always changing," said the chief prosecutor of Villa Nueva, a sprawling suburb of Guatemala City. "We cannot differentiate between maras, narcotraffickers, and other organized criminal groups."[73]

Given the immeasurable difficulties of investigating crime in postwar Guatemala, a retreat to cold numbers is not surprising. There are dead bodies in the street; some have been tortured, and many of them have tattoos. Too often these are the only material facts available. Almost everything else is hearsay, including much of the "data" produced by state offices and NGOs.[74] So everyone is subject to a "regime of rumor" under which "everything becomes patchwork; an infrastructure of hidden bricolage floats to social

FIGURE 3. Former Barrio18 member in his quarters in Canada prison, Escuintla, Guatemala. Notice the dolls he keeps for family visits and his self-portrait with his four-year-old daughter.

consciousness like a submerged, stitched together body."[75] And nowhere is the power of rumor more influential than inside mara networks and the neighborhoods and prisons they inhabit. After all, "rumor is the language of risk," and gang members face more mortal risk on a daily basis than I (and most probably you) will experience in a lifetime.[76] Indeed, anecdotal evidence suggests that fewer than 20 percent of mareros survive into their twenties. As among any population caught up in constant violence, a Hobbesian state of war, "torture and assassination frequently are rumor materially enacted on other people's bodies."[77] During my fieldwork I heard stories of gangsters and gang-involved youths being murdered because of rumors concerning their loyalty, negligence, or some real or imagined slight. Rumors produce dead bodies, and dead bodies produce rumors. Stories bloom from every corpse to explain (away), justify, or otherwise make sense of the death.

Navigating this landscape of risk meant, first of all, finding spaces in which gang-involved individuals felt safe enough to talk with me. Curiously, many chose to meet in fast-food joints—McDonald's, Wendy's, Pollo Campero—in the historic zone, a part of the city easily accessible via public transportation. These restaurants tended to be bright, loud, and crowded with middle-class families. Even so, such meetings were difficult to arrange and often fell through. There was only one space where I could rely on relatively secure and consistent access to gang-involved individuals willing to speak with me: prison.

The prison became a primary fieldwork site as well as a key institutional space for understanding the production of violence well beyond prison walls. To ensure I could get to prison whenever I wanted, I became a "facilitator of projects" with gang-rehab organizations. On a few days each week for more than a year I participated in community-building exercises with groups of incarcerated ex-mareros and other convicts. Through this constant contact, I slowly developed a network of gang-involved men willing to open their lives to me. Many of the stories you will read in this book were recounted in prison yards, recorded on a voice recorder smuggled in my underwear through the prison gates and hidden from prying eyes beneath a trucker cap placed carefully between myself and the narrator. Over the years I have come to count several of these men as friends, and they have invited me to meet their families, which in turn gave me access to new street networks that included the few women whose voices also appear here.[78]

When I wasn't in prison, I was pursuing contacts and information on the other side of the law. My aim was to collect, *Rashomon*-like, as wide a variety of perspectives on gangs and criminal violence as possible. To carry this off, I had to assume many roles and manage a schizophrenic existence. I tagged along with pastors in parishes of gang-dominated neighborhoods. I spent weeks in police precincts, occasionally accompanying police raids on criminal safe houses. I got journalist gigs in order to get a press pass and access to government hearings. I built an archive of newspaper, radio, and television reports of allegedly gang-related crimes. I spent months sitting through somnambulant eight-hour extortion and homicide hearings and pursuing coffee dates with judges and prosecutors. And so on. By moving back and forth between sustained conversations with gang-involved men and digging into the representations of gangs and gangsters in the press and in everyday conversation, I came to understand how mareros themselves incorporate—self-consciously or not—the phantasmagoric image the maras strike before the public eye. That is, gangs play a part in forging their symbolic power and are in turn forged by it.

Clearly I had to be careful crisscrossing the blurred divide between the state and its underworld. I always introduced myself as a scholar/writer, emphasizing my interest in life histories and personal perspectives while eschewing direct questions about particular criminal activities. Hewing to the "outsider" role—one with no stake in the clumsy struggle between law and outlaw—was the best way I knew to preserve my safety and that of those who spoke with me. But after a year in the field I too was pulled into the vortex of vicious, sometimes deadly rumor circulating in and beyond the prisons. It happened at a conference in San Salvador while I was talking to a respected crime journalist. For months I had tried to track him down, and I asked him if he would give me an interview or at least have a drink with me and exchange notes.

After a long, calculating look, he replied, "Before I talk to you, I have to know one thing. Are you Interpol?" I laughed, but he went on. "I have heard that you are working for Interpol, passing them the information that you get. Is this true?"

"No!" I exclaimed, perhaps a bit more forcefully than I meant to. I wanted to seem nonchalant—"How ridiculous!"—but I could hear my pulse throbbing in my ears, and my mind was racing—flipping through all the people I knew whom he might have spoken to, all my gatekeepers, friends, and informants. Who would have said such a thing? Who was this journalist? Whom would he have talked to? Though I was able to clear up the rumor after returning to Guatemala—and no one, thankfully, got hurt because of it—the episode was an important lesson. In utter ignorance, I had been recast by rumor into the role of a transnational cop. That this role was entirely invented—to my knowledge Interpol doesn't have agents in the field anywhere in Guatemala— mattered far less than the fact that this was how some of those I interacted with in prison chose to make sense of me. The consequences of my entanglement with these webs of rumor and suspicion could have been far, far worse.

Given how precarious the situation could be, and because informants and opportunities to enter prisons or mara-dominated zones could arise and disappear very quickly, I had to jump down every rabbit hole I found. Such was my "research plan." Slowly, my network of friends and contacts grew beyond gangsters to include police, prosecutors, human rights activists, prison directors, social workers, taxi drivers, church pastors, journalists, and many others. Over the years I have done my best to keep in touch with this network, though many of my gang-involved contacts and friends have disappeared. There are few avenues by which to escape the violence of gang life. In their desperation to find a different way to live, some became protected witnesses in high-profile murder cases, evangelical converts, antiviolence activists, freelance hitmen, or drug addicts. Some still survive in prison or eke out a living on the street, while others have been killed by the police, their rivals, or their old gangs. It may be true that they were once perpetrators of the violence to which they fell victim. But as you will see, the violence for which the maras speak, or are made to speak, has a way of conscripting into its ranks all sorts of unexpected accomplices, erstwhile and otherwise.

PART ONE

Truths and Fictions

FIGURE 4. Where city and cemetery meet.

Bring Out the Dead

Guatemala City, May 2012. Calavera eases open the door and eyes the street he grew up on. Blurred figures slip beyond his peripheral vision down an alley.* Children from the neighborhood? Or perhaps not. Tinkling laughter. Nothing to fear. Then again . . . he knows well enough the demons lurking in children's smiles. They make the best lookouts. Watching, just watching, they go. And didn't Casper once call you his little *chucho.* Just let the dog off the chain and see . . .

Across the street the *tiendita* he knew as a child has been painted blue, "TIGO" stenciled in white block letters. His own Mara Salvatrucha tag is somewhere beneath those layers of paint. Behind the tiendita's black metal grate, a small girl sits on a stool among Doritos and Lays potato chip bags strung up like baitfish among sacs of fried pigskin, plantain chips, and *suaro* for babies sick with fever. A refrigerator glows behind her, brown glass bottles sweating within, and beside the refrigerator rusted propane canisters are stacked like ordinance from a forgotten war. The girl watches the street without blinking, her lips pulled back in a half smile, gold teeth glinting in the sunlight slanting over the tin rooftops.

I stand before the arches of the cemetery entrance, waiting for Calavera. I have a small silver voice recorder, a camera, and a journal in a green US Army

---

* This narrative is an experiment in ethnographic storytelling. It splices conversations and information from several interviews with Calavera and sublimates analysis into the narrative arc. Names, dates, and details have been changed to protect the subjects.

surplus satchel. Flower vendors clog the sidewalk. The scent of carnations and roses wilting in piles filters through the stench of burning garbage on the breeze. Further down the boulevard, the city morgue is abuzz. Men in white lab coats haul forensic equipment in and out. A line of silent visitors stretches out onto the sidewalk, waiting to identify the recently dead. Funeral home operators—wearing dark glasses and tattered blazers—linger among the aggrieved, handing out business cards. A month from now I will pose as a mourner and come to find the body of a young man named Andy. Government officials will not answer my queries. Eight years ago Calavera stood here holding his sister's hand as she waited to identify her murdered husband. Then as now, coffin makers and stonemasons bend to their labors across the boulevard, their hammers echoing through the traffic. I mull over my plan: walk with Calavera to his brother's grave and record his memories of growing up, his brother's death, and their time running with the Mara Salvatrucha.

Calavera steps out and shuts the door quietly behind him. For a few heartbeats he lingers, tracing in his memory the constellation of bullet holes above the door long plastered over. Then he's on the street, watching the neighbors' shuttered windows as he walks. Few of his old compatriots remain who might recognize him. Except for Casper, who hardly ever leaves his safe house in El Trebol. Still, Calavera wouldn't have even come here if he didn't long to see his sister and nieces. Quickening his pace, he walks past a handful of boys kicking a rumpled blue plastic ball. They stop their game and watch him disappear down a cement footpath winding beneath electricity wires strung like sad nets to catch the falling sky.

"Hey, Anthony."

I turn and Calavera is standing before me. We clasp right hands and embrace. He has lost weight since leaving prison, and he was skinny to begin with. His shoulder blades are sharp against my arms.

"What's the vibe?"

Calavera shrugs. "All good."

"Well, uh, shall we go?"

"Right on."

We walk through the cemetery's vaulted entrance and down a paved boulevard lined with ornate mausoleums and cypress and walnut trees. The street noises quickly fade.

"So . . .," I begin. Last night I wrote down a list of questions—probing, intelligent questions with a subtle, penetrating arc. But now I feel like a clumsy stranger prying into another's pain. I hold the recorder awkwardly between us, the red light blinking. "Have you been here since you got out?"

"No." Calavera shakes his head. He has passed the last six of his twenty-five years languishing behind bars. The previous five he spent snorting, smoking, and selling drugs and shooting at rivals. The gang told him it was the way to avenge his brother's murder.

We walk past the wealthy dead. A forty-foot-tall knockoff of an Egyptian pyramid looms on the left, replete with a pharaoh's head and stylized hieroglyphs. It belongs to the Castillo family, who it is said became fantastically rich by monopolizing the national beer industry. *Gallo, la cerveza mas gallo!* An elderly couple—a woman wrapped in a rainbow shawl, a man in overalls stiff with mud—peer out from beneath the pyramid's granite awnings.

When we reach the end of the main boulevard, Calavera stops. "My brother was a good person," he says. "And a good *ranflero*.[*] He joined the gang really believing in the whole brotherhood thing, and when he was the leader he didn't run when all the rest abandoned him. But I know he was sick of it at the end too. Come on, this way." We turn down a pitted stone walkway lined with mausoleums crumbling into anonymity.

After a few minutes we walk past the mausoleum of General Justo Rufino Barrios, the great dictator and liberal reformer of Guatemala. The stone pillars are mottled green and white with mold. A giant rusted padlock hangs from the wrought-iron gate, and shards of green glass make ragged teeth in the façade. In 1885 General Barrios declared war on the isthmus to create a single great nation. He died in the first battle. Ambitions to unite Central America were buried with him. Horseflies buzz through the broken windows, feeding on rat corpses unearthed by recent rains.

"You know, it's because of my brother that I have no tattoos," Calavera says. "Giovanni was blue with ink. He said his body was a prison."

"Uh, did his tattoos have anything to do with his murder?"

"No . . . well, it's not so clear," Calavera says. "He was the leader and the last of Los Adams Blocotes Salvatrucha. The war with the narcos took the rest. I told you they shot him on the patio of our house with an AK-47. But you see, it was only a leg wound. My sister says he was laughing and joking when they loaded him into the ambulance. But when she went to the hospital the next morning they told her he was dead. They said it was an asthma attack.

[*] Gang leader.

Or something. Sandra—she's my sister—thinks that maybe the doctors let him die, or overdosed him or something."

"Where were you when all this happened?"

"I was in the orphanage in Xela."

"Why?"

"My uncle put me there after our grandmother died. My dad was in prison, see, and no one knew where my moms was. It was my sister who buried him, and then she came to tell me what had happened. But I already knew."

"Really?"

"Yeah."

"How did you know?"

"Well . . .," he says, smiling vaguely, "you might not believe me."

"Try me."

"Okay then. On the night he died I had a nightmare. They said I was screaming in my sleep. When I woke up, I felt this like emptiness, like something had been stolen but I didn't know exactly what. After that, and when Sandra told me . . . well, it made sense."

"I believe you," I say. "I also have brothers."

We walk down a long corridor between massive sepulcher walls stretched out before us, plots stacked in columns eight high to protect them from the rain. There are dozens and dozens of these tenements for the dead forming a vast labyrinth through the cemetery, and few signs with which to distinguish one tenement block from another. Calavera thinks Giovanni is interred in one somewhere in the northwest corner of the cemetery. We pass an old woman dressed in black, a bouquet of carnations clasped to her breast, and a man atop a wooden ladder polishing a plaque. We pass children cavorting with a puppy down the corridor.

"A few months after my brother died, my sister brought me home from the orphanage. But when I got to the old neighborhood, she was afraid for me to leave the house. She enrolled me in school, and when I wasn't in school I was supposed to be with her, helping her little business selling tortas. I didn't know why until a couple weeks after I was back."

"What happened?"

"I was walking home when a bunch of kids came out of an alleyway. The war between my brother's gang and the narco-traffickers was supposed to have ended with his death, but my sister told me that things were still crazy. We all know it never really ends. The kids started pushing me around. I was even

FIGURE 5. Children and puppy playing in the Guatemala City General Cemetery.

skinnier than I am now, but quick. 'It's him!' they shouted. 'It's true! It's true!' They made a circle around me. I could tell they wanted to beat the shit out of me, but they were also afraid. I saw my chance and rushed the smallest one, and he jumped away like I was a leper or something. I ran all the way back to my house. They didn't follow me."

"What was it all about?"

"Well, I told my sister what happened and asked her what the fuck was going on. She wouldn't look at me, and then she started crying. 'Some people believe that your brother's death was fake—that he didn't die in the hospital, and that we all hid the truth to protect him.'

"I was shocked, you know, like I was almost crying, too. 'But you showed me his grave,' I said to her. And my sister looked so sad. She's tough, and I've only seen her like that a couple of times—when she first told me about Giovanni, and when they killed her husband. 'They say I only buried dirt,' she said. 'They say it was all a charade so that he could escape.'

"'Well was it?' I yelled. And then she slapped me hard. I knew why. She never would have done that to me. Never, and I felt bad." Calavera looks up into the cloudless sky where vultures turn slow spirals far, far above. Then he closes his eyes.

"So," I say, trying to work it out, "they thought you were your brother? Or your brother's ghost?"

"Yeah, one or the other. Or they just wanted to kick my ass because I was my brother's brother. Anyway, soon after that I joined with Casper's Northside crew and that sort of thing never happened again."

We walk past a purgatory of gray concrete boxes and come upon an old man in a worn cowboy hat and fine-tooled leather boots. He slouches on a wooden stool, dozing, surrounded by half-carved stelas, protean angels, incomplete Virgins, and a rough-hewn Jesus hauling a bulbous cross. The crude savior crouches beneath his terrible load. He has no face. A mongrel of uncertain parentage is curled at the old man's feet. Their eyes snap open as Calavera and I draw near. Without moving, the old man tracks our progres-

FIGURE 6. A mass grave in the Guatemala City General Cemetery.

sion. We nod and say good day, and he nods. The dog sniffs the air before curling once again into its tail. The man picks up a marble plaque and after studying it briefly, lays it across a palette nailed between two wooden horses and begins polishing it with a bit of rag. I have a passing vision: the blank headstones and plaques etched with the names of dead friends, informants, and murder victims I read about in the newspaper. Maria Siekavezza. Juan Carlos "Chooky" Rodriguez. Maria Tzoc Castañeda.

We turn right onto another long, straight corridor. Bright flowers and succulents grow in plastic planter boxes garnishing the cubbyholes of the dead. Solemn, washed-out portraits return my gaze. A young man with a goatee and shaved head, stained blue with rain and time, poses grimly in a dark suit. A girl child smiles, one hand raised as if in greeting or farewell, from beneath a carved elegy. The wall rises up twenty feet, and many of the cubbyholes are covered over in rough plaster, service numbers scrawled on them in black paint. Others are empty and open, mortar and broken brick, here and there a scrap of faded crinoline. They await the newly deceased to replace those whose families have stopped paying their cemetery dues. Each day cemetery workers haul away the desiccated remains of the indigent dead in wheelbarrows and toss them down a forty-foot hole where the cemetery borders the ravine of trash. Here, at the cemetery's outermost edge, nature too takes part in erasing the past. Each year, as the rains wear away the earth, one by one the abandoned mausoleums and broken sepulchers tumble down the muddy slope to mingle their remains with the refuse of the metropolis.

CHAPTER I

Portrait of a "Real" Marero

Guatemala City, May 2012. A few days after Calavera and I met in the cemetery, I found myself sitting across from a young man slouched in a desk chair in the corner of a prosecutor's cluttered office.

"What can you give me?" he asked. He had a wispy mustache and smooth, olive skin, a Miami Marlin's baseball cap pulled over long black hair tucked behind his ears. The sliver of a roughly etched tattoo on his chest peeked out from under a short-sleeved button-down.

"Not much," I said. Having grown accustomed to this question, I was careful not to promise more than I could fulfill. I repeated an offer I had made to others. "I can tell your story far from these streets where you have seen so many like you die."

He gazed at me silently for several seconds and then nodded. "Right on (*Órale*). Ask me your questions. You ask and I answer."[1]

So began my first interview with Andy, a seventeen-year-old member of the Mara Salvatrucha (MS) and protected witness for the Guatemalan government. After more than a year of living and conducting fieldwork in Guatemala City, I had gotten to know many young men caught up in gang life, like Andy, and many more struggling to leave gang life behind. But few were able—or willing—to tell about their lives with such clarity and detail, and none were in quite the predicament in which Andy found himself. Since the age of eight Andy had extorted, killed, and tortured for the MS clique Coronados Locos Salvatrucha (CLS) the most powerful clique of Guatemala's most-feared mara. As a protected witness in the prosecution of gruesome

FIGURE 7. Andy, protected witness for the Guatemalan government, May 11, 2012.

murders he claimed to have helped commit, he crisscrossed the blurred boundaries dividing the "criminal underworld from the law-abiding world that rests upon it."[2] Straddling the uncertain divide between a weak, corrupt judicial system and the criminals it is meant to bring to justice is dangerous business. When we met, Andy seemed to be making a stand against—or at least reconsidering—the brutal realities that had shaped so much of his life. But whatever personal transformations he might have been experiencing were cut short. A little over a month after our first interview and three days after our last, the MS found and executed him.

Before he died, Andy gave Guatemalan investigators detailed testimony describing his gang's modus operandi, their strategies, and the motives behind unsolved murders both mundane and spectacular. Through our conversations I tried to record his history and map out his beliefs and reflections about the world he grew up in and his current predicament. Oral histories are inherently unstable, always "floating in time between the present and an ever-changing past, oscillating in the dialogue between the narrator and the interviewer, and melting and coalescing in the no-man's-land from orality to writing and back."[3] The conditions of Andy's life, the circumstances of our encounter, and his violent death place his story in the most volatile and treacherous zone of this "no-man's-land."[4] Threading it together requires pivoting back and forth among Andy's recorded voice; the memories, myths, and fantasies it invokes; and the fact that he is gone.[5] His is a story shot through with lacunae and ellipses. Perhaps if he had lived, I could have distinguished more truths from untruths. But this confusion is in a sense precisely the point. Such a fractured narrative is entirely appropriate for a tale of violent life and death. Andy's story is about how a young man survived and learned to use violence. It is also about how this violence dictates how that story can and should be told. The complex interplay between truth and rumor, the facts of the matter and the inventions of the imagination, illuminate the possibilities and pitfalls of the search for order in the midst of chaos.

Both the real and imagined violence of Central America's gangs makes delving into the gang phenomenon extremely difficult, for at least two reasons. First, as gangs have become more insular and more violent, getting past collective fantasies about them by getting "close" enough to gang-involved youth has become far riskier. Second, such fantasies are deeply a part of gang culture itself. In twenty-first-century Central America, maras have become erstwhile emissaries of extreme peacetime violence. They have come to distill in spectacular fashion the fear, rage, and trauma swirling around out-of-control crime. Young mareros like Andy are drawn in by and work hard to re-create the phantasmagoric figure the maras cut in social imaginaries, linking the acts of violence gangs perform to the ways gang members (and others) collectively and individually make sense of this violence. This entanglement between symbolic meaning and material violence was starkly illuminated in Andy's courtroom testimonies. Even as he engaged in flights of fantasy, his testimonies provided the locations of real cadavers, decapitated and quartered, and revealed in precise detail acts of violence no more gruesome or farfetched than the deeds he claimed as his own.

By the time I met him, Andy had become expert in playing the part of the "real" marero, a patchwork figure sewn together from the facts, fears, and fictions swirling about criminal terror. In drawing an image of himself for me, he seemed to swing back and forth between self-consciously acting out this role and searching for some alternative means of representing his life. I will not—I cannot—parse truth from fantasy. But neither do I wish to simply reproduce and reify the fetishized spectacle of gang violence that seemed so integral to Andy's sense of self.

Instead I follow Andy's lead. Since he seemed to fold fantasy and experience so seamlessly in his narration, I have written this account of Andy's life and death in a similar vein. I will not arbitrate between the truth of his stories and the lies, half-truths, and flights of fantasy. By walking in Andy's footsteps I show how his forays into fantasy cannot be understood as solely his own. "Men do not live by truth alone," writes Mario Vargas Llosa, "they also need lies."[6] The fiction of the "real" marero Andy worked so hard to fulfill also served the needs of those who would use him for their own purposes and who in turn take part in the layering of fantasy into Andy's tales. These exchanges— between gang leader and gang wannabe, investigator and witness, writer and subject—illuminate how essential shared fantasies and falsehoods are in the production of knowledge about criminal terror, as well as in the making of violence itself.

ANDY'S UTILITY

A month before I met Andy, I climbed the fifteen stories of Guatemala City's Tower of Tribunals. I went to court to witness the sentencing of Rafael Cita- lan, a twenty-three-year-old *guero* (light-skinned man) with slicked-back hair and a jutting chin. He was one of several MS members allegedly responsible for murdering four people, decapitating them, and placing the heads at various locations around Guatemala City. He sat in chains in a glass and metal cage, wearing a white T-shirt, jeans, and plastic clogs, head bowed before his own reflection. As the judge droned out a long list of his crimes, pronounced his guilt, and handed down his sentence in minute detail, Citalan kept shaking his head.

Back in June 2010, incarcerated leaders of the MS had ordered gang mem- bers on the street to decapitate five people. In the end, one clique failed, and they only managed to kill four. Gang members placed the four victims' heads at various locations around the city. With each head they left a note— supposedly written by Citalan—attacking the government for "impunity" and "injustice" in the prison system. Media outlets across the country flocked to publicize the grisly affair.

Before the trial, I'd spoken with Edgar Martinez, the lawyer for the prosecution. He is a tall, balding man, amiable and ready to talk. "This is the most spectacular and frightening gang case I have been involved with," he said. "This was a political act. They wanted to terrify the populace and intimidate the government so they would get better treatment in the prisons. It's the first case I've worked on that has had such political overtones. It's like terrorism."

For nearly two years the crimes remained unsolved. Maras are notoriously difficult to infiltrate. "They have their own language, their own style," said an eager young Guatemalan gang expert working with an FBI task force. "It is their subculture that makes them harder to infiltrate than even organized crime or drug traffickers (narcos)." Besides, as they have admitted to me time and again, Guatemalan security officials have very little experience in undercover operations. Martinez told me that the case broke open with the testimony of a secret witness, another MS member who, for reasons he did not explain, confessed and turned on his compatriots. This witness, I would learn later, was Andy.

"He's really something. He's a real marero," exclaimed Martinez, his eyes wide with excitement, while we were sitting over fried chicken, his bodyguards sitting stolidly beside us. "And a good witness. A fine witness."

The only reason Andy seemed to matter to Martinez and nearly everyone else with whom he worked was his utility. For the government prosecutors reveling in his authenticity, he made possible a deeper understanding of the MS than they had ever had. Guatemalan investigators are often woefully ignorant regarding the criminal structures they face, making a "real marero" witness like Andy a rare treasure indeed. A paranoic state and terrified society have long targeted poor young men who happen to have tattoos, wear baggy pants, or use certain slang as potential mareros.[7] And the illicit businesses in which gangs are involved—extortion, drug dealing, hired assassinations—incorporate people and networks far beyond the gangs themselves.[8] The maras are not a discrete "thing" separable from structures of violence linking, among others, organized crime, poor urban communities, and corrupt state officials. Distinguishing living, breathing mareros from their brutal public image reproduced in the media and everyday conversation is also difficult.[9] Gangsters and gangster wannabes alike work hard to mirror the monstrous figure the marero cuts in the collective consciousness. Yet more often than not, both the victims and alleged perpetrators of "gang violence" are not even gang members.[10] Andy, however, was. He also had a remarkable memory for detail and was able to provide an accurate insider's perspective on how the MS operates.

The gleam of excitement in Martinez's eyes when he touted Andy to me— "a *real* marero!"—spoke volumes. By giving the government the case of the four heads, Andy offered prosecutors a chance to show they were not the corrupt, incompetent bureaucrats most Guatemalans believe them to be.

But even as Andy helped prosecutors take apart the Mara Salvatrucha's most powerful clique, the government failed to give him cover. Andy's murder only months after helping investigators break open one of the most sensational mara cases in history epitomizes the state of justice in Guatemala today. As part of the witness protection program, officials locked Andy and three other gang associates who had followed him into exile in a room for three days with little food. The stipend money they were promised never materialized. When the boys complained, no one listened, and when they complained more loudly, officials kicked them out of the program. After Andy's death, Federico, a young, earnest investigator who had taken Andy under his wing, waved a sheaf of papers in my face. "These are applications to get him back in the safe house," he said, shaking his head. "All rejected. He hadn't even begun to give us 1 percent of what he knew."

When I met Andy, he had already been kicked out of the witness protection program and was seeking his own security by joining a Barrio18 clique. From our very first encounter, I did not need to cajole Andy into telling me about his life—he readily agreed to my using a voice recorder in each of our interviews—but that does not absolve me from having used him as well. I am using him now. When Martinez mentioned the possibility of meeting him, I jumped at the opportunity. "A real marero!" While my reasons for wanting to meet Andy were distinct from the government's, I shared a similar dilemma. Reliable informants were hard to come by and harder to keep. Throughout my fieldwork, my network of people involved in criminal groups was in constant flux. Friends and contacts were transferred into maximum security prisons, were killed, or simply disappeared. I was careful to keep my correspondence with Andy—and his situation—secret from my networks in prison. I confided only in Calavera and gave him no details. He warned me in no uncertain terms that Andy's cooperation with the government would get him killed. Still, although I pursued Andy, at the time I did not realize just how short-lived our relationship would be. It took a couple of weeks of repeated phone calls to Federico to finally set up an interview.

Federico introduced me to Andy as an American (*gavacho*) scholar who wanted to learn about gang life. I emphasized that I was not a cop, nor did I have any connections to law enforcement, but was merely a researcher and writer with no stake in the struggle between the Guatemalan government and the gangs. Careful not to promise more than I could fulfill, I never pledged more than to write his story. In retrospect, however, even this paltry promise may have shaped how he chose to represent himself. Did he improvise and edit his tale to match what he imagined would keep me coming back for more? He already knew that his usefulness to the government was all that kept him out of prison. He was used to being used. Before I used him for my research, before the government used him to take apart the Mara Salvatrucha, gang leaders used him to commit many, many murders. Children who kill do not risk the same legal consequences as adults. For years his usefulness kept him alive when everyone about him was dying. And a week before his death, Andy fantasized that *he* was using the government to wipe out his enemies.

"More than anything . . . look, I'll explain," he said. "What I want is that they catch all those assholes so that I remain as the commander. To govern, you understand! Once I'm in charge it's gonna be another deal, *loco* (dude). No more extortions. . . . Well, there will be extortions, but you won't see any deaths. We'll go to the homes and tell them, 'Look, we're going to take care of you, but we don't want the violence.' To reach an accord without the violence."

At the time, I shrugged off this declaration as so much brash naïveté, the foolish musings of a young man. In retrospect, I was blind to just how skilled Andy had become in bending his words to manipulate those around him, including me.

FINDING AND LOSING ANDY

I did not fully comprehend while he was alive just how precarious a position Andy was struggling to maintain, nor all the roles he was playing at once. He was a protected witness against the MS while undergoing initiation with their rival, the Little Psychos, a powerful Barrio18 clique, in another part of the city. He was saving his skin from prosecution for quartered corpses dumped in front of his house while claiming revenge against the MS for killing his family, who were Barrio18 members.[11] Andy would brag about killing enemies and innocents and in the next breath be cursing his old clique for hurting children. The complexities and contradictions of his life only came into focus as I pieced together what I could from our recorded interviews and the transcripts from his court testimony.

Take, for example, the constellation of aliases he used in his short life. Andy, aka El Fish, aka El Niño, aka El Reaper, aka José Luis Velasquez-Cuellar. Each of his names addressed an aspect of his self and his history. He said that before she died, "my mother called me Andy," and that's how he introduced himself to me. When he was a toddler his neighbors and family called him El Fish because of a funny hairstyle he wore for a time. "They called me El Niño because I was the youngest 'homito.'" Homitos are little gang-bangers, who emulated the Barrio18 members who controlled his neighborhood before MS killed them all. When he was a gang wannabe trying to pass his chequeo—an initiation period in which the gang measures a wannabe's worth—with the MS, "they called me El Reaper [as in the Grim Reaper], because I collected the most lives," he said. He claimed they also called him El Enigma, because they could not fathom his true desires. To the legal system and the press, he was Jose Luis Velazquez-Cuellar.[12]

I have kept two pictures of Andy. The first I took at our initial meeting in the public ministry building. Federico had introduced us perhaps an hour earlier. In the photograph Andy looks into the camera without expression—no smile, nothing—as if he were looking through me. I had asked to see his tattoos, and he lifted his shirt up to his skinny shoulders, exposing his chest. There were two: a gaunt female face wreathed in flames and a roughly etched marijuana leaf. The latter I have seen many times. It is a popular "subversive" symbol among disaffected Central American youth.

"My first tattoo," he said with pride. "I got it when I was eight."

"And the other?"

"My mother. They shot her eight times."

The second photo was taken about an hour after he was gunned down with five bullets to the back of his skull. It's a grainy, black-and-white image snapped by the police who retrieved his body a few blocks from the McDonald's where we had our last interview. Andy is lying on his back, eyes staring off to the right, lips parted, exit wounds swelling the left side of his face. A triple slash across the front of his black sweatshirt looks at first like some brutal injury, but on closer inspection is merely the trademark logo for Monster Energy drink. Monster Energy . . . the irony is just too much. Federico gave the photo to me along with the rest of the police report on Andy's murder. "Here, do something with this for your book," he said. "Don't let him be forgotten."

A month before his murder, Andy said he knew he must die. "Anyway, I don't give a shit. I'm already dead. I lose nothing. When my time comes, they better come at me from behind, because if not . . ." And this was precisely what they did. "These are my streets," he had said to me as we walked out of the McDonald's into the five o'clock sun hanging low over the concrete boulevard where his body would be found. He wasn't looking, but he must have known they were coming. An hour earlier they'd taken out his friend, El Gorgojo, a fifteen-year-old kid who was often slouched in the corner of the prosecutor's office to support Andy while he made his declarations. Gorgojo had followed Andy into exile when he left the MS, so he would share his fate. After they shot Gorgojo, Andy called Federico.

"They killed my *carnal* (buddy). They killed Gorgojo."[13] He was sobbing.

Federico told him to go home, but Andy kept repeating, "They killed him, those sons of bitches. He never did anything to anybody."[14]

The phone went silent midsentence, and Federico heard no more from him. It seems as though Andy's concern for his friend was his undoing. Gorgojo's killers had seen him in the crowd milling about the body. Perhaps killing Gorgojo was simply a ploy to draw Andy out of hiding. An hour later Andy, too, was dead. That's when Federico called me at home. "I have bad news for you," he said. As he spoke, I pictured him sitting in his office, linoleum floors cluttered with case files, requests for Andy's reentry into the protected witness program stamped "denied" and piled in a cardboard box. And I already knew Andy was dead. Of course he was. Federico sounded terrified. "He told me they're going to come for me, too," he said. "They have videotapes, he said. They know my face and they know where I work."

I told Federico to be careful, and then there was nothing else to say. We hung up, and I slumped back in my shoddy wooden chair in my barely furnished apartment. Stupid boy, I thought, and clutched my belly and cried, but only for a few seconds.

BECOMING A REAL MARERO

This is how Andy said he came to join the MS. He grew up in Ciudad del Sol, Villa Nueva, an urban sprawl bordering Guatemala City's southern edge. His

FIGURE 8. Andy, June 20, 2012. Photo: Anonymous.

parents were both Barrio18 gang members. He never knew his father, but his uncle was of the "Clanton 14," one of Los Angeles's original *sureño* gangs that still has mythological status among Barrio18 folk in both US and Central American cities.[15] Andy started with Barrio18 when he was just six years old, and he said he was leader of the homitos, the little homies, the gangsters in training who hung around their older, bloodier brethren. When Andy was eight the MS clique CLS—led by El Soldado, a man who would become nationally famous before he died at age twenty-three—captured Ciudad del Sol in a hostile takeover. Andy's mother was shot eight times and died a few days later, and they killed his uncle with a gunshot to the head. So, Andy said, at eight years old he decided to go on a mission to infiltrate the MS clique that had taken out his people. He joined with a plan to bide his time and kill those who had killed his family. At least this is what he told me after he'd become a government witness. I was never sure whether he was trying to justify—to me or to himself—betraying his gang. I suspect the truth was rooted somewhere else, somewhere deeper and too painful to admit. I believe that after making Andy an orphan, El Soldado took him under his wing. The Coronados killed off his family and then replaced it.

I asked him what the MS meant to him while he was still part of it.

"It was a family that didn't leave me to die," he said. "When I needed it most they gave me a hand and gave me food to eat, you understand. So I couldn't bite the hand that fed me."

"So they were your friends?" I asked.

"Not my friends. They were *family*," he insisted with what strikes me now as ineffable sadness. "They were my family when I had no family. It was all I had. I had no father, no mother, no brothers or sisters. They were my family."

With no one to turn to except the very authors of his disaster, eight-year-old Andy had to reconcile insuperable emotional contradictions. Rendering the ordeal into a simpler story line such that his eventual betrayal became a successful conclusion to a tale of righteous revenge ties up the loose ends quite elegantly. In this version of his history, both Andy's past and present selves retain agency and control that one suspects were absent in his "real" life.

In any case, he said that for years he couldn't get his revenge because they knew where he came from and kept him closely monitored. He underwent a particularly long and strenuous chequeo—a period in which the aspiring gang member demonstrates his worthiness—being tested with ever more difficult missions. When he was nine, he said, already a year into his chequeo, he had to kill another kid who had tried to run away:

> They dropped the kid from chequeo, and for his failure they were going to drop me too. It all went to shit because of this dude. He took off and was in a discotheque here in zone 5. He never imagined that I would come to zone 5 to find him, and I came, and another homie came with me. He was like, "Look at (*watchea*) that dude, look alive and go hit him."
>
> "Son of a (*a la gran*)!" I said. "No way bro, the dude backed me up (*el vato me hizo paro*)."[16]
>
> "What do you mean 'no' you sonofabitch," he said, and he got on the phone with the chief, El Soldado. "Look, Soldado," he told him, "the vibe (*la onda*) is that the Reaper doesn't want to hit Casper."[17] And then he turned to me, "Look here you sonofabitch, if you don't shoot him I'm gonna shoot you."

"*A la gran*, okay," I answered, and so I had to shoot the guy. I shed a tear because he was just a baby. I still had a heart, you know. Since then they showed me how to not have a heart, so I didn't have feelings about anything.

This was Andy's first murder, and given the circumstances, it seems that killing the boy was a matter of self-preservation. This was the "choice" Andy's victim had refused to make by running away, a move the gang interpreted as a decision to die. How does a nine-year-old make sense of such a brutal zero-sum calculus? Age-old philosophical puzzles—the parsing of guilt from innocence, for example, or the possibility of rational choice and free will—become moot, even absurd, when applied to the moment in which Andy took the gun too heavy for his thin wrists and shot another child.

When we spoke, Andy blamed El Soldado for making him into a killer. Like Andy nearly a decade later, the CLS chief would die while apparently cooperating with the government to reduce gang violence in Guatemala City. The reasons for his death remain unclear to all but those who ordered it. El Soldado had played some very dangerous games: becoming a lead negotiator with the government to start gang rehabilitation programs and meeting with and giving talks to the police, the media, and low-level government officials in which he advocated the need for reconciliation, that gangs could be part of peacemaking, and that police profiling was violating poor youths' human rights. His message made him both a celebrity and a target for other gang leaders (and as the rumors go, for the police as well), for whom gang war was far too profitable to give up. For a short time, national media referred to him, with thinly veiled sarcasm, as the next "savior of Guatemala" for his role in trying to bring peace to the streets.[18] A few years before he died, an Associated Press photographer snapped his picture hunched over his baby son at his home in Ciudad del Sol—the neighborhood where Andy's family once lived—kissing the child's head and holding a .45.

El Soldado's celebrity made him the very personification of the MS and all its contradictions. The savior of Guatemala was, according to his contemporaries, also a central player in institutionalizing the practice of *descuartizamiento* (dismemberment), torture, and other forms of extreme corporal punishment against captured rivals as well as homies who betrayed the gang, wanted to leave, or couldn't cut it anymore. This kind of violence is performed in a group, a communal act in which aspiring or newly initiated members must take part to prove their mettle. Andy said he participated in a *descuartizamiento* for the first time when he was ten.

FIGURE 9. El Soldado and his son in front of their home in Ciudad del Sol, Villa Nueva, in 2003. Photo: Rodrigo Abd (API).

"I had to kill a homie from my old *barrio* (gang).[19] We had to dismember him, just me and the *ramflero* (gang leader)."[20]

"You had to kill and quarter him?"

"Nope. Dismember him alive. Torture him, make it a party."

"Where did this happen?"

"Over in Ciudad del Sol, Villa Nueva in a *chantehuario*. *Chantehuario*, that's what you call the houses of war, you understand, where all the homies will be, see."[21]

"Were the others around when you were doing it?"

"Yeah. All the homies of my clique: El Extraño, El Huevon, El Shadow, El Brown, El Maniaco, El Delincuente, El Fideo, El Aniquilador, El Hache, El Chino. All of them, you understand."[22]

"What were they doing?"

"Marking the wrath (*marcando la ira*), seeing if I had heart, mind, and balls. All they ask of you in the *Barrio* is that you have mind, heart, and balls, because if you don't have any of them you're not worth dick. That's right, and I had been a little vato since I was six with Clanton 14. Now they were seeing what I was capable of, testing me. So with faith and joy I had to do it."

"How did you feel?"

"Look, carnal, the way I grew up, I grew up in the gang. My dad was eighteen, my mother was eighteen, you understand, ok. I had already grown up with a gangster's outlook, so I took pleasure in killing dogs, going around killing cats. So when I killed a human it was like I was killing an animal. I was already a beast (*bestia*) for that kind of thing."[23]

I still find it difficult to stomach Andy's glib reproduction of himself as beast, as the devil personified. I wanted some other explanation—something more nuanced and reflective, perhaps. But none was forthcoming, at least not from him. Again and again, he claimed the virtues of a "real marero." Whether he in fact embodied this image and did so out of habit or was simply playacting is impossible to say. The idea that mareros are essentially different from other criminals, and from other human beings, is an important part of their public persona. It is also a notion the maras have taken on and self-consciously cultivated. The key distinction, the way to "recognize" a marero, is his capacity for violence without the psychological baggage that would paralyze a "normal" human being.

In our last meeting, Andy sat across from me in a McDonald's, a chicken burger and fries untouched before him. Middle-class parents eyed us nervously while their children shrieked in the ball pit some thirty feet away. "Human beings have five senses," he said. "The marero will have a sixth. The sixth will be that he has no heart, that he doesn't give a damn about anything. You will dismember for your gang, you will kill for your gang, you will die for your gang. This is how you describe a marero."[24]

It was as though he was reciting from a script. The cadence was measured and precise, with emphasis on the action verbs: *descuartizar, matar, morir* (dismember, kill, die). He seemed to be describing a sociopathic subject freed of the empathies expected of "normal" humans: for others' suffering, for the value of human life, for the need to be considered human at all.[25] "I am more than human," Andy seemed to be saying, "because I am less." To identify so closely with the inhuman, the beastly, the demonic is to reject all facets of belonging in wider society—worldly, spiritual, and otherwise—since "one's worthiness to exist, one's claim to life, and one's relation to what counts as the reality of the world, all pass through what is considered to be human at any particular time."[26]

Such wholesale alienation cannot be invoked with mere words. It must be created through ritual and repetition. The urge to fetishize the violence of

Andy's world is strong: to hold it at arm's length and convince oneself that it is not ours, it belongs to some other realm, some other time, some other species. I know. I have done it. The image of grown men performing similar acts—in a war zone under military orders, perhaps—seems to me more palatable, or at least less world-rending. Children who kill, children who learn to glory in death, embody an ethical and even existential set of dilemmas for human societies. They invoke a deep-seated sense of horror, an internal scream pleading "How could this happen in the world I live in?"[27] And yet by reacting this way, we ignore how children like Andy learn to do what they do through an *education*. Andy's life demonstrates how this behavior is taught. Accepting this fact means accepting that any one of us could be molded in exactly this way.

Through the brutal acts the MS made him perform, Andy made himself in the image of the unfeeling killer that mareros are so widely imagined to be. He became not only a child who has killed, but a child who assumes he must be a killer in order to be anything at all. Once he was caught up in this image of himself, all possibility of a different life and a different way of being seemed to disappear. But at least some of his brutal braggadocio was pretense. Several times Andy seemed to let slip the suffering hidden behind the facade of the unfeeling killer, admissions quickly swallowed back again.

"I'm already grown and I'm always shedding tears, loco," Andy said the last time I spoke with him. "Because one knows that loneliness attacks, and one has a heart. Maybe not for caring for other people, but for caring about oneself. . . . To not have a person who will listen to you, to be able to talk and have a peaceful life. . . . But whatever, it's the life that I chose and so it has to be cared for."

"Chose?" I asked. "Do you think at the age of eight you can really choose?"

"Like I said, I didn't know the deal then." He shrugged. "I didn't know what I would get myself into. But here are the consequences, you understand, and I'm grown. All that's left to me is to tighten my belt and continue forward, with my chest high. This is what destiny wants."

"Would you say you were a victim?"

"No way, I'm no victim. No way, carnal."

"A victimizer then?"

He paused for a moment, and then laughed uncertainly. "That's it. Other people are my victims."

Andy's outright rejection of victimhood sutures him tightly to the carefully nurtured and hyperaggressive machismo typical of the maras. But refusing the mantle of victim, to my mind, only reifies his victimhood. His stubborn insistence on his own agency required turning a blind eye to the lifetime of brutal exploitation that he had survived until then, not to mention the complex assemblage of violent structures and structural violence that framed his life.[28]

Upon reflection, however, my urge to think of Andy as a victim may very well stem from my need to empathize with his dilemma and so bridge what too often feels like an insuperable divide between my perspective and his. I cannot deny that I was, to borrow a phrase from Antonius Robben, "seduced" by Andy's being a "real" marero, drawn in by his eloquence and bravado before so much risk and violence. Over the years of writing and contemplating Andy and his fate, I have gained a modicum of distance from this seduction, but it was woven into all our conversations and still shapes how I convey his story to you. Andy and his story can only emerge through the lens of my recollection and reflection, warped by my own sentimental image of his life and death.

KILLING INNOCENCE AND BEING SOMEBODY

Before Andy entered adolescence, he was accustomed to killing. Once accustomed to killing, he claimed, the distinctions between the "innocent," the relatively sacrosanct, those-who-deserve-to-live, and those who do not all but disappeared. In his short life, Andy learned that the categories of innocence and guilt and right and wrong cannot be and never are stable.

As Andy grew from a child into an adolescent, gang war in Guatemala intensified, and CLS expanded from the territory in Ciudad del Sol won from its rivals to running extortion rackets in La Paz, El Alyoto, Linda Vista, and numerous other neighborhoods. It became the dominant gang in Villa Nueva. Its success was underpinned, at least in part, by turning the violent techniques used against enemies and traitors onto extortion victims residing and doing business in its territories.

In conversation with me, Andy made no distinction between innocent victims and enemy combatants. When I asked him if it was difficult to kill people who posed no threat to him, he replied, "No way. It was a luxury for me. It was a luxury to go killing people, go collecting. In the clique we had this thing of seeing who would kill more people. So every day we would go. One day I would kill two and another guy comes and he's killed three."

"So it was a competition between you?"

"Exactly. It was 'who's the best?' The best sniper, you understand. That was the game."

"What type of arms did you use?"

"Guns. M16, AR-15, 9.40, 380, 357," he said, ticking them off on the fingers of one hand. "Whatever there was, even machetes, to use to take a person's life when the time came."

He claimed this was his expertise. Not for nothing, he said, did they call him El Reaper. He was for a long while one of the youngest in his clique, and as the youngest he was often given the dirtiest jobs. El Soldado and those working beneath him knew that the police could do little against a child. Another member of the MS serving multiple life sentences recalled getting hauled in a half dozen times as a minor for homicide. Once a policeman jerked him by the handcuffs off the pavement, muttering, "Just wait 'til you're eighteen, you son of a bitch," while the boy grinned in his face. Andy said the police picked him up a few times, but no witnesses ever came forward to testify against him, and he never spent more than a few days in police custody before the charges were dropped for lack of evidence.

Andy hurt and killed his share of victims, but no matter what he said, he certainly was a victim himself. But for Andy, and countless others caught up in such violence, an act of killing can be about far more than simply ending another's life. The most cogent summary of what death and violence does to and for boys like Andy came from another MS member named Mo. "This world is not like your world," he said in a quiet voice, sitting in the prison yard, staring at his hands. He had been incarcerated for over a decade, and with forty years left of his sentence, would likely die in prison.

"What do you mean?" I asked.

"Here death plays into so many social necessities, to your very identity, that it becomes an addiction—addiction to the money, the pleasure of it, but it's a pleasure that comes from the respect you get, from your name entering the myth of the street. This is the way to be somebody—but as you build up your name on the street you are also building up your own prison, because the bigger you become the more of a target you become. And then you're only thinking that if they do come to kill you, they shoot you in the head. That's the best way out."

Money and addiction, myth and identity, pleasure and death are hopelessly entangled when hurting and killing become the ultimate means of fulfilling a sense of power and importance.[29] Encoding oneself into the myth of the street means becoming one more rider of the self-consuming Ouroborous, taking a trip on the never-ending cycle of death and revenge that gang war has become.[30] Among mareros, killing, and making sure the world knows you are a killer, have become key to being somebody.[31]

And yet the telling is never an exact copy of the doing. The entangled causes and conditions that drive a person to commit a violent act, or any act for that matter, are not the end products of some rational choice game. Pressed to explain himself, Andy supplied a coherent narrative, a chain of events that made the act inevitable. For gangsters like Andy the act of killing—to choose who lives and who dies—has to seem like a choice, but it is precisely because violence becomes a point of pride and the fodder of myths that the excessive brutality so many mareros claim as their own must remain suspect. If the circulation of personal myths, if being somebody, is a key aspect of why mareros kill, then stories of killing may simply be the raconteur's fantasies grown from the desire to reflect this brutal paradigm.

THE REAL, THE TRUTH, AND THE DEAD

How do we provide accounts of ourselves to others? What do we expose, and what do we keep hidden? And how do the stories we tell about ourselves entangle what we have done with how we imagine ourselves to be?

These questions hinge on the complex relationship among agency, event, and acts of narration that materialize the event in the moment of its (re)telling.[32] That is, no event is accessible outside of its narration; nothing that happens has any meaning separate from how it is "remembered, recounted, and mediated."[33] This means that an event's existence does not remain locked in linear time. Its temporal contours shift each time it is narrated. What's more, this intimate entanglement between the doing and the telling also constitutes an essential process in how people imagine themselves to be, in the very making of the subject himself. The narrator is as much a product of the story as he is its purveyor, and in the moment of telling he reinvents his own place in the world.

For Andy, the ability to reinvent himself by performing carefully crafted narrations of self was always a matter of life and death. He struggled for years to pass his chequeo and become a bona fide homie of the Mara Salvatrucha, to show his gang that he was really one of them. Playing the role of the real marero had become his life's work and key to his survival. But how much of his narration was self-conscious performance reciting the experiences a "real" marero ought to have? That is, if Andy understood me as a conduit through which his story might live beyond his particular place and time, then what was invented to fulfill the image of the spectacular real?

One often-repeated "truth" is that no one escapes the MS. The exit routes once open to Central American mareros—having a kid, going straight, becoming a devout Christian—have crumbled in the face of heavy-handed policing and society's unwillingness to forgive mareros' tattooed skin and stained souls. Andy mouthed the words he had heard hundreds of times: "You can run, but you can't hide." Years before, El Smokey, the CLS leader before Andy became part of the gang, had run to the United States. Andy said El Pensador, the man who took control after El Soldado died, issued the order to have El Smokey tracked down and killed.

This was in 2006. The SUR, a prison pact between Barrio18 and MS, had been broken the year before, and it was a new, harsher world. Former mareros, labeled "Gayboy Gangsters" and *pesetas* (meaning "pennies," because they aren't worth a damn) by their old comrades, who had slipped away in the preceding years, would no longer be so lucky. "The *culero* (faggot) who runs gets a green light. Period." A green light is like the mark of Cain. A message filters out via cellular phone and word of mouth among every clique in the country, ordering execution. Every homie, chequeo, and gangster wannabe has the duty to shoot the person on sight. This is why Andy said El Smokey had run to the North, to escape the web that surely would have ensnared him had he stayed.

As the story goes, El Pensador wanted that loose end tied up. And so in 2007 he sent Andy, along with a boy named El Pícaro, to kill El Smokey. Andy had been in chequeo for almost four years due to his young age and suspicions that he might still have loyalties to his Barrio18 roots. "If you want to end your chequeo, go find that son of a bitch and kill him. That's your mission," the ramflero told Andy. The homies in Guatemala knew El Smokey had gone to Los Angeles. According to Andy, it was his women who gave him away.

This is how Andy described the journey: on their way north, he and El Pícaro, newly minted *missioneros*, passed from clique to clique across the Guatemalan border and into Mexico. From Tecun Uman they crossed the Suchiate River in a truck driven by Mexican MS members. They then traveled up to Veracruz, Mexico, and so on, always escorted by a local MS member who knew the area and could navigate the local authorities, always checking in with El Pensador back in Guatemala, who dealt with the local Mexican clique, ensuring the two boys had food and money. It took three months to complete the trans-Mexico journey and enter the United States.

When Andy and El Pícaro caught up with their target in Las Vegas, some local MS homeboys pointed him out and gave Andy a knife. El Smokey was wearing a turtleneck to cover the MS tattoo etched in gothic letters across his neck.

"They told me, 'Look at him, that's the dude over there. Hit him here and he'll die slowly,'" touching his belly. "'Hit here and here and he'll die instantly,'" touching his neck and his temple. "One time, *bimbim!*"

"Do you remember where you were?"

"In front of a casino. I hit the guy and he went like this." Andy clutched the right side of his neck. "He took a half step, and boom, he fell. When I left there was a helicopter, tatatatatatata."

"What kind of gun did you use?"[34]

"No man! Over there you use a knife. Like I told you, we didn't have permission to take him with bullets. It was a place of real cops (*mero juras*) so finfinfin!" He stabbed the air with an imaginary knife. "So he was just left there. That's right. It was a job for the gang (*barrio*)."

El Smokey died from the knife wounds in the neck he had tried to conceal, in front of a Las Vegas casino. At first the passersby thought he was fallen-down drunk, a common enough sight in that city. Andy's mission accomplished, he returned to Guatemala and finally ended his long chequeo. At least this is how he recounted the story to me a few days before MS murdered him.

A month after Andy was killed, I finally got around to watching the film *Sangre por Sangre* (the English title is *Blood In, Blood Out*). It is a fictional account of the birth of the Mexican Mafia—a Mexican American prison "super gang"—in Southern California prisons, written by Jimmy Santiago Baca, an accomplished ex-con writer and poet who found his muse in the early years of incarceration. The film—produced and distributed by the Walt Disney corporation—can be found all over Mexico and Central America. I bought a pirated copy in a Guatemala City market. Alongside *American Me*, it ranks as one of the most popular and "accurate" film accounts of the Mexican Mafia, which to this day holds sway over Latino street gangs like 18th Street and the MS in Southern California and parts of the US Southwest. I watched it alone in bed, drinking a beer.

A third of the way into the film, the main character, Miklos, a half-Caucasian, half-Latino youth desperate to join the prison gang "La Onda," must demonstrate his worth by killing a white prisoner who has double-crossed the gang. "Show him the book," the gang leader tells a tall, mustachioed prisoner named Magic. The book looks like a small, black Bible, but hidden in its pages is a human figure marked with black dashes. The dashes are kill points.

"Hit a man here and here," says Magic, pointing to the stomach and the chest. "And he will die slowly, painfully. Hit a man here or here," he continues, pointing to the neck and the head, "and he will die instantly."[35] I rewound the scene and watched it again and again. Astounded. Angry. Laughing in confusion.

Did Andy see *Sangre por Sangre*? Did twelve-year-old Andy travel all the way to Las Vegas to kill an escaped ramflero? Did he knife the man in the neck on a busy street in front of a casino and escape before the police helicopter arrived? Does it matter whether this boy did this thing in this place? Or whether he and his homeboys spun it out of a collage of their experiences, Hollywood films, and the internal stories circulating and transforming endlessly in the unstable myths of the MS?

Of course it matters. Let us assume, for a moment, that his story is true. That Andy did make this trip north, and his US compatriot parodied the film scene to the young *missionero*. The film itself is based loosely on the very real spaces, events, and even personalities that spawned the Mexican Mafia. It is also a "foundational text" of gang culture. Central American cliques connected to both MS and 18 present the film to new recruits to teach them the ethos, history, and meaning of the Latino gangs. It became the script through which Andy performed this murder. All of them—Andy, the US homeboy, and even El Smokey—became actors reinventing a piece of theater that itself is a simulacrum of real events. Art imitates life, life imitates art, in a chaotic circuit that never seems to end.[36] And in telling the story to me, Andy spun the cycle onward, drawing me (and through me, you) into a performance of violence that is not locked in time and place, but is staged again and again before new audiences while drawing on a Hollywood invention that has now become an intimate element of the real. Or he lied to me sitting in the prosecutor's office. Why? Did he lie so that the poor chance at immortality I offered would be commensurate with his imagination? Because the invented story shines so much more than the violent drudgery much of his life in actual fact was? Such glaring uncertainties are not separate from the violent acts they obfuscate, but in fact are integral to how this violence becomes woven into the world. That is, these fantasies and falsehoods are irrevocably linked to both the rationale for and consequences of acts of violence. Together, the act, the narration, and

its reception tie the dead bodies to efforts to justify, mourn, or exalt the violence and enhance the sense of power that, no matter how fleeting, the story
can provide the teller, who, no matter how he tells it, may or may not be the
doer. Approaching the scene from the "outside," one can watch the bloody
drama and count the dead and sometimes identify the actors and even analyze
their roles. But how is all this violence and suffering scripted, and to what end?

Ultimately, the meaning of this story goes deeper than whether Andy
actually did this thing in this place the way he said he did. Andy, speaking to
me, answering my questions, caught up in the maelstrom of his last days,
explained his life to me this way, using these words and these symbols as
anchors in the story. Storytelling always entails an act of self-creation. Whether
the Las Vegas story was true, a flight of whimsy, or an allegory for something
else too painful or too mundane to tell, it exposes a brief fragment of the self
that Andy invented and reinvented to survive and, perhaps, to survive beyond
his time and place among the living. In my effort to capture and convey his
experience, I have become another purveyor of Andy's life and death, adding
one more degree of separation and sowing one more set of sutures to keep the
whole thing from coming apart at the seams. Still, I cannot stop the narrative
from unraveling. Every facet of Andy's life, every version of his life story that
he told and that I inferred, every lie, flight of fancy, and grim confession recede
into the event horizon of his murder, from whence they cannot be reclaimed.
That Thursday afternoon when another youth about his age blasted five bullets through his skull forms both the beginning and the end of Andy's story.

————

After killing El Smokey, Andy returned to Guatemala and was finally "jumped
in" (*brincado*)—officially accepted into the gang. He was thirteen years old, a
bona fide homie belonging to the MS's bloodiest and most powerful clique in
Guatemala. Three years later he helped organize the crime of the four heads.
Shortly afterward he walked in on El Pensador, his ramflero, snorting cocaine,
an act prohibited by MS internal rules (alcohol and marijuana are okay; anything else receives swift punishment). Andy reported his ramflero's violation
to the other homies, but El Pensador denied everything, threatening to turn
Andy into ceviche. Andy knew well enough not to hang around after his
ramflero made this kind of threat. He split with three other guys, Gorgojo
and two other young chequeos dissatisfied with their indentured servitude,
leaving CLS forever.

A year later, a dismembered female body in a trash bag appeared in front of Andy's house in zone 5 of Guatemala City. His "marero-ness," it seems, was obvious to his neighbors, and someone fingered him to the cops. He roundly denied his guilt—"How could I be so stupid as to leave a corpse in front of my own house?"—but no one listened. Fearing the real possibility of going to adult prison and seeing an opportunity to get back at the MS, Andy told the police he could give them the perpetrators of the quadruple decapitation. In exchange, they promised to make him a protected witness.

Three months later, under armed escort on his way to give testimony in the Tower of Tribunals, Andy said, he caught sight of a CLS member waiting outside the underground entry, watching the media and prosecutors streaming in. His collar was pulled up high to cover the tattoos on his neck. They locked eyes for a second, Andy said, and that's when he knew. He walked on through the warren of tunnels beneath the Supreme Court, into the cramped, stuffy courtroom. Sitting before the sweating judge, he put it all down on tape, all he knew of the MS: the leaders, the structures of command, the weapons caches, the fronts, the accountants, the soldiers. Extortion networks. Murdered children. Bodies buried in basements.

Andy's story is a collection of memories twisted by trauma, fantasies of power, and Hollywood invention, lies and myths that he drew upon in his narration of his life. This layering of truth and fantasy was by no means his alone. Storytelling is always an exchange between the actor and his or her audience. This exchange takes place as much through the fantasies we project upon one another as it does through the truths we believe we are sharing. As Andy engaged with his violent past and impossible future, he fulfilled law enforcement officials' fantasies of protecting society from gang atrocities. And through our brief encounter, he fulfilled my own dream of delving into the life of a "real" marero. His violent death permanently blocked the possibility of continuing this exchange, providing an abruptly certain sense of closure to a narrative filled with lacunae and ellipses. And now, the only way I know to give back what is owed is to keep the promise I made to Andy of a poor kind of immortality. I have constructed a hall of mirrors out of the shards of Andy's life to reflect how acts of brutality are etched into life through the endless blurring of truth and fantasy, memory and myth. And though Andy's story may appear singular, it is not. As I explore in the next chapters, the processes of violent creation and destruction that shaped his life, his death, and his story are in fact layered into the making of the maras, and of the world itself, on a far grander scale.

FIGURE 10. Sepulchers in the Guatemala City General Cemetery.

Brother's Bones

Calavera and I climb a ragged stone staircase up a low rise in the middle of the cemetery. He talks of how he wishes he could forget much of his past, but also how so many memories slip away no matter how hard he fights to hold them close. In prison, it was easier to simply not think of the dead or of problems beyond his capacity to solve. Having witnessed so many men lose themselves raging against their past and the present it had made, he became adept at forgetting. But since walking free, his past has mounted a clandestine assault. Ghosts mark him from the shadows, from just around a corner, and in strangers' sidelong glances. They are whispered reminders of all he survived and the unlucky bastards who did not. The cemetery is rife with these ghosts and their stories. Some of their stories he lived, too. Some he heard from his sister, Casper, and others, repeated so many times they became his own, slipping into his dreams.

One such story begins with his brother Giovanni walking through the old neighborhood more than a decade before. Where the path forked a young man sat on a broken cement bench, staring at his hands. It was Casper. When he saw Giovanni, he straightened up, calling out, "What do you think they have waiting for us, carnal?"

"El Soldado said it was to make peace with the Boyz 13."

Casper spit. "Those motherfuckers. I'd sooner skin my dick."

"Well, we'll find out," Giovanni shrugged. "I'm just glad you came."

"Of course I came," Casper blurted, then caught himself. "Where the fuck could I run?"

Giovanni looked at Casper and then beyond him into the ravine of trash and the slums clustered against the steep hills on the other side.

"Come on," he said. "It's time." The left fork cut between two weather-beaten and crudely graffitied tin warehouses, then made a precipitous drop to a packed gravel road worn by dump truck tread and the soles of trash pickers. Giovanni started down the right fork that twisted across a desolate space pocked with crabgrass, broken bits of masonry, and scrap metal. Casper followed. More and more debris appeared as the path wound on, as if they were approaching the foundation of some blasted edifice, until it swung up sharply and into the cemetery's outer border.

After a minute a plateau of broken and eviscerated crypts came into view to the left down the slope. They could see a cluster of dark figures gathered there among the ruins, some sitting, others leaning against scattered gravestones.

"Wait up a moment," Casper said.

"What is there to wait for?"

"Just hold on, will you."

"OK."

They huddled against a mossy concrete slab. The sun had dropped into the hills cresting above the ravine of trash, swinging beams of light upward through the warship clouds strung in ragged columns across the sky. Suddenly the clustered figures threw their heads back and a shout of laughter echoed faintly, and Casper and Giovanni could hear traces of a deep voice speaking in rapid cadence. Then the men all rose, throwing up their hands in a salute, fingers cocked like claws over their heads.

"*Vivo te quiero*," Giovanni murmured under his breath. "Look alive." Then he stepped out onto an uneven dirt path. Muttering a prayer and crossing himself, Casper hurried to catch up. As they crossed the barren decline, the voice ceased and the figures turned together, marking their approach.

The one who had been speaking was El Soldado. He stood apart from the others, shaved head shining in the fading light.

"You are here," he said.

Giovanni shrugged. "I told you."

"Why did the others run?"

"They do not want to kill their neighbors. We've known those boys since we were kids."

"They would kill you if it suited them."

"Perhaps."

"*Órale*," Soldado said, signaling to the other homies. Several ducked behind a concrete mausoleum and emerged dragging three figures, wrists and ankles bound with wire. They were so bloodied and beaten it took Giovanni a moment to recognize them. They were all that remained of the Boyz 13.

———

As Calavera tells the story of the Boyz 13, we stand atop the low rise amid mausoleums marked with Mandarin characters, looking out onto the cemetery. Below us, long corridors of the dead cut through dense stands of broken pillars and concrete crucifixes. The cemetery ends abruptly above the ravine.

In this telling, Calavera has put himself in Giovanni's place, making his brother's story his own. He points toward a plateau at the cemetery's edge, hazy in the distance. "It was right over there, on that patch of grass just before the garbage dump. El Soldado called the two of us over, Casper and I, while the others kept watch on the Boyz 13. El Soldado had this terrible smile on his face. 'Look here,' he said in a low voice. 'Right now you have a choice to make. Put an end to this charade once and for all, or . . .' He nodded at the boys, all bloody and tied up, and said, 'This has gone on long enough.'"

"Wait, who were the Boyz 13?" I ask.

"They were another clique belonging to the Letters like us, and they had gotten deep into drug trafficking, but for a dude named El Marino. El Marino controlled Barrio Gallito, over there, on the other side of the cemetery. We fought with them for years over drug *puntos*." Calavera pauses, looking out over the ravine. "So I say, "Right on then,' and ba ba ba! Pistols for the two of us. Just revolvers, 38s. 'Vivo te quiero,' El Soldado told us. 'Blast 'em, because if not I'll be right here behind you and you too will stay here.' Then he turned back to the other homies and told them to free the Boyz 13, that they could go.

"'Your mother,' I thought. And so the meeting ended and the locos started to leave. I don't know what they thought was going down. They were just walking back along the way we had come. And we're walking after them, and El Shark and El Soldado are walking behind us. And I'm like that, almost trembling with that feeling.

"And when those locos turn back and look at us, one asks, 'What's up dude?'

"'Nothing.' I said. Then I started firing. One of them fell, I made one fall. And then Casper started firing, and he put down another. But one of them got away."

"Up that path there?" I say, pointing to a footpath leading back toward a cluster of rundown warehouses.

"Yeah, up that way, but it was higher then, less eroded. I could hear the sirens, the police already coming and I knew I had to get out of here, so I ran toward 26th and jumped the cemetery wall and from there to my house. But with the idea that one of them was still alive. 'Sonofabitch, what a shitshow,' I thought. They're going to come for us. But it wasn't so. The last one had three bullets in his stomach, and he died. He couldn't take it. Ah."

Several seconds pass in silence broken only by the sound of my scribbling in my notebook.

"I should have recognized then that it was all bullshit," Calavera continues with a sigh. "That all the talk of blood brotherhood and loyalty and giving your life for the Barrio was just a charade. Soldado and the others were just trying to get El Marino's influence out of zone 3 so they could control the drug houses. That's it. So they made us kill each other like dogs." He shakes his head, grimacing. "I'm just glad it wasn't me who took three bullets in the stomach."

We descend the stairs and turn onto a narrow path twisting between modest family plots overrun with creeping vines. Degraded by time, wind, and rain, many resemble ancient midden mounds. We turn a corner and nearly overtake a man dressed in ragged clothing bent over the pitted stone, pushing an empty wooden wheelbarrow. A boy walks before him carrying a battered metal bucket in each hand. The path is too narrow for Calavera and I to pass, so we slow and fall in line behind the two laborers. The old man smells of sweat and earth. A long knife in a cracked leather sheath hangs from a belt around his waist, softly slapping against his thigh with each step. Both man and boy are covered in a chalky dust from attending to the resting places of the dead. It is they who excavate the paupers' graves, ferry the bones and tattered funereal finery, and fling them down the hole, human dust floating in a final wake.

We turn down another long corridor, and then another. Calavera knows, or thinks he recognizes, several of the dead we pass. He points a few out to me.

"These are the vatos who weren't lucky enough to get arrested." He laughs ruefully. He tells me how the police nabbed him at a checkpoint as he was moving crack across the city. Casper was the leader of Los Northside by then and promised to care for Calavera's family. But the stipend Casper pledged never materialized, and Sandra was left to fend for herself and her daughters.

Casper started going crazy, killing anyone who stood in his way. And he didn't care when little kids or pregnant mothers got caught in the crossfire. Calavera read the newspapers, and his sister told him what was going down. He tried to talk sense to some of his old homies, but they were all scared of Casper.

"The way I saw it, killing women and kids was bad for business, bad for our reputation." He shakes his head, "Don't we all have brothers and sisters and children we want to protect? But Northside's territory grew, and you can be sure that the Big Homies who were still around didn't give a shit. And no one else either. There was plenty of newspaper reporting, but no one did anything."

We reach a break in the wall, where Calavera signals for me to follow him to the right. The man and the boy walk on toward a water tower rising above the grounds. The boy joins a line of others stooping to dip their buckets in a well of murky water and draw them out again.

We enter a forest of concrete crucifixes, some broken and bent at rakish angles. Calavera halts suddenly, looking first one way and then the other.

"What's wrong?" I ask.

He shakes his head and resumes walking slowly down a path that carves a slight descent to where the cemetery ends above the garbage dump. We reach the edge of the precipice. Motley debris is tangled in the vines and brambles carpeting the slope. Twisted rebar and concrete, battered coffins with bits of gray crinoline spilling out. A plastic baby doll sits upright among shards of shattered crockery as if a child's tea party has gone awry. A greasy, cloying stench fills my nostrils. It is the smell of vultures. They perch on the limbs of trees and on every crucifix above every grave, black wings spread wide to dry in the sun, gray heads cocked to inspect newcomers. I inch out to stand on the exposed foundation of an abandoned mausoleum jutting out above the ravine. Below, diesel trucks rumble over the packed refuse, delivering the garbage of the heaving metropolis. Trash pickers move across the waste, tiny figures stooping and rising beside pools of metallic green water leaching through the dump and into a black river coursing into the bowels of the city.

I back away from the edge and follow Calavera along a sepulcher wall facing out over the precipice.

"He's here, I know he's here," Calavera mutters to himself. "He should be here." Again he halts and stands for some time facing the wall, closely inspecting each plaque. A name, a simple prayer, a life reduced to a hyphen. This one is faded by the elements. This one is favored with a flowering succulent. This one is carved in flowing font. A few plots have been bricked up and plastered

FIGURE 11. Tenements for the dead, Guatemala City General Cemetery.

over. One remains open, a blank blackness occupied by a vulture, head cocked, inspecting us with a single beady eye.

"I must have it wrong," Calavera says. "Let's go to the next one." The path ahead ends abruptly where the cliff has crumbled away into the ravine. We backtrack and turn down another corridor, surprising an adolescent couple necking, the boy pressed up against the girl against the wall. She giggles. The boy looks up, then nuzzles in closer. They cling to each other, ignoring my awkward greeting. Vultures perch atop the walls on either side like sentries, wings rustling and talons scraping against the plaster.

For the next hour, as the sun sinks in the west, we wander like that, criss-crossing the northwest section of the cemetery, vainly searching for Giovanni's plot among the tens of thousands interred and innumerable missing. After a while, Calavera stops pointing out people he knows and trudges along in silence.

Finally, we stand side by side above the path leading to the old meeting place at the furthest corner of the cemetery.

"It's confusing here," I say. "And it's been . . . well, it's been a long time."

Calavera just shakes his head.

"I'm sure your sister wouldn't have let anything, uh, happen."

"No."

I fiddle with the recorder and jot a few words in my journal: "Forgotten? Discarded? Dead or not?"

Calavera pauses, and then, suddenly resolute, turns to head down the path to the old meeting place. "Let's go, Anthony. Let's see what's down there now."

A flock of vultures has gathered around a corpse of one of their own stretched out like a patient etherized upon a table beside a pillaged grave. They flap away lugubriously as we approach, dispersing among the scattered trash and headstones worn indecipherable in the undergrowth. Calavera pokes around, looking for his name and others he and his old compatriots graffitied long ago. I walk the perimeter and stop suddenly before a ruined mausoleum.

"Oh shit," I say, and call out to Calavera. "Look here."

Calavera joins me. The mausoleum wall has been graffitied in black spray paint. An M and an S, a 13, and a cartoon crown and skyscrapers. A date is scrawled beneath: 21 May 2012. That is two days ago.

We both turn to look out from the plateau toward the footpath leading back to Calavera's neighborhood. After a few moments, I say in a low voice, "Perhaps we should be leaving."

Calavera's gaze lingers on the graffiti. "Yeah, OK." He shakes his head. "What a shitty tag. I tell you, kids these days don't know shit."

––––––––––

As Calavera walks with me away from the meeting place at the edge of the cemetery, one more memory rises up unbidden. It was the last time he saw his brother. Giovanni was driving a Honda civic with tinted windows on the outskirts of Xela. The air coming through the windows was hot and dry. Casper—already ramflero of Salvatrucha Locos de Northside—sat in the front passenger seat. Giovanni had invited him against Sandra's wishes. Sandra was in the back with her infant daughter suckling at her breast, sitting next to Calavera. Calavera watched the baby breastfeed while pretending to look out the window: her lips straining at the nipple, her eyelids squeezed shut as if the light flitting through the car were blinding. Sandra was listening distractedly to Giovanni and Casper talking, when Casper suddenly turned around and fixed Calavera with a grin.

"One more to feed the nation, huh," he said, turning back to Giovanni.

Giovanni looked over sharply at Casper. "What did you say?"

"I said, one more little vato to make the mara strong."

Giovanni jerked the car to the side of the road and skidded to a stop in the gravel. "Listen, dickhead," he said in a quiet, charged voice, "my brother will never join the gang. I do not want this life for him. He is better than this. Do you understand?"

"Calm down, brother. I was just . . ."

"I said, do you fucking understand?"

"Yeah yeah, of course. Don't worry man. I was just joking around. Why don't you smoke your joint and chill out, hey?"

Still glaring at Casper, Giovanni shoved the car into gear and pealed out onto the road. Sandra and Calavera exchanged a startled look, both too afraid to speak. Casper stared stolidly out the window at warehouses of sheet metal, unpainted, boxy things where men covered in grease moved like ants among the carcasses of dead tractors, semis, and other machines strewn about the gravel lot.

As they drove, Calavera watched his brother's face in the rearview mirror, the tattoo tears etched at his right eye, the gothic script down his neck. In those days he was always angry about one thing or another, stuff he never

FIGURE 12. Mara Salvatrucha graffiti on gravestone, Guatemala City General Cemetery.

discussed with Calavera, or with any of his family, if what Sandra said was true. As Calavera watched, Giovanni looked up into the mirror and for an instant they were caught in each other's reflected gaze. What Calavera saw there he was never able to name: an infinite sadness, a secret window into his brother that he'd never seen before and never would again. Perhaps it was all the hopes and fears that would break Giovanni to pieces if he let them loose. Calavera wanted to wrap his arms around his brother's neck and cry. Then Giovanni turned his eyes back to the road. For a long while, no one spoke.

CHAPTER 2

Emissaries of the Violent Peace

Like the decomposing landscape where the Guatemala City cemetery meets the city dump, mara history makes for treacherous terrain. Telling the story of the maras' rise means reckoning with the breathtaking mortality rates among gang-involved youth. Death's specter materializes in the symbols with which maras and mareros mark their bodies and neighborhoods. Take, for example, the *tres puntos* (three points) tattoo, once a trademark of Southern California Latino gangs. Composed of three dots in the shape of an ellipsis or an equilateral triangle, it is usually tattooed on the back of the hand or at the corner of an eye.[1] For some it references the Holy Trinity. For others it is a trifecta of sex, mourning, and death. Among the maras of Central America, the tres puntos has taken on another meaning as well. It is said to stand for the only three certainties in *la vida loca*: the hospital, the prison, and the cemetery. Over the years, as violent death has steadily become more certain than survival, the cemetery has come to loom larger than life among the maras.

Today, relatively few gang members, it seems, survive their twenties. For example, José, a former Barrio18 member, claimed that of the ninety homies he saw initiated into the gang between 1998 and 2000, only three are alive today. Little Fat of the Mara Salvatrucha (MS) believed that he was among five men who survived out of the sixty he ran with in the early 2000s. El Cholo Cifuentes may be the last man alive from his Barrio18 crew that was active in the mid-1990s. They are survivors of peacetime war zones in which thousands of youths kill and die each year in the name of imported symbols tattooed on their bodies and graffitied on neighborhood walls, only to be replaced by others too brash, too ignorant, or too vulnerable to resist the maras' allure. In recent years, if official statistics are to be trusted at all, the killing has only accelerated.[2]

How did this happen? How did the maras come to influence the lives and deaths of so many urban youths growing up in postwar Guatemala City?[3] And how did groups of youths fighting in the name of symbols imported from US street gangs become such central figures in the making and mooring of peacetime terror? In this chapter I piece together a few key elements of mara history that set the arc of the maras' dystopian evolution and made them into harbingers of a new age of violence. Drawing from the stories of former gang members and gang associates, as well as journalists' and scholars' accounts, I map the political and social ferment of Guatemala City when the maras first took root; how decades of US involvement in Guatemala gave the maras' "made in America" style an irresistible magnetism for some urban youth; and finally, the ways that this "new way of being a gang" seemed, for a moment, to structure and regulate internecine gang violence before it too fell apart.

Exploring the rise of the gangs in Guatemala means linking irrefutable historical phenomena—US imperialism and Cold War atrocities, transnational migrations and deportations, and so forth—with the multiple and contradictory ways people remember and make meaning out of the past. That is, this chapter tacks back and forth between documented material history and how people remember and symbolically render the past in the present. The point is to provide a relatively clear context and background to contemporary struggles for order, but also to show how in the end, material and symbolic histories are absolutely inseparable. Neither should be valued over the other.[4] What *actually* happened in the past only gains power and meaning through how it is imagined in the present, and such memories are always uncertain and under contestation.[5]

To put it another way, making history is a process of creative destruction, of remembering *and* forgetting.[6] Many of the stories in this chapter were recounted to me by former gang members and gang associates stuck in prison or struggling to survive on the street. They came filtered—consciously or not—through memories twisted by time and trauma. Some have been passed down from generation to generation, tweaked and embellished countless times before reaching me. Some are fragments of memory that fit, like rough-hewn puzzle pieces, more or less awkwardly with the mishmash of newspaper and scholarly reports that pass for the "historical record." These stories of the gang past, like any historical account, should not be taken as "merely" history. The maras' evolution in Guatemala has been concomitant with the rise of out-of-control crime, and these stories reflect collective efforts—made by myriad actors besides the maras—to stabilize the present by pinning down the past. As the harbinger of a dystopian present and future, gang history reflects collective anxieties over Guatemala's descent into peacetime chaos. This history of the ever-receding past conjures forth dreams and nightmares animating contemporary struggles with severe insecurity.[7] Indeed, one of the only certainties to emerge in these stories is that the past was more orderly and secure than the present, mirroring the widespread sense of nostalgia at work in Guatemala City (and elsewhere) for long-lost orders of violence. Whether these stories tell the truth about the past is an open and unanswerable question. But even if the old ways of ordering violence never existed as they are remembered, such memories provide a foundation, shaky as it may appear, upon which to construct a sense of order.[8]

NOSTALGIA FOR A FAILED REVOLUTION

Among large swathes of the urban population today, out-of-control violence and insecurity have given rise to an odd sort of nostalgia for the ordered violence of civil war.[9] That such nostalgia exists at all is disturbing, given that the endgame of Cold War conflict was state-perpetrated massacres, disappearances, and genocide. But in the late 1980s, when the signs and symbols associated with the maras are purported to have first appeared in Central America, the armed conflict that had simmered and periodically erupted for more than thirty years was grinding to a close. The threat of state violence was still very much on people's minds, though armed confrontation between the military and what was left of the guerrilla forces was rare, and the nation was groping hesitantly toward peace and the return of nominal democracy. During this period several robbery and kidnapping rings developed in Guatemala City, including Los Pasacos, the Kangooroos, Agosto Negro, and the AR15s, to name a few. The AR15s became famous for using high-caliber weapons in shootouts with urban police; its rank and file were probably deserters from the army. Youth gangs also existed but were for the most part scattered, unaffiliated, and isolated from one another. There were *brekeros* (break-dancers), decked out in Michael Jackson-esque glitz, tight pants, and jean jackets, dancing to US funk and hip-hop. There were (and still are) the *niños de la calle* (street children)—orphans and runaways living together for companionship and protection, huffing glue and gasoline, panhandling, snatching purses, and picking pockets. Military police are said to have targeted them for social cleansing.[10] Stories still circulate of *el panal blanco* (the white van), into which police hustled street children and common thugs. Some claim these people were sent into compulsory military duty, others that they were simply killed.

El Cholo Cifuentes—who would eventually become the leader of a Barrio18 clique in zone 1 of Guatemala City—came of age in the late 1980s. He also claimed to have served a stint transporting cocaine for Guatemalan middlemen involved in the Colombian trade. For more than a decade he has made his home in Granja Penitenciaria Pavón, Guatemala's oldest prison, known to inmates simply as Pavón. This is where I made his acquaintance.

At first, he said, he resided with the general population, commingling with other Barrio18 members and *paisas* (non-gang prisoners). However, toward the end of his sentence he requested a transfer to an isolation block. The young gangsters entering the prison were getting too crazy, he said, too out of control, and he didn't want to risk getting caught up in their bad trouble. In mid-2012, when we spoke in his private cell, he was sick with hepatitis, patches of skin yellow and inflamed, wearing a grease-stained, secondhand Izod golf shirt. I asked him how he first became involved in the maras.

"Ah, yes," he said, flashing stained yellow teeth. "I was waiting for that question. We were a *banda* (band or group), not yet a gang. We called ourselves *los Guerreros* (the Warriors). This was before the maras had become the maras. We got a group together of ten, fifteen guys. And when we saw a man acting dishonorably, like abusing a woman on the street, we shut him up." He held up a swollen finger in righteous admonition. "'Calm down, man. Women are not to be touched.' And we were young, but that's how we were. Doing the work of heroes."

Like other aging gangsters, Cholo's stories are sticky with nostalgia for a more moral, even heroic past.[11] To hear them tell it, early gangs hewed to a spirit of communal protection and ethical mores that have all but disappeared today. These accounts blur the idealized memories of popular revolution with the birth pangs of a new era and the criminal phenomenon that would dominate it. In the mid- to late 1980s, although the guerrillas had already been effectively defeated in the highlands and stamped out in the capital, revolutionary zeal was still something palpable in Guatemala. The children and youths who would become involved with gangs carried with them a political awareness rooted in working-class solidarity and leftist politics that had helped spark and sustain the social movements and armed efforts against the government.

Working with a team of Guatemalan researchers in the mid-1980s, historian Deborah Levenson interviewed dozens of Guatemala City youths involved in this early generation of maras.[12] She found that they were growing up in shantytowns populated by refugees displaced by war and in working-class neighborhoods terrorized by the counterinsurgency. The refugee families had fled scorched-earth campaigns in the countryside, while death squads targeted urban trade unionists, students, and other urban-based "subversives" for disappearance and torture. Lingering fear silenced the survivors of these movements and engulfed entire communities. As a result, their children would have few tools and little opportunity to understand the politics or legitimacy of the violence that made their world.[13] The youth who formed the street gangs that would later be subsumed into the MS and Barrio18 inherited both the vestiges of progressive politics and shades of nightmarish violence of the continent's bloodiest, dirtiest war.[14] This toxic cocktail of failed revolution and ingrown terror still courses through the veins of postwar society.

———

Silence grew up in zone 5 of Guatemala City. He is a tall, light-skinned man with a big belly and scarred hands. He showed me where the knuckles were disjointed and the small bones in his left wrist broken. Today he goes by Juan Gabriel, but when he was fourteen and joined a Barrio18 clique in zone 5 of Guatemala City, they gave him the *apodo* Silence because, he says, he never shut up. People who knew him when he was an active gang member speak of his violent temper. For an imagined slight, it is said, he macheted a man across the collarbone in broad daylight on a crowded street. To proclaim his undying allegiance to Barrio18, he had tattoos etched up each arm and across his neck. He was thirty-two when I met him and had left the gang ten years earlier. He had spent these years trying to burn away those tattoos. Blurred shadows and mottled skin were all that remained.

It was during popular protests in the late 1980s, Silence said, when he was about five years old, that he first heard the word *mara*. "Look, it was toward the end of the main violence of the civil war," he told me in a Wendy's across from the National Cathedral, the orange pillars catching the day's last light. "When Vinicio Cerezo came and . . . bus fare was at 15 cents and he changed it to 85 cents. An egg cost 5 cents, and he wanted it at 10 cents." Vinicio Cerezo was Guatemala's first democratically elected president of the modern era.[15]

"How do I explain?" Silence continued. "It's like, if today they come and say bus fare is Q1, and we're going to put it at Q5! Who of the people would allow that? But it was a transition government moving toward democracy. There still existed all that military repression. So people went out to protest and were attacked by the military police. There were many jailed and beaten, and some were even disappeared. In those days no one knew a thing about the maras of Guatemala, absolutely nothing." He paused to survey the other patrons, then went on. "But gang members had been arriving since the '70s and organizing in an anonymous way. And in the time of Vinicio Cerezo, the opportunity presents itself for the gangs to make themselves known in Guatemala. The gangsters who were organized here in zone 6 of Guatemala City, they came out to respond in favor of the people, to support the protest because, most of all, many of those who had been incarcerated or beaten or killed were their family members. So, the army is subjugating the people—and the gang comes out and pushed back the army. And that was when one heard about . . . searches from house to house, cars were upturned, busses set on fire, etcetera. This was—," Silence paused again, searching for the appropriate word. "This was *unstoppable*."

"So the news comes out, and it comes out that the Barrio18 gang announced that they weren't going to allow the rights of the people to be abused and that they were there to defend the pueblo. So when I heard that story I was five years old, and I told myself, 'Damn!'" He pounded a scarred fist on the Formica table. "'When I'm big I want to be like that.' Not wanting to be a gangster, exactly, but to be someone who fights for the rights of others. That's how I conceived of the vision."

No historical record exists of Barrio18 members secretly organizing throughout the 1970s and 1980s. But in his story Silence draws an organic link between the transnational gangs that would become a zeitgeist of postwar disorder and a prior generation of urban youth who embraced a vibrant mix of countercultural solidarities and styles. The term *mara* itself emerged in connection with the same protests that Silence remembers so vividly. In a 1985 press interview a police chief referred to the mass of youth taking part in these protests as *marabunta*—swarming army ants—and the term quickly caught on in public discourse and eventually among the maras themselves.[16]

Levenson's research in the 1980s was and remains one of the few existing scholarly accounts of this lost generation of maras. The stories she collected speak of poor urban youths searching for and finding a deep sense of belonging with one another. These young people carved out social spaces in which they could express themselves—politically, artistically, and even sexually— with more freedom than the edicts of mainstream culture allowed for.[17] And for many of them, whatever violence came from being part of a gang—fights with rival groups, robbing middle-class youth, and so on—paled in comparison to the brutalities they witnessed in their homes and the counterinsurgent terror of massacre and disappearance that destroyed so much of the country's politically minded underclass. In retrospect, however, the vibrant and ambiguous mix of social forces that compelled these youths to join together proved extremely volatile. Revisiting their accounts thirty years later, Levenson herself seems overcome by a sense of nostalgia for what was or might have been. This generation of mara youth, she writes, today appears "almost suspended in historical time between what now seems like a shutter-shot moment of an urban popular movement's peak and its quick bloody demise."[18]

Nostalgia for communal solidarity against an abusive authoritarian state saturates collective memories of the last years before peace was officially declared.[19] During this period, Gato—a former thief and drug addict who reformed in prison and became a government social worker—was the leader of a street gang in zone 1 of Guatemala City. Gato was my first real contact and one of my closest friends in Guatemala. One evening in 2012, as Gato, his wife, and I were drinking beer in their home, he recalled how his crew collected protection money from the local drug dealers, prostitutes, and thieves working around the Parque Concordia, about ten city blocks from the National Palace. These were fond memories. He claimed his gang was strong enough— and he had enough personal cachet—to hold the respect of the local underworld. He could rob police of their guns with just a knife, he bragged, and twirled a fork in the air to demonstrate.

His wife, Catalina, who grew up with him on the streets, clicked her tongue. "He gave all of that money away," she said, shaking her head, "or drank it."

Gato laughed and told a story of getting caught by three cops in the Parque Concordia. "One of them was a policeman we knew as Chino, who would extort the street kids and if they didn't pay he would arrest them. Chino put his gun to my head and the gun went off. It was probably an accident, a misfire, or just nerves. It snapped my head back." He put the fork down and massaged a small white scar on the side of his head. "The bullet is still buried there.

A crowd gathers around me, people from all over the neighborhood—shop-keepers and transvestite prostitutes, men and women crying, 'Gato is dead.' A little boy leans over me and Gato opens one eye. 'Gato is alive,' the boy shouts. He puts his hand on my other eye, 'Ay Gato, your eye, it's still there. It's just covered in blood.'"

After the shot rang out, an angry mob attacked the police, sending them running. Gato said his people lifted him up and whisked him away to the dump to hide him in the trash. He burrowed into the garbage, sniffed some glue, and fell sleep. Hours or minutes passed, and he poked his bloody head out. An old woman was sitting there, quiet and serene. She shushed him, telling him it was not safe and that he should go back to sleep.

Gato is a born storyteller, and in all the time I have known him, he has never hesitated to blend facts with more convenient or entertaining fictions. This story bears uncanny traces of *El Señor Presidente*, the opus of Guatemala's Nobel laureate Miguel Angel Asturias. In the book, el Pelele, an idiot clown, accidentally kills a military officer and runs away to hide in the trash dump, where the vultures pick at his exposed limbs. He is a hapless victim who, in a moment of blind rage, strikes out against a figure of state power. Later, he dies ignominiously, doomed in Asturias's allegory of life under military dictatorship.[20]

Though Gato's life today seems far more stable and secure than were his days leading a street gang, he mourns the past, when, he says, "things were better because we were in charge." Regardless of the facts, Gato's story is also an allegory—an allegory for a lost or imaginary past in which his community stood up against abusive police to defend its own. Today, such sentiments of solidarity seem sorely missing, replaced by far more brutal and opportunistic modes of competition and survival. However uncertain and violent the past may have been, from the perspective of the present this history arcs toward one particular certainty: things are far worse now.

Emerging out of a past roiled by social movements that once seemed to hold the promise of a better future, the maras have since eclipsed them. This was brought home to me at an international conference on the maras hosted in San Salvador, El Salvador. It was March 2012, shortly after imprisoned leaders of the Barrio18 and the MS in El Salvador had announced a truce, dropping the national murder rate by an unprecedented 60 percent.[21] This was big news, and I found myself mingling with journalists, scholars, and members of law enforcement from all over Central America, as well as many from the United States and Europe. José Luis Sanz, an investigative journalist with *El Faro* who has spent more than a decade delving into the gangs and their histories, addressed the cosmopolitan crowd. "In a matter of years the gangs have achieved a virulence beyond anything else that has followed," he declared. "Probably not even . . . the epic revolutionary movements of the 70s and 80s spread like such wildfire, leaving its mark on so many generations in such a powerful way as the gang phenomenon has done."[22] This awe-inspiring ascent was intimately entangled with the circulation of bodies, images, aspirations, and violence between the United States and Central America.

MADE IN AMERICA?

Pavón Prison, Guatemala City, 2012. A dozen or so prisoners gathered around cement tables in the prison courtyard, stringing plastic beads on fishing line to make tiny, floppy-eared dog ornaments. Juande, former leader of the MS clique Los Salvatruchas de Normandy, was in charge of the arts and crafts workshop. He slouched on a bench, wearing an immaculate, bright yellow hoodie. He was thirty-three, the age of Jesus when he died on the cross.

"If you make it one more year," I joked, "you'll prove you aren't Christ's second coming."

He flashed a gold-rimmed smile, as if to say "what a farce." Since age seventeen he had been in and out of prison seventeen times. When we met, he was a decade into what he hoped would be his last stint, a twenty-five-year sentence for homicide. In three years he would be up for parole. With a wry smile, he proclaimed that he did not commit the murder for which he was sentenced. But there were plenty of others they never pinned on him.

Juande had a way of holding himself that let you know he could pound your face into the pavement without thinking too much about it. I saw him once feign a back kick hard to the chest of another prisoner who had appeared suddenly behind him. He was quick and flexible for such a big guy. But he always claimed he had left it all behind.

"When you're up in the mix, you got to be tough on the street," he said. "You don't ever show weakness. They'll take advantage of you." He jutted out his chin at the other prisoners crowded around the table, then looked down at his hands. "But when you're lying down in bed you think of all the ways they could kill you. And when a homie dies—well, you don't cry. You find out who did it, and you make a mission to go kill them. And if you can't find out exactly who, well you know which gang. Eventually you find out. Nothing stays secret." For all his aggressive talk and performance, I found Juande to be capable of great patience and generosity. In prison he was Calavera's closest confidant, and other inmates respected him as a fair and disciplined leader. Over the years I have come to call him my friend.

In the 1990s, Juande said, his family struggled financially, but his sister had a decent job as an accountant for a Korean-run factory, and she provided him with pretty much everything he needed. He was into stylish clothes. "I already had my loose pants, my Nike Cortezes, which was the style back then." When he was fourteen, she offered to pay his way to the United States because he was getting picked on by a group of guys in the neighborhood. Either that, or to buy him a gun so he could protect himself. He chose the gun because, he said, he didn't want people to think he was scared.

After we'd been hanging out for almost a year, Juande told me the story of how he joined up with the MS. We were sitting out on the prison patio, my recorder hidden beneath a baseball cap between us, the sun blazing on the concrete as a cool breeze wafted through. His storytelling style was always intensely cinematic. I felt like I was listening to an improvised script of *West Side Story* set in Guatemala City. He was fifteen, he said, when he first made contact with MS—back in 1993, when hardly anyone in Guatemala had even heard of MS or 18. There was a girl in his high school that he really liked, and he was always bothering her, trying to get her to pay attention to him. He performed a snippet of their courting.

"'I can't go with you,' she would tell me.

"'But why? You're a woman and I'm a man.'

"'No! It's that there are other people behind me.'

"'What, your parents don't let you have a boyfriend?'

"'No, that's not important.'

"'Then what? You don't like me?'

"'No, I like you. I just can't.'"

He kept pursuing her and pursuing her. Finally, she told him that if he really liked her, he should come to a party where she would be:

When I got there, I saw at the back of the room a ton of cholos standing around. But since I had come for her, I went in, and walked to the back of the room, and found her.

"Right on," I said.

"You came."

"Like I wasn't gonna come?"

So I was in the middle of all the cholos, and they're watching me, right. I see that they're riding with beanies, baseball caps, earrings, all tattooed. They dressed like I dressed. "These are my people!" I thought. I'm looking at them. The guy who had the command (*ramfle*) in those days was El Ice, may he rest in peace. El Frio of Normandy.

"Yo, *morro*, come here."[23]

"What the hell?" I say. I thought that . . . well, in Guatemala faggots (*huecos*) are called morros, but in El Salvador morros, or *bichitos*, are boys or kids. Like "*huiros*" or "*patojos*."

"No," he says. "It's just our slang (*calua*). Like saying, 'yo patojo.'"[24]

So I come up to him. She's standing there with him.

"And so you like Clowney?"

That's when I learned that she was Clowney of MS of Normandy. She had hidden it. Later I saw the letters "MS" underneath her bellybutton.

"This was why I couldn't pay attention to you. Because I am the Clowney of Normandy. And who are you?"

"My name is Juande," I said. "And I am not anything."

"Really? You're nothing?" she says. El Ice, the deceased, is watching me.

"No, I'm nothing."

"Then why do you dress like that?" El Ice asks me.

"Because I like it."

"But who have you seen dressed like that?" He was trying to find out where I come from.

"Look, I'm from section A," I say. And all of the dudes are looking at me now. "And my friend Pocholo lives there. . . . He dresses like this with loose clothing (*ropa floja*). And I like how he looks. But it's not a sin to dress like this, is it?" And everyone laughs.

"It's all good, don't worry." And he says to Clowney, "OK then, the dude is pleasing to you?"

"The truth (*la neta*) is that yes, he is pleasing to me."[25]

"So then, do it. Let him inside, and you see what you do, but don't be careless. You know the process to follow. Tell him." It was about bringing me in, involving me with the gang.

So I'm dancing with her. "*Simón carnal* (Right on, brother)!" They're all yelling.[26]

"Carnal?" I say to myself. These aren't my brothers, I think to myself, but okay.

Juande went to more parties and brought in other youths from his neighborhood. The fact that he had a gun and knew how to use it impressed other gang members, and he had a natural flair for giving orders and intimidating people. He took part in the business side of things—robbing stores and setting

up modest extortion rackets—and became a bona fide member of Los Salvatruchas de Normandy. Eventually he helped raise and discipline other MS
cliques.

Juande was one of tens of thousands of youths across urban Central
America enamored of the style, the exotic language, and the confidence and
coolness he saw in the cholos he met and associated with the image they struck.
In the gangsters at that party he glimpsed a vision of himself, a reflection of
what he was, he thought, already aspiring to be. The language, the girl, the
clothes: "These are my people!"

How did US-style gangsters become the archetypes of "cool" for Juande and
so many others like him? Where did this aspirational image come from? In
the early 1990s groups of youths naming themselves after Los Angeles street
gangs—La Mara Salvatrucha, Barrio18, White Fence, Latin Kings, and so
forth—suddenly seemed to be in every major city in the Northern Triangle
of Central America.[27]

When they first emerged before the public eye, politicians, security watchdogs, and the media quickly labeled the maras a transnational phenomenon.
Worries of an internationally networked "super gang" mushroomed and
persist to this day.[28] However, cribbing and copying imported gang styles and
structures is not the same as forming a transnational criminal network. While
deported gangsters were important conduits for this transnational transfusion, they were not the only ones, and official estimates of their initial presence
have proven to be greatly inflated. A series of studies conducted in late 1990s
and early 2000s in El Salvador—the Central American nation with the greatest gang presence—seemed to show that less than 17 percent of gang youth
had ever been to the United States, and less than 11 percent had even been
gangsters when they lived there.[29] In Guatemala, where many of the founding
gang members were Salvadoran migrants, proportions would have been even
less. Flesh and blood deportees would play important roles in founding early
gang cliques in Guatemala and across the region. However, whatever respect
and admiration they inspired was by no means wholly their own. Their influence took hold through the symbolic power of all things "American" in Guatemalan society. This power stems from long histories of exchange between
the United States and Central American societies and reverberates far beyond
the street gang phenomenon.

From Hollywood movies to Maytag washing machines, from the Cold War to the War on Drugs, the influence US society has exercised over its Central American neighbors is inescapable. In 1954, to protect US corporate interests, the US government engineered a coup to oust Guatemala's second democratically elected president.[30] The Central Intelligence Agency (CIA) used the coup to develop its Cold War playbook and made the tiny country a testing ground for a new kind of psychological warfare drawing on techniques developed in the US advertising industry.[31] The CIA would go on to perfect the methods developed in Guatemala and apply them in Cold War conflicts around the world.[32]

The damage done to Guatemala was deep and lasting. The coup permanently crippled Guatemala's nascent democratic institutions. Political conflict raged for the next forty years, and US cold warriors lent a hand by training and nurturing right-wing death squads that decimated the moderate Left in Guatemala. The result was a deeply polarized political landscape in which anticommunist demagogues and military men would rule until the return of nominal democracy in the late 1980s. And perhaps ironically, throughout Guatemala's long history of civil strife, the United States has also been the primary destination for Guatemalans fleeing poverty and violence. The American dream, the dream of El Norte, the land of decent wages and a chance to "get ahead," is deeply etched into Guatemalan society.[33]

In the aftermath of the Cold War, US cultural and economic influences over Guatemalan society have only deepened. The nation's economy is tied to providing raw commodities—sugar, coffee, and silver—to US markets. Jobs in factories making goods for US consumers are highly prized. Customer service telemarketing, employing fluent English speakers, most of them deported from the United States, is one of Guatemala's most dynamic growth industries.[34] Over 80 percent of cocaine bound for the "insatiable North American nose" passes through Guatemalan territory, corrupting security forces and politicians and transforming both urban and rural economies.[35] Guatemalan authorities must fight against or collude with narco-traffickers enriched by US dollars and armed with weapons manufactured on US soil.[36] Meanwhile, the richest Central Americans go on weekend shopping trips to Miami, Florida. The point is, in both historic and contemporary terms, as both a driver of bloody chaos and the site of sanctuary and prosperity, the United States has played essential—if schizophrenic—roles in Guatemala's development.

The story of the maras in Guatemala emerges out of these transnational entanglements, but in ways that blend fantasy and reality in endless loops and feedback effects from beginning to end.

Transnational Birth Stories

In the 1970s and 1980s, when Guatemalans and other Central Americans began migrating en masse to the United States, Mexican Americans dominated Southern California's Latino gangs. For the most part, these gangs looked down upon and discriminated against Central American youths looking to join their ranks. They were too country and had funny accents, making them unfit for the gangs' standards and easy targets for ridicule. Neither were they allowed to found their own gangs. However, as more and more Central Americans settled in the Los Angeles area, the story goes, one gang saw an opportunity for expansion and opened its arms to these newcomers: 18th Street, or Barrio18. 18th Street was not the largest Hispanic gang in Los Angeles, but it was among the largest and among the oldest as well, claiming a direct lineage to the Clanton 14, a prestigious Latino gang with a history dating back to the 1950s.[37]

Guatemalans, Hondurans, and especially Salvadorans began to swell 18th Street's ranks. Joining meant gaining the respect, the companionship, and most of all the protection that went along with belonging to one of Los Angeles's biggest gangs. But it also meant sublimating their distinctive national identities into the dominant Mexican American subculture. They had to dress like Mexican cholos, speak like cholos, and so on, if they wanted to be accepted. Then, sometime in the late 1970s, a group of Salvadoran immigrants decided to go their own way.[38]

In 2012 investigative reporters Jose Luis Sanz and Carlos Martinez interviewed retired members of 18th Street and the MS in Los Angeles about the history that gave rise to the ongoing feud between the two gangs. "The Salvadorans who would form the first Mara Salvatrucha gang," Sanz later said,

> decided they didn't want to do what other Salvadoran youth who arrived before them had done; integrate with the Chicano gangs and conceal their Salvadoran identity by speaking like Chicanos, hiding or denying their origin, their place of birth, and dressing exactly like the cholos dressed—Sanchez pants, long dress shirts, a belt, slicked hair, this young man who has been caricatured so much and continues with the passing of time . . . and they were distinct as well because they didn't look like gangsters, they were groups of youthful fans of heavy metal music.[39]

These Salvadoran youths would consolidate into their own gang and call themselves La Mara Salvatrucha, becoming one more Los Angeles gang fighting for turf, drug distribution networks, and respect. Sometime later, not too much later according to Sanz and Martinez's sources, the MS and 18th Street turned on each other. How the break between the two rivals occurred, and how it escalated into an ongoing blood feud, is lost to history. It is said that Salvadoran members of 18th Street asked for permission to leave and begin their own gang, and when 18th Street refused, the Salvadorans left anyway, creating a schism that widened and hardened over the years. Another version has it that the MS killed an 18th Street member by accident in a drive-by, and the tit-for-tat killing never ended. Yet another version links the definitive break to a fight between the two gangs' leaders over a particularly beautiful woman, tying the age-old myth of feminine temptation leading to man's downfall into the gangs' origin stories.

Perhaps none of these stories is true; perhaps they all are. In any case, the making of profound enmity never occurs in a single moment. Love and hate, allies and enemies—these relationships form and crystallize over many actions and many years until the layers of sediment harden into bedrock, until that hatred is a natural, unquestioned thing. But gang history is an oral history, and as such, particular events are pulled out of the flow of time or thrust back into it, becoming watershed moments changing the course of history itself. But we know that history doesn't work like this; it only becomes so when we try to go back and reconstruct it to make sense of the present.[40]

The Flow of Fantasy and Flesh

In the early 1990s, riding a tide of national consternation in the wake of the Rodney King riots, the Moral Majority in the United States targeted Latinos suspected of gang membership for arrest and deportation. They were the vanguard of the "alien threat": foreign criminals destroying the inner cities of America. Men and women picked up in raids or culled from US prisons found themselves fast-tracked into deportation, loaded onto planes, and sent back "home."[41]

Most had never returned to their country of origin since leaving as small children and now found themselves adrift in a harsh, alien environment. Mainstream Guatemalan society rejected them wholesale. Central America's civil wars were grinding to a close, and these deportees represented the deeply entrenched troubles of the new democracy, the libertine-ism spawned by the arrival of liberty. For gang-involved deportees, setting up gangs in the style of those they had left behind was a strategic means of survival. They found many youths willing and eager to join, even if they had no idea what being part of a mara would mean. As Silence mused, he and other boys he knew growing up poor and abandoned were "ready for a future in which we could join a transnational gang, but we were really just aficionados. It was more like a hobby."

Coming from the United States and all it stood for, these deportees found they had a marked cultural cachet among poor urban youth. Their allure was rooted, at least in part, in the Hollywood images they so closely resembled. As planeloads of deportees touched down in Guatemala, Latino gangster films made in Hollywood—films like *Sangre por Sangre* and *American Me*—inspired Guatemalan youths to emulate what they saw. Such films may even have been key conduits in the transnational transfusions that brought the mara phenomenon to Central America. For example, I was talking to Estuardo—a Barrio18 member approaching the end of a six-year sentence for involvement in an extortion ring—about a recent prison riot when he abruptly shifted the conversation to the clique he had joined twenty years earlier. He claimed it was the first Barrio18 affiliate in zone 5 of Guatemala City, and the members called themselves Los Vatos Locos.[42] In the film *Sangre por Sangre* (the same movie Andy seemed to reenact), Los Vatos Locos is the name of the protagonist's street gang, caught in turf battles with the Tres Puntos. These were fictionalized amalgams, drawing their names and styles from early Los Angeles Latino street gangs. Soon after *Sangre por Sangre*'s 1993 release, groups of youths calling themselves Los Vatos Locos emerged in zones throughout Guatemala City.

Forged in feedback loops between the "real thing" and its Hollywood simulacrum, this new way of being a gang was defined by more solidarity, more brotherliness, and distinct forms of self-expression.[43] Acolytes of this new order hewed to an imported ideal of deathless brotherhood and barrio pride, sporting the clothing, language, and of course, tattoos of the North. They were eager to learn the logistical organization and strategies that had made Latino street gangs in the United States sustainable, even multigenerational organizations. "Snyper was his name," recalled José, one of three surviving members of an early Barrio18 clique in zone 18.

> He was an 18 of Hollywood Gangster . . . from the United States. When we met him he came talking half Spanish, half English. He would tell us that we had to learn to speak like that to be more involved and focused with the gang. He came

with this ideology of expanding ourselves, to make our territory bigger. We only had the actual park, it was the only sanctuary that we had, and we were living on the brink of war all the time. From there, it was only about four blocks to where the MS were. El Snyper organized us. He began organizing the money to gather when somebody got arrested and needed a lawyer to get him out, or to buy weapons. Because our clique had no guns. I had a shotgun, but it was homemade. . . . And so we started making contacts with the police, and they would sell us arms and bullets.

Like the vast majority of this generation of mareros, Jose's former compatriots are dead and gone. But the logic of solidarity and organization that they took on would spread beyond particular gang cliques, transforming into allegiance to gang pacts and codes that seemed, for a time, to order when, where, and against whom gang violence could occur. By joining up with the MS or Barrio18, the gangs that would come to dominate and subsume the rest, newly minted mareros were supposed to take on their gang's codes of allegiance and revenge, imported from the streets and prisons of Southern California. The first was the age-old feud between Barrio18 and the MS, which would map onto and transform already present street rivalries in Guatemala City. The second was the ideology of the Southern United Raza (SUR), an unstable but influential article of faith enforcing solidarity among imprisoned Latino gang members in Southern California. The introduction of these two doctrines in Guatemala City and other Central American cities would integrate into and transform the "architecture of enmity" that carved up urban space, prisons, and postwar society itself.[44]

MS13, BARRIO18, AND THE SUR

I met Triste while he was serving a five-year sentence for armed robbery in Canada prison, located sixty kilometers southwest of Guatemala City. We would talk in his quarters—a tin-roofed shack—as prisoners came and went asking him to etch tattoos into their skin with his homemade rig. When he was nine years old, sick of the squalor and his abusive father, Triste made the journey solo from a Guatemala City slum to Los Angeles to join his mom. He got into trouble in middle school and more in high school, and after a few years in juvenile hall, he joined a gang called Widmer Sreet. At twenty-two he ended up in adult prison for selling drugs, and it was there that he had his first contact with the Mexican Mafia.

The birth of the Mexican Mafia (MM or La Eme) is another canonical story in US gang history. The Mexican Mafia is said to have originated in Deuel Vocational Institute (DVI) in Tracy, California, in the late 1950s.[45] It was an adult facility but also became the last stop for the California juvenile detention system's worst youthful offenders. According to gang intervention specialists, youth entering DVI called it "gladiator's school" because of the need to constantly fight in order to hold your own. Housed with adult criminals, youth prisoners were constantly picked on. A group of Mexican Americans is said to have founded La Eme as a means of self-protection. As the story goes, Rodolfo Cadena, a seventeen-year-old from East Los Angeles, recruited other young toughs into a cohesive group to defend themselves against older inmates: against the bullying, sexual molestation, and general victimization that were and remain an everyday part of US prison life.[46]

Today, La Eme has become a prison "supergang" that controls prison black markets throughout the California prison system.[47] La Eme founded and enforces the SUR, a code of solidarity among imprisoned Latino gang members in the United States.

"In prison in California they teach you discipline, they teach you respect," Triste said, speaking a mix of English and Spanish typical of deportees who grew up in the United States. "You graduate from just being a gang member." Triste said that during his stateside incarceration he had no personal contact with known members of La Eme, who were in isolation lockdown. But the entire prison population understood the raison d'être of the SUR. "The Mexican Mafia are the ones that made the SUR," he explained. "The unity. Us Hispanics, if everyone of us stands on his own in prison, we won't stand up to anybody. We're small, fat, *chaparritos* mostly." He laughed and slapped his ample belly. "You have to stick together to have power. If you're on your own everyone knows. If you don't stick together you'll get raped, become somebody's bitch."

Arising out of sordid histories of officially sanctioned racial violence in US prisons, the Mexican Mafia would eventually play a crucial role in governing California prisons. To put it simply: La Eme and the SUR provided—and still provide—the promise of protection to imprisoned Latino gang members through the threat of imminent violence. The Southern United Raza is the crystallization into "law" of a strategic solidarity among Latino gang members in prison who, on the street, would be at one another's throats. "Southern" refers to Southern California, the geographical hub of Latino gangs and home to most Mexican Mafia members.[48] "Raza" (race), as in *la Raza*, encompasses all those who identify as Latino and conveys the central role of race in casting the lines of opposition between warring factions in urban California and in the US prison system. As for "United," the SUR dictates that blood feuds between rival Latino gangs in Southern California must be left at the prison gate. They have no place inside, because in prison everyone is already suffering. Those gangs who pay homage to the Mexican Mafia—in loyalty and other currencies—have long been known as sureños. Sureño gangs often attach the number "13" to their title to show their affiliation with La Eme ("M" is the thirteenth letter in the alphabet).

In California, La Eme has upheld the SUR primarily as a means of maintaining its dominance in prison, and the protection La Eme offers to incarcerated Latinos is also a clear and present threat to those who refuse to accept its rules.[49] The logic is quite simple, and ironically, depends on effective law enforcement. Given the intensive police targeting of gang members in California, every gangster knows that sooner or later he will end up behind bars. It might only be a few weeks in county lockup, or it might be a life sentence in a state penitentiary, but once incarcerated they are in La Eme territory. If a gang member or his gang has done anything to offend La Eme—refusing to pay the requisite kickbacks, cheating on a drug deal, or failing to carry out La Eme's orders—he will have a rough time behind bars, if he even survives.

The SUR in Guatemala

"The northerners know the why and how of the philosophy, the colors, the history," said Gato, who had learned the codes of the SUR back in the mid-1990s. "They know the need for control, why we are not mafia, because they are constantly inside their history, what the objective is of being here, why we are a family, a family of kings, and that we have blue blood, and that we are revolutionaries because we are constantly against the established norms." Gato's is an atavistic awe belonging to a short-lived moment in gang history, when being a marero in Guatemala meant following the SUR and believing in the maras as a cohesive community abiding by a separate set of laws, the product of a history alien to their environs. It meant taking on the sureño identity and investing in the mythic history of Southern California gangs transplanted to Guatemalan society.

The stories circulating on Guatemala City streets and in the prisons about the SUR recall an era in which mareros, as a nascent community, all adhered to the same myth of deathless brotherhood and mutual defense against a hostile world. It was far more than simply a pact of prison nonaggression; it was a central tenet of gang *clecha*.[50] Clecha means, roughly, "gang wisdom" or "knowledge of the gang." It is a philosophy, a way of seeing the world, an ideology formed by a deep relationship with the history of Latino gangs in California. It is composed of stories, parables, codes, signs, ethics, handshakes, clothing styles, language, and attitude—in short, an entire script for how to be a marero.

This code of racial solidarity in California prisons, violently enforced by a prison gang with a powerful presence across the state, became a defining code of ethics for gangs in Guatemala. This happened despite the fact that the racial rivalries in the US prison system do not exist in Guatemala, and no "super" gang like La Eme existed to enforce the peace. Still, for a time mareros from opposing gangs would repeat "the SUR is genesis" and maintain a careful détente in prison even as gang war raged in the streets. While the SUR was intact, the maras' united front in prison made them a force to be reckoned with.[51]

The story of the rival leaders Psycho of Alpha and Omega, an MS leader, and El Spyder of Barrio18 captures the mythic status of the SUR and the early gangsters who upheld it. It came to me in various versions from marero and paisa inmates who had been incarcerated in the early 2000s.

"El Spyder. I knew him. He was sureño," said Carlos, an ex-military policeman imprisoned for stealing cocaine from a government depot. Before his 2004 release, he served time with both Psycho and Spyder in various prisons. I interviewed him in a cavernous cantina where we were practically the only patrons. Carlos seemed nervous and never stopped scanning the space as he spoke rapidly beneath the booming ranchero music I had put on the jukebox. He also never stopped drinking. "Spyder had been a cholo who fought in Los Angeles, in the US 18th Street gang. He was one of the first to be deported and one of the first to come and strengthen the gangs here in Guatemala, where he gained much respect." Carlos gulped noisily at his beer. "El Psycho of Alpha and Omega became famous for doing one of the first decapitations in Guatemala. . . . Military intelligence kept El Spyder and El Psycho in the same cell so that they would eliminate each other because they knew that on the street these men were mortal rivals. But because of the dominion of the SUR, they didn't touch each other or do each other any harm." Tipping the bottle back, he finished the beer and wiped his mouth. "The authorities kept them together in el Infiernito in isolation lockup with the idea that they would kill each other. But they didn't do it, because they kept the brotherly pact, because they were of the two barrios. They kept the pact of the SUR in force, and all the other homies did the same. Psycho and Spyder gave an example of brotherhood between what are known as the MS and the 18. Eventually [in 2004] the authorities separated the two leaders." Carlos grabbed another bottle from the ice bucket between us. "Spyder, my little buddy, they killed him in Mazatenango," he sighed, suddenly mournful. "They hung him and stabbed him. They returned Psycho of Alpha and Omega to el Infiernito [prison] and there they strangled him."

While mara leaders kept the SUR's peace in the prisons, the imported rivalries between Los Angeles gangs entangled with and mapped onto gang wars on the street. The age-old feud between the MS and Barrio18 entered Guatemalan street history.

"Two years after I joined Barrio18 I met a clique that kept the SUR with MS on the street," said Silence, the retired gangster cum evangelical, as we sat drinking coffee in my apartment.

"Fuck," I say. "This is illegal for a gang."

And they say to me, "No, you got nothing to say here. Sorry but we keep our own rules."

"No way, bro," I said. "You all are blind and are gonna get beat down. And look, better not to be insulting but to just walk away, cuz we won't leave one of you standing."

I was known to seven or ten cliques, and I told them about it, and they tell me the whole clan will kick their ass. And so I say, "How about this, how about I go and blow shit up, and you give me the privilege of raising this clique."

They tell me OK, that I have the mission and if I don't fulfill it, I die. So it's the final word. So I go to pull in six or seven soldiers, and I go to the MS territory to plug them up, to make them run and hide in their ratholes. . . . And those that we found, well, they didn't live to tell it. So we return to the 18s.

"Look bro, the truth is that now things are going to blow up here."

"Why?"

"Because we just got back from blowing shit up. And now if those fucking dogs don't do anything, it's because they're worn out pussies (*tapados chavalas*). So now you know that here and now blood will run."

And they say to me that I had fucked shit up.

Behind me there were vatos who were ramfleros and more than this, men who had shown they had balls in different zones and different cliques. They had authority, and they had the backing of the Barrio.

So I say, "You know what bro, the only truth is that here the SUR will no longer flow. The SUR flows only in the prison. Here outside it's illegal in the Barrio to keep the SUR. We are different gangs." And I say, "Look here, the only truth is he who doesn't want to break any eggs walks away. The only truth is that we are not playing with water pistols. Here we are playing with real life mortars. And here there will be war, and war means death. And he who wants to just play around, once and for all, let him go suck his mama's tit."

"The truth is we're not going to put up with your charade," said one of them.

And those who came with me jumped up, and I said, "So the whole clan is gonna fall on you if you don't line up."

And so they decided to change, they had their eyes opened. They realized what the vision of the gang is. They say, "The truth is I have a lot of years living here and I won't leave my corner (*punto*) like that. And now I understand what the heart of the Barrio is (*corra del Barrio*), and I want to stay. Forgive me, homies, if I offended."

Silence told this story with pride—obviously enjoying the recounting—but like others of his generation, he knew all too well the dire consequences such compulsive violence would have.[52] Today Barrio18 members still repeat, almost like a mantra, "La Mara Salvatrucha is the Eve of 18th Street." That is, Eve was born of a rib plucked from Adam's chest, and it was she who led him, and the human race, into damnation. But the feud between MS and 18 has become only one of several factors driving gang violence—and violence against gangs—in Central American city streets.

By the late 1990s, youths suspected of being mareros became the targets of police and social cleansing organizations across the region.[53] As the gangs struggled to maintain internal discipline and criminal rackets in the face of such pressure, they turned their violence inward. After talking of all the boys that he had recruited into the MS, all his conquests, and all his street cred, Juande shook his head sadly. "Most of the boys I brought up, almost all of them are dead." Most of those he came up with are also dead. He rattled off two dozen names. I couldn't catch all of them: Sleepy, Speedy, Dopey, Killing, El Extraño, El Cosa, Topo, Travieso, El Viejo. "All dead and buried," Juande said. He believed most of them had been killed by their brethren. "That is the greatest shame," he lamented. "If I had been there I would not have allowed them to be killed by their own Barrio."

Ashes, Ashes, We All Fall Down

Gato and I were drinking prison moonshine with former Barrio18 members in El Jocote prison in Zacapa, discussing the old days, when Gato, red-faced and slurring his words, slammed his cup down on the makeshift table. "The SUR was just Mickey Mouse!" he exclaimed. "A Salvatrucha killed my brother. Bap bap! My brother is with God. And later, I see the guy in prison and all of a sudden it's, 'The SUR! The SUR! Gato, we're both sureños!' Okay then, the SUR, homeboy!" He flashed a sureño hand sign. "When he kills Gato's brother and I'm a bitch because I cry from the pain of his death, and the SUR doesn't allow me to kill the man who has killed my brother. . . . I have to bow my head to the SUR when my brother is dead. That's the SUR." He slumped in his chair and shook his head morosely while others around the table nodded along. "But then, his own gang puts the green light on his head because he's robbed Q500 worth of drugs . . . and I say, 'Ah! Q500 is my brother, that's how much my brother is worth.'" Gato snorted. "But, really, how much is he worth? How much?"

The bifurcated world ordered by the SUR did not last long. Throughout the early 2000s, elements in both gangs pushed to break the pact and be done with the charade once and for all. But each time influential gang leaders in both gangs argued to keep the peace. Finally, on August 15, 2005, members of the MS, using weapons smuggled into the prison, opened fire on Barrio18 members performing their morning exercises in El Hoyon prison in Escuintla, Guatemala. Before they died, the 18s tried to get warnings out to their homies in other prisons, but it was already too late. Leaders of the MS housed in all nine prisons had held a conference call that morning, and they attacked their rivals simultaneously throughout the prison system. In total, thirty-six Barrio18 members—including many of the most respected leaders—died that day, and the SUR with them.[54]

In a little over a decade—from the mid-1990s to 2005—a code of solidarity that was an organizing principle for Guatemala's maras took hold, degenerated, and collapsed. Today the SUR, along with the real or imagined transnational allegiances from which it was born and the world it seemed to have ordered, are lost. All that remains are the bittersweet memories of its existence and scattered, contradictory explanations for its demise.

Like Gato, some former gang members believe the idea of sureños as a cohesive community was undone by the violence, mutual rage, and hatred intensified by each murder, each friend, sibling, and neighbor killed by the enemy. Once in prison, young men from communities separated by a single city block who were at war with one another, engulfed in the pain and suffering pushing these feuds onward, found themselves face to face with their mortal enemies. How were they supposed to suspend their hunger for revenge?[55]

Agents of the Guatemalan security forces claim credit for escalating the tit-for-tat vengeance of gang war. A police official who worked in President Oscar Berger's (2000–2004) office of security (known as the G-2) told me that his office intentionally sowed mistrust to sharpen the mutual hatred between incarcerated members of the two gangs. The SUR's demise, they hoped, would break the gangs' power in the prisons. I pressed him for details, but he refused to explain any further.

In any case, the MS may have had more calculated motivations for destroying the prison alliance. Surviving MS leaders claimed that for reasons of business they had long planned to end the prison truce. Through the late 1990s and early 2000s, Barrio18 grew frenetically in Guatemala City's most populous urban neighborhoods, and MS leaders feared that the balance of power—in the street, but most of all in the prisons—was shifting against them. Guatemalan prisons had already become the "corporate headquarters" for Barrio18 and the MS. The most respected leaders of both gangs managed their business—extortion rackets, drug distribution on the street and in the prisons, and so forth—from behind bars. The war between MS and 18 was no longer solely about vengeance or preserving barrio honor. In 2012 the MS leader El Diabólico told Martinez and Sanz that the primary reason the MS members turned on their rivals in prison and broke the SUR was to stop Barrio18 from duplicating and moving in on the extortion networks MS had pioneered from inside the prisons.[56]

Some surviving mareros claim that leaders of the MS in Los Angeles attempted to save the SUR by sending a homie on a mission to kill Guatemalan MS leaders who had advocated breaking the truce. The emissary's name was El Snyper of Adams Blocotes (Calavera's brother's clique). His target was El Shark of Los Salvatrucha de Normandy, an influential leader who pushed hard to break the SUR. But before he even arrived in Guatemala, recalled Calavera, who heard the story from his brother, "the charade was known." Upon El Snyper's arrival, MS leaders took him to the meeting place in the general cemetery, where they forced a confession out of him.

"There, all of the homies were present, the whole Barrio, because they had called a general meeting," Calavera said. "Everyone was already informed of what was going to happen."

"They tortured him," Calavera continued in a quiet voice, "taking out his fingernails, right, and from his feet. The dude *yelled*. But he wouldn't confess. So they start to go to work on his penis with a Gilette [razor]."

"'Look brother,' Calavera pitched his voice in a high-pitched squeak. "'For the love of God, brother.' And he let out some screams. 'You don't have to do that. Yes ok! They sent me to kill El Shark and stop the breaking of the SUR.'"

El Snyper begged for his life, but, Calavera said, El Shark and El Soldado and the other leaders had already decided his fate. "'It skinned your dick for you to come and take Latino blood,' El Shark said. 'It will skin your dick to die for it.' Then they bathed him in gasoline, they lit him on fire, and they threw him in the dump. That's how our buddy El Snyper of Adams Blocotes died."

Speaking with Martinez and Sanz of *El Faro* in 2012, the MS leader El Diabólico denied that any Snyper from Adams Blocotes ever came to Guatemala. Unsatisfied, Martinez and Sanz went to Los Angeles to see if they could find more information on the breaking of the SUR in Guatemala. They found that veterans of the MS in California recalled a homie named Snyper who disappeared from Los Angeles in the early 2000s. "[Snyper] was a weird dude, who thought he was sharper than he really was. One of those who speak thinking it is great knowledge, right? But it's only bullshit," said one of his old homies. "One time we gave him a big beat down because he didn't come to the meetings and wasn't acting right. That was the last time I saw him."[57] But Sanz and Martinez's Los Angeles informants denied that the MS sent Snyper on a mission to kill Shark and defend the SUR, or that sureños in Los Angeles were the least bit concerned about the status of the mythical pact in Central America.

Whatever the combination of causes, the SUR's demise spelled the end of an era for the gangs of Guatemala. The united sureños were a thing of the past, and the last vestiges of the myth of solidarity also faded. Those who would become leaders of both gangs would self-consciously reject such traditions. Movies like *Sangre por Sangre* and *American Me* would continue to be used as "training videos" for new recruits, but flesh and blood deportees would no longer find refuge in Guatemala, since they had come to represent a way of doing things, a way of being a marero, that no longer applied there. And survivors of the earlier generations of homegrown gangs and maras—men like Juande, El Cholo Cifuentes, and Silence—must now find shelter where they can, left only with the memories of the way it once was or might have been.

The history of transnational connection and deathless brotherhood, once so respected and fetishized, has faded away so quickly that it is difficult today to know the true extent of its influence or, indeed, reality.

———————

The skein of history and memory out of which the maras emerge entangles legacies of civil war; stories of migration, incarceration, and return; and the circulation of images, aspirations, and symbols between US and Central American societies. Drawn into contemporary struggles for survival, this past becomes part of a disordered dance between fact and fiction, memory and myth that is integral to the making of the maras and the new order of violence they have come to represent. This order of violence is distinguished by a never-ending conflict between profound doubts over the source and meaning of daily murder and collective efforts to carve a sense of security back into the world. And as the tales of the SUR suggest, the prison has been a key space in this struggle. Mass incarceration has been essential to the maras' dystopian evolution, and most survivors of gang war are alive only because they have been preserved in prisons. This makes the prison, like the cemetery, one of the few certainties left to mareros. But the prison is more than simply a place to preserve criminal bodies and reproduce criminal cultures. The prison is also an essential emblem of social order. In part 2, I go to prison to explore how this structure and symbol of law and order is in fact a space in which a blurred divide—between the free and the incarcerated, law and outlaw, world and underworld—comes into sharp focus.

PART TWO

Worlds and Underworlds

FIGURE 13. Child's doll strung up on the outer fence of Canada prison, Escuintla, Guatemala

The Road to Prison

I take a deep breath and knock three times on a black metal door.[*] Inside there is a slow shuffling inside, and the door swings open. A young woman stands blinking in a pool of light.

"Good morning," I say. "Is Gato up?"

She smiles and nods, retreating into the shadows of the house. I come in and sit down heavily on an overstuffed couch, and a swarm of flies rises and settles again. Dozens of cages covered in heavy gray muslin hang about the room, and dozens more are hidden down a dark hallway, swaying almost imperceptibly. One cage is uncovered, and I can see an owl's black eyes burning into the gloom.

A quarter of an hour goes by, and the owl moves only once, swiveling its gaze down the hallway and then back again at me.

Deep in the bowels of the house someone is hacking and spitting and swearing. A few moments later, Gato emerges into the living room red-eyed and shirtless, his belly hanging over his boxer shorts. There is a tattoo of Emilio Zapata etched across his back. He got the tattoo, he always says, in the days when he ran with the Mexican Mafia in Mexico City. When he was still a

[*] Like the first two stories, this is an experiment in ethnographic storytelling. It splices conversations from several interviews and prison visits and sublimates analysis into the narrative arc. I do this in order to give a sense—psychologically and emotionally as much as intellectually—of how prisons are made porous on multiple scales. Certain details, including subjects' names and the timing of events, have been changed to protect my subjects.

dedicated thief, before he went to prison, before he leveraged his experience in the criminal world into a government job. He started out teaching classes in various Guatemala City juvenile detention centers. This was in the early 2000s, when Guatemala, following a regional trend, began targeting suspected gang youth for mass incarceration. Through his work in youth prisons, Gato made connections with the gangs that he still relies upon today—for the social work he carries on in the prison system and as a fixer for international journalists (and researchers like me) who want to make contact with real-life mareros.

"*Borracho asceroso.*" I laugh. Dirty drunk.

"*Culero,*" Gato grunts, which translates to "asshole" or "faggot," depending on the context. He ambles back to the bathroom. I get up stiffly, walk out the door, and lean against the chalky whitewashed wall. The sun beats hot on my skin through the last of the morning chill. I close my eyes and tilt my face upward, the light streaking orange across the inside of my eyelids. I check my phone for messages. There are none.

When I come back inside, Gato seems to be engaged in a staring contest with the owl. He turns and grins. "You're late again *pinche* Gringo."

"Your mother. I've been here almost half an hour. You told me we were leaving for the prison at 7:30."

"Looks to me like you just walked in."

"You shithead."

"What's the matter, Anthony? You okay?"

"Ah . . . just problems with my woman."

"She found out you're a big GAY?"

"Something like that."

Gato laughs and claps me on the back. "Well, don't get mad at me. I didn't tell her."

There is a knocking at the door. We turn to see a silhouette of a small man peering into the gloom as if waiting to be invited further.

"Cheeky! Culero!" Gato exclaims.

Cheeky is Gato's loyal assistant and the butt of his cruelest jokes. Cheeky's mother volunteered for syphilis injections administered by American doctors in the 1960s. Cheeky's father is from Chernobyl. Cheeky likes little boys. And so on. After a moment, he limps the rest of the way in and stands awkwardly among the cages. His right leg is twisted from a motorbike accident, a mottled red scar carved across his shin, the muscle withered down. One night he and I went drinking in a lonely cantina where an outsized Wurlitzer was flashing like the days of disco. Shouting above the raucous oompah-pah, Cheeky told me about his drunkard father, who would only come home to beat his mother because there was no dinner. And so Cheeky grew up huffing solvent and robbing yokels commuting from the highlands to sell their wares in the city.

"Get up! I'll show you!" he shouted, lurching out of his chair and embracing me from behind. "Grab them like *this!*" He shoved his hand under my ribs. "And the knife like *this!*"

He's been out of prison for two months. By the smell of him, he's been up drinking all night. I tell him so, and Cheeky twists his orc's face into a rueful grin, knotting the pitted scars across his forehead, puckering the web tattoos around his mouth. The man is missing half his teeth. He reaches into his coat pocket and pulls out a plastic bag of clear liquid that smells like rubbing alcohol.

"For my hangover," he says. "No problem."

At Gato's order, Cheeky fetches the goods destined for mareros stuck in the isolation block of Canada prison, in the hot lowlands some sixty kilometers southwest of the city: two garbage bags of deflated soccer balls and T-shirts with a government ministry logo stamped on the front and back. As he limps past the owl's cage, Cheeky pauses uncertainly.

"Cheeky," I ask, "are you okay?"

"I'm okay," he shrugs, "but I think the owl is sad."

Out in the street, the sun has burned off the morning mist and beats down on Gato, Cheeky, and me. We're waiting for a bus. A man huddled against a shuttered storefront, pants around his ankles, calls out. Gato knows him. He knows all the drunks, street urchins, prostitutes, and drug addicts residing in this part of the city. He was once of them. He started as an eight-year-old runaway, stealing to survive on the streets. When he was twenty-four he held up an old man at knifepoint. The man had a heart attack and died. The judge convicted Gato of manslaughter and sentenced him to fifteen years behind bars. After serving seven, he came up for parole. At the hearing, he spoke of intent and repentance, of man's mutable soul and God's divine will. The judge set him free.

"Anthony," Gato whispers, "can you give him some change?"

We catch a rust-red bus trailing black plumes of smoke and disembark in a labyrinthine bus station at the southern edge of the capital. Three tiered platforms connect overpasses snaking above sprawling concrete apartment blocks. Diesel engines, worn brakes, teenage boys calling out destinations in high-pitched chants. We run to jump on a chicken bus—a decommissioned

Bluebird, painted purple and red and hung with Virgin Mary talismans and Looney Toons stickers—as it pulls out for the lowlands between the capital and the Pacific Ocean. It will pass the entrance of Canada prison. The wives, mothers, and children of the incarcerated fill row after row. Cheeky and I maneuver the frayed garbage bags as best we can. The women have bags of food, clothing, and other sundries held in their laps and arranged along the aisle. Some carry infants in their arms. Some are sure to have tightly wrapped packets of marijuana or cocaine ensconced deep in their vaginas. We sit down in the last row. I remember vinyl seats just like these sticking to my seven-year-old thighs on hot, just-before-summer-vacation afternoons in Watson-ville, California. The bus driver—a disheveled fat man with a thick mustache and red-rimmed eyes—cranks the engine and fiddles with the sound system. The steel hull vibrates with the thumping bass of a reggaeton top 40 station.

After grinding through the last of the suburban sprawl, we descend out of the mountains and onto the hot lowland plains. A boy sitting with his mother spends most of the journey with his face pressed up against the window, watching the sheet-metal and concrete buildings give way to tin and mud shacks and then to fallow fields, sugar cane, and dense jungle. I watch the landscape flit by through his reflection. Every few minutes the bus stops to pick up passengers who signal from the roadside.

Sapling thin, with long, wispy hair to her waist, an adolescent girl walks slowly up the aisle. She turns and steadies herself on a seat and raises her right hand before her as if blessing a congregation, then begins to speak. Her voice is small and reedy, her words all but lost beneath the music, the engine, the wind.

Then the bus driver brakes violently, and the passengers lurch together. In the momentary hush, I hear her prayer—"in each of our veins. The Virgin Mary protects with her sorrowful hand. The agony in the garden is ours, for it is we who scourged him on the pillar. He was crowned with thorns so that we might live in peace. Carry the"—and then the engine cranks, the bus lurches forward, and her voice is lost.

I close my eyes and rest my head against the window. A rosary strung along barbed wire floats out of the darkness and dissolves into a woman with dark hair and blue eyes, huddled naked and crying on yellow sheets. I press my thumb against my ring. Then Gato is speaking into my ear.

"Listen, Anthony, listen," he hisses, "do you want to know a secret? You want our secrets to write them down and become famous? I know. I know your kind. Well, here's a secret. At the end of every sector in every prison a devil has been scratched into the wall. Sometimes a Christian, one of these evangelicals, will find it and erase it, but always it reappears within a few days. Do you know what it does? It has a dark magic. Want to know? Do you? Ah, you don't believe me? You think I am a liar?"

"I know you're a liar, Gato. But I like your lies. They have a lot of truth in them."

"Ah! Very good, very good," Gato chortles. "You're smart for a gringo. So here it is—if properly asked, the devil will bring anyone into the prison. Cause them to arrive inside—willfully or no. It is the tool of last resort for the men trapped inside. All you have to do is take an old shoe in your left hand, holding it just so, and say the person's name three times while—ah, we've arrived!"

The bus pulls into a gravel lot. Gato jumps up as Cheeky and I fumble for our things. We hurry after him to join the others, lugging the garbage bags down the aisle. Outside the sun is blazing. Above an empty roadside cantina, a torn canvas banner sporting a black rooster lolls in the breeze. The assistant thumps the side of the bus and whistles, and the Bluebird pulls out again, leaving the visitors standing in the dust. At our feet, a rooster struts back and forth pecking neurotically at its own raw, pink neck.

I hoist a garbage bag to my shoulder, Cheeky grabs the other, and we join the ragged column of visitors walking past the cantina and up a dirt road. Forty meters further and I am soaked with sweat. A hand-painted wooden billboard announces EL INFIERNITO MAXIMUM SECURITY FACILITY, hung above a black metal gate flung open. The other visitors pass beneath the sign and continue on up the road. Gato leads us into the shade of a concrete guard station beside the gate, where uniformed men sit around a low metal table. A man in a black uniform stretched tight across his belly stands up from the table and hails Gato with a toothy grin. Two young soldiers in fatigues stand behind him, M16s slung low at their waists. A shirtless boy in flip-flops slouches in a chair, staring at me.

"Ah, Gato, welcome once again," the guard says, smoothing down a luxurious mustache.

"My Captain! A pleasure of course." Gato reaches over and grabs a deflated soccer ball from Cheeky's bag and hands it to the guard.

"Ah, thank you, Gato."

"Of course, of course."

We continue up the dirt road, blinking against the dust stirred up by other visitors trudging through the shimmering heat. Like good mules, Cheeky and

I lean forward under our loads. El Infiernito, the Little Inferno, is on the left, walls painted an incongruous baby blue. Electrified barbed wire fences, thirty feet high, mark the outside perimeter. Guards in ski masks and bulletproof vests walk atop the walls, their Israeli Tovars and M16s trained on inmates sunning themselves in the prison courtyard.

"Gringo!" Gato hisses in my ear, "stop looking!" I turn my gaze back to the road and keep walking.

The pilgrimage stretches out along the hard-packed dirt track, past empty checkpoint kiosks, whitewashed rocks piled in rough squares below slanted tin roofs. As we trudge along, a woman walking against the tide appears up ahead and shambles past us hugging herself and crying. She does not look up. I turn and watch her stumble under the weight of the cloth bag she carries.

Ten minutes later the prison gate looms at the end of the road. The mothers, wives, lovers, sisters, and offspring of the incarcerated stand in a long line snaking out from the gate. It's nearing 11:00 in the morning, and many have traveled through the night to arrive with the sun already burning high in the sky. There are also prostitutes arriving for work, heavily made up in high heels and sequin skirts. Some visitors talk in little groups, but most keep to themselves, their attention trained on the prison gate.

A triple barrier establishes the prison perimeter, surrounded by stands of palm and fallow fields. There are two twenty-foot-high fences of metal mesh festooned with barbed wire. Posts run between them, strung with thick coils of electrified wire. A dozen prisoners stand in the courtyard on the other side, anxious sentinels peering into the knot of visitors. Their longing is palpable, insistent and strong, as they await a woman's touch, a child's voice, the money or drugs smuggled in that will make the days, weeks, months, years, lifetimes pass less harshly. Each second brings freedom closer and death nearer. An anonymous inmate has scrawled the epithet for this place where the prisoners wait: *Porton de los Desesperados. Se Sufre y es Duro* (Gate of the Hopeless. One Suffers and It Is Hard).

As we approach the entrance, Cheeky pauses. He stares at the gate and at the women, then looks back down the way we have come.

"What's the vibe Cheeky?" I ask.

Cheeky looks up with a sad smile and hands me his bag, slowly shaking his head. "I don't want to go in there."

"Afraid you might get stuck on the other side again?"

FIGURE 14. "Gate of the Hopeless. One Suffers and It Is Hard."

"No." He hunkers down in the roots of an almond tree across from a ramshackle restaurant where an old man sits eyeing the women. He leans back against the trunk and pushes his baseball cap over his face.

I walk over to the restaurant and give the old man Q2, and he points me toward his outhouse. Holding my breath against the sweltering stink, I quickly take my Canon Powershot S-90 out of my satchel and slip it into my underwear so it sits snugly between my legs.

When I emerge again, the air feels cool and clean, and the line has started to move. Many of the younger women wear halter tops, and all of the women are in short skirts or dresses. They steel themselves for the ritual of entry. Before they meet their men, guards will search their belongings and their bodies. The women will step into a closet-sized cell, and a female guard wearing latex gloves will probe their insides for drugs, weapons, cell-phone parts, and other contraband.

Behind the bars of the prison entrance, men in uniform sit at old metal writing desks. After passing through the first gate, I flash the government ID card Gato made for me and hand over my driver's license, house keys, and cell phone in exchange for a small laminated piece of paper with the number 6 scrawled in felt pen. I write my name, date of birth, and an invented passport number in a clothbound tome, the pages yellowed and curling with age and moisture. No one will check to verify my ID. A wiry, mean-eyed guard slides his hands along my shoulders, under my armpits, around the belt line, and down the inside of my pants legs to my ankles. He misses the camera tucked snug against my crotch. They always do. Even so, my jaw slowly unclenches as I walk through the last gate and enter the guards' outhouse. I unzip my pants and transfer the camera from my underwear back to my satchel. When I emerge again Gato is waiting for me, head cocked to one side, a smile on his lips. Even after all this time, getting into prison is always a bit harrowing. But once inside, an uneasy calm reigns. The prison may seem a space for monsters to the viewing public, but I feel safer here than I do walking down my own street in Guatemala City. Gato and I wait together as two female guards finish searching the garbage bags. They each ask him, rather petulantly, why he hasn't brought them the kid-sized T-shirts he promised.

The men in the isolation block have already spotted us when we walk out onto the courtyard. Arms thrust between the bars wave and gesture. They start to shout, "Gato, Gaaaato! Gringo, Griiiiingoo!"

CHAPTER 3

Porous Prisons

We think of the key, each in his prison.
Thinking of the key, each confirms a prison.

—T. S. Eliot, *The Wasteland*

On February 14, 2012, a fire ripped through Comayagua prison in Honduras. 377 inmates were burned alive. More than half of Comayagua's inmates were in pretrial detention, still awaiting their day in court. Along with horrific images of bodies split open like burned sausages and anguished family members gathered at the prison walls, rumors quickly surfaced that elements in the Honduran security forces had started the fire.[1] Prison guards reportedly shot at prisoners attempting to escape the blaze. The conflagration was the third of its kind in seven years, and the deadliest. When the news hit the airwaves, I was on my way to court in the Tower of Tribunals in Guatemala City. While I was riding up in the elevator, a prosecutor turned to his colleague. "It's a message from God!" he exclaimed. "What a shame we don't do it like that here. We could finally be done with all the mara filth (*lacra*) and their extortions."

The next day I sat with Juande in Pavón prison judging a Valentine's Day card contest organized by the gang rehabilitation organization for which I volunteered. The three finalists' creations featured Tweetie Bird, Tigger, and a sad little blond boy. While the winners collected their prizes, Juande pored over front-page photographs of the charred dead. I recounted the conversation I had overheard. He sat mulling it over, then cracked a sad smile. "They think they can burn the devil out," he said. "But wouldn't that mean setting fire to the whole world?"

In the last thirty years, humans have built more prisons and incarcerated more people than at any other time in history.[2] Driving this surge in

FIGURE 15. Newspaper article on the fire at Comayagua prison:
"Inferno in Prison," *Nuestro Diario*, February 16, 2012.

imprisonment is a set of harsh but simple arguments: criminals must be quar-
antined to protect the social body from the contagion of crime, their suffering
is payment for their sin, and imprisonment serves as a warning to others who
would consider breaking the law.[3] In this way, prisons are not merely concrete
structures for "warehousing" criminalized bodies.[4] They are also invested with
powerful political and social meaning essential to the functioning of many
modern societies.[5] Prisons help create a sense of order against a gnawing sense
of uncertainty and insecurity. Built to serve the ideals of certainty, classifica-
tion, and hard and fast boundaries, they etch these ideals into the social body.
That such ideals are false idols does not stop the institution from carving into
prisoners' flesh and into public consciousness the notion that the "good" really

can be distinguished from the "evil," feeding the fantasy of clearly defined categories of personhood. But legal classifications of innocence and guilt tend to elide all sorts of factors driving social conflict, including historical inequality and contemporary conditions of violation.[6] Overwhelmingly, the "evil" are drawn from society's poorest and most marginalized populations.[7] And so prisons are spaces and symbols in and through which the deep socioeconomic inequalities, abiding prejudices, and power dynamics defining contemporary life are distilled and become all too visible.[8]

As essential as prisons are for providing a sense of security, they do not, by and large, actually make societies safer.[9] This is especially so in Guatemala and other parts of Central America, where the belief that prisons can actually quarantine criminals and protect society is widely understood as a misbegotten fallacy.[10] "It all comes back to prisons," lamented Walter Villatoro, a respected Guatemala City criminal circuit judge, "and no one wants to deal with it." Collective rage and frustration over Central American states' failure to punish evildoers—which may have fueled the Comayagua fire and certainly inspired celebratory reactions like the one I overheard—belie how deeply implicated institutions of punishment are in the rise of peacetime crime. As a case in point, the penal state has been an unwitting midwife to the maras' metamorphosis.[11]

For mareros, prison has long been both an expected way station and a central point of organization and cultural reproduction.[12] Beginning in the late 1990s and growing into the early 2000s, Guatemala was caught up in regional hysteria over the unprecedented growth of post–Cold War crime. Pantomiming Honduras and El Salvador, the Guatemalan government organized a massive assault on the "gang threat." Plan Escoba (Plan Broom), Guatemala's 2003 anti-gang legislation, did not have the far-reaching judicial and enforcement initiatives of its neighbors' full-blown mano dura (strong fist) policies.[13] However, government efforts still resulted in the arrest of thousands of poor urban youths. Some were bona fide gangsters, but most were not.[14]

By the early 2000s, prisons in Guatemala, as in Honduras and El Salvador, were packed full of mareros alongside young men who became easy fodder for gang recruitment as they took on the group identity foisted upon them by police profiling. They found themselves trapped behind bars, fighting for survival against rival prisoner factions. United by the SUR, rival gangs learned to cooperate with each other to survive and profit from the ebb and flow of prison life—the constant game of tug of war (tira y floja) between prisoner factions and agents of the state. Imprisoned gang leaders formed the first "Wheel of the Barrio" (Rueda del Barrio), through which the most powerful ramfleros met and coordinated trade in weapons, soldiers, and territorial claims on the outside.[15] Surviving leaders even claim to have ordered homies on the street to intentionally get arrested. Through calculated misbehavior and disruption, they sought to have marero prisoners be transferred to select facilities in order to gain numerical dominance. Such strategies helped make the maras a force to be reckoned with throughout the prison system.

I went to prison to understand the maras. After all, prison helped make the maras, and the maras are a perfect example of the world that prisons make.[16] Over the years of conducting research behind bars, however, I learned that prison life can provide a powerful lens for observing social relations and political dynamics that order life beyond prison walls and beyond the maras, too. The prison's role in driving the maras' dystopian evolution is only one example of its profound failure as an institution of isolation and order, and exchange between the incarcerated and the free goes far beyond gang networks. Like the infrastructure of any border, the prison's concrete walls and electrified barbed wire fences form a porous membrane across which all kinds of exchanges—both licit and illicit—take place. This chapter maps the symbiotic relationships among prisoners, the state, and the free to show how deeply the world and the underworld upon which it rests interpenetrate and produce one another. These relationships and this exchange undermine the ideals of isolation and certainty the prison is meant to provide and reveal how struggles for control over prison life feed into the making of meaning and power far beyond prison walls. Maras, of course, have played an important role in exposing such connections, but they are in rich and varied company. Prison guards and prisoners' lovers, the media and politicians, the military, and the highest echelons of state government all feed and feed upon the prison: for power, for profit, or merely for survival. Such porous prisons require constant policing to reproduce, reperform, and prop up commonsense distinctions between the lawful and the criminal, the Good and the Evil.[17] By mapping the flow of bodies and goods, desire and violence, information and influence across prison walls, I track the constant friction between the ideal and the real of prison life. This friction can and often does ignite into violent conflict. Just as prisoners depend on the free for survival, the brutalities of prison life inevitably impact society in ways both spectacular and clandestine. The urge to punish backfires, the infrastructure of isolation fails, and the whole world burns.

FLOW

Concrete walls, electrified fences, guard towers, high-wattage searchlights, and miles and miles of razor wire form the physical boundary between the "street," as prisoners refer to the outside world, and the space of the prison. Masked guards wielding M16s, cell-phone signal blockers, and a broken-down byzantine bureaucracy buttress and extend this boundary. But all of this is not enough.[18] Every day, countless acts both licit and illicit penetrate the prison border. The primary vector of exchange is the stream of visitors crossing in and out of the prison. In prison parlance, these visitors—most of whom are the wives, girlfriends, and lovers of the incarcerated—are known simply as *la visita* (the visit). Through la visita, cash, food, and medicine enter the prison, along with drugs, weapons, and cell phones. Messages and money for street networks, as well as goods wrought by prisoner labor, leave with them. Also present are love and desire, devotion and bodily fluids, and the babies conceived inside the prison to be born and raised on the outside.

La Visita

Access to la visita is the prisoners' most valued privilege and is essential for the survival of the prison system itself.[19] It is the first privilege prison authorities rescind when punishing troublemakers, and this is the punishment most likely to cause prisoners to revolt. Unlike US prisons, in which visits from the outside are largely limited to bona fide spouses, immediate family members, and legal counsel—and even then, in most prisons only once every few months—the Guatemalan prison authorities (known as *el Sistema* [the System] in prison parlance) allow visitors to come several days a week in all but a few maximum security facilities.[20]

At the time of writing this book, the Guatemalan prison system is operating at 276 percent of capacity, with pretrial detention facilities at over 500 percent. State investment per prisoner comes to roughly Q50 ($6.25) per day. Feeding one prisoner costs Q12. The remaining Q38 per prisoner is supposed to cover staff salaries, infrastructure maintenance, medical care, and all other services.[21] Given how radically overcrowded and woefully underfunded these prisons are, most prisoners depend upon la visita to survive. El Sistema also depends upon the women visitors, who nurture a booming underground economy. Both prisoners and agents of the state seek to straddle and profit from the terms of trade dictated by the border the visitors must cross each day, a border at which licit and illicit economies entwine. Without la visita, prisoners would revolt, and the system would fall apart.[22] These women triage the state.

What do they bring? They bring food, soap, toilet paper, toothpaste, razors, magazines, batteries, stereos, tools, watches, jewelry, and raw materials for inmate artisans. The food—from fresh vegetables, to home-cooked meals, to candy and snacks—supplements the poor and often unsanitary fare provided by el Sistema and stocks the shelves of prisoner-run stores.

Visitors also bring cash into the currency-starved prison economy. Those inmates without support from their families or street networks must earn money if they hope to survive inside. Prisoners run restaurants, bakeries, barbershops, laundry services, shoe-repair shops, and hammock-weaving factories. In Pavón prison, located some fifteen kilometers northeast of Guatemala City, there are inmate-run jewelry boutiques, clothing shops, and portrait-painting studios. These laboring prisoners do their best business, if not their only business, on days when the prison gates are flung open to welcome la visita.

Prison businesses depend heavily on visitors to restock raw materials, merchandise, and equipment. In many prisons, one can buy electronic equipment, paintings and furniture, the latest Hollywood films on pirated DVDs burned on prison computers, gold and silver jewelry, raccoon pelts, fighting cocks, hammocks, homemade cakes and pastries, . . . and the list goes on.[23] Even if the visitors don't bring their own cash, they inspire prisoners who have money to purchase gifts on their behalf. During his last decade in prison, for example, Juande maintained himself by fashioning children's nightlights out of wood and plastic, which he sold to guards and other inmates to give to their families.[24] They featured cartoon characters: SpongeBob SquarePants, Tweetie Bird, and Disney princesses, among others.[25]

Prisoners with no outside support must labor for others. Many are underpaid workers for entrepreneurs looking to cash in on inmates' isolation. Denizens of Pavón earn about Q6/day (about 75 cents) gluing plastic soccer balls, weaving nylon nets, or knitting hammocks for sale by vendors on the outside. This is time-consuming and repetitive labor. Those who sell prisoner-made goods on the outside tend to present their work as philanthropy, providing desperate prisoners with much-needed work to pass the time. However, given how abject the inmates are—how little they earn, how long they labor, and how few options they have—much of their work smacks more of indentured servitude than wage labor.

Illicit Exchange

Earning a living wage can be just as difficult for the free as it is for the imprisoned. Prison guards earn little more than the national minimum wage of Q2,644.50/month ($346). To offset the chances of corruption, el Sistema may rotate guards among facilities around the country every six months. This does not work, however. Forced to live and work far from their homes and families, guards can rarely rely on the home-cooked meals, shared living spaces, and other support that family networks provide. In a sense, prison guards live under the same conditions their charges do. They work and sleep in the same space. They eat the same food. They depend on the same prison markets—legal and otherwise—for their well-being. To pad their paltry salaries, up to 30 percent of guards work with or take bribes from narco-traffickers, arms dealers, and others involved in smuggling contraband into prison.[26] But not all corruption is so nefarious and profitable. For example, just inside the entrance to Pavón Prison, I once watched a gaggle of guards standing around a pile of secondhand shoes delivered by a church group. A male guard picked up a pair of black faux leather stilettos. Turning awkwardly to a female guard beside him, he asked, "Do you think these will fit my wife?"

The entry of illicit goods is, of course, much riskier and far more lucrative for guards, visitors, and prisoners alike. Visitors and guards regularly smuggle drugs (marijuana, crack, and cocaine), cell phones, and cell-phone parts into the prison. Prison directors manage some of this flow for the most well-connected prisoners. But the vast majority of men behind bars—who cannot afford to keep prison staff on their payrolls—must depend on their female visitors if they want to compete. Every day hundreds of prisoners' wives and girlfriends smuggle contraband through prison gates inside their vaginas. This is not the only method, but it seems to be the most effective. Except at Guatemala's two maximum security facilities, there are no metal detectors, body scanners, or drug dogs. There is only one way for el Sistema to identify smugglers: to search for contraband, female guards don latex gloves and perform body-cavity searches.[27] To facilitate such clumsy violations, female visitors must wear dresses or skirts. "It feels like a kind of rape," said La Shadow, a female sex worker who trafficked drugs into prison for years before getting caught. "The guards use the same gloves with each girl, one after another."[28]

As in any illicit market, the cost of a commodity rises in relation to the risks involved in transport and distribution. Licit goods like food, soccer balls, hammocks, and secondhand watches can be purchased inside the prison at and sometimes even below street-market prices.[29] Marijuana is generally priced at about three times street-level value, and cell phones, cell-phone batteries, and SIM cards go for at least ten times what they cost on the street. In "random" cell searches, guards regularly discover and confiscate cell phones and drugs, punishing prisoners with prolonged stays in isolation blocks. However, these momentary disruptions only serve to stimulate further sales of the confiscated contraband, while maintaining the performance of state control.

Alongside illicit drugs, cell phones are the prison's most valued commodity. Cell phones allow prisoners to stay in contact with their families, which is especially important for those whose relations are too poor, too preoccupied, or too far away to make regular visits. Access to a cell phone is also the only way for prisoners to keep love affairs with female visitors alive in the days, weeks, or months between each visit. The cell phone is also essential technology for the most lucrative and violent prison business: extortion rackets.[30]

Spurred by region-wide anger and frustration, the Guatemalan government has tried to shut down prisoners' capacity to communicate beyond prison walls. Again and again, these efforts have proven ineffectual. In 2015, for example, the government cut a deal with major cell-phone companies to build signal blockers around prison facilities. But necessity is the mother of invention, as they say, and inmates always seem to find their way around the state's clumsy efforts to cut them off. In some cases, gang leaders and other powerful inmates have simply bribed or cowed prison directors into surreptitiously shutting down the signal blockers for certain periods. More common, however, is the use of improvised mechanisms for bypassing the state's efforts to cut off cellular communication. In one prison, inmates are said to have constructed a telephone "booth" from scrap metal in a hidden corner of the grounds, which boosted the cell-phone signal enough to break through the blocking mechanism. In any case, six months after the signal blockers were erected, veteran prisoners I spoke with were confident that eventually the technology would fail. "The government doesn't have the money or the know-how to repair that shit," said a deported gang member who made his living running extortion and telepromotion scams from his cell in Pavón. "Just wait 'til the next big thunderstorm. The machine will break and we'll be free to do business." While special police units dedicated to tracking down imprisoned extortionists have had a modicum of success, the ease with which guards are corrupted, extortion networks raised, and new cell phones smuggled in puts the state at a decided disadvantage.

The authorities have managed to curtail cell-phone use in some maximum security facilities housing gang leaders and other powerful inmates.[31] Incarcerated leaders of the MS and Barrio18 continue to be key decision makers in extortion rackets, murders, and other gang activities. For these men, la visita is absolutely necessary to keep business going. Their visitors often carry messages—known as *wirlas* in prison argot—for operatives in the street secreted away inside their clothes or, more often, inside their bodies.[32] I have translated the text of one such message here. Prison guards discovered it among the belongings of a Barrio18 chief's girlfriend as she left sector 11 of the Preventivo prison, and investigators transcribed it for use as evidence in court:

> Hi mamacita, I hope you are well. You know what? I'm going crazy to get free and make love to you. You got to look alive with the lawyers and my papers. And tell *Chamarra* to get busy with the wirlas that will be arriving, that he doesn't act like an idiot and doesn't be doing drugs, and that he motivates the locos that remain. And if he can jump in more guys, then do it.

The writer continues with instructions to collect tithes (*la renta*) from extorted neighborhoods and businesses, to acquire weapons with the money collected, and to not screw up because he will punish his second in command if he gets out of prison and everything is lost. The message ends with a threat and a promise to his girlfriend, "and you already know, if you cheat on me, I will kill you."

A mixture of love letter, rambling threat, and concise directives to street operatives running protection rackets in Guatemala City neighborhoods, the message reveals how varied and entangled exchange across prison walls can be. Indeed, gangs' and other organized criminal groups' dependence on street rackets for survival has made la visita a strategic tool, enmeshing prison policy and criminal command structures with love, the bonds of family, and physical desire.

Prison Time and Desire

Incarceration dilates time. Again and again, my imprisoned friends and interviewees spoke of how time spent with someone from the outside can be a chance to escape, or enjoy the illusion of escape, from the painfully slow passage of one moment into the next.[33] La visita is as essential for providing this sort of relief, especially for those with life sentences, as it is for prison economies.

A few months after he got out of prison, Calavera and I were sitting in El Portal, an old Guatemala City bar once frequented by Che Guevara. Sipping an *ojo rojo*, Calavera reflected on his companions still inside. Mo, the MS member facing a double life sentence, had recently disappeared from the rehabilitation program I volunteered with after a brief romance with one of the social workers went sour. Every morning for six months he had been at the gates to greet her and the rest of the crew and escort us inside, until one day he was not. His compatriots said he'd gone back to using crack and bullying other prisoners, even cheating Juande out of money he owed him.

"Ah, my buddy," Calavera sighed, "his life is already given away. That's not a good vibe. That one still thinks like he's in the game. He can be really cold. But maybe it's because of how many years he's got. With that many years I don't know what I would think."

"Yeah, me neither," I said.

"And that's why I guess I understand why he is the way he is. These are things that one cannot withstand so easily. Day after day with a life sentence, every day passing feels heavier, right, instead of feeling like one day less."

Prisoners must find ways to endure the torture of time. Some enlist in reforming their souls with the vision of Christ. Some pass their time with secular rehabilitation programs in arts and crafts and "community-building" exercises.[34] Others twist time with the help of hard drugs like crack cocaine and paint thinner. For a few prisoners, staring down the barrel of a lifetime behind bars can breed a dangerous kind of nihilism. These men ensure that the suffering incarceration causes will reach far beyond prison walls. Since they have no hope of walking free, it is said that gang leaders and other powerful inmates carrying life sentences become crueler and more prone to outrageous violence.[35] When imprisoned rivals cannot strike at each other, for example, gang war continues by proxy. To make their enemies suffer, Juande claimed, "ramfleros will order their boys on the street to go after their enemies' families." Isolation in maximum security prisons is the worst the state can do to such men. With little to fear from further punishment, intense, even spectacular violence has proven to be a useful tool for them to expand extortion rackets and other illicit businesses, or simply for vengeance.

The last time I saw Mo before he disappeared into drug addiction, he was wearing a T-shirt with the logo "Sonic Blonde" stenciled across the chest, and underneath in flowing script the words, "We have more fun, just harder." I asked him why his gang had become so violent. After giving it some thought, he

FIGURE 16. A prisoner and his family on visiting day, Canada prison, Escuintla, Guatemala.

replied, "The gang leaders facing life in prison are interested first in ensuring that they and their families can live well, and they are willing to use anyone and do anything to make it happen." From distributing drugs inside prison to organizing extortion rackets on the street, criminal enterprises are, for many prisoners, the only possibility to earn enough money to soften the squalor of prison life and care for their loved ones on the outside. Preying on others becomes the best, if not the only, means of remaining a provider from behind bars.

But to merely focus on the violence and suffering la visita helps enable misses the point. Whether they promote violence beyond prison walls or not, prisoners must rely on the love and support of their female visitors to make the time pass less harshly. The care, love, devotion, and physical contact la visita provides are as important to inmates' lives as the goods, money, and information that they pass in and out of the prison. The image of the sacrificing mother who faithfully visits her incarcerated son and stands by his side through the years wasted behind bars is deeply etched upon the prisoners' collective consciousness. Meanwhile, wives, lovers, and sex workers provide prisoners with the chance for female companionship, lovemaking, fucking.

FIGURE 17. Ex-marero inmates preparing for la visita.

Given how important la visita is to prisoners' survival and sense of well-being, many incarcerated men work hard on developing their capacity to woo female visitors. These efforts take up much of their time. Even when female visitors are absent, their influence is still palpable. "Prisoners spend all week in expectation of their next visit," explained Elena, a social worker with whom I worked in Pavón Prison. "They plan for it. Prepare for it. A lot of guys don't have regular visits. But whether you have a visit or not, every dude is getting a haircut in preparation, washing the sector." She drew on her extensive experience with both the prisoners and their partners: "They make phone calls all week long. 'Are you going to come? When? What time?' The visits also feed the economy." She swept her arm out, gesturing toward the prison yard, at its haphazard collection of tents and men standing about in little groups. She added: "Maybe you don't have a nice space to share with your visita. So you rent a room from a guy who does. You do *everything* to ensure that things go well with her."

Many prisoners I met were quick to stress how enlightened their treatment of women is in comparison with men on the outside. "On the street, men treat their women badly," said Mike, a prisoner in Pavón, a few months before his release. "They only want them there so they will serve them. They do not take the time to care for their women. But we prisoners, we can be very romantic. We write love letters. We take baths with our women. That is why they come back and want to be with us." Mike spoke from experience—he was preparing to move in with his fiancée, whom he had met and wooed while incarcerated. Later that day I watched another prisoner approach Elena and a few other social workers and inquire in the most respectful of tones, "Are you happy in your marriage? Are you sure? Does your man pay attention to you? Does he give you enough time?"

Though such sentiments and overtures may smack of utilitarian manipulation—men desperate for outside help performing for survival's sake—traditional gender dynamics do seem to undergo an odd trebling in some male prisons. For some female visitors, the prison can be a space of welcome transgression in a highly conservative and *machista* (misogynist and patriarchal) society, a place where they can express themselves in ways forbidden on the street.[36] By trapping men behind bars, the prison becomes, in a surprising inversion, a space of rare freedom and emancipation for some female visitors.

"Watch the women cross the threshold of the prison," Elena urged. "On the outside they are demure, staid, 'yes sir,' 'no sir,' good little women. But as soon as they enter something comes alive, something is awoken." She put her hand to her chest. "They find freedom. As soon as they cross the frontier of the prison they can lose their etiquette. You won't be judged. No one will judge you. Not for how you act." She flashed an enigmatic smile. "You can even desire a man with tattoos without your parents telling you it is wrong. On the street you are under constant surveillance. In the prison, no one is watching." She herself carried on a romantic relationship with Juande for years while organizing rehabilitation programs inside prison, and she relied on his cachet with other prisoners to ensure these programs had at least a modicum of success. At the same time, he relied on her for the materials he needed to keep his carpentry and other small businesses alive.

The prison, constructed to trap and keep a watchful eye on criminal bodies, is also, in a way, a space of liberty and hidden pleasure for women trapped by the machismo of their society.[37] Able to come and go more or less as they please and dictate the terms of their relationships with men desperate for their companionship, they get a taste of equality rare for most poor women in this country. And for these women who sustain prison life, the prison can offer far more than romance and a sense of freedom. It is also a space of entrepreneurial opportunity, where some earn their livelihoods and support their families by taking on the risks and rewards of smuggling contraband. La Shadow, who was serving a five-year sentence for trafficking, said, "Smuggling drugs was the only way I could support my kids and also care for them." She shrugged and smiled sadly, saying, "but look where it got me." Despite the prevalence of marijuana and crack in Guatemalan prisons, legislation inspired by the war on drugs still nominally governs El Sistema, and those caught smuggling contraband face a stiff prison sentence. Escaping detection requires painstaking hyperawareness as well as meticulous manipulation of the body, emotions, and social interactions to get past prison guards. While the Guatemalan prison system has no metal detectors, no drug-sniffing dogs, and no imaging technology, prison guards do deploy full body-cavity searches at random. The arbitrariness of such searches makes passing undetected contingent not only on careful strategy, but also on some degree of luck.

To escape detection, female smugglers have to maintain both physical control and emotional discipline. 'Every time I go, I have to think about it,' said Sofía, who ran a drug-smuggling operation in Pavón Prison with her imprisoned partner. 'It's dangerous. There's a little room just for women. The guards are there with their latex gloves. They wear them all the time just to intimidate you. They have the glove on already just to see if you get nervous. If [the drugs are] not well-positioned, they will feel it, and it's 'Ah ha!'" She snapped her fingers. "I know, because I've seen it happen. And it's straight to the central office. Then they take your picture, and take you to the police." Sofía took a moment to evaluate the risk: "If you really don't love the person," she said, "I don't see why you would do it." Drawn in by their need to support themselves and their families, caught up in the risks and romance that male prisons make possible, women like Sofía effectively uphold a prison system in a state of perpetual crisis. And they do so by trespassing the nominal boundaries that are supposed to isolate the incarcerated from the free.

In addition to taking on enormous risks in the name of survival, many of these women must also bear the burdens of single parenthood. I met several prisoners who had fathered children while serving their sentences. For example, it was said that in the three years he spent in Pavón, one smooth-talking former MS member had four children by three different women.

Most prisoners, however, are not lucky or capable enough to woo new lovers, and many do not have families able or willing to care for them. For these men, life in prison is difficult indeed. They are known as *rusos*, meaning Russians, blighted commies, isolated and embargoed in Siberia.[38] These men are left to fend for themselves, and they covet the women who come to be with others each visiting day. Trapped in their solitude and their poverty, they are left to listen to the hushed gasping of lovers echoing from cramped cells down dark sector hallways.

While state surveillance inside all but a few maximum security facilities is extremely haphazard and easily sidestepped, it is not true, as Elena claimed, that "no one is watching." Agents of the state may be largely absent, but prisoners are *always* watching one another. In this space where rumors born of fear, hunger, or jealousy spread anew each day, knowing your neighbors' business can be key to survival. Information, after all, can be the most valuable currency. But the atmosphere of envy and distrust is palpable. The gifts la visita offer, the spell against the pall of prison time they can provide, are not apportioned equally. Appeasing one man's hunger will feed another's.

"Envy controls everything in the prison," said El Gordo, Calavera's father and a prison old-timer. "This one eats well, this one does not; this one is always high, this one is not; this one has visitors, this one does not; this one has a woman on the outside, this one has no family at all. This one is a ruso, and this one runs an extortion racket."

In Guatemalan prisons, the famous ideal of the panopticon—the carceral dream of making prisoners transparent before a disciplining authority—takes on new meaning.[39] Rather than the specter of an all-seeing state authority ordering prisoners' bodies and souls, the only ones watching and keeping careful notes on the prisoners are the prisoners themselves. Too often it is the most ruthless and well-connected inmates—those most willing and able to use violence to get their way—who direct the most lucrative kinds of exchange with the outside world, thereby dictating the conditions of prison life. Linked up with agents of the state, powerful prisoners attempt to profit from the prison's porousness by imposing unofficial, unregulated control over the entangled flows.

FRICTION

Prisons are the ultimate expression, if a clumsy one, of the state's claim to govern. By stripping the criminal of his community, his rights, and his humanity in cages of concrete and razor wire, imprisonment is the endgame of carefully orchestrated rituals of crime and punishment.[40] Such rituals are essential scripts in the state's performance of power. In Guatemala, as elsewhere, prisons are meant to create the illusion of order out of the chaos of rampant insecurity.[41] However, while the state may create the prison's physical infrastructure, once inside state agents are only one of several groups vying for control over prisoners' daily routine and their exchange with the outside world. Authority over prison life flows along networks linking state authorities to powerful prisoners; together they reap profits from the constant exchange between the prison and the outside world. Through violent coercion, these networks establish authoritarian hierarchies over the rest of the population. Controlling prison space means more than simply wielding power inside prison. It means straddling the porous membrane between the prison and the outside world and regulating the constant flow of goods, bodies, and information across prison walls.[42]

For their part, prison officials often find themselves locked in an uneasy détente with their prisoners, able to maintain only the barest shell of control. The director of Pavón Prison, who gave me a lunchtime interview on one of his last days working for El Sistema, characterized the state's tenuous control in particularly stark, personal terms. "I know perfectly well what is going on," he said. He then proceeded to list all the illegal activities in which prisoners, with clear collusion from his guards, were involved: the constant flow of drugs, cell phones, and other black market goods; the extortion networks organized and directed by prisoners; and the illegal businesses run inside the prisons that take advantage of the inmates' depressed wages. He understood some of this flow as a necessary pressure valve. "I know how much marijuana gets smuggled in here. But let them smoke their joints. It calms them down, makes the time pass. If I were to seize all the marijuana tomorrow, I would have an immediate riot on my hands."

He also made it clear that if he tried to plug up the porous membrane, even his own guards would turn against him. As we spoke, a uniformed guard brought the director a *sopa de mariscos* (seafood soup) for lunch. The guard saluted, and as he left the room, the director nodded his head meaningfully toward his retreating back, then looked down at the soup, then fixed me with a stare and muttered, "If I mess too much with [the guards], what's to stop them from poisoning my soup?"

The one thing that must at all costs be prevented, he said, was an escape. If even one inmate escapes, the director himself must take the blame, and he could end up incarcerated. And so, agents of the state maintain a careful facade of daily control in order to avoid the very real possibility of ending up behind bars themselves. Indeed, over the last decades five out of the last seven ministers of the interior (the directors of the state organ that oversees prisons and law enforcement) have ended up in prison for fraud and criminal negligence. I met one of them in Pavoncito prison. When I asked him how he got there, he shook his head ruefully and sighed, "As soon as I got in office they started sawing the legs off my chair."

Powerful prisoners also represent a mortal threat to prison officials. Just weeks before my interview with the director of Pavón, masked assailants gunned down the newly appointed director of el Infiernito, the maximum security facility on the way to Canada Prison. The man had tried to tighten control inside Infiernito by limiting visits and increasing cell searches. He angered powerful inmates, so they ordered his execution. After recounting this story, Pavón's director slumped back in his chair. "A week before he died, we tried to warn him that he was sitting on a time bomb. But he didn't listen." Such events are common enough that prison directors and guards know that they must carefully walk a line. Caught between the need to maintain the appearance of control to appease their superiors and powerful prisoners willing to kill to maintain their privileges, prison officials' authority is tenuous indeed.

The Authority of Abuse

Under such precarious circumstances, prison guards' fear and anger give rise to periodic acts of violence against prisoners. This is not the kind of disciplinary power associated with the "totalizing institutions" we have come to imagine in advanced industrialized societies.[43] In every prison, el Sistema regularly carries out searches for drugs, weapons, cell phones, and other black market goods, but the targets are often only the most vulnerable prisoners, making such efforts seem more like symbolic gestures—or futile gesturing—than organized regulation. Still, the use of targeted violence against prisoners deemed too weak to retaliate is integral to the performance of control inside the prison. Even as such actions exemplify the effort to build authority through abuse, they are also about state agents lashing out against the constraints on their power. The line between instrumental, tactical violence and reactive rage fades away. Too many brutal acts are alloyed by both.

In 2013 I finally got the chance to meet Captain Byron Lima, Guatemala's most powerful prison strongman, in Pavoncito Prison, his base of operations. Carlos, the ex-military policeman, had worked for Lima while incarcerated with him, and he introduced us. I had hoped to interview Lima about his decade-long feud with imprisoned mareros, but on this occasion (as on every occasion) he had his own agenda. It seems he wanted to highlight for me how deeply abusive el Sistema could be. And so, at Lima's behest, I found myself sitting across from a young man I will call Xavier, a short, muscular, Ladino prisoner. Mottled third degree burns rippled across the left side of his neck and face, and his left ear was nearly gone. He lifted up his shirt to show where a mass of whorled scar tissue ran down his left shoulder. A year earlier, he had spent fifteen days in Fraijanes II (F-2), a maximum security facility just over the wall from where we were sitting. Xavier had been housed with several recently arrested members of the Zetas, a powerful Mexican-based drug cartel.[44] They had made international headlines by murdering and decapitating twenty-seven farmworkers employed by a rival and writing messages in their blood across a farmhouse wall.[45] After the Zetas' arrival, the director of F-2 and several guards received death threats via cell phone and scribbled notes, setting them on edge. One night, to demonstrate their authority and their own capacity for brutality, hooded prison guards cornered Xavier in his cell. A man claiming to be chief guard oversaw his torture. Guards kicked him into submission and pulled out his fingernails. After stripping off his clothes, they dumped gasoline on him. Other prisoners heard Xavier's cries and tried to intervene, but the guards forced them back with kicks and rifle butts. Then the chief stuck him in the shoulder with a cattle prod. As Xavier lost consciousness in a flash of heat and light, the chief screamed, "I'm in charge here!" Unable or afraid to directly threaten more powerful inmates who could retaliate, the guards' fury—conveniently, tactically—found Xavier.

The chain of command gets no cleaner or clearer higher up. Dive beneath the surface effects of some of the government's most spectacular efforts to impose its authority over prisons, and the waters get ever murkier. In the early 2000s, for example, Pavón Prison was known as the "Hilton" of the prison system.[46] El Sistema had long ceded everyday governance to the Comité de Orden y Disciplina (the Committee of Order and Discipline, known as the COD), organized and staffed by a tight-knit prisoner clique. Prisoners associated with the COD—several of whom were connected with transnational drug-trafficking organizations—had built cottages on the banks of a soccer field that became an artificial lake each rainy season. Their residences had hot tubs and guesthouses, and there was a nightclub connected to the central cafeteria.

Association with the COD allowed prisoners to organize a wide variety of illicit businesses on the prison grounds. Prisoner mechanics ran an auto-body shop that received stolen vehicles for refurbishment, while extortion and kidnapping rings used Pavón as a base from which to operate. Kidnapping victims were allegedly held in Pavón's cells until their families paid ransom. A prisoner I will call Rosario, who has resided in Pavón since 1998 and whose crack habit made him prone to late night wanderings, recalled the clandestine comings and goings. "I saw when cars would enter in the night," he told me as we spoke in Pavón's courtyard, my recorder hidden beneath a baseball cap between us. "Sometimes they were full of guys with guns. The room where they kept the victims was about fifty meters from my house, there in front"—he pointed toward a collection of hastily built structures about forty meters from the director's office—"so I heard when the cars passed before dawn, when they let the people out, when they left again down the road. And a few times I saw the dudes bringing in the kidnapped victims."

Because Rosario was a skilled soccer player, he enjoyed the sponsorship of one of Pavón's richest inmates, a Guatemala City drug dealer who set up a crack lab on the premises and cooked crack for sale inside Pavón. Networks of prisoners and guards allegedly distributed his product in other prisons and on the street. His wealth made him an influential prisoner linked with the COD, and he maintained close relations with another prisoner, known as El Loco Batres, a Colombian who ran cross-border transport for drug shipments. El Loco Batres was a leading member of the COD.

In 2006 the Guatemalan Ministry of the Interior, in cooperation with the army, mounted a full-scale assault on Pavón Prison. The invasion was code-named Operation Peacock and was depicted in the media as the "retaking of Pavón" (la retoma de Pavón). Heavily armed troops and armored vehicles stormed the prison grounds. As riot police rounded up prisoners en masse for transport to another facility, Rosario and other survivors saw masked troops checking a list of names and searching out leading COD members. The police dragged El Loco Batres from his residence half naked and in handcuffs. Later, authorities "discovered" his body—now fully clothed—murdered execution-style, along with six others. To escape the ensuing investigation, top officials fled the country. In 2014 Austrian courts found former police chief Carlos Viellman, the man in charge of the raid, guilty of human rights abuses for his role in torturing and assassinating these inmates.[47]

Was the retaking of Pavón simply the state enforcing law and order by reining in powerful prisoners and reestablishing nominal government control? The answer is a murky "no." Rumors in prison and among journalists allege that before the raid and executions, former interior minister Alejandro Giammatei visited El Loco Batres and other COD leaders and demanded a major cut of their profits. Rosario's sponsor tipped him off to what was going on, and he claimed to have overheard their conversation from a hiding place near the auditorium where Giammatei met with the COD. "[Giammatei] already knew everything that was going down in the prison," Rosario said, and slipped into an impression of the former minister. "'Look, I know you have stolen cars, that you're making crack, that you have kidnapped victims and all that shit. I have video of what you are doing in here. So let's make a deal. I'll let you keep on doing your work in exchange for Q100,000 a week. You do what you want, there will be no cell searches, nothing.'"

Angered, El Loco Batres and other leading members of the COD protested that Q100,000 was too much, and in the ensuing argument they threatened to kill the minister. Giammatei, Rosario said, refused to back down. As he left, limping out on the crutches he used for multiple sclerosis, Rosario heard him shout, "You will see, I'm the one that's gonna kill you first!"

If this story is true, rather than trying to curtail the power and profit prisoners gained from their ability to reach beyond prison walls, Giammattei (and likely his subordinates) simply wanted their piece of the pie. In any case, two days later Giammatei ordered the retaking of Pavón, and government agents murdered El Loco Batres and his colleagues.

Talacha: Prison Taxes

The pursuit of profit in the name of state authority is a given in Guatemalan prisons, and there are much more prosaic methods of extraction and abuse than the examples already given. The profits reaped from the ebb and flow of goods, information, and bodies in and out of the prison form the very glue that binds the networks of state agents and prisoners who dictate the conditions of prison life. First and foremost among the commodities taxed by these networks are the prisoners themselves.

In every prison, prison strongmen (known as *voceros*, or spokesmen) direct some version of talacha, a system of taxation and indentured servitude. When a new inmate enters a prison, the vocero or a consortium of voceros will require a one-time payment. The payment usually depends on the new arrival's perceived wealth, which voceros determine from his rap sheet, furnished by prison officials. For example, a prisoner accused of petty theft will usually get off by paying a small fee, or more likely, will simply have to work off his debt.

Calavera was nineteen when he was arrested and convicted for transporting crack cocaine. Having followed his brother's advice to never get tattoos, he was able to hide his gang affiliation. Upon his arrest, he was sent first to the Preventivo prison in zone 18 of Guatemala City to await his trial. "Well, my dad had already been a prisoner for many years," he recalled when we spoke shortly after his release. "He knew a man who was in charge named El Ruco, and recommended me to him. 'Good,' I thought. 'I'll be in good shape here.'" Calavera acted out the conversation that ensued.

"'Who is Samuel?' El Ruco asks.

"'Me!' I say.

"'Ah, you're Gordo's son. What problem do you come with?'

"'Ah, for a little bag of marijuana,' I say.

"'Ah, that's fine,' he says to me. He opens the door and I go below with him. In his little office he has my identification, my file, what I'm accused of, trafficking and all that. The old man looks at me, 'Trafficking!' he says. I know he's thinking, 'Ah, this one has money.' Then he says, 'Here you have to pay Q6,000 ($800), and you're going to live well. If not, you won't live well at all.'

"But I, obviously, came from the street, and as we say vulgarly here, I wasn't going to tolerate their bullshit. 'I'm not gonna pay you,' I told him. 'I'm used to people paying *me* the rent. I'm not the one who pays.'"

Calavera resisted paying the "rent" for a week. During that week, El Ruco and his henchman forced him to clean out the latrines and mop the floor on his belly. They did not allow him to sleep until his chores were done, and these chores often took most of the night. When he refused, they beat him. After a week of this, fearing he might be killed, Calavera gave in. Using his father's connections, he negotiated the payment down to Q2,000. "But El Ruco told me not to tell anyone he let me get away for so little," Calavera told me. "He had to pay off the guards, the director, other voceros, and I don't know who else."[48]

Calavera's story is typical for newly arrived prisoners, most of whom are not as well connected or as savvy as he.[49] Across the prison system, voceros expect the inmates' families to raise the talacha money. Anxious to protect their loved ones, families who have the means inevitably come through with the demanded payments.

Rarely are prisoners executed for refusing to pay talacha. In prison, there are other means of coercion. Those who cannot pay must work off their debt or face beatings, isolation blocks, and even torture. Powerful voceros have been known to threaten and even kill prisoners' family members to enforce proper payment. In return for tolerating these abuses—and supplying the information needed to assess how much each prisoner ought to be charged— prison directors and other officials often receive a cut of the profits. Some version of these state-prisoner assemblages dictates prison life throughout the prison system and can only be displaced through organized revolt.

Visiting Day at Canada Prison, Escuintla, Guatemala, 2012

On the surface, life in Canada Prison appeared normal. The same interminable line of visitors at the gate. The same quiet desperation on the prisoners' faces as they waited for their loved ones. The same suffocating heat. But rumors whispered to me through air vents spoke differently. The population was furious. La Comité (the Committee)—favored convicts appointed by Director Latona to ensure internal security—had committed unforgivable abuses. It wasn't the kickbacks they paid to Latona from taxes collected from newly arrived prisoners that caused the anger; this was standard practice. Nor were the newly imposed "sanitation control" levies cause for revolt. But in recent months certain members had commandeered shops and other prisoner-run businesses. And far worse, they had demanded money from la visita and had even molested women come to visit other prisoners. Abusing visitors was the last straw. "We will see what happens," a voice muttered from inside an isolation cell.

Two days later the storm broke, but as often happens, nothing went as planned. Latona caught wind of the riot organized to kill the most hated members of La Comité, and in the night he removed his allies from the general population. During roll call the following morning, he threatened to permanently take away visiting privileges. Minutes after he returned to his office, a riot erupted. Several shots were fired, stores were looted, and one man—a well-to-do shop owner named Javier—was killed. Triste related what happened next:

> Latona came out of his office yelling like crazy and firing an AK-47 over our heads. Everyone hit the deck. He went down below with a team of guards and came back out with *Enano*,[50] the bald guy who everyone knew had killed Javier. . . . Out on the street Enano had been an associate of Barrio18, but the dude wasn't anything

inside. Latona came out holding Enano by his shirt with the AK pressed against the back of his head. The crowd started screaming for him. "Give him to us, give us Enano." They yelled. "He killed Javier."

"You want him?" Latona yelled, shaking Enano like a doll.

"Yes, yes, yes," they yelled.

"You want him?"

"Yes. Yes. YES.

"Here, take him," Latona yelled. "Eat him." He pushed Enano into the crowd of prisoners. They hit him, kicked him . . . hit him with sticks. I saw the skin peeling off his head and his face. . . . They were going to kill him. He was holding onto the fence with both hands. A dude was carrying a big rock, walking over slowly to smash Enano. But he tripped and dropped it too soon, and Enano got away from the crowd and ran towards the guards.

The prisoners' attempt to resist the authority of powerful prisoners and corrupt officials momentarily fractured the state's nominal control. Director Latona fanned the explosive spark to punish those attempting to throw off the oppression that he had helped to organize and profit from. Thus a single inmate became the scapegoat for the prisoners' helpless rage, a body made abject among a thousand abject bodies.[51]

FIRE

Prisons are central nodes in a continuum linking the state, the incarcerated, and the free into a single, uninterrupted whole. Thus far, I have explored how exchange among prisoners, state agents, and the free dictates the flow of everyday life inside the prison, and how conditions in prison reverberate far beyond prison walls. The coproduction of law and outlaw, however, goes well beyond everyday life behind bars, and the networks linked through the prison reach well above gangsters, guards, and girlfriends.[52] It is only through moments of violent rupture—moments when the facade of isolation and order is ripped away—that the deeper matrices linking prison power to state sovereignty become detectable, effectively dragging the state back into the pit designed to isolate criminals from society.

In Guatemala, the maras have played an important role in achieving such ruptures. Their history of conflict with incarcerated members of the Guatemalan military—a powerful subset of the prison population—illuminates how prison power flows back and forth across prison walls and can insinuate itself into the highest echelons of state power.

Maras and the Military

Most prisoners must remain servile before the prisoner faction–state agent alliances that maintain what passes for law and order within the prison. Over the last two decades, imprisoned mareros and ex-military members have become vicious competitors, leveraging very different forms of violent capital in their fight to dominate the prisons. Their confrontations have led to the most spectacular prison riots in Guatemalan history.

The authority and power some military men accrue in prison is based on a number of complex factors. According to a United Nations study, the military today remains the most highly respected and trusted government institution in the country.[53] This is despite—or because of—its role in massacring and disappearing hundreds of thousands of suspected "subversives" and guerrilla sympathizers during Guatemala's long civil war. This violent peace has disgraced the National Civil Police, and respect for the military has only grown. Today many Guatemalans believe the military to be the only institution capable of bringing peace to the streets. This prestige is even more powerful inside prison, where many guards have themselves served a stint in the military, and where daily routine—from morning roll call to sector cleanup duties—mirrors barracks life.[54]

Military men are also on the other side of the law. Two-thirds of the Guatemalan military was decommissioned by order of the 1996 peace accords, and many former soldiers found their way into the burgeoning trade and transport of narcotics, formed kidnapping rings, and engaged in other illicit activities.[55] Some of them, of course, ended up behind bars. There are also those found guilty of war crimes in the trials that followed in the wake of the civil war. Based on their shared identity and history—and for their own protection— former military men often band together to form a distinct stratum among the prison population.

This brings us back to Byron Lima, former *kaibil* captain and the most infamous prison strongman in Guatemalan history. The kaibiles are the most feared and respected of Guatemala's special forces.[56] Trained by US and Israeli military, they were responsible for the worst massacres of the civil war, and today the Zetas and other drug trafficking organizations seek out soldiers with kaibil training to work for them.[57]

In many ways, Lima embodied the Guatemalan military's powerful and multifarious role in the continuum of violence between war and peace. He served in some of the civil war's bloodiest theaters and, linked through his father to hard-line military leaders, segued from war to peace by becoming a darling of Guatemala's economic elite. As the war officially ended, widespread kidnappings for ransom terrorized the rich. Lima was part of the government's antikidnapping unit, working closely with these families to rescue their sons and daughters. He even became head of President Alvaro Arzú's (1996–2000) security detail. But his rise was seemingly cut short in 1998 when he, his father, and Sergeant Obdulio Villanueva were convicted of the assassination of Archbishop Juan José Gerardi two days after Gerardi published an account of the military's wartime atrocities.[58]

For Captain Lima, however, incarceration was the beginning of a new career. Over the next seventeen years he leveraged his power in prison to accumulate wealth and influence national politics in astounding ways.[59] His rise to power began in El Preventivo prison, where within a year Lima became the de facto leader of eight out of ten sectors.[60] He controlled these sectors with an iron fist while dipping a hand into virtually all prison businesses to funnel money to himself, his father, and his lackeys. He taxed the tienditas (small convenience stores), and inmates had to obtain his permission to sell merchandise like smokes, sodas, and snacks. He collected "rent" from the restaurants, the production of twine and rubber soccer balls, and myriad other prison businesses. Prisoners incarcerated in Preventivo during his reign claim that he also gained control of the lucrative drug and cell-phone rackets by paying off the guards and strong-arming rivals. Just how he managed to do this so quickly is not clear. Archbishop Gerardi's murder was a politically motivated military plot involving many more conspirators than the Limas and Villanueva. Some say their refusal to implicate others was rewarded with behind-the-scenes favors.[61] Prisoners and journalists (off the record) muse that his connections to the highest echelons of the Guatemalan military were essential in his rapid rise to power in the Preventivo prison and in the four other facilities he has since occupied.

Prisoners who lived under Lima's reign recalled having no one to turn to for help against him.

"We couldn't denounce him to the police, because [Lima and his men] were police," explained Juande, who spent his first few years behind bars in Preventivo. "I couldn't complain to the guards, because he had the guards in his corner (sombreaba a la guardia). He had control of the guards, and would order them about. 'Ah! My Captain!' they would say." Juande mimed a cartoonish military salute, then broke into a grin. "I don't know how he got so much power being a prisoner, or what privileges he had . . . but he bought the guards boots, uniforms, everything. So, how to say to a guard, 'Look, excuse me, but Captain Lima does this and this to us?'"

Juande slipped back into his prison guard impression. "'Ay, okay,' says the guard. 'We'll see what we can do about this!' and then a second later, 'Look, my captain, so and so is complaining to us that you are harassing other prisoners, that you are hitting them for no reason.'"

Then Juande pulled an evil grin. "'Ah, thank you,' says Lima, 'here's Q100 for your trouble.'"

The maras, for their part, have leveraged a very different kind of violent capital in their rise to prison dominance. By the early 2000s they had become a force to be reckoned with throughout the prison system. Their capacity to disrupt prison hierarchies made them anathema to state agents and fellow prisoners alike.[62] "The cholos are the only ones who are down to ride," Triste explained. "If you ask anyone else, they'll say they don't want no trouble. . . . Everyone else is scared, that's just how it is. In riots they'll do their get backs, but never face to face or in the open. But cholos will. And that's one of the big reasons other prisoners don't like them and treat them bad or try to get them kicked out."

The maras turned the government's policing efforts to strategic advantage by gaining overwhelming numbers inside the prison and by developing a highly coordinated network linking prisoners with the street. The military's prestige in Guatemalan society has served imprisoned soldiers well, and some, like Lima, have been able to rely on help from outside the prison and from prison officials. In hindsight, confrontation between these groups was inevitable. In a series of riots between 2000 and 2005, gangsters and paisas led by former military decapitated, quartered, burned, and otherwise disfigured each other, parading mutilated bodies before the news cameras that gathered en masse outside the prison walls.

The first spectacular clash occurred on Christmas Eve, 2001, in Pavoncito Prison, when gang members rose up against former army sergeant El Negro Beteta.[63] The media flocked to publicize it, and images of massed mareros, masked and rioting, flooded the airwaves. Twelve years later Sanz and Martinez interviewed prisoner witnesses and wrote the following account of events.

> On the 23rd of December a young leader of la Mara Salvatrucha, *El Vago de Coronados*, spearheaded a riot in Pavoncito prison, on the outskirts of Guatemala City. While a hundred sureños demolished walls and opened bars to take control of the

prison block, El Vago launched himself in search of Julio Cesar Beteta, who for years had been the leader of the paisas in this prison. According to newspaper reports from those days, El Negro Beteta, as he was called, accumulated more than Q50 thousand (more than $6,000) a month in taxes on other prisoners, he had an office next to the director's, and those who did not follow his rules he enclosed in isolation cells in which they would stay for up to 15 days in water up to their knees.

Lupe is a shy, soft-spoken man who spends his days carving wooden figurines for sale in Pavón. He was once an MS member and had been transferred to Pavoncito four days before the riot started. He had just turned eighteen and begun a life sentence for involvement in a paid assassination he committed with his father. He found himself in the middle of the maelstrom when an MS leader handed him a pistol and told him he would have to defend himself. "I heard a lot of things," Lupe recalled. "One guy kept shouting, 'You killed my family just because I refused to do the cleaning!' They killed families, man! These military guys wanted people to pay like Q10,000 at a time. And who has that money? I'm lucky if I have Q50 in my pocket. And to pressure people to pay, they killed people's family on the street. Their rule was, 'The family will pay—whether with money or with their lives.'"

Out of this riot, El Vago would emerge as the very face of the avenging mareros. As Sanz and Martinez wrote:

> [E]l Vago lashed mattress scraps to his chest and back as improvised armor, grabbed a machete in each hand and made his way to sector 5, where Beteta was quartered. A few hours later he posed in front of cameras from every news-station in the country with the head of the paisas' leader stuck on a long stake. This Christmas eve, El Vago de Coronados changed his *apodo* (gang alias) and decided that from then on he would be called *El Diabólico de Coronados*. His name would resound in the decade to come. It still does.[64]

This was one of the first widely circulated mara decapitations, and the first prison riot to receive such intense media attention in Guatemala. As such, it proved a pivotal event, thrusting the maras and their prison power before the public eye. Toppling the prison strongman Beteta, along with the media frenzy his decapitation engendered, helped transform El Diabólico from a minor player in the MS into a widely recognized and respected leader both within and outside the prisons. His influence, as we shall see in later chapters, can still be felt today. Not only had he spearheaded what became a prison coup d'état, he also increased the fame (and infamy) of the MS across the nation. For the MS, such a decisive move, and its media spectacle, proved to be an effective "branding" technique, spreading the kind of fear and intimidation that undergird the extortion rackets that are its bread and butter. El Diabóli-co's "method" also became a model for mara revolts against abusive prison strongmen in other prisons.[65] A year later, mareros in the Preventivo prison attempted to take down Captain Lima in the most spectacular prison riot in Guatemalan history.

The Anatomy of a Riot

Riots are integral to the chaotic rhythm of rupture and reformation through which prison power is established.[66] Riots are the end product of the endless frictions and frustrations produced by the systems of domination shaping prison life and are moments in which everyday violence breaks out into the spectacular. They are also deeply confused, confusing events. Sometimes, powerful prisoner conspirators carefully plan riots. This process can involve weeks or months of preparation, but when the time comes, the riot always takes place within and relies upon conditions of total chaos. For prisoners, such chaos can present opportunities for revenge, enshrouding the event in a smokescreen of countless and contradictory motives. For prison officials, riots represent a failure to manage the precarious balance of power inside the pris-ons essential for maintaining a facade of control.[67]

In our interviews and in his statements to the press, Lima claimed loudly and often that he had gained authority in Preventivo and the other prisons he has occupied through his leadership qualities and his selfless dedication to improving prison life. But his fellow inmates remembered things differently.

"We wanted to kill Captain Lima because he was such an asshole," recalled Juande. "He had military training, and if one answered him disrespectfully, the dude would have you whipped—he would have all his dogs on you. . . . He had a vato named El Buffón of Santos [an MS clique], who told him everything about the maras." He spit and wiped his mouth. "So he thought, 'Ah, I can dominate them.' What Buffón didn't know was that the moment would arrive when we would say, 'No more, now you're going to die too!' But Buffón was lucky, he escaped with Lima. He appeared in news photos with Lima yelling his head off."

Lima's most despised associate was Sergeant Obdulio Villanueva, an enforcer who targeted newly arrived mareros for abuse. "He was terrible with the cholos," recalled Carlos, the ex-military police officer. Carlos shared quar-ters with Villanueva, and Lima employed him in one of his father's prison convenience stores. "Everytime a cholo was imprisoned he treated them horribly and hit them, threw them in the *pila* (isolation torture in a tub of cold water), broke broom handles over them. . . . [H]e tortured the cholos, and they hated him. They were waiting for an opportunity to kill him."

Whether the mareros revolted of their own accord is not clear. Some witnesses claimed that a hidden adversary manipulated the mareros. Some said it was organized crime and cartel bosses in the two sectors yet to fall under Lima's control who paid marero leaders to kill him in order to protect their black market businesses. Lima himself swore that the same human rights organizations that had pressed charges against him pushed incarcerated mareros into a berserker rage.[68] Whatever the truth, on February 12, 2003, more than three hundred mareros went on a coordinated rampage. They tore through the Preventivo prison on their way to sector 7, where Lima, Buffón, Villanueva, Carlos, and dozens of incarcerated police and military men were housed.

A decade later, Carlos sat across the table from me, getting drunk in the same cantina where we first spoke.

"On the 12th of February, 2003," he said, eyes flitting about the place as if someone might be eavesdropping, "if I'm not mistaken, at 9:00 a.m. the mareros took advantage when a baker entered their sector. They took the *llavero* (holder of the keys) hostage and many gangsters got out. They organized themselves and went to free all the gangsters from their sectors . . . because every gangster already knew the mission and what was going to happen that day."

Juande was, he said, an unwilling participant in the riot against Lima. He said that two gang leaders—Psycho of Alpha and Omega (an MS clique) and Spyder of Barrio18—led the riot. "They were in front of everyone. Since they each had 50-year sentences, they told us they would throw themselves into the fight. 'Don't worry,' they said, 'but we want you to look alive.'" Other witnesses claimed that the two leaders were already in sector 7 with Lima's people when the riot started and helped the homies enter.

Lima was their ultimate target, but the sureños had other scores to settle. On their way to sector 7, mareros targeted others who had abused them. They went after a man named La Vaca Pinta, a Brekero thief on the street who in Preventivo had become an enforcer for a pair of narco-trafficking brothers known as Los Cruces. "They would beat you with wire whips," Juande exclaimed, "in the head, PLOW! They mistreated you, they abused you, they humiliated you."

The rioting gangsters took their revenge. "'Ay, there's Vaca Pinta'," Juande exulted in a grinding voice, "'remember when you were with los Cruces?'"

"'No, carnal, those were different times,'" Juande mimicked in a high-pitched whine, then slipped back into himself. "But he had had the time to put on a ski-mask and mistreat the cholos, and this was our time."

The gangsters stabbed Vaca Pinta to death. They had no firearms and few machetes. Mostly, they used *fizgars* (prison-made knives) and objects they found as they moved through the sectors toward sector 7. Juande described how they killed another narco-trafficker named Baudilio by severing his head at the jawline with dumbbells. "I didn't even know you could do that with dumbbells," he said, shaking his head.

Carlos and the other men in Lima's sector heard the mareros coming and shouting for Lima. But Captain Lima was nowhere to be found. He had disappeared an hour earlier. Carlos would not say so, but others who were there hinted that Lima knew what was coming—having been informed of the impending riot by a guard—and only bothered to save himself. He had two pistols stashed among his things. In desperation, as the cholos approached sector 7, Carlos and his compatriots searched for them, but to no avail.

Others claim that Lima just got lucky. He had simply gone to greet visitors in the area reserved for conjugal visits on the other side of the prison when, as Carlos recalls, "The cholos descended upon sector 7 with the idea of eliminating all of us. They tried to break open the doors, but they couldn't because we barricaded it with mattresses and lit them on fire." He brought a hand to his chest. "I participated in defending my fellow prisoners, and got hit in the face with a rock, broke two ribs." With sudden delicacy, he touched a scar above his eye, then finished off another Corona. "So, anyway, since they couldn't get in through the doors they started to open holes in the wall. While they did this, we, using some dumbbells Captain Byron Lima had, opened up holes to save our lives. Once we opened the holes, the older prisoners began to leave. Soon after, thank God, I left too. Obdulio Villanueva tried to escape, but he got stuck in the hole because he was very fat and was carrying a fanny pack." I couldn't help myself, and started laughing at this detail. Carlos laughed too. "It's true, it's true!" he insisted, then became serious again. "So the cholos entered and they were like piranhas."

The gangsters grabbed Villanueva's ankles and pulled. He wouldn't let go, so they cut at his thighs until he did and then hauled him back. Inmates taking shelter in neighboring sectors heard his screaming. "It was Psycho and

Spyder who decapitated him," Carlos said. "They did it in less than two minutes. It was something with the devil inside it."

Juande remembered them sawing off Villanueva's head with his own Rambo knife while other mareros swarmed in. I asked him what he was doing during all this.

"I was there," he said, suddenly shy. "Watching, nothing more. Those guys were crazy. It was like, you couldn't even get in, neither to hit nor to help. There were so many, it was like they had become ants, ya know?" He vividly recalled how Villanueva's fanny pack ripped open, and thousands of quetzales—allegedly Lima's talacha money—came spilling out, flying everywhere, soaking up the blood. For his part, Carlos said the fanny pack held Lima's logbooks of all his dealings, who owed him what, and other information on new prisoners.

Every time I visited Captain Lima, he gave me a tour of the grounds with two of his bodyguards—one from the army and the other from the air force—walking point and muttering into walkie-talkies. On one such visit, I asked him what Villanueva had in that fanny pack that had made him hold onto it. "It was just his radio," he said, pulling his lips back from his big white dentures. "He always carried it, and when he tried to escape, he panicked."

When I had finally built up the courage to ask Lima how he escaped the riot and the three hundred odd gangsters gunning for him, he countered with a question of his own.

"Do you believe in God?"

"What?" I replied, confused.

"Do you believe in God?"

"Uh, well, sure."

"Well then," he said slowly, that grin widening, "I walked out before all the cholos, and they didn't see me. God made me invisible to them."

At the time of this conversation, Lima was Pavoncito Prison's undisputed strongman. He ran the prison cooperative, *Torre Fuerte* (Strong Tower), which manufactured police and prison guard uniforms. Under Lima's reign, Pavoncito became a model facility, where prisoners could learn to use computers, receive English lessons, and earn a high school diploma. In mid-2013 El Diabólico and other MS leaders spent a week in Pavoncito to learn what could happen if they would cooperate with the authorities, even though, as a general rule, Lima allowed no gangsters or even ex-gangsters inside his prison.[69]

I was not alone in seeking an audience with the famous former kaibil cum prison reformer. Prison officials and technocrats from around the world paid him visits to learn from his success in making prison and prisoners productive. Under Lima's command, all inmates had to work, even those locked in the high-security wing. The prison also boasted a Pizza Hut and a Pollo Campero, Guatemala's most popular fast-food franchise.[70] Lima employed a full-time security detail of incarcerated former soldiers, who screened all incoming visitors just inside the prison gate. Unlike their official doppelgangers, these men used metal detectors and were thorough.

Meanwhile, Lima worked to secure his release through his connections to the highest echelons of Guatemalan government. Torre Fuerte provided former general Otto Pérez Molina's Partido Patriota (Patriotic Party) with party shirts and flags for his victorious 2011 presidential campaign. Through his connections to the Perez Molina administration, Lima was able to direct the nomination of prison officials, filling six out of the seven subdirector positions with men who had graduated in his class from the military academy. When we had our meetings, Captain Lima liked to show off the pictures taken before his arrest of himself with President Pérez Molina, which he kept on one of his many smartphones.

In 2013 Lima publicly announced his intention to run for president in 2015, based on his success in bringing order to the prisons. One of his promotional videos—which he helped edit from prison—opens with scenes from the riot in the Preventivo prison. I found it on YouTube. Bloodied, distraught riot police are filmed tending to their wounds. Masked prisoners scream, throw rocks, and brandish machetes. Cut to three severed heads arranged in a row at the feet of enraged prisoners yelling threats at the camera from behind a prison gate. The heads look like melted wax masks, and anonymous hands gouge at their eyes. Above them a masked man holds a child's doll dressed in army fatigues and garroted by the neck. "Liiimmmaaa," he screams, shaking it, "we come for you Liiiiimmmaa."

But a year after our meeting in Pavoncito, Lima fell on troubled times. An investigation by the attorney general's office resulted in the seizure of real estate, dozens of cars, and hundreds of cell phones belonging to Lima. Over the following months, the investigation revealed how for years he had used his influence over prison officials to organize a complex bribery and extortion system targeting the richest prisoners. Incarcerated narco-traffickers, government officials, and others could pay him exorbitant "fees" to be transferred

FIGURE 18. Byron Lima presidential campaign poster (www.byronlimapresidente.com).

into Pavoncito Prison, where they received "VIP" treatment.[71] Those who refused his offer he ordered beaten and tortured by prison guards. Kickbacks from this scheme circulated into the highest echelons of the prison administration. The fallout from the investigation resulted in a shake-up of the entire prison system and the firing and arrest of dozens of prison officials. Lima was transferred out of Pavoncito—losing access to his carefully built prison empire—and remanded to a cell at the Matamoros Air Force Base. But though his rise to power was cut short, as we shall see, Lima's dominant role in prison life was not over just yet.

FIGURE 19. Marero in the isolation block of Canada prison, Escuintla, Guatemala.

The Prisoners and the Cascabel

Back in Canada Prison, Escuintla, Guatemala. "Gato! Hey Gaaaaato, did you bring balls this time?" "Gringo! Griiiingo! Welcome back! We missed you!"

The men in the isolation block shout and wave as we make our way toward them across the courtyard. I glance back toward the prison gate, where hundreds of women still wait in line under the burning sun. Through the layered metal fences, I can just make out Cheeky, propped between the roots of the almond tree, baseball cap pulled down over his face. He appears to be sleeping soundly.

Before Gato and me, the newly whitewashed isolation block gleams incandescent, and its inhabitants' faces pushed between the bars come into focus.

There is Doble Cara, half his bony face tattooed in a grinning skull, wearing the same DARE T-shirt that an avuncular policeman once handed out to my fourth-grade class. There is Soto, who shot and killed a bus driver because his boss didn't make extortion payments. Mouse, tiny tattooed Mouse, who they say is gay, is somewhere inside nursing the HIV and tuberculosis that will kill him. There is El Maniaco, who, they say, killed and ate part of the director of Chimaltenango prison on orders from incarcerated Barrio18 leaders. Or perhaps he simply murdered the man, or threatened to, if not something else entirely. He has a pronounced lisp and an empty, crackhead stare. And there is El Buffón, Captain Lima's old ally. He has a wide mouth, protruding eyes, narrow shoulders, and a potbelly. He was arrested in 1999 for killing his four-year-old stepdaughter with a drunken punch. They say it was an accident.

FIGURE 20. Mouse (RIP) in the isolation block of Canada prison,
Escuintla, Guatemala.

All of them have been expelled from the general population because of their
tattooed faces, because they made too many enemies, because they angered the
wrong people. Buffón's gang green-lighted him for having helped Lima in Preventivo prison, and he has only survived the last thirteen years by moving from
isolation block to isolation block. The one called Blacky is a witness to a high-
profile prison murder. On orders from the outside, Maniaco attacked a deported
Mexican Mafia member with a baseball bat. It is known that Mouse has HIV.
And so on. These are a few of so many stories of uncertain provenance whispered
to me in cautious conversations, in boasts, in passing moments of trust or need.
A question lurks in every exchange: Who will I tell these stories to?

Arms reach out between the bars to greet us. High fives and fist bumps all around, and the guard keys the padlock, motioning for Gato and me to enter. The metal door clangs shut behind us. The concrete floor has recently been washed; the caustic smell of bleach mingles with the stink of unwashed bodies and greasy leftovers. There is a flimsy side table in one corner with a TV and an Xbox on it, jerry-rigged wiring spilling out. A fresh coat of peach paint is drying on the interior walls near the entrance. Farther back, near the cell doors, are images drawn in pencil and charcoal on dirty whitewashed walls: a grinning grim reaper with scythe, the Virgin Mary of Guadalupe, a cartoon gangster weeping on his knees.

Gato takes the plastic bags of shirts and soccer balls from me and hands them to El Brown, a thickset 18th Streeter with olive skin and piercing green eyes. Brown signals to El Nica—who has "666" tattooed on his forehead in ugly block letters—who disappears into a cell and emerges a few moments later with an empty two-liter Coke bottle. With a shy smile he hands it to Gato. Gato holds the bottle in two hands close to his face and breaks into laughter. Inside is a snake about a foot long, black and green diamonds along its length.

"It's a cascabel," El Nica explains. "I caught it in the courtyard beneath the mango tree. It's for your zoo."

"Ah yes, a cascabel," Gato says, as if he were an expert on the species. He hands the bottle to me. I take it gingerly, watching the snake flick its tongue against the plastic, and hand it back to Gato.

"Be careful," El Nica says. "It is only a baby, but it's really poisonous. One bit my daughter and she almost died."

For several minutes Gato and Brown stand apart from the rest of us before the barred window, talking in low voices. Holding the bottle horizontally in both hands, Gato turns it absentmindedly. The snake slides sideways again and again to rest on the shifting bottom. It writhes madly for several seconds, slithering in place, burrowing forward, its tongue flicking at the inside of the plastic cap. Then it falls still, flopping stiffly as if a dead thing, with each turn of the bottle. I lean against an adjacent wall, elbows resting on the rough plaster.

Buffón sidles up to me, eyes flitting from my baseball cap, to the rose gold ring, to my dusty Adidas running shoes. He cracks a smile. "Look, Gringo," he says, speaking quickly. "You know I'm alone here right? No one, not my family, not the homies, nobody cares if I live or die. I am a ruso among rusos.

I have nothing, no visits, no work. Nothing. You come here to see our lives, right? Well this life is shit. Give me some quetzales, man. Make a donation."

"Buffón, sorry man, I don't have any money left. I spent it all coming up here." This is only half true. I have about $20 worth of quetzales in my frayed wallet. But no change, no small bills.

Buffón stares at me, then turns away. I see him again in a grainy video recorded nearly a decade before, shouting and gesticulating, bleeding from a head wound after escaping the Preventivo riot, in which his former homies tried to knife him to death. On several occasions I have tried to talk to him about his time with Lima, his perspective on the riot that almost killed him. But he always just smirks at me, says he's no rat, and jokes loudly about me being an FBI informant.

When I turn back to the rough semicircle of men, El Nica is there, his eyes fixed on the floor. He speaks so quietly I can hardly hear his words. "My daughter will turn three next week and my woman is bringing her from Chimal to visit me. I have nothing to give them. Could you help me?"

"Man, I don't have anything with me now. I'm sorry. Next week. . . . Next week I'll bring you some photos okay? Photos you can give to your family if you like."

"OK."

I take out my camera, but El Nica shakes his head. He wants to change his shirt first. He disappears down a corridor that smells of mold and wet paint.

While I wait for El Nica to return, there is a sudden commotion at the barred windows. Doble Cara and Blacky are catcalling at a woman with peroxide blond hair and heavy makeup crossing the courtyard. Her sequined miniskirt shimmers with each high-heeled step. She doesn't bother to look back. Waving a hand dismissively, she passes through the side gate to where the general population resides.

Turning away from the window, Doble Cara addresses me from across the room. "You know what we really need?" he says. "What we really need is some putas, man. That's what we need up in this place." Some of the others laugh, and Doble Cara starts gyrating, grabbing his crotch and rocking his hips. "This is how we do it you know, this is how." The others start in, shouting encouragement. I laugh and join in with the shouting, perhaps a little too loudly.

Suddenly, Buffón appears again at my side. "Yes Gringo, that's right. That's what we need. We need some whores man. You'll get us some putas, won't you."

"Putas!"

"Some girls to fuck!!"

"Yeah, putas, Gringo," Buffón continues. "We're fucking desperate in here. A man needs to fuck. A man needs to fuck a lady. It's not right. We have needs."

I laugh and shrug, trying to hold Buffón's gaze.

"No Gringo. I'm serious," Buffón says. He breaks away and walks over to Gato, who is grinning and seems tremendously entertained by all this. They confer for a moment, and Gato, like a game show host presenting the grand prize, announces, "Gentleman, the ministry will take care of everything. We can offer transport to and from the prison. I will collect the ladies," he fixes me with a sly grin, "and all the Gringo has to do is put up the money."

Thanks, Gato, I think. Thanks a lot, you bastard.

Gato's words seem to touch off a current in the room. The men gather in closer, forming a rough semicircle, some shouting and laughing, others quietly alert, curious. Buffón's eyes seem to be popping out of his head, and he leans in close to me, hissing into my ear, "Gringo, listen okay listen, I'll take care of everything. I know the girls okay they're from my barrio, don't worry I'll just give them a call and you bring the money. We need, . . ." he pauses, "we need four girls—that's one for five prisoners apiece, and 200 quetzales paid to each one."

"One girl . . . one girl for every five prisoners?"

"Yeah, that's it, Gringo, that's it. No problem."

Doble Cara shouts, "Just get some girls in here for a show. Get some to dance for us, yeah boy!"

Buffón spins around. "No mames, cabron," he yells. "Don't fuck around, dumbass. Look at my hand. Do you see the blisters on my hand? What we need are some women to fuck."

"Okay, okay," I say, "how about this. How about we dress Gato up as a transvestite and send him in here on a visiting day and you can all fuck him." Doble Cara and some others guffaw.

But Buffón will not let it go. "Just make sure you bring them on a visiting day okay—you have to let me know in advance and it's got to be a Wednesday, a Friday, or a Saturday, okay?" I shake my head, but Buffón continues. "Wednesday, Friday or Saturday so that I can get permission for them from the guards."

I hold up a hand in mock seriousness. "Guys," I say, "you all need some condoms if you're going to be sharing women. You have to protect yourselves."

"Condoms!" Doble Cara shouts triumphantly. "You want condoms? Fuck man, we got condoms." He crosses the room and disappears into a cell. In the sudden hush, a skinny, smooth-faced prisoner emerges from a cell leading a woman by the hand. She turns to him, brushing some lint off his T-shirt, which reads, "Senior Weekend 2010, Dubbington High School." He gives her a timid kiss on the cheek and signals to a guard outside the window, who unlocks the door and opens it for her. The men standing about remain silent until the door slams shut behind her. Then, as if on cue, Doble Cara returns clutching a black plastic bag in one hand. He reaches in and takes out a handful of silver-wrapped condoms and lube, flinging them like confetti across the floor. "We got all the condoms we need, see. We just don't have any way to use them."

There is more shouting and jeering at the window. Another woman, perhaps skinnier than the first but practically her twin from this distance, is crossing the courtyard with the same rocking gait.

"Bring her over here," Doble Cara shouts to no one in particular, "the gringo said he would get us some whores. She works here. Hey, Gringo, you talk to her." The others are hooting and jeering behind me as we all peer out between the bars at the woman. I try to smile in order to hide the fact that I am absolutely terrified. What would I do if she actually came over? But she only smiles and waves and disappears through the gate.

"Hey Gringo, you'll do it, right? We're suffering man. It's not right."

"Okay, Buffón, okay. Jesus man, calm down." I think for a moment. Joking it off still seems the best solution. "Well, you know I am here doing a study. We have to do this scientifically. If we're going to do this right, I would need to interview you before and after, and probably take pictures of the whole thing." Their howls of laughter drown me out.

"We'll make a pinche video!" Doble Cara shouts. "Prison pornography!" He commences dancing and grabbing himself again, to much hooting and cheering. For a moment I think I'm off the hook.

But Buffón is undeterred. "Look, Gringo. When are you going to bring the girls? 800 barras. That's all we need." He is staring hard into my face, but I am looking at the object Buffón holds in his right hand: the cascabel in its bottle. The creature starts wriggling madly as Buffón waves the bottle around like a baton. Planting himself squarely before me, he raises it as if in accusation. I attempt another grin.

"No man. I can't," I say.

"Gringo."

"No."

"Gringo," Buffón thrusts the bottle with the cascabel at my face, cap first. There are three dots tattooed in a tiny equilateral triangle on Buffón's hand. "Gringo," he says again, more softly, "we need the girls. It is what we need more than anything in all the world. Do you understand me?" He pushes the bottle, cap first, up against my sternum. He's almost whispering now. "You don't know what it's like to be trapped in here. To know you're going to die without ever walking the street again."

The snake inside writhes with its flat head burrowed against the cap. A smile is fixed on my face, and my eyes are fixed on Buffón's forehead, where a vein seems to be pulsing in time with my beating heart. What a coincidence, I think.

"Ah Buffón, man, I understand. Believe me, I understand," I say, knowing I do not and knowing that Buffón and the rest of them know it too, "but I can't help you."

"Gringo. Please."

I shake my head, and Buffón abruptly turns toward the light and spits between the bars, wipes his mouth, and walks away. I watch him go, and will my heart to slow down. The others, Doble Cara and the rest, are still for a moment, as if someone had asked a question to which no one knew the answer. Then they disperse singly and in pairs. Some disappear into their cells. A few approach Gato with whispered inquiries. Left alone in the corner, I find I am holding the coke bottle with the snake in it. The creature lies still, its tiny eyes hooded. When I look up, El Nica is there again, smiling timidly, ready for his picture. He has donned an immaculate white T-shirt with words printed in English: "Stick a Fork in Me, I'm Done!"

Soon after that we bid good-bye to the men in the isolation block, and we spend the rest of the day visiting other prisoners in other sectors. Several hours later, Gato and I collect our things from the guards at the prison gate and undergo a final, cursory search. We pick up Cheeky, who sits chewing raw almonds he has collected from the tree, and walk back down the dirt road. Gato and I take turns telling Cheeky about Buffón and the cascabel. "You should have seen how scared the Gringo was," Gato chortles, "I thought he was going to shit himself!"

Three weeks after the cascabel incident, I return to visit the men in the isolation block and meet the new committee that took over after the riot that killed

Javier and got Director Latona fired, but they are on lockdown and are not allowed any visitors, period.

A sympathetic guard gives me entry to bring a message to Brown from his brother, incarcerated in Pavón prison. "Gringo, Gringo," the others call softly. "Gringo, pssssssssst, Gringo!" Disembodied hands thrust out of small air vents in the cell doors, holding greasy bits of mirror. They reach out to me for soft high fives. El Nica, I think it's El Nica's hand, clasps mine for a second.

Light streams through a barred window into Brown's cell, making his green eyes shine out of his wide, placid face. He hands me a plate of fried brown rice.

"Give it to the guard."

For a moment I'm confused. But Brown knows what he's doing, and this guard is showing kindness.

The guard is leaning in the open doorway, and I bring him the plate of rice. He thinks it's from me, but then I explain and he takes it and shrugs.

"Why are they locked up in their cells?" I ask.

"Ah," he says slowly, "supposedly they had relations with a prostitute and they did not treat her well. Or some of them abused her. Who knows?"

"What happened?"

"Supposedly they did not pay her. It's a shame because some of them are good guys."

"So did they abuse her? Or simply not pay her?"

He shrugs again and chews a mouthful of rice. "Who knows? But they weren't all involved. Some of them are good guys."

Later, I find out that Doble Cara, Buffón, and several others gang-raped a girl who came to visit a skinny, shy prisoner named Juan Carlos. When he left to get her a Coke, several of them—not all, but several—cornered and raped her in his room. They had done it to other visitors, but this time the girl went directly across the courtyard to the director's office and made an official complaint. Investigators from the prosecutor's office arrived later that night.

The guard looks out onto the concrete plaza toward the gathering crowd of prisoners and government clerks. The vocero of the new prisoners' committee, a grinning fat man with a heavily pomaded hairdo, is making a welcome speech to Gato and other government folk. Gato makes a joke I can't hear, and they all burst into raucous laughter.

"Did you bring soccer balls this time?" the guard asks me between mouthfuls. "I was promised a soccer ball."

"I don't know."

Porous prisons dissolve any hard and fast boundaries dividing the incarcerated from the free, revealing how deeply the state, the law-abiding world, and the underworld overlap and depend upon one another, how illusory the dream of their separation is. Such porous prisons bring the collective struggle for a sense of order into stark relief by revealing how violently carceral ideals of order and isolation clash with prison actualities. In this way, the prison's symbolic power is deeply significant for the mutual making of law and outlaw, since both the flow and the friction between the ideal and real of the prison are necessary for the very survival of the system. Networks linking the incarcerated with prison officials regulate the terms of exchange between prisoners and the outside world, profiting from inmates' desperation and the state's silent dependence on prisoners' families and loved ones. These networks reach beyond everyday survival to co-opt the highest echelons of state power. Who knows what webs of command and profit were hidden behind Lima's toothy grin? Meanwhile, those prisoners without access to help from the outside—men like El Buffón— are left to fend for themselves by whatever means necessary.

The enmeshed material and symbolic nature of prison life produces a reality in which prisoners remain largely invisible to the outside world and are forced to police themselves. They survive in a space where the most violent and ruthless tend to dominate all others. Such conditions make prisons ideal ground for the strong to violate the weak, weaving acts like the gang rape in the isolation block into a context of everyday violence and victimization. Indeed, the integral role violence plays in prison life explodes the notion that prisons are an effective means of protecting society, much less the idea that they can reshape deviant subjects into productive and law-abiding citizens.

The state's misguided efforts to punish and contain the criminal threat have instead led to the warping and spreading of violence and fear into new spaces. Today in Guatemala City, collective fear and paranoia over the terms of everyday survival have been etched into the landscape. Police stations in some neighborhoods are barricaded behind sandbags; twelve-foot-high, barbed-wire walls protect even humble homes; those with money live in

FIGURE 21. Denizens of the isolation block, Canada prison, Escuintla, Guatemala.

enclaved communities; and heavily armed private security guards patrol every mall, gas station, and hotel. Even small businesses—toy stores, family-owned restaurants, stationary vendors—have a shotgun-toting guard in uniform. Violence and fear isolate people and fragment communities by corroding the possibility of trust between neighbors and strangers alike. In this era of mass incarceration, life for "the free" is becoming ever more prisonlike.* One clear continuum in this diffusion of prison-made violence into public spaces can be found in extortion rackets, the maras' most lucrative and bloodthirsty business. Gang extortion networks were grown and corporatized from inside Central American prisons, and they mirror the systems of extraction prison authorities utilize to profit from incarcerated populations. I now turn to the phenomenon of extortion and its consequences for life in Guatemala City.

---

* Diverging from the "carceral continuum" highlighted by scholars of US prisons, which links prison life and state surveillance practices to certain bounded spaces beyond the prison (see, e.g., Wacquant, *Punishing the Poor*), the boundaries of this continuum are far more diffused and difficult to pin down. See, for example, Fontes and O'Neill, "*La Visita*."

CHAPTER 4

Extorted Life

Guatemala City and Villa Nueva, September 2011. Jorge is a taxi driver.[1] We spoke as he ferried me across the bridge between Guatemala City and Villa Nueva. Three years before I met him, he had a job driving a bus, making a "decent" living, he said, enough to own a small home in a gated community and to send his kids to school. Then the violence against bus drivers started ramping up, violence that seemed to be connected to extortion rackets, and he had to abandon the job. "Too many compatriots killed," he said. So he went to work as a guard for a private security company. While working, he was attacked by thieves, who broke his collarbone. He spent his savings on medical bills. Then he started working as a taxi driver. This does not pay well, and he eventually had to give up the home in which he had already invested his life's savings. Now he and his wife are struggling to keep their children in school. "I don't think I will be able to pay for the next semester," he said morosely. "My wife is going to start a little *atol* stand to make some money, but . . . ."

A year earlier, alleged extortionists had executed his mother. It's not clear why, but he thinks she refused to pay extortion tithes for her little fruit stand outside a Villa Nueva school. "It might have been gangs," Jorge said over garbled radio voices and the rush of traffic, "but I think the police were also involved. I saw my mother on the pavement under the plastic tarp they put over her and I wanted to take revenge, but I know this is not my work. *Mano dura, mano floja* (iron fist, weak fist), we end up with the same thing. It is up to God and God alone." He leaned over and pulled out a newspaper clipping

FIGURE 22. Newspaper article on the murder of an elderly fruit vendor: "They Kill an Old Lady: She Sold Fruit at a School," *Nuestro Diario*, May 21, 2010.

about his mother's murder from the glove compartment. "Here, take it for your book." I snapped a photograph of it and gave it back.

The dictionary definition of "extort" is "to obtain from another by coercion or intimidation." It can mean to overcharge, to blackmail, and to engage in "protection rackets." Protection rackets have been called "organized crime at its smoothest."[2] Here, the term *protection* has a double meaning, depending on one's relationship to a given danger and the offered means of shelter from that danger. "'Protection' calls upon images of the shelter against danger provided by a powerful friend, a large insurance policy, a sturdy roof" or "it evokes the racket in which a local strong man forces merchants to pay tribute in order to avoid damage—damage the strong man himself threatens to deliver."[3] One way to understand the modern state is as the racketeer that has, over time, managed to monopolize the power to "protect" within its territory by co-opting completely the legitimate use of violence against its taxpaying populace.

But the Guatemalan state, like so many struggling sovereigns, has never had such a monopoly over "legitimate" violence.[4] The rise of gangs, organized crime, private security, vigilante groups, and narco-trafficking organizations patrolling and controlling bits and pieces of Guatemala presents open challenges to the state's claim to govern its territory. In certain Guatemala City neighborhoods—el Limon, la Limonada, and Barrio Gallito, to name a few— criminal organizations form a kind of underground authority that competes with or subsumes local state authorities. One result has been the rapid proliferation of protection rackets in poor urban neighborhoods.

Today extortion is the most common of crimes in Central America and the most despised. Its ubiquitous presence is both a symptom of and answer to the collective experience of living with profound doubt over the terms of everyday survival. In the absence of viable state security, it is often difficult to determine just who is in charge. Such conditions are rife with opportunities for entrepreneurs who accrue power and profit by subsuming the sovereign threat of violence, combining it with a promise to protect (for a fee) and imposing their own brand of order.

La Mara Salvatrucha and Barrio18 are widely considered the primary culprits of extortion. The maras were among the first to organize efforts to extract *la renta* (the rent)—the colloquial term for extortion tithes—from residents and businesses in their respective territories. Extortion now appears to be one of the central activities driving gang violence in Guatemala City and in many other cities across the Northern Triangle of Central America.[5] But as Jorge hinted, the business of extortion has become profitable for a wide array of actors beyond the gangs. Mareros, the extortionist subjects par excellence, are in fact the leading edge of a cannibalistic approach to survival that threatens to tear apart the already frayed social fabric. They have become a commonly mimicked model and a smokescreen obscuring vast networks of state agents, financial institutions, private businesses, and countless civilians feeding off the extortion economy. The diffusion of extortion beyond "traditional" criminal networks links the terror in poor neighborhoods with considerable profits for agents who will never need to carry out violence. This terror and these profits, however, remain intimately linked to the maras' symbolic power. As extortion's spectral face, the maras are key figures through which people from all walks of life make sense of this bloody business and its brutal consequences. The newspaper clipping Jorge handed me, for example, named Barrio18 as the only suspect in the police investigation.

Tracing the maras' footsteps, this chapter maps Guatemala City's expanding geographies of extortion to track the entanglements among the evolution of gang extortion rackets, the profits of the extortion economy, and collective efforts to cast and recast a sense of certainty upon extortion's terror. The struggle to fix such fears by way of the maras gives rise to diverse opportunities for material gain through terror, even as it continually fails, disrupted again and again by unmanageable forces feeding and feeding off so much insecurity. The maras may order society's fear of extortion, but in places like Guatemala City, extortion orders the world.

THE RISE OF MARA EXTORTION

Mareros still refer to la renta as *impuesto de guerra*, meaning "war tax." Whether they reference the revolutionary past is not clear. In an internally circulated publication, the Guatemalan justice department traced the practice of collecting "war taxes" back to civil war guerrilla operations in the Guatemalan highlands.[6] Ex-military commanders and indigenous peasant troops would threaten to burn down rich landowners' plantations unless they paid in food or treasure.[7] However, the document fails to explain the lines of historical inheritance that brought this practice to urban gangs.

In some neighborhoods, residents trace the use of the term *impuesto de guerra* to an epoch when the local gang clique collected tithes to fund ongoing feuds with enemy gangs in other barrios. It was meant to fund the community's self-defense and was distinct from robbery, which was practiced, among the more conscientious cliques anyway, strictly outside the barrio. Mara efforts to collect money from their own communities started with businesses and families residing in the neighborhood, then targeted vendors' trucks delivering in mara territory. Today, however, gang war, as reason or excuse, is rarely mentioned. Extortion rackets, as I will show, have become unhinged from other exigencies and have a raison d'être all their own.

Like protection rackets run by the Sicilian Mafia and various organized criminal groups in the United States, demands for la renta implicitly entail the possibility of violence.[8] But when gang extortion first became a widespread urban phenomenon in the early 1990s, the maras emphasized the softer side of protection.

Like gang veterans, many experienced observers hew to a nostalgic version of history, drawing a decisive break between la renta of yesteryear and contemporary extortion rackets. Before he passed away in 2014, Emilio Goubaud was the director of one of the oldest gang rehabilitation organizations in Guatemala. In 2011, sitting in his ramshackle office in a neighborhood where extortion threats had closed down all but a few family-run businesses, he told me that when gangs first started exacting tribute from local businesses— mostly corner stores, the ubiquitous tiendita found in every poor Guatemala City neighborhood—"la renta was a kind of primitive taxation scheme where the 'clients' paid the gangs for round the clock protection as they would pay a private security firm to guard against intruders."

This comparison between gangs and the security industry, which has been postwar Guatemala's fastest growing legal industry, is a common refrain among former gang members, civilians, and gang experts. In the ever-receding golden past, if you were rich enough to afford the Q700 ($90) a week for a shotgun-toting, uniformed guard to stand outside your place of business for twelve-hour stretches, you hired private security. Otherwise, you contracted with the local gang for a homie, or more likely a chequeo, to provide a similar service. Instead of a shotgun, he might have a black market handgun tucked into his jeans.

Of course it was never that simple. During the five years he worked the streets (in the late 1990s), Juande and his homies collected la renta from store owners in Mixco, a suburb of Guatemala City. He claimed it was a peaceful operation, even if he had to engage in underhanded coercion from time to time to make it profitable. "In that time, we only sold protection—and the people came to us to tell us that someone was bothering them," he said as we watched fellow prisoners play soccer on a concrete court in Pavón. "Perhaps we gave the right to protect to another homie, and he took care of it. . . . When a store wouldn't pay, we sent a dude from another corner to do a coralina, that is, to rob without assaulting . . . but we only did it to convince them that they needed protection." He trailed off and then shook his head. "We should have finished with it then, but we didn't know we would go to cannibalizing other poor people like us."

This is the crux of the matter: even as some gang members still mouth the refrain of protecting the barrio for a fee, almost everyone, including mareros themselves, know this is pure fiction. Whatever communal solidarity maras once claimed has been lost or discarded. The maras' role in protecting their neighborhoods from hostile intruders has been sublimated into the pursuit of extraction, plain and simple. Even in those neighborhoods where gang protection rackets began as a kind of communal response to insecurity, in less than a decade the dominant ethos became one of profit through violence. And this violence broke the boundaries of what are remembered as hallowed rules of combat.[9] Underpinning this shift was a growing sense of alienation between the gang and the neighborhood communities where they operated. This communal fracturing had a lot to do with the state's efforts to deal with the "gang threat." The same heavy-handed policing that packed the prisons with mareros also made the state complicit in the increasing violence of mara extortion.

Prison life was key in nurturing the transformation. From the isolation of prison mara leaders leveraged their ability to raise funds from the street. Is it a coincidence that the daily operation of the prison system itself depends on an informal taxation scheme that is extortion in all but name? Recall that talacha—the prison taxation scheme discussed in chapter 3—forces every newly arrived inmate to pay a tax, and refusal to pay this tax results in hard labor, physical punishment, or worse. Whether or not incarcerated mareros learned from this model, extortion appears to have been the quickest—and certainly the easiest—means of establishing a steady cash flow to soften life in prison, feed their families, and keep themselves armed against their enemies on the street. At the same time, consolidation of command structures inside prison meant that the business of extortion could be corporatized. Mass incarceration of mareros helped turn gang extortion into a viable business model.[10]

The prisons were crucibles forging new relationships among gang members from various urban zones and cities. But by separating gang members from their home neighborhoods, mass incarceration weakened and even severed the communal ties that once seemed to have grounded and regulated gang violence. To escape heightened state pressure, both Barrio18 and the MS began circulating homies to conduct gang business outside the neighborhoods in which they grew up. To organize a hit against a rival gang in a neighboring *colonia*, for example, an incarcerated gang leader might exchange soldiers with another gang leader because they wouldn't be recognized as neighbors. "You could just walk into a group from the enemy gang and start firing," recalled a former MS member. "And no one would know what you were until you were gone." Such strategies were highly successful, even as they sharpened the fear and paranoia of daily life.

Ramfleros employed the same strategy in collecting extortion payments and threatening or killing recalcitrant clients. The "rights" to extort a given neighborhood were often negotiated between hardened convicts inside prison, and mara youth on the street could be called to conduct hits in barrios they had never seen before. Driven by the economic imperatives and conditions of possibility created by incarceration, maras' repertoire of violence shifted from an ethos of combat (defending against or attacking a threat to the community) to an ethos of extortion—that is, coercing tithes from innocent victims by any means possible.

"Killing innocent people became part of la renta," said Mo, who lived through the transition into the more violent era, committing more murders for the MS than he was willing to admit before he fell out with his colleagues. "Before you could intimidate just with words, but then people didn't listen so much, so you had to really scare them. . . . People today don't even pay attention if you kill someone with a shooting. It's just a lost bullet. Today you have to dismember and terrorize the people . . . if you want to have power."[11] Whereas la renta was once an exchange between business owners and local youth who pledged to stop outsiders from robbing in the neighborhood, it transformed into alien and alienated agents threatening to hurt anyone who refused to make regular installments.

For maras today, extortion has become far more than simply a means of making money; it has become a signature facet of their claim to power, which, like most forms of governance, is hooked to territorial control.[12] In the face of heightened police scrutiny, the old methods of advertising gang dominance over urban space (graffiti) and over members' bodies (tattoos) have noticeably diminished. Today, they measure their power by the number of households they tax, the earnings the gang treasurer logs.

Before Andy abandoned the MS he was, he claimed, a primary enforcer of extortion threats, killing those who refused to pay. In one of his courtroom interrogations, a prosecutor asked, "During the course of your declaration you indicated that the Mara Salvatrucha is dominating the world. Can you indicate to what you refer with this expression?"

"Of dominating the world?" he replied. "More than anything, how can I say it, from pure extortions they are controlling territory. They are a big gang. . . . [T]hey have a ton of soldiers. What I'm telling you is that they are expanding like rats, throughout the world. The vatos have a great power."

Killing "clients" who refuse to pay their dues is only the beginning. To instill the proper fear, maras employ more sophisticated forms of intimidation. The brutal corporeal violence that Mo referred to—decapitation, dismemberment, and so on—has been accompanied by evolving methods of psychological terror. A workingman struggling to support his family, when threatened by a fifteen-year-old with a gun, might be willing to risk refusing to pay up, in the hope that the gang won't bother following through on the threat. But, the logic goes, menace that man's family—threaten to rape his daughter and torture his son, and make sure he knows you have done it before and will do it again— and he will be on his knees begging for mercy. A man's love for his family makes him vulnerable, and such exposed weaknesses are extortion's bread and butter. Indeed, the most ruthless and successful mara cliques have spent the last few decades honing their capacity to identify and exploit exactly these sorts of vulnerabilities. Some have become so adept that they do not even need to explicitly threaten violence to convince extortion victims to pay up.

Tower of Tribunals, Guatemala City, June 2012. Andy sits on a raised platform before a panel of judges and an army of prosecutors. One of the lawyers is asking him, for the record, to define certain key terms he used to describe his gang's activities.

> Prosecutor: What does "la renta" mean?
>
> Andy: La renta. La renta is when the ramflero gives an order to go and set up an extortion, ask for bills (*barras*), ask for money from a corner store. For example: it's a big store, you understand, they come with a letter with a number that the dude has to call. When the dude calls, you give the vibe that you're gonna care for them and you'll give them protection and at the same time the dude will report with the gang (*plebe*).[13] So, they ask for approximately 5,000 bills ($650) for entry for which they give a maximum term of ten days for the dude to pay, and then they put it at 400 bills weekly you understand. With the dude you speak nicely (*de pinta*) . . . and if the dude doesn't want to collaborate with the plebe, the ramflero will be told and the ramflero gives the order to go and kill him. This is what extortion and charging la renta means.

At their smoothest, mara extortion schemes resemble formalized business models. The gang expects clients to pay an established rate, though as with all transactions in the informal market, payment is subject to barter. The promise to protect is a formal article of the contract, and the gang presents this protection in conciliatory terms. There is a preferred tone and friendly approach. If the client cannot produce the entire sum up front, he or she can go with the payment plan. Often the mortal threat attached to the request need not be openly expressed. But it is the red thread running through every transaction between maras and those they extort.

Contemporary gang extortion rackets only function with such smoothness in spaces where they have established unrivaled control over the use of violence. These neighborhoods are legion, scattered throughout the poorer zones of the city and concentrated in peripheral areas that have always fallen outside both the formal capitalist economy and the state's promise of protection. Everyone in mara territory knows the score. For example, during the years Katherine Saunders-Hastings spent conducting ethnographic research in a Guatemala City neighborhood dominated by the Barrio18, she found that children and youths were well aware that no one—not the government "authorities" or their own parents—could protect them if their family failed to pay. These children must also carve out their own security.[14] Often this means getting close to someone inside the gang in the hopes that amicable association will provide a buffer against the gang's demands. But how can they remain on the periphery when the gang's gravitational pull is so strong? And so in these neighborhoods, extortion rackets often employ significant subsets of the population. Most of those involved in its day-to-day business are not even bona fide mareros.

While local gang members and incarcerated leaders dictate how much tax to levy and from whom to collect it, it is often their neighbors, relatives, girlfriends, and wives who deliver the written demands or hand over the cell phone with an incarcerated marero waiting on the line to threaten a victim. In a zone 18 neighborhood built into a ravine and dominated by a Barrio18 clique, children as young as eight work as watchmen (banderas), taking note of what goes on in the neighborhood, while grandmothers collect la renta on the gang's behalf. As in other mara-dominated neighborhoods, the only individuals able to run corner stores or other small businesses are gang members' kin, girlfriends, or other gang associates (paros) on friendly terms with the gang. Everyone else gets taxed or threatened into bankruptcy.[15] Today, as much as one-third of residences in this zone 18 neighborhood have been abandoned due to extortion demands that residents would not or could not pay. Other poor urban neighborhoods exhibit similar patterns.[16]

Field Notes, 15th floor of the Tower of Tribunals, May 2012
Waving my press pass at guards in blue uniforms, I enter the courtroom with the vaulted ceiling, the cage of the accused, the lawyers' tables set before the judge's platform. Opposite the entrance a bulletproof glass window affords a panoramic view of the city below.
There are thirty-two defendants on trial for involvement in an extortion ring. Four of them are Barrio18 gang leaders already jailed for other crimes, their heads

FIGURE 23. Six alleged members of an extortionist ring directed by incarcerated mareros.

shaved and faces tattooed. Two in white, two in orange jumpsuits, they sit chained by the ankles in the glass and metal cage. In the gallery sit two dozen women handcuffed to each other in pairs. All but three are young, wearing heavy makeup, boots, tight jeans. They sit in silence, except for a girl with thick, smiling lips and heavy silver mascara. She giggles and makes jokes, communicating in gestured signs with one of the caged leaders. The oldest woman—in her late fifties I would guess—sits heavily in her chair wearing a blank stare. Her daughter sits beside her, occasionally leaning her head on her mother's shoulder.

I wonder how it would be to be handcuffed to my mother—or to my daughter—facing the state's accusations and all its portents.

Defense lawyers crowd a table set before the judge's raised platform. They bump elbows as they shift about, reaching for the shared microphone. A single lawyer for the prosecution sits facing them across the room. He spends most of the time reading text messages and inspecting his fingernails.

Along the gallery's perimeter stand dozens of heavily armed police. Men in gray uniforms and gray caps hold old machine guns with wood panel grips. Men in black uniforms and black berets hold Israeli Tavor assault rifles, heavy clips jutting out like tusks. They all have 9mm pistols in hip holsters or shoved into the front of their bulletproof vests. They are here for our protection, I suppose, standing around so tense and bored. But what the hell do you do with that much firepower in one room? Any one of them starts firing and we're all dead, I think. I take my seat behind three male defendants without visible tattoos, sitting across the aisle from the women.

The day wears on with much shuffling of papers. With so many defendants, the piles of evidence get confused, and each defense lawyer is in charge of several defendants, so the documents must be divvied up among them. Inside the cage, the gang members shift about in their chains. The women talk in hushed voices and take turns holding a toddler. She crawls beneath their chairs across the linoleum floor.

Judge Walter Villatoro is reviewing the enormous pile of documents set before him. According to his summary, the caged men allegedly selected the companies to target and made the extortion threats via cell phone. The women picked up the payments in small increments—no more than $500 worth of quetzales at a time. The three men sitting in the row before me were allegedly enforcers—shooting bus drivers when their bosses failed to make timely payments. The whole operation depended entirely on the transportation company being too cowed to report to the police. All of this is laid out in recorded phone conversations, bank records, victims' testimonies, rap sheets from the prosecution. The defense has merely provided a motley collection of affidavits attesting to this and that woman's character, along with pay stubs and birth records. These are good, hard-working mothers, they bleat. No one is denying involvement in the racket. No one is fighting, only asking for mercy.

A white-haired defense lawyer interrupts the judge's study. Could the caged prisoners, whose mothers and wives and sisters sit accused and handcuffed to each other some twenty feet away, get the chance to talk to their loved ones while the judge reviews the files?

Judge Villatoro is nothing if not a humanitarian. "Seeing how today is Mother's Day, and while these prisoners have lost their right to liberty of movement they remain subject to all the other constitutional rights provided to Guatemalan citizens, it seems to me they should be able to talk and interact with their relations as long as security is not compromised. So please, those who wish to visit with their loved ones may do so in groups of two."

In many poor urban neighborhoods, mara-directed extortion rackets constitute a brutal form of taxation and spatial control with little pretense of "governance" beyond the terror necessary to ensure smooth and timely extraction of la renta. The gangs do not seek to mold their clients beyond instilling fear in ways that will not soon be forgotten. However, the kin networks, neighbors, and other gang associates through which the maras collect la renta make extortion far more than merely a brutal criminal business or even a "parallel mode of production and profiteering" that appropriates or mimics some aspect of state sovereignty.[17] Rather, extortion constitutes a pivotal social relation in the communities where it has become entrenched. Residents survive by either taking part in or capitulating to the maras' rules, by either preying upon their community or being preyed upon.[18]

THE PROFITS OF EXTORTION

The networks through which extortion rackets spread terror and extract profit go far beyond mara territory. Most of the money leveraged from such suffering does not remain in the pockets of accomplices, rank-and-file mareros, or even gang leadership. Instead, it flows into the hands of state agents and financial institutions, while communal efforts to defend against extortion threats almost inevitably profit private security corporations. And so extortion rackets feeding upon poor, insecure space generate significant wealth for many who never need threaten or kill in order to reap dividends.

Let us return to the prison. The most well-developed, prison-based extortion schemes can generate profits far greater than what is needed for daily existence behind bars. In maximum security facilities, where most gang leaders are housed, there are few diversions on which to spend money besides the bribes and kickbacks necessary to keep the system running.[19] The profits of extortion join the flow of money, information, and other commodities across the prison system's porous boundaries. In exchange for allowing gangsters and other inmates to communicate and exchange with their street networks, prison staff get a cut of the profits. Police are also often involved, receiving their cut in return for looking the other way or even taking an active role in identifying potential victims. Beat cops and rank-and-file prison guards earn little more than the national minimum wage of Q3,300/month (about $400), and the bribes they receive can easily double or triple their monthly income.

State agents are not merely tools of criminal-run extortion networks. Incarcerated extortionists, street operatives, and government agents form symbiotic networks to extract profit through terror, and it is often unclear who, ultimately, is calling the shots. "These poor gangsters are only the lowest on the ladder," exclaimed an evangelical pastor working in a gang-dominated Guatemala City suburb. "I have no motivation to tell the police the things that happen, because they are often running the charade themselves. I remember one night at 2:00 a.m. a policeman came to one of the boys' houses and started beating him, yelling, 'I asked for a good cellphone, not this piece of shit!'"

Government agents are not the only "outsiders" to profit from the extortion economy. Once collected, extortion monies filter through gangs' networks as quotas for homies; it might only be Q1,000 (about $125) a month, but it's regular. Money also flows to lawyers to represent homies in legal trouble; doctors and nurses are paid a retainer to be on call; and in the last few years, gang "treasurers" have been reinvesting in working-class businesses: car washes, bus lines, microbuses, and so on. Thus, extorted profits work their way back into the licit economy, suturing it to the fear and suffering this cold-blooded business requires and reproduces.

But this is only the beginning. Arturo Aguilar was assistant to Claudia Paz y Paz, Guatemala's former attorney general (2008–2013). When I asked him in 2013 about the obstacles his office faced in prosecuting extortion cases, I expected him to talk about police corruption, bureaucratic intransigence, and the widespread fear victims have of reporting crimes. But to my surprise he replied, "Look, most of the money goes through the banks, and it is impossible to trace . . . because we have virtually no way of forcing financial institutions to reveal their records." As extortionists move more and more money electronically, the extortion commodity chain increasingly involves Guatemala's largest financial institutions. As in the case described above, in which more than two dozen women collected money extorted from a bus company, banks make considerable profits off the regular deposits victims make into anonymous bank accounts.

After the court hearing for the thirty-two alleged extortionists, when the defendants had all been bussed back to their respective prisons, I joined Judge Villatoro in his office. We discussed the plight of those two dozen girlfriends, wives, and mothers handcuffed in his courtroom. A tall, bulky man with a thick black mustache and an avuncular kindness, Villatoro cut an impressive figure in his black robe. He spoke regretfully of the female defendants. "They should never have let themselves get involved!" he said, but then abruptly switched the subject and his tone. "Ah, I can send the mareros away just like this," he exclaimed in a stentorian baritone, snapping his fingers. "But the banks! No one goes after the banks. And, believe me, they *know* what is going on."

In recent years various Guatemalan banks, many of which do not require clients to register personal information when depositing or collecting funds, appear to have made untold millions off the 10 percent surcharge on each extortion payment transferred through their systems. To date, no bank has been prosecuted or even investigated for its involvement in extortion schemes.[20] According to government officials who chose to remain anonymous, this is because Guatemala's richest families maintain ultimate control over national banks. Congressional efforts to pass stricter financial oversight laws have repeatedly failed because the political and economic consortiums representing elite interests will not let them go forward.[21] As Aguilar said a few months before he and Paz y Paz were forced out of office: "Every case we decide to pursue involves a calculation, and this calculation must always take into account what big powers we are going up against. When we go up against the banks, we can do nothing." Extortion, so often defined as "the poor eating their fellow poor," cannot be disentangled from systemic impunity and considerable profits reaching up to the highest levels of society.

———

While extortion has been the fastest growing illicit business since the end of the civil war, private security, its legal doppelgänger, is the region's number 1 growth industry. The maras' extortion profits are nothing compared to those reaped by private security. In 2005 Guatemala spent $574.3 million—approximately 1.8 percent of its gross domestic product—on private security.[22] Although there is a dearth of reliable data pertaining to private security profits in subsequent years, it is clear that spending on private security has continued to grow. Today there are 141 registered private security companies in Guatemala employing 48,240 guards, as well as 30,000–40,000 additional "clandestine" private security agents working for illegal companies.[23] The Guatemalan government's efforts to regulate this industry—which has been accused of criminal ties and involvement in extrajudicial killings—have failed spectacularly. The ongoing windfall for security corporations has provoked new assemblages of criminal threat, government intervention, and private profit.[24]

Villa Nueva and Guatemala City, January 2012
Colonia Castañas is a small neighborhood located just before the bridge between Villa Nueva and Guatemala City. Elizabet, a prison social worker and longtime Colonia Castañas resident, told me that nearly every single household

in her neighborhood received an extortion letter slipped under their door at the end of November 2011. They were distributed by *ladroncitos* (little thieves) from the nearby community of Mezquital. She thought they were Barrio18, but she was not sure. Up until these threats, Castañas was unclaimed by Barrio18 or the Mara Salvatrucha and thus fair game. This group was trying to make its move. In response, young and middle-aged neighborhood men donned ski masks and mounted patrols armed with bats, knives, and the occasional firearm to defend the community.

But the vigilantes were a short-term affair, because meanwhile the neighborhood committee lobbied the city government to provide protection. In February of 2012 the government granted them permission to close off all but one of the entrances to the neighborhood to through traffic, motorized or otherwise (the ladroncitos came in by car and motorbike), and establish a private security checkpoint at the remaining entrance. Now, everyone must carry an ID card to get in. Elizabet showed me hers, a simple pink plastic card that could have been a gym membership. Each resident now makes a monthly payment for the new system.

The gang did not take long to attempt revenge. Edwin Ortega, the Villa Nueva police chief had done little more than act as middleman between the community and the private security firm. Nevertheless, Ortega told me, the frustrated gang sent two seventeen-year-old chequeos on a mission against the local police station. Eager to earn some recognition, they lobbed grenades over the station wall into the courtyard, where a dozen or so civilians waited in line. The boys panicked, however, or had a crisis of conscience, and never pulled the pins.

The Colonia Castañas community banded together to protect itself and eventually found a long-term solution by isolating entry and exit to one avenue guarded 24/7 by private security. Thus, an ad hoc "enclave community" was created and the costs of this newfound security were paid out of pocket by the enclave's residents.[25] In the final analysis, Barrio18's attempt to extract extortion ended up providing new profits to a private security firm. This is typical of "successful" efforts to stave off the threat of extortion.

In order to profit from public fear, both private security companies and maras depend on the government's failure to secure the city. Both extract payments from urban communities with the promise to protect. Gangs depend on their reputation for hyperviolence to scare off would-be rivals and thieves while coercing timely extortion payments from clients. Private security firms arm their guards with 12-gauge shotguns, the highest caliber weapons that nongovernment personnel can legally carry. Finally, both employ poor, uneducated young men, give them guns, and put them in harm's way. Today, nearly the entire young male populations of some rural villages seek employment in security firms, leaving their communities to work in Guatemala City and other urban centers for the pitiful wages these companies offer.

The differences between private security and extortion rackets are, of course, obvious, especially with today's brutal version of la renta. Gangs siphon money from their fellow poor (albeit slightly less poor than most) and create some part of the terror from which they promise to protect their clientele. Security firms merely leverage general fear into moneymaking opportunities, while their investors, many of whom are drawn from the rich elite, lobby successfully against raising Guatemala's 12 percent tax rate, ensuring that the national police force will remain underfunded, undertrained, and out-gunned.[26] If gangs have become parasites, then perhaps private security firms are merely symbiotes. But I cannot help seeing this distinction as somewhat superfluous. Both self-consciously feed off the same overwhelming collective fear, the same pervading uncertainty that has spread far beyond the "red zones" and mara-dominated spaces to engulf the city itself.

MARA MASQUERADE: FROM CRIMINAL ENTERPRISE TO POSTWAR ZEITGEIST

In August 2012 I accompanied a police raid on a house in a suburban enclave just outside the city. Armed with AK-47s, the swat team stormed both entrances and captured two men and three kilos of cocaine in plastic baggies. The lead investigators were immensely satisfied, slapping each other on the back and talking of promotions. "It's the famous (el famoso) Scrappy," they whispered as police dragged a shirtless man in boxers into the courtyard. "El famoso Scrappy!" Later, the presumed gang connection would prove false. These were simply low-level drug runners betrayed by a colleague or competitor. The press arrived soon afterward, shooting pictures and video of the two arrested men handcuffed, huddled in a sliver of shade in the concrete courtyard. A child's stroller and baby toys were strewn about, and a small dog lay loyally at the men's feet. Aware of the rumor that they were gang members, one of them begged, "Just don't call us extortionists in your report. We're just men trying to make a living."

As the most feared and despised criminal enterprise in a time when rampant insecurity defines urban life, extortion has become the zeitgeist of the post–civil war era. Many urbanites consider extortion to be worse than immediate bodily violence. As Isabel Aguilar of Interpeace Guatemala, an antiviolence organization, said, "Extortion leaves one without hope. Why are you going to work if they're going to take away the little you earn?"[27] Today, maras are the phantasmagoric face of extortion. The image of the tattooed gang leader residing comfortably at home, or even behind bars, as his network of extortionists terrorize and suck the lifeblood out of good, law-abiding citizens has been etched into the public consciousness. Hence the poor fools above were desperate to be seen as hardworking drug dealers rather than as marero extortionists.

Mass media have played a key role in forming and feeding this image. Virtually any day of the week, one can pick up a newspaper or turn on the TV to a flood of images and stories of gruesome murders, massacres, and mutilations. This murky "death porn" has become standard fare for the Guatemalan public and an important vector for enhancing extortion's profitability.[28] Indeed, exceptional violence (dismemberment, rape, etc.) has proven an incredibly efficient business practice. The more spectacular the brutality imputed to the maras, the more widely the fear of extortion circulates in the community and in the press, the further the maras' message of intimidation travels, and the more willing their "clients" will be to make timely extortion payments.

The image of the marero extortionist, and the terror it transmits, also serve as a means of papering over the uncertainty swirling about urban crime and insecurity.[29] For example, when I asked Villa Nueva's chief prosecutor what part of the daily crime in her district could be verifiably connected to gang extortion, she replied, "It has become impossible to know because it is always changing. Neither can we differentiate between maras, narco-traffickers, and other organized criminal groups." It is widely believed that some gang cliques regularly carry out murders and other business at the orders of narcos and organized crime, and besides, with less than 5 percent of violent crimes ever prosecuted, many victims, along with the viewing public, are left to identify the predators by themselves.

The urge to root all this murder in the maras and their extortion rackets has made it possible for extortion to expand in astounding ways, drawing in a diverse set of perpetrators and victims far beyond the maras and their "clients." Anyone willing and able to perform the role carved out by mareros in public perception can get in on the extortion game. Instead of impersonating the state to pull off "counterfeit crimes"—as a variety of illicit actors in post-colonial societies are known to do—countless anonymous extortionists instead choose to play the "mara masquerade."[30]

The chief of PANDA, Guatemala's anti-gang unit, cited a dozen examples of extortion rackets run by individuals pretending to be gangsters. One of the most successful was a man named El Nica, an inmate in Fraijanes 2 maximum security facility, who had become particularly adept at the mara masquerade.[31] He would peruse the newspapers each day looking for murders involving taxi drivers or other employees of commonly extorted companies. "I only call up the big ones," he said. "Hotels, taxi companies, that kind of thing." After finding the company's phone number, he would call in the threat.

Ostilio Novegil, the investigator who finally caught El Nica, made little effort to hide his amusement as he recollected the prisoner's tactics. "That shithead could speak pure marero slang," he laughed. "He would tell them, 'This is El Smiley of Barrio18'—or some other famous marero—'Did you read the newspaper? Well you know we killed your driver. If you don't want anyone else to be killed, deposit Q15,000 in such and such account.'" According to police records, El Nica managed to bring in as much as Q20,000 (about $2,500) a week. "He never killed a single person," the investigator said. "The guy didn't even have any hitmen on the street."

This sort of masquerade is not limited to the incarcerated. Anyone clever, desperate, or ruthless enough to emulate the gang approach can reap the profits. Former members of the military have been caught pretending to be mareros making extortion threats. Disgruntled employees have made extortion threats against their employers, and estranged family members have targeted their own relatives.

In rackets targeting public transportation, rival bus and trucking companies are thought to be responsible for up to 40 percent of the associated murders.[32] Bus inspectors, quasi-government functionaries who coordinate bus schedules among various private contractors, often act as middlemen between extortionists and bus companies. They facilitate the exchange of money and demands and a take a cut of the profits. Bus driver's assistants, often young men drawn from gang-affected neighborhoods, have also been blamed for passing information on daily profits and bus schedules to extortion networks. Such violent competition has made driving a Guatemala City bus arguably the "most dangerous job in the world" over the last several years—with more than five hundred bus drivers gunned down between 2007 and 2011.[33]

Though still moored in the image of the maras, fear of extortion has practically gone atmospheric. The ever-present possibility of extortion, like political terror, makes everyone feel they need to watch their backs, watch their words, watch their neighbors. But unlike under political terror, one's suspected ideological affiliations mean little; it's not what one thinks that matters.[34] If extortionists consider their target at all, it's how much money they imagine one earns and how vulnerable one appears that make one a potential victim. While urban poor remain the most abject before the threat of extortion, the field of potential victims has expanded far beyond their neighborhoods.

Ostilio, the investigator who caught El Nica, is a former military sergeant who worked for the prison system investigating extortion threats emerging from behind bars. By Guatemalan standards, he made a decent income— enough to own a modest home in a middle-class neighborhood—and when we spoke in 2013 he had recently bought a new car. His office walls were plastered with maps of criminal networks, marero mug shots, and blueprints of various Guatemalan prisons. But when, sitting at home one afternoon, he answered his phone to hear a stranger threatening to kill his family unless he deposited Q10,000 (about $1,200) in a bank account within three days, he was caught off guard.

"This asshole spoke with utter politeness," Ostilio grimaced. He mimed holding a phone to his ear. "'Look, we don't want to have to kill any of your kids, but we know your schedule, we know where they go to school. . . .' I told him to shut his damn mouth and never call me again, and then I hung up. Then the phone rang again, and when I picked it up he started yelling and threatening, and I replied, 'Look, I know where you're calling from. I can have the guards pick you up in two hours. You don't know who you're dealing with. Never call my house again.' And you know what? He never did."

Impressed with his chutzpah, I asked him how he was able to face down the threat with such aplomb. He grinned ruefully and shook his head. "He threatened to kill my 'kids'," he said, "and I only have one child. That is how I knew, and could answer with such confidence. If he had not given himself away . . . oof, I would have been in trouble."

Receiving cold-call threats from strangers riffling randomly through telephone directories is increasingly common for residents of Guatemala City and other parts of urban Central America. If you own a cell phone in Guatemala City long enough, in all likelihood you will receive such a threat. Ostilio had the knowledge, experience, and luck to identify this would-be extortionist as a fake. Others, far too many others, do not, and must negotiate without ever knowing for sure whether their survival is on the line.

Cold-call extortion schemes are mostly sporadic, once-off affairs—a threat is made, the money is collected—or not—and that's that. They do not require the maras' territorial control and street operatives, or even the clever opportunism of someone like El Nica. Rarely do they pose any "real" threat, but in a sense, that is beside the point. How is one to decide which threats are real? Cold-call extortion merely requires a certain percentage of victims made docile by fear. Perpetrators need not cull money from every call. "Out of every one hundred calls I made," said Juande, who supported himself for years with cold-call extortion, "if one or two agreed to pay, that was enough."[35]

For many residents of Guatemala City and other parts of Central America, there is no sanctuary. Extortion threats can arrive at any hour, anywhere, against practically any kind of victim. Schools, humanitarian organizations, and even church parishes have received demands for la renta. The ever-present threat of extortion corrodes the pretense that personal security is possible.[36] In the never-ending calculations of risk all city dwellers—rich and poor alike—must make as they navigate urban life, such unaccountable randomness destroys the capacity to judge whether, when, and where one can feel safe. While this fear is still concentrated in poor urban neighborhoods where illicit actors dominate, today it has also spread across the city, the nation, and the region.

Indeed, by taking advantage of the lack of oversight on financial institutions and the ease with which money can be electronically moved across borders, extortionists in Central America and Mexico can today work transnationally. The Transnational Anti-Gang Unit (CAT)—an initiative trained and funded by the US Federal Bureau of Investigation (FBI)—has traced extortion demands made from southern Mexico and El Salvador to Guatemala City, and inmates in Guatemalan prisons have extorted businesses and families in El Salvador and Honduras. Demands for la renta can arrive from any quarter: business rivals, police, one's own family or employees, or random strangers based hundreds of miles away.

Maras, with their gothic tattoos and brash embrace of brutality, provide extortion with a recognizable face. They may mask the myriad actors feeding off the extortion economy, but in so doing they help make extorted life livable by providing an anchor for the otherwise floating sense of terror and impotent rage. In the end, however, they are not nearly enough. The maras cannot mask the fact that extortion has become a way of organizing life on the most intimate of scales. It is an alternative livelihood and a zero-sum game in which, willingly or not, knowingly or not, the majority of Central Americans must participate. And the deeper one digs, the harder it is to trust that anyone's hands are clean.

Zone 8, Guatemala City, September 2011

It's 2:00 a.m. For the last several hours I have been hanging with Tommy and his workers in his carpentry shop. Tommy maintains a number of small businesses, including this shop, a laundromat, and several corner stores, among others. He also runs cocaine and marijuana as a low-level, freelance transporter with a consortium of cartels, and is, as I will learn much later, a middleman for assassination contracts. As a matter of charity, he says, he also gives ex-mareros temporary jobs. To get them on their feet, he says. But right now, Tommy is singing karaoke—mostly Mexican ballads and *narco-corridos* (drug ballads)—in what passes for his office.[37] Everyone else is bored stiff, which doesn't bother Tommy. A former Barrio18 member sits in a plastic chair drinking Coca Cola, nervously tapping his foot. He has "Fuck God" and "Fuck Love" tattooed across his neck. He leaves early. Tommy's other workers get drunk on the beer I brought. But once the last bottle empties, a few of them leave to huff solvents. With the room stinking of paint thinner, I figure it's time to make my exit. But then "Linkon," a guy with an Abraham Lincoln–style beard, asks me to follow and leads me out to the car. Tommy is in the driver's seat, letting the engine idle.

"Are you hungry?"

"Sure, but I spent all my bills on the beer."

"Don't worry about that. That's not a problem."

"And I have to get back to my apartment—"

"Ah don't be a *gringo*, Gringo. Don't worry. I'll get you home."

I get in the front passenger seat and Linkon gets in the back. Tommy peels out. We drive a couple blocks to a hole-in-the-wall restaurant. A bare yellow bulb lights the scene. A young boy mopping the floor looks up as we enter and then quickly down again. We sit down at the table nearest the street and an old woman wearing a checkered apron approaches from behind the counter.

Tommy orders soup for everyone. Linkon fixes me with a bloodshot stare and jerks his head toward a pair of police trucks parked thirty yards down the street.

"You see that? That's a police station. The fucking pigs act like they're in charge, but we're the ones who rule here. You'll see."

I nod, unsure what else to do.

The soup arrives and we eat quickly. Tommy alternates between making crass jokes and singing snippets of his favorite melodies. He orders a Coca Cola he does not drink and needles me about my gringo accent. When it's time to go, I search my pockets again for any remaining money and find none. Not good. You don't want to be out of cash in this city—you never know when you'll be robbed or have to pay off the cops. Tommy and Linkon are already in the car and I get up to follow. The old woman follows me out to the sidewalk and stops. She just stands there. I turn and say good night. She nods but does not smile.

"Sorry, Tommy," I say, shutting the door behind me. "I'll pay you back tomorrow when I can get to an ATM."

"Pay?" Tommy shakes his head. "I don't have to pay. They pay me a rent just to stay open."

"That's right!" Linkon crows. "We charge the rent while the pigs eat shit!"

It suddenly dawns on me. I've just participated in extortion—a mild, everyday extortion. I don't like it. Not at all. I feel angry and embarrassed, but most of all, I feel stupid. It must show because as he speeds through the night Tommy slaps me on the back, saying, "Ah Gringo, don't worry. You did nothing wrong. You were only riding along. And all this. . ."—he waves his hand vaguely, gesturing back toward the restaurant, the police station, the deserted street—"All this is normal. I am lucky enough to be the one who charges, and not one of those who pays. As they say, 'would you rather hear the sound of weeping in your neighbor's home, or in your own?'"

Years later, Tommy is gone—dead or on the lam, I do not know—but his question lingers. I had no answer then, and I have no answer now. From what Archimedean point of morality does one cast judgment on Tommy and his ilk when the terms of survival seem to be etched in such stark, unforgiving terms for so many living and dying in Guatemala City? Not that extortionists of any stripe should be absolved of the suffering they wreak. But too often, living under a regime of extortion means taking part, one way or another, in its brutal calculus.

The following chapters examine and extend this disturbed blurring of innocence and guilt, structure and agency, through the lens of violent spectacles perpetrated by the maras. Such acts are essential to the maras' symbolic power and have helped launch them onto the world stage. At the same time, this kind of spectacle has a way of drawing supposed outsiders, both distant and close, into the very heart of the terror the maras represent.

PART THREE

Spectacle, Structure, and Agency

FIGURE 24. One of the messages left around the city by the Mara Salvatrucha. Photo: Anonymous.

Make It a *Global*

Automariscos is a popular water park off the highway between Guatemala City and the Pacific Ocean. Two giant plastic dolphins are suspended like sentries over the front gate. Inside, children splash about in the wave pool, squeal down the waterslides, and cavort around giant metal mushrooms spraying water into the air. Vendors push carts loaded with balloons, beach balls, water pistols, and brightly colored pinwheels spinning in the hot breeze. An old man sells ice cream, ringing a small cowbell among the trucks and RVs parked on matted crabgrass.

In the early morning on June 9, 2010, before the grounds filled up with vacationers, members of the MS gathered around some unused barbecue pits on the far side of the parking lot. Representatives from every major MS clique in the country were there. The day before, Jorge Jair de Leon, aka El Diabólico, had sent messages via cell phone from El Boquerón prison to operatives on the street for a "Barrio level 'Meeting.'"*

Andy was there among the men gathered in the parking lot that morning. This was two years before I met him in May 2012, when he had already become a secret witness for the crimes planned, ordered, and executed that very day. In clear, precise language, he narrated the day's events before a judge and a dozen prosecutors.

---

* El Diabólico entered prison in 2001 as a little known *sicario* for the CLS, the same MS clique to which Andy belonged, and one of Guatemala's most infamous. Today he is widely regarded as an important leader of the MS in Guatemala. El Boquerón is a prison facility housing only active MS members.

"I was already jumped in," he testified, "so it fell to me, El Pensador, El Scrappy and Maniaco to go to the meeting. When we arrived we were some of the first of the homies. Afterward, homies arrived from Gangster, Parking, Bichos, Bandidos, Puiguis, from Normandy, Souza, Little Psychos, from Chapines, from Little Malditos, Leeward, from Vatos Locos. A shit ton of homies from various cliques came. It was a big meeting. From Little Psychos came El Sleepy, El Serio was there, El Little Loco, and El Demente. From Little Malditos a chequeo who's called El Cruz. From Chapines there was El Verdugo and a guy called El Willy. From Crazy Latin there came El Viejo Strong, the only one of his clique outside. From Gangster there was El Mentiroso and El Droopy, who was calling inside to Boquerón. . . . There was El Travieso, El Nero de Parking, El Shadow de Leeward. Once the meeting was started El Pensador put the cell on speakerphone so that all the homies at the meeting would hear."

El Diabólico explained the situation. Months before, prison authorities had revoked prized privileges, chief among them access to la visita. In protest, MS prisoners staged a series of riots. The prison authorities seemed to capitulate, promising to reinstate conjugal visits and other privileges—and then reneged. To punish this duplicity, El Diabólico instructed the homies to find and kill five people, decapitate them, and place their heads around the capital with messages attacking the government. The victims should have no relationship whatsoever to the MS or its rival, Barrio18. The leadership wanted the message pure, untainted by gang rivalries. After all, it's relatively easy for the general population to dismiss murdered gangsters. But killing random victims strikes fear, because *they* could be *you*. El Diabólico and the other imprisoned leaders, in fact, wanted their message to go beyond Guatemala. "Make it a *global*," El Diabólico told the gathered gang members. That is, make it an act of violence that gets taken up into the international news stream.

Andy, El Pensador, and the others returned to Guatemala City that afternoon and immediately put the plan into action. Andy claimed that he did not participate in hunting down their victim. Instead, he said, he was patched in via cell phone. This strikes me as unlikely, but I never had the chance to clarify my doubts.

"'Open a hole in *chante huario #3*,'" Andy recalled El Pensador saying, "'because there's going to be a party.'" It was time to go get the person from whom they had to take the head. They left in two cars from La Paz and went towards Alyoto. They wanted to pick up a dude, but they couldn't because a patrol came and since the vatos only carried 9mms they didn't want a shoot-out with the *juras*. So they went to La Riqueta. In Riqueta they ran over a dude, and acted like they were gonna take him to a hospital, but the vato didn't want to get in the car and another patrol arrived. From there they went to la Primavera, and there they found nothing. The vatos were pissed.

"And from there they went to La Frutal where I heard el Pensador say, 'Look at that dude. Look alive,' to Maniaco. They got out and said to the dude, 'We're from the National Civil Police. You know who charges extortion around here so get in the car!' They put a cloth and a bag over his head so he wouldn't have a clue where he went. Since we could still hear everything he said over the line, they said, 'now get ready because we're going to arrive.' I was in La Paz, and the vatos in Frutal brought this person to the pad. When they arrived in La Paz, TNT calls and El Pensador, he says, 'Look alive and open the gate because we're here with the present.' I opened the door, and they entered the garage of chante huario 4."

After cruising slipshod and reckless through the ghetto, Andy and his compatriots captured their victim by masquerading as police desperate to enforce the law against gang extortion. They continued the charade long after the victim could effectively resist.

"El Maniaco, El Pensador, El TNT, and la Madrastra come in and throw him on the floor.

'What's up with this dude?' I ask.

'He's the guy,' they tell me.

'And here La Mara Salvatrucha,' I say.

'No way,' says one of them. 'This is the National Police.'

'Ummm, okay,' I say."[*]

They moved quickly to execute their victim by garrotting him, using the same technique by which military death squads killed subversives disappeared during the civil war.[**]

---

[*] Andy claimed he did not accompany the men searching for a victim, but that he overheard everything on speakerphone. This seems highly suspicious: Why would they stay in telephone contact the entire time? Andy, I believe, was distancing himself from the affair as much as he could without ruining his worth as a witness. Thankful for the information he provided, the prosecution did not question him more deeply regarding this disparity.

[**] Jorge Suasnavar, interview with author, Guatemala City, March 1, 2012. Beheading, on the other hand, was never a popular military method, according to forensic anthropologists who have spent decades combing through the remains of civil war victims. Where the maras

"'Look alive then,' says El Pensador to El Madrastra, a chequeo of Little Psychos, 'tie a lasso.'"

"So El Madrastra tied a lasso. Then he grabbed a piece of broken broom handle. I was just checking the vibe, you understand, since I was already jumped in and the dude was a chequeo trying to do the work because he wanted to get out of his chequeo. The dude put the lasso around his neck. And with the piece of wood he starts to turn it, making a tourniquet until he kills him.

"From there El Pensador comes and says, 'Look alive, take him to chante huario number 3.' They get into the car again, the green Mirage, polarized four-door. We take it to the Chante La Paz, the chante huario number 3. A hole had already been opened. They threw him on the floor by the hole. El Maniaco went to bring a machete, a big machete, ok, and then he tells TNT and La Cuca, a chequeo from little Psychos, to take the clothes off the body. They do it, and they put him with his mouth facing down and a block under the head so that it would stay hanging. From there they start to cut the dude." Andy makes a harsh sawing sound. "He passes the machete to Cuca, and says, 'take it and cut him,' and the vato starts to cut him.

"El Maniaco asked again for the machete. He just cut a little bone that one has here, and the head fell off. A ton of blood came out and they put a wash bucket underneath so that it wouldn't spray all over the room. Then El TNT starts to cut pieces out of the face, the head, with a knife, and he throws gasoline on it and lights it on fire to disfigure it. . . .

"El Pensador and El Maniaco went to chante number 1 with a piece of paper on which they were going to write a note since they were the ramflero and the second in command, and the treasurer too was going to see what they put on the note. Around 4:30 or 5:30 in the morning, El Pensador comes and says to El Mike that he put the head in a backpack, inside the plastic bags, and they put in the paper. And he says, 'Right then, go leave the package, you already know where.'

"'Right then,' he replies, and he puts the backpack on and gets on a motor-cycle. It was a Surna Escobar 125. The vato gets on and goes, and at like six in

---

got the idea to chop their victims' heads off remains unclear and probably always will be. American security analysts have traced the practice of decapitation in Latin America to "viral videos" produced by Muslim extremists, eliding the long history of colonial brutality in the Americas. (The Spanish conquistadors used decapitation and other forms of dismemberment against captured Indians for centuries.)

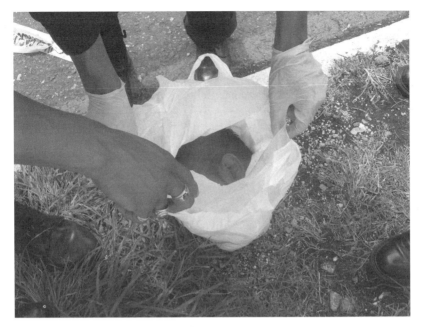

FIGURE 25. One of the four heads placed around Guatemala City. Photo: Anonymous.

the morning he gets back. He says to the homies, 'Right on, carnal, I turned in the package.' And from there we watched the news that came out when the four heads appeared here in the capital. And the homies started feeling good, they were happy and relieved."

Working through the night, three other cliques captured and decapitated their victims, all of them men. A fifth clique did not come through with their head, a failure for which they were subsequently punished. As dawn approached, the cliques placed the four heads at various locations around the city: one in front of a popular shopping mall, one at the entrance to the congressional building, one at a fire station where journalists were known to congregate, and the last in a working-class neighborhood (*barrio popular*). With each head they left a note addressing the government. One read simply, "No More Impunity," misspelled in a clumsy scrawl.

Another said: "This is happening because of all the impunity and injustice that exist in the prisons of this country. If you do not pay more attention to these mistreatments, we will hold the Ministry of Government and the penitentiary system responsible for what happens going forward because of their abuses of authority." In a bizarre parody of popular protest, MS sutured claims of defending human rights against state tyranny to the decapitated heads of innocent victims chosen at random.

The government labeled the quadruple murder an act of terror, and the national press flocked to publicize the grisly affair throughout the region. However, despite intense media and police scrutiny, it would be two years before investigators made any arrests connected with the case. The break came in early 2012 when Andy—who had severed ties with CLS leadership shortly after the crime of the four heads—agreed to testify against his old gang as a protected witness.

CHAPTER 5

Made-for-Media Murder

The apparent motive, the principal motive was, of course, single. But the crime was the effect of a whole list of motives which had blown on it in a whirlwind (like the 16 winds in the list of winds when they twist together in a tornado, in a cyclonic depression) and had ended by pressing into the vortex of the crime the enfeebled "reason of the world."
—Carlo Emilio Gadda, *That Awful Mess on the Via Merulana*[1]

In the crime of the four heads, members of the MS inscribed their rage into the public sphere through the mutilation and exhibition of bodies chosen at random for execution. As excessively callous as this act may appear, it draws from what has by now become a standard, even well-worn script: murdered, mutilated bodies put on public display to communicate some message to some audience. Today in Guatemala, terror is often spoken through corpses chopped up and left in garbage bags in the street; female bodies raped and tortured and quartered; and charred gangster corpses placed in certain police-designated locations signalling no need for an official investigation. In the midst of skyrocketing homicide rates, such strategically brutal demonstrations—circulated in the media, infiltrating everyday conversation—take on a starring role in the bloody drama of Guatemala's peacetime order. Time and again in my conversations with friends and informants, gang members and government ministers, taxi drivers and waitresses, they would turn to a computer or take out a cell phone to show me yet another body undone and rearranged for public viewing. It was as if, as words failed them, the images might convey what they could not say.

In a sense, acts like the crime of the four heads are terribly simple. The perpetrators employ a brutal, efficient logic to give their violence maximum circulation before the public eye. More often than not, the message they wish to convey is nothing more than blunt, unvarnished intimidation and terror. This kind of violence is not simply a matter of killing and mutilating bodies. It is violence "employed to create political acquiescence. It is intended to make

terror, and thus political inertia. It is intended to create hierarchies of domination and submission based on control of force."[2] But mere motives are not
nearly the whole story. Acts like the crime of the four heads must be recognized
as part of a *conversation*, a cacophonous, often incomprehensible exchange and
struggle waged for power and survival between interlocutors who, more often
than not, remain mysterious to the public. This conversation manifests as a
confused *discourse of suffering bodies*: mutilated corpses offered up to the public eye—in the flesh and in staged images—transform into surfaces bearing
some message for some audience.[3] Such messages do not transcribe neatly into
collective comprehension. While violent perpetrators may intend their actions
to have a specific political effect, that intention is not always realized, and the
repercussions will always range far beyond what they may have conceived.

Complicating the matter further is the fact that the loops and feedback
effects between such acts of violence and their symbolic representations before
the public eye revolve endlessly. This muddies any easy distinctions between
structure and agency, robbing stark labels like "innocent" and "guilty" of the
certainties they are meant to convey. It is true that maras are often active
agents of such violence, engaging in this discourse to spectacular effect. The
savviest and most powerful among them—men like El Diabólico—capitalize
on their underlings' aspirations and capacities for violence to initiate the
spectacle. Spectacles, however, are not mere images or collections of images.
They are produced through social interactions and relationships.[4] Therefore,
rooting this public brutality in the maras elides how the crucible of postwar
Guatemala—alongside global media hungry for violent sensation—has forged
maras into the "limit-point" of criminal violence.[5] As mareros continue to kill
and die in breathtaking numbers, they have become a kind of shorthand in
the vernacular of peacetime brutality, and this has consequences. Their will
to excessive violence cannot be disentangled from how the maras—as both
the source and target of murder—have come to moor the floating sense of fear
and uncertainty haunting postwar life.

From gang leaders' sociopathic disregard for human life, to rank-and-file
mareros' eagerness to become the killers they are told they are supposed to
be, to the public's horror at and hungry fascination with such deeds, such
violence has ways of ensnaring us all. The Guatemalan (as well as the global)
public keep coming to the coliseum, so to speak. In so doing, they (and we)
are drawn into this discourse of suffering bodies and participate in both its
circulation and savage erasure. Whether intended as performance or not,

murder, once drawn into the public sphere, becomes a grotesque act of theater. Like all performances, meaning and significance are determined as much by the audience as by the actors staging the spectacle.[6] The crime of the four heads and other acts of violence that become spectacle, then, are central to the never-ending struggle to create and prop up a sense of order, even as peacetime terror blurs commonsense distinctions between innocence and guilt, witness and perpetrator. From the Cold War conflict into the present, violent death has been an intimate companion of everyday life in Guatemala City.[7] But today the meaning of violent death—and thus the meaning and value of human life—has been thrown into a new kind of cacophonous confusion. Certain deaths can count and others do not, and the maras expose the brutal calculations of this economy of suffering as they strive to make murder matter to a public strung out on criminal brutality, pulled into hysterical excitement and numbing shock with every new act of spectacular violence.[8] The maras are not alone. Such violent and confused meaning making emerges in the public sphere as a babel of blame, prejudice, and fear. This chapter wades into the maelstrom to interrogate the ethical scripts and political dialects at play in the production and consumption of all this death. I dig beneath the bloody spectacle to probe how its stage was set. From indifference to horror, fascination to fatigue, made-for-media murder, like T. S. Eliot's magic lantern, "throws the nerves in patterns on a screen," exposing, in gory detail, collective conceptions of unjust suffering and deserved death circulating through Guatemalan society and beyond.[9]

MAKING SENSE OF SENSELESS SUFFERING

The maras fit too perfectly into all sorts of pre-existing fears and prejudices. The history of extreme racism towards the dark Indian, the class fears still clung to by the rich and the ambitious middle classes. Everyone finds their answers in the maras: business interests and their fear for continuing profits, the middle class fear of the raging poor, politicians searching for a topic that will mobilize their populace.

—Francisco Jimenez Irungaray, former public security minister[10]

In Guatemala City, violent terror is not new, and brutal histories have left painful scars upon the social body. The state-perpetrated, US-funded massacres and disappearance campaigns of Guatemala's civil war have become the subject of countless books, war crimes cases, and NGO fund-raising pamphlets. This history of violence manifests in myriad ways; witness the continued impunity of the rich, the widespread acceptance of violence as a means of resolving conflict, and ongoing war crimes prosecutions and public protests to break the silence and suffering of the survivors.[11]

This history is essential to understanding the present scene, but it is certainly not enough. Memories fade and contort collective understandings of history, especially when those in power have little interest in dredging up a past that incriminates them.[12] Today, public concern over past atrocities must compete for media attention and psychic space with contemporary horrors. For many residents of Guatemala City, everyday worries leave little time or energy to devote to the ghosts of historical injustice.[13] As Elena, my colleague in the gang rehabilitation program, wondered aloud, "Why should I care about someone who was killed thirty years ago, when I have to worry about my daughters getting raped and killed on their way home at night?" Or as Calavera commented a few months after he got out of prison: "Look at how the people live, rushing from home to work, work to home, hiding in concrete boxes and scared of their own shadows. The city feels like just another prison!"

A litany of macabre questions without easy answers haunts city life: *What does it mean* when a baby's severed head is discovered on the outskirts of the city? Is the precipitous rise in bus driver murders linked to gang extortion rackets, or is it a matter of right-wing political maneuvering to convince people to vote for hard-line, mano dura candidates? Why was the dismembered corpse of a seventeen-year-old girl left on a brand new commuter bus platform? Such questions inspire a profusion of contradictory answers. "What really arouses indignation against suffering," Friedrich Nietzsche long ago observed, "is not suffering as such but the senselessness of suffering."[14] Faced with so much suffering that appears so deeply senseless, we are left, more often than not, to contemplate these signs written in blood and viscera like fraudulent seers muttering over tea leaves. The ruined corpses on parade each day become a set of unsettling referents, public wounds inviting any Doubting Thomas to probe them.[15] For many, they reveal how deeply insecure and violent the present has become and how apocalyptic the future appears. Public reactions tend to make the bloodshed more palatable, as those who must live with this violence day in and day out fall back on blanket assumptions. The perpetrators are "beasts." The victims "must have been involved in *something*." The maras, of course, have become essential to anchoring this otherwise vague and overwhelming sense of despair, fear, and horror by providing an easy target for reactive rage.

Guatemala City, November 2013. I caught a taxi outside a mall in the zona viva and asked the driver—an affable, quick-witted fellow named Juventino—to take me across town to Calavera's family's home near the general cemetery. I was fighting a fever. After navigating typically horrendous traffic, we made it to the historic zone, passing rust-red buses idling in their own smog as young men called out destinations in cartoon falsetto. I looked for smiley faces sketched in soap on the windshields, which, I had been told, signal that the owner has paid the required extortion tithes to whichever gang is owed. I asked Juventino what he knew about such things. He shrugged. "I don't know about that, but I wouldn't be surprised. The gangs will do anything to anyone!" In zone 3, approaching the cemetery, we passed cinderblock residences crouched behind wrought-iron-barred windows, heavy metal doors, and barbed wire festooned along the second- and third-floor terraces. A private security guard, silver epaulettes shining, stood stiffly beneath a cement awning, holding a 12-gauge shotgun across his chest, index finger resting on the trigger. My brother at arms, I thought, and giggled. Juventino looked over at me askance and said something I didn't catch.

"Sorry, what?"

"The cross streets, friend! Where am I taking you exactly?"

"5th Avenue and 38th Street," I replied, "a few blocks down from the cemetery, on the way to Verbena."

He glanced at me sharply. "That's a . . . well, a complicated neighborhood. Full of mareros. You should be careful."

"Yes sir," I struggled to rouse myself from my stupor. "Full of mareros, you say. Which mara? Letters? Numbers?"

He shrugged. "Who knows? Who can tell them apart these days?"

At the next intersection, Juventino hit the breaks as a police truck careened across our path with lights flashing, but no siren, and disappeared.

As we drove on, Juventino grinned at me. "You know, I have trouble sleeping sometimes. I suffer from insomnia. Often it happens that I watch too much television, and afterward I can't sleep. So to relax, instead of counting sheep, I shoot mareros." His grin widened. "Just line them up, take aim, and shoot them. And you know what? It works, I suppose, because there are always more," he laughed, shaking his head, "always more. I must have killed thousands and thousands of them. But only in my thoughts." Then he was suddenly earnest. "But really, it would be okay to really kill them because the Bible says, well, 'He that does not listen to me shall be pulled out by the roots and thrown into the fire.'"

Juventino's observations mirror sentiments prevalent across the Northern Triangle of Central America. Regional governments' spectacular failures to stamp out the maras have helped inspire widespread support for vigilante groups that target youth suspected of gang involvement for extermination.[16] They are typically made up of off-duty policemen and military, once again blurring any hard and fast distinction between the state and its underworld, and tend to employ techniques and tactics of terror perfected by Cold War–era security forces. No policeman I interviewed admitted to involvement in such groups, though some made oblique references to carrying out clandestine killings. When I asked a police chief about mareros' famed fearlessness before death, for example, he chuckled and shook his head. "I have been with them when they are about to die," he said, "and believe me, they were afraid."

Even so, the collective sense that mareros are fit only for extermination seems to pivot on the fact that they are categorically different from other humans, a notion that the maras themselves have proudly taken on.[17] In a society in which violent death has become a defining feature of everyday life, maras are the inhuman killers who have lost the oh-so-human fear of death. Speaking in utter seriousness, an antiviolence adviser for the US Agency for International Development in Guatemala told me that "the gangs' biggest advantage, the reason they create such horror in the population and they are so difficult to combat is that their soldiers have reached a point where they no longer fear death. Death has no power over them." But as deviant as they may appear in the eyes of some analysts and the viewing public, mareros' apparent bravado regarding death and killing cannot be reduced to some pathological root. Or so said Rodolfo Kepfer, a psychoanalyst and researcher who worked for several years in juvenile detention centers with young killers of all stripes, marero and otherwise. He found that the gang members under his care managed themselves with far more discipline and less erratic behavior than other minors incarcerated for homicide. We spoke in his office at the University of Landívar, tucked away in the steep green hills above Guatemala City where the rich keep their homes.

"Most of the young men who had a higher degree of psychopathology were not mareros," he told me over cups of watered down Nescafé. Kepfer always seemed to have a twinkle in his eye and a smile on his lips, evincing an impish good humor even when discussing the most macabre subjects. "'The marero', so to speak, was quite socialized," he continued. "It was difficult to give a marero the diagnosis of, for example, a social disorder. Difficult because he did not fulfill the criteria, nor was his conduct so antisocial. Interestingly, there were groups of *paisas* [non-gang-affiliated prisoners] who were *really* violent and dangerous."

Gang violence is not the work of pathological deviants. One might even call them "structured psychopaths" if the term *psychopath* weren't so heavily laden with images of serial killers muzzled and straitjacketed and mad. Kepfer offered an alternative psychological analysis, one that takes into account the conditions of violation and insecurity in which gang members find themselves immersed every day of their short lives. Surviving day in and day out under the constant threat of death, mareros become "thanatophobes." "These are young men who fear death so deeply that they seek it," Kepfer concluded, and for once his smile sagged. "They try to beat death to the punch."

Though gang violence is no longer defined by the SUR's strict edicts, it still seems to follow a set of rules, relationships, and hierarchies that dictate who can be killed and why. Echoing my police and gang informants, Kepfer claimed that the MS's structure imposes an ironclad discipline on its rank-and-file members, and to step outside these rules is to invite brutal punishment. "Something that one noted a lot in mareros, especially in the MS members, was how dominated they were by the rules," Kepfer said. "The rules for them are everything. The 'marero rules.'" He shrugged and shook his head. "You sit with them for an hour and they would talk to you about all kinds of things, but then you ask about something specific and it's, 'No, no I can't say because of the rule.' In this sense they have rules that are as strict as the military. Like kaibiles."

A willingness to perform extreme violence within an organization that exacts extreme discipline; it *is* a military model. Kepfer's reference to kaibiles—the US-trained and -funded special-forces responsible for many of the Guatemalan civil war's worst atrocities—is apt.[18] Their brutal training regime and thirst for violence are the stuff of legends. It is said that in the 1980s, their training program included raising a puppy during boot camp. At the end of training, their final test was to drown the dog and eat its heart.[19] Even so, in peacetime Guatemala the military has remained the most widely respected and trusted public institution, and many of the top leaders in the country, including former president Perez Molina and his security minister, are former kaibiles. So was the leader of the Zetas in Guatemala when the narco-cartel went to war with Guatemalan drug transporters associated with their rival, the Sinaloa Cartel, in the early 2010s.[20] Mareros also claim that those who become gang leaders often have received military training. The marero, the personification of criminal chaos in the popular imagination, in fact emulates the rigid, authoritarian models that have become the paradigms of order in post–civil war society.

At times, mara violence bears the mark of militarized conflict. Clearly defined goals and ruthless strategy drive some of the maras' most gruesome and spectacular acts. In late 2011, for example, the Guatemala City government opened a new TransUrbano bus station in El Limon, zone 18 of Guatemala City. The neighborhood had long been bypassed by public transportation because of gang extortion rackets and lack of security. The new commuter line displeased the local gang, Los Solo Raperos, one of Guatemala's most infamous Barrio18 cliques. The TransUrbano route would displace the *tuk-tuk* drivers who provided local transport for commuters, as well as extortion tithes and valuable information for the gang. To express their anger, Barrio18 members kidnapped, tortured, raped, murdered, and dismembered a seventeen-year-old girl chosen at random. They put her undone body in a garbage bag and placed the garbage bag in the newly minted TransUrbano bus station on the day the route opened.[21]

With some maras and mareros hewing so eagerly to the role that has been written for them, maras as social symbols become ever more tightly sutured to the death and violence they have come to represent.[22] Mareros are "psychopaths" addicted to killing, and they are "thanatophobes," so afraid of death they try to beat it to the punch. They are demon worshipers deaf to God's edicts. They are organized and intensely disciplined "like kaibiles." They are the perpetrators of senseless suffering and the targets of desperate rage. Clearly, maras have come to symbolize the worst excesses of peacetime society. But the horrors that haunt everyday life are too numerous and too ambiguous to know or name with such specificity. In the figure of the marero, brutal agency and overwhelming structural violence are hopelessly layered. And so maras have become a kind of floating signifier embodying the messy collection of rumors, fantasies, and nightmares about violence and its consequences in postwar life.[23] But the sense of order the marero helps edify is always fleeting. Today, having become the answer when no answer suffices, the marero's utility in mooring collective confusion is already waning.

As we turned onto Calavera's street, I asked Juventino how the mareros appeared in his fantasies of execution. He shrugged, laughed, and said they always had tattooed faces, they threw up gang signs with their hands, and they wore baggy clothes. But then he sighed. "Anyway it's just a fantasy. In real life, it's impossible to tell if someone's a marero or not. Today . . . even someone dressed like you, a white guy (*guero*) in a nice coat, can be a marero. You just don't know, so you are always risking yourself." I thanked him, paid him, and got out of the taxi. "Be careful," he called out as I walked away. "This is a bad neighborhood."

And so the plot thickens. Even as the press, the police, and civilians look for the tattoos, clothing style, and other telltale signs to link daily death to gang involvement, the maras have largely exchanged these symbols for more subtle codes of belonging. Today bone fide members maintain a much lower profile. They stick to more formal clothes, and many cliques—especially MS cliques—have discontinued altogether the use of body tattoos for their members. This blending appears to make the already incalculable fear and insecurity more pervasive. Police chiefs and prosecutors claim the maras have begun to infiltrate government positions, becoming clerks in offices in charge of making national identification cards and cadets in the national police academy. Since the marero is both the paradigmatic killer and the most easily excused target of violence, the category of the "innocent" victim has shrunk as collective fear expands. A homicide victim must be presumed innocent in order to be publicly mourned, to invoke outrage, as well as to garner the publicity necessary to make the killer's message register before a wider audience. But who, in this age of assured blame and collective fear, can be innocent?

THE VIOLENCE OF IMAGES

Images—digital and print—have become a primary vector through which violent death circulates in the public sphere. "Narratives can make us understand," wrote Susan Sontag. "Photographs do something else. They haunt us."[24] Certain images have a way of etching themselves into consciousness with more precision and power than perhaps we would like to give them. Today, global media culture saturates everyday life with endless images defining collective aspirations, fears, and desires, and sensational violence has long been an essential ingredient of this culture.[25] A raw, flamboyant species of "death porn," increasingly prevalent across the Americas and in other parts of the world, has become standard fare served up to the Guatemalan public.[26] Images of such suffering do more than haunt. Death porn, whether "real," for "entertainment," or both, so shocks and titillates that finding a measured, ethical response sometimes seems impossible.

By its very nature, photographic imagery offers only fleeting glimpses of the world as it is. "Photographs don't explain the way the world works," writes the critic Susie Linfield. "They don't offer reasons or causes. They don't tell us stories with a coherent, or even discernible, beginning, middle or end."[27] This makes the photograph a volatile means of communication, appealing first and foremost to our emotional selves. And when a desperate awareness of insecurity and violence dominates everyday life, images of murder, torture, and massacre become totemic symbols of the status quo. Such images circulate so widely that they seem to be everywhere, intruding upon one's field of vision even when one is trying to look away.

For example, in November 2011 I was on a trip to the Pacific coast of Guatemala with Gwendolyn, my fiancée. As the bus pulled up to the southernmost village along the coastal road, I could hear the waves lapping on the shore. It had been a long, hot journey, and I was looking forward to an ice-cold beer. As I reached up to pull down a bag from the overhead compartment, a crumpled newspaper fluttered down to rest among our things. Gwendolyn picked it up. She smoothed it out and looked at it, shook her head, and handed it to me. The headline announced, "They find the decapitated head of a baby." And there it was, a baby's head cradled in two yellow gloves, the eyes swollen shut, the lips parted slightly, the skin mottled and discolored. The head was tiny in the gloved hands, about the size of an apple, and horribly misshapen except for a perfectly articulated ear no larger than my fingernail.

By way of such imagery, sensationalist journalism has fed upon daily violence to become the most popular and powerful venue for informing the public of its daily dangers. A prime example is the enormous success of *Nuestro Diario*, the country's leading newspaper.[28] *Nuestro Diario* is a "blue collar" paper with extensive circulation chockfull of bright and often bloody images and short on text.[29] It often dedicates a full third of its pages—more than any other newspaper—to the *nota roja* (red note), a subsection focused entirely on crime and violent death. *Nuestro Diario*'s consistent attention to violent death and catastrophe has earned it the nickname "*Nuestro Muerto Diario*," or "Our Daily Death." Many who peruse this paper are barely literate. Along with several pages dedicated to Latin American and European professional soccer and the requisite scantily clad models, the nota roja is Nuestro Diario's bread and butter. There is an implicit politics in this kind of sensationalized reporting of violence. With echoes of Baudelaire, pitched to resonate with the bloody present of Guatemala City, Colussi observes:

Nuestro Diario transmits violence wherever one looks, in general terms associating violence with criminality. There is no critical analysis of the delinquent acts presented daily; only report and the image (macabre in every case) of the situation in isolation and without contextualization. The first few pages are impactful; a victim killed in an assault, a marero dead in a coup de grace, a woman raped and dismembered, a lynched delinquent... all of which is nothing but the regurgitation of the facts—without doubt real, since there is an efficient journalism at work here—but that, repeated day after day, nourishes a collective imaginary in which the violence is identified with an abundant delinquency that is master and mistress of these lands, without presenting causes of these processes, and much less, alternatives.[30]

The effects of this kind of reporting, sharpened so poignantly with images of death and massacre, can be deeply confusing. The urge to look contends with the urge to look away, numbing shock shot through with mystified fascination. Over time, public reaction to daily murder circulated in this way cycles through horror to titillation, from titillation to indifference, and from indifference to exhaustion, until some new atrocity breaches the defenses to start the process all over again. This violence becomes woven into the fabric of everyday expectations.

The image of the dead gangster is conscripted into collective efforts to deal with all this death. Photographs of marero bodies—or bodies labeled as such—have become central nodes through which a frightened public metabolizes a creeping sense of helplessness, confusion, and despair. Such images and reactions colonize and contort the politics of mourning.[31] Mareros' suffering is easily justified, and murdered mareros are not, on a public level, "grievable."[32] The urge to blame trumps any presumption of innocence in the public sphere, and the messy play of images helps push the refusal to grieve beyond "real" mareros to encompass considerable portions of the daily dead. Any sign of "gang association"—determined by myriad factors relating to age, dress, geography, and so on—can make a victim unmournable.

Field Notes, September 19, 2011

Today, like every other day, the first four pages of *Nuestro Diario* are dedicated to reporting murder and violence of every kind—dismembered bodies dredged up outside of Mixco, "MARERO KILLED" (*ASESINAN A MARERO*) spelled out in huge capitals, and a close-up of the cadaver's tattoos. . . . The faces of a woman and a girl child and boy child on his bicep, "Gaby" drawn in gothic calligraphy, a gun on his belly. Somewhere else, the *Santa Muerte*. The headline claims he was the head of a gang that conducted extortion rackets, though the 100-word article contains nothing to back this up.

NOTICIAS al 1177   LUNES 19 DE SEPTIEMBRE DE 2011 · NUESTRO DIARIO

IMPACTO

JEFE · MARIO RECINOS. *mrecinos@nuestrodiario.com.gt*

Como Carlos Alonzo García, residente en Tierra Nueva, fue identificado el fallecido.   La Policía cree que la causa del crimen es una venganza.

ASESINAN A MARERO

Jefe de pandilla que extorsiona a comerciantes en Tierra Nueva y Minerva aparece estrangulado.

Marta Muñoz
★Nuestro Diario

En un terreno desolado, envuelto en sábanas y ponchos amarrados con un cable y lazo de nailon, fue localizado en la zona 11 de Mixco el cadáver de un hombre con señales de tortura.

Vecinos de un sector de Planes de Minerva que se dirigían a un servicio religioso encontraron el cuerpo y le avisaron a la Policía Nacional Civil, la cual lo identificó como Carlos Leonel Alonzo García, de 26 años, residente de la colonia Tierra Nueva.

Algunos comerciantes del lugar comentaron que se trataba de uno de los jefes de las pandillas que se dedican a extorsionar negocios, así como a pilotos del transporte colectivo y ruteros, lo cual fue ratificado por inves-

tigadores de la Policía.

Según los peritos del Ministerio Público, el cuerpo de la víctima estaba boca arriba con dos bolsas negras en la cabeza y varios disparos.

POSIBLE VENGANZA

Agentes de la comisaría que funciona en ese sector indicaron que el crimen podría deberse a una venganza personal o bien a la lucha interna entre pandillas.

Fiscales del Ministerio Público constataron que los delincuentes cometieron el crimen en otro lugar, donde habría sido torturado y estrangulado.

La víctima tenía varios tatuajes, entre estos uno de la santa muerte, el rostro de una mujer y dos niños, y un fusil en el pecho.

En las bolsas del pantalón le hallaron marihuana, las llaves de su casa y una billetera con sus

documentos personales.

Pobladores pidieron a las autoridades más seguridad en ese sector, el cual, indicaron, siempre se ha catalogado como un lugar tranquilo, y nunca había sucedido algo similar.

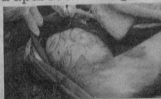

A Carlos lo vinculaban con quienes extorsionan a choferes.

"Tengo 25 años de vivir aquí, y jamás había pasado algo así de terrible", dijo Clementina Rojas, quien, con asombro, llegó a verificar quién era la persona que estaba muerta entre los matorrales.

FIGURE 26. Newspaper article on the murder of an alleged marero: "Marero Killed," *Nuestro Diario*, September 19, 2011.

The next page shows two separate "massacres." Two women were killed with multiple gunshot wounds in zone 21 of the capital. There is a quote from a local business owner. "Sadly, some girls get involved with the gangs, and this kills them." (*Lamentablemente, algunas patojas se meten con las maras, esta las matan.*)[33]

A tortured, tattooed corpse immediately becomes a gangster's body, an extortionist's body. The body is intact, but the selective use of imagery robs the corpse of its human wholeness by showing only his tattoos, focusing in on these symbols of social subversion that for many Guatemalans are prima facie evidence of his guilt. The other stories relate without detail the murders of two women, with only a glib quote linking the girls' deaths to association with gangs. It is the association that kills, whoever the perpetrator might be.

A history of violence, exclusion, and erasure is written into—or rather, out of—this skin-deep rendition of death. Bodies stained with mara markings, so intensely visible as killers and signs of social subversion, make the violence they have come to represent more easily metabolized. As murder rates have risen exponentially, the collective struggle to create distance from so much death has pushed many victims into the same category as the killers. These people, as the saying goes, "must have been involved in something." The overwhelming urge to "differentiate the image of the criminal as far as possible from oneself" extends not only to violent perpetrators but also their victims.[34]

IMAGES OF INNOCENT SUFFERING AND THE POLITICS OF MEMORY

Contemporary killers are not the only actors deploying dead innocents for political gain. While one species of death porn dominates the daily news, activists and left-wing politicians use another in campaigns to reshape collective memory of unresolved and unpunished civil war atrocities. War crimes trials are perhaps the most public venue for these struggles. Court cases prosecuting the military's worst human rights abuses have become public stages upon which a cast of actors—lawyers and human rights organizations, the media and politicians, survivors and perpetrators—debates and refigures civil war violence before a public that, like most publics, is largely ignorant of its own history.[35]

The lines of opposition in this struggle fall messily along those of the civil war: the fragmented, progressive "Left" arrayed against military watchdogs defending the interests of the oligarchs who still rule this country. Typical of human rights–based demands for justice, these cases follow a framework made from three interwoven discourses: the primacy of *innocent* victims over any other subject, making justice claims visible by strategically deploying innocent suffering, and the importance of punitive justice against certain perpetrators chosen as much for their symbolic value as for their deeds.[36]

Zone 1, Guatemala City, March 2012

On a quiet, shady side street in Guatemala City's historic quarter, I discovered a tiny war museum. Inside, a tall man with braces on his teeth and an awkward smile introduced himself as Samuel Villatoro. This provoked something of a *Twilight Zone* moment for me. Samuel Villatoro was a union activist disappeared during the civil war and recently identified by forensic anthropologists. A month earlier, I walked with mourners in the man's wake, staged outside an NGO office in zone 2. I stared at the man, dumbfounded, before I realized he was the *son* of the deceased.

Black-and-white portraits hung on a wall in a tiny room. They showed the faces of the forty-two disappeared "subversives" identified in military diaries recently unearthed by human rights investigators. Many looked scared and exhausted. Alongside their faces were their capture dates, and the date they "went with Pancho" (*se fue con Pancho*), the military's euphemism for execution. And there among the doomed was Samuel Villatoro the father. He wore dark glasses, and his hair was swept back like his son's. The resemblance was striking.

Samuel Jr. launched into a rehearsed speech. His father became the head of the rubber farmer's union after the military disappeared twenty-seven leading members from a union meeting. On January 30, 1984, he left his home in Guatemala City to attend classes at the Universidad de San Carlos. A few blocks from his home, a specially trained police unit kidnapped him and immediately turned him over to military intelligence. He spent fifty-seven days in military custody undergoing torture, until his captors executed him by garroting. Decades later, forensic anthropologists found his skeleton in the same Levi's jeans he was wearing when he was captured, the jeans Samuel Jr.'s mother remembered him wearing when he left the house thirty-one years before. Today, Samuel Sr. is one of thousands of victims featured in cases against military and police officials allegedly involved in their disappearance, torture, and execution.

After finishing his speech, Samuel Jr. led me into another cubbyhole of a room. An enormous glass box, polished and immaculate, dominated the space. Inside, his father's skeleton lay in repose. With the bones spread out the man looked to have been a giant. Placing his hand delicately on the glass, Samuel Jr. said, "I know it's strange for a body to be left out like this . . . but it's just that we lost him so long ago and now we want [to] always have him near. And we want to send a message to Guatemala and the world about what happened here. We want to make sure that such violations of human rights never happen again." He paused and looked down at the bones. "This is only the beginning. We are getting funds for a full-fledged museum, full of information about the disappeared."

I wonder how full of bodies it will be.

Such efforts to expose the injustices of the past are geared to redirecting the moral compass of the present, and they depend on making the suffering of innocents intensely visible, often on the national stage. International and Guatemalan NGOs have spent millions digging up, identifying, and presenting the bones of the massacred dead to the public eye. Paired with survivors' narratives, these efforts have been absolutely essential in the pursuit of justice.[37] In the 2013 genocide trial of General Efrain Rios Montt, for example, Guatemalan and international human rights advocates lauded the prosecution for giving the innocent victims of civil war atrocity a stage upon which to present their suffering to the world.[38] They did so in graphic detail. More than one hundred survivors of military massacre took the stand against Rios Montt and described the litany of abuses they had witnessed and suffered. Human rights advocates have hailed this as a victory in and of itself, despite the fact that the testimonies did not result in any kind of punishment for the former general.[39] A three-judge panel found Rios Montt guilty of genocide and crimes against humanity, but under severe pressure from ruling elites, the Constitutional Court nullified the proceedings on a technicality.

Guatemalan society is today suffused with images of suffering bodies. Corpses and photographs of the civil war's massacred and disappeared contend for a place in the public imagination with today's murdered and dismembered. The former's haunting portraits and unearthed bones have become key instruments with which human rights organizations and their supporters attempt to make the bloody past matter. *These* innocents are mourned, their suffering fetishized and mobilized, while the possibility of even being *considered* an innocent victim of contemporary violence seems to diminish a little more each day.

Such ethical contradictions have helped make human rights a target for considerable misuse and abuse. In the crime of the four heads, the MS played off the power of innocent suffering by deploying human rights discourse in perverse fashion. The demand for "no more impunity," spoken through an act of awe-inspiring impunity, smacks of grim satire. Whether the MS evinced a dark sense of humor here or just clumsy misapprehension is an open question. Either way, it played nicely into the hands of those who portray the inflammatory power of human rights speech and justice claims as a key factor in the explosion of violent crime. Right-wing politicians and frustrated civilians claim that international human rights groups have defenestrated the Guatemalan security forces. A bereaved father of a murder victim in zone 18 said,

"All this talk of human rights has made it impossible for parents and police to keep the young people in line." A middle-aged taxi driver lamented, "Human rights only help criminals escape justice." Even those who work to make peace in neighborhoods struggling with gang violence blame the discourse of human rights for hamstringing local responses against wrongdoers. "Everything started with the human rights," raged a former gang member who became an evangelical pastor. "We confuse liberty with libertinism! The [human rights ombudsman] looks out for the rights of people who kill and dismember others, and so the parents and the police have lost their authority."

Blaming human rights for criminal violence is a common refrain across Latin America and other parts of the world. The political Right in Central America, Brazil, and other Southern Cone nations, as well as postapartheid South Africa, elides human rights struggles with criminal chaos as a means of undermining a discourse that has become the global language of resistance to elite impunity. It is a simple but shrewd strategy: mobilize the specter of extreme peacetime violence to snuff out struggles against environmental degradation, land grabs by multinational companies, government corruption, and so on. In societies where collective desperation for a sense of order has reached a fever pitch, such strategies have been highly effective.[40]

MAKING MURDER MATTER

We want to know the reasons a person died violently, because, we think, such knowledge will help us to place that murder in its appropriate category; just or unjust, deserved or tragic. This is not simply a matter of satisfying curiosity. These reasons, we might secretly hope, will explain the murder as a matter of the victim's personal history, making him in some way an agent of his own destruction. Making sense of a stranger's violent death in this way creates a buffer between his suffering and our own existence. All the well-worn categories of human difference—race, class, gender, faith, age, geography—come into play, harnessed to distance ourselves from the specter of violence and to diminish its terrifying reality. When so many murders can be made to fit so easily with preconceived notions of deserved death, how do maras and others seeking to speak through violence ensure their message won't simply be ignored, shunted away, and made invisible?

Discounting the suffering and death of certain social types has been integral to the rise of made-for-media murders like the crime of the four heads.[41]

The "making invisible" of certain victims of violence has a hidden history, a history of which I have only been able to collect disjointed fragments. Francisco Jimenez Irungaray, a former government adviser for public security, emphasized the role of police profiling. "I spent years reviewing the daily police reports made on a twenty-four-hour basis," he said as we ate crepes and sipped cappuccinos. "There were two categories that came out as falling under direct suspicion with little or no additional provocation. These were 'young' and 'tattooed.' If the victim of robbery, homicide, shooting, or what have you, either was young or had tattoos or both the case would be immediately archived and forgotten." He shook his head. "These were not cases worth pursuing because clearly it was an issue of gangs, and therefore did not bear police intervention. Here we see prejudice rising to the level of repression."

This "prejudice rising to the level of repression" effectively erased the murders of poor young men from the public record, allowing the public to turn away, and signaled to the killers that they could do what they wanted. "I've killed for respect, for money," mused Mo, an MS member incarcerated for multiple murders. "But also just to keep up the practice, to not lose my touch. Once I learned that I could kill without anything happening, well then . . ."

The government's intentional ignorance about the deaths of poor urban youth was paired with heavy-handed policing efforts that took on extrajudicial savagery. Vigilante groups, staffed by off-duty military and police officials, took matters into their own hands, targeting suspected mareros for torture and execution.

Shortly before his release, I sat with Triste in Canada prison. He had his homemade tattoo rig set up, but no clients to work on. As we idled away the afternoon, he told me the story of two friends of his who had been executed by vigilantes. "Two guys I knew, deportees like me, used to hang with Barrio18 guys named Travieso and Spider," he recalled, speaking in a mix of English and Spanish. This was in 2000, shortly after Triste was deported from the United States. "They weren't in the game, you understand, just friends. One day two cars from SIC [a police division] picked up my buddies outside my house." Triste flashed a rueful grin. "Lucky for me, I had just been arrested for receiving stolen property, or else they would have gotten me too. My buddies had come around the house looking for me, but since I never came back, they left. The police got them just around the block. They were both tattooed dudes, one 18th Street, the other Kansas Street." Triste traced his friends' tattoos across his chest and down his right shoulder. "The police put them against the wall, and then two or three days later they showed up real crispy a few blocks from my house."

"What do you mean 'real crispy'?"

Triste raised an eyebrow. "I mean *crispy*. Like Kentucky Fried. They burned those dudes to death."

By officially ignoring murder victims who appeared to be mareros and unofficially taking part in murdering and terrorizing suspected gang members, the Guatemalan state has helped make mareros into easily excused, even celebrated victims of violence. When mareros die, no public mourning is necessary, and the tragedy of youth killing and dying in such breathtaking numbers transforms into unfortunate but necessary violence to heal the diseased social body. This goes some way in explaining why maras will go to such great lengths to inscribe their messages into the public sphere. In the crime of the four heads, for example, the MS's victims were poor young men living or working in urban slums. The neighborhoods through which the killers drove in search of their victims are poor urban settlements that have been left largely abandoned by both the state security services and the formal capitalist economy. These are spaces that are, for the most part, "invisible" to the public eye. Imminent violence—connected to gang warfare or extortion rackets—is a virtual constant. The victims were poor young males living and working in poor urban neighborhoods: a cook, a day laborer, and a corner store clerk (tellingly, authorities never identified the fourth victim). Their sex, class, and geography made them more or less typical targets and perpetrators of violence, and thus nothing special.[42] Since these murders were geared toward making the mara demands as intensely *visible* as possible, the bodies, so easily culled from the ghetto, could not remain there. In the political economy of daily murder, poor male corpses appearing in poor urban space create no more than minor blips on the public consciousness. The MS acted on these unwritten rules of visibility and value, to stunning effect.

While young men are by far the most common victims of murder, female bodies have become the favored means of transmitting messages to a rival, a community, the state, the nation, and even the world. Maras have taken the blame for the rising tide of "femicides": murders targeting females that show evidence of sexual abuse, torture, dismemberment, and other signs of excessive brutality.[43] The increasing frequency of this kind of crime has garnered national and international attention. Signs seem to indicate that maras and others target women precisely for this reason; in 85 percent of femicides, no effort has been made to hide the body.[44] A disproportionate number of murdered female bodies also show signs of torture.[45] Maras are said to target women in the game of competitive cruelty between rivals or as part of their initiation rituals.[46] Tortured and undone, female corpses sometimes function as "internal memos" meant to circulate within the gang. Sometimes they are messages meant to reach a broader audience: a community, the government, or even the nation as a whole. Again, this is a recent page in an old story. During the civil war, when the military targeted men, the men were more likely to be disappeared.[47] When they massacred women—most often in rural villages—the corpses were often left in public view. In Guatemalan culture, as in much of the world, the female is symbolically linked to the home, a space of intimacy, and she is the primary bearer of cultural reproduction.[48] To violate a community and make sure that violation lasts, to make a message indelible in the public sphere, female corpses have proven a most effective means of communication in war as well as in so-called peace.

The MS leveraged its otherwise unremarkable victims into spectacle by strategically placing the severed heads in locations associated with political, economic, or mediatic importance. Thus three of the four heads ended up before the congressional building, at the entrance to the Tikal Futura shopping mall, and near a congregation point for journalists. To pull it off, the mareros masqueraded as police and mimicked a military execution. They attached to these bodies messages echoing the language of resistance expressed in human rights vernacular. By playing at police cum death squad, mouthing the refrain of rights, and speaking their grievances through innocent corpses, the MS took on multiple and schizophrenic roles in this postwar pageantry. All this to make its demands heard amid the cacophony of everyday violence, if only for an ephemeral media moment. It turned out to be enough for the murders to become a nationally circulated event. The MS failed, however, to perform a "global," to break through into the international media. A stringer for Reuters in Guatemala tried to run this story, but his editors in the Mexico City office required at least ten undone bodies for a Guatemalan massacre to become newsworthy. Fewer than that, he said, and it was not a story worth telling.

Clearly the global marketplace for spectacular violence is cutthroat competitive. The capacity of twenty-first-century violent actors like the maras—operating within the confines of local social orders and with limited territorial reach—to stage spectacles that gain instant worldwide circulation has undergone a marked evolution. Maras are decidedly less adept at garnering global attention than other more powerful, more media-savvy groups. To the north, for example, Mexican narco-cartels have staged massacres, multiple beheadings, and online torture videos in their struggles with each other and with the Mexican state.[49] Images of their victims' bodies hung from city bridges or coiled together in rural farmhouses have become iconic of the ill-fated War on Drugs, incessantly reproduced online and appropriated in Hollywood films.[50]

Both maras' and Mexican cartels' efforts at global exposure pale in comparison to the attention Islamic State (ISIS) has garnered. ISIS has demonstrated consummate skill in staging and editing slick, made-for-media online beheading videos, which have been useful for international recruitment to its cause. But more to the point, ISIS has maximized its media exposure (and leveraged its political import) by playing to the global moral economy of suffering. The handful of US and European citizens ISIS has so far beheaded on video have provoked more media outrage and geopolitical maneuvering than tens and hundreds of thousands of innocent victims of war lacking the proper citizenship (or faith, skin color, ethnicity, etc.) for more globalized grief.[51] Far more than the maras, ISIS self-consciously capitalizes on massive differentials in our capacity to grieve, counting on our quickness to mourn and rage at the suffering of those in whom we recognize ourselves. If we were capable of collectively mourning the pain of alien others, a more peaceful world might be possible.[52] For now, our role as distant witnesses to such atrocities will remain alloyed with a vague and maddening sense of complicity.[53]

LA DESCUARTIZADA (ANONYMOUS)

I have tried to interpret the crime of the four heads—and hypervisual violence more generally—through various lenses to understand how such events map onto and shape perceptions of unjust suffering and deserved death embedded in personal, communal, and national anxieties circulating throughout the postwar order. By peeling back the layered dialectics—between the past and the present, material acts and symbolic representation, actor and audience—haphazardly exposed in acts of public brutality, I hoped to reveal how the maras are throwing back distorted reflections of the social and ethical order of our world.

And yet, by assuming the privileged role of interpreter, the speaker for the dismembered dead drawing on all manner of epistemological tools, have I not also constructed an intellectual bulwark against such crimes?[54] It allows me to duck their nightmarish force and visceral impact, the way they can become lodged in the nether regions of consciousness. I have conveyed the brutal language and economy of suffering that inspires made-for-media murder while sidestepping my own complicity in such horrors. I have masked the confusion and shame that arise with the urge to look upon such suffering and then to look away because it is beyond my powers of comprehension and troubles my empathy.

How do I navigate the ethical and existential quandaries of witnessing, and asking you to witness, this kind of violence and suffering? I have refused to shield myself (and you) from images of violence in order to explore the confused struggle over representation they provoke. However, by circulating such images and trying to make sense of them, do I not also participate in the perpetrators' dreams of recognition? Am I not helping the MS perform the "global" it initially failed to achieve? But giving in to the desire to turn away and remain silent is itself a savage erasure of cruelty and suffering that cannot and should not be ignored. In the end, both the histrionic circulation of such images *and* the urge to suppress and ignore the reality they expose are part and parcel of what gives acts of spectacular violence their inimitable power.

The crisis of bearing witness to extreme violence and cruelty that ought not to exist but does—and in massive proportions—should not be dismissed. Such ethical and existential quandaries are integral to how violence circulates in the social body and key to the struggle to carve a sense of security and order back into a chaotic world. As I have shown, however, the search for certainty can accelerate cycles of violence that refuse to be fixed in time and place. Another means of confronting the questions without answers that arise from such overwhelming pain and suffering must be found. This, to me, means sitting with acts and images that I would rather suppress, accepting the shock and horror that are their due, and seeking a way of understanding this violence that gives in to neither silence nor hysteria, nor to the urge to blame and explain.

Villa Nueva, Guatemala, August 2012

I have just finished an interview with the police chief of Villa Nueva. Late for another appointment, I'm trying to make my exit as politely as possible when he turns abruptly to his computer—a huge flat screen mounted behind him—and pulls up an image of a man's half-charred body lying face down in a wheelbarrow in the blazing sun, a broken length of pipe protruding from the anus. A half dozen police are gathered in the background, with only their black uniform pants and boots visible, and one man's latex-gloved hands. Then the police chief commences flipping images rapid fire across that giant screen, images from his personal data-base. There are smashed heads and headless bodies in San Jose Pinula minors' prison from when MS broke the SUR, and in Pavoncito prison when the paisas rioted and killed a bunch of mareros; a pile of half-clothed male bodies, some of them headless, piled promiscuously on top of one another; and a severed head caught in a shaft of light in an otherwise pitch-black room. Many, many others flicker across the screen in a horrible blur. He shows me pictures taken from Zeta200 cell phones of a man posing with a human heart in his hand, a dead nine-year-old boy, and ghoulish grins on decapitated heads lined up one next to the other. He flips through them quickly, occasionally turning to me with a grave expression as if I should understand, until he stops on the last image: a teenage girl, the photo labeled *La Descuartizada* (the Dismembered Girl). Her legs have been severed at the hips, her arms at the elbows. The stumps are layered with fat and muscle like meat in a butcher's shop, laid out on a blanket. The remains of her body seem to be glistening. For a moment I imagine she is covered in tears. But then on closer inspection it turns out to be only rain or dew. I ask the police chief if he can give me the photos. He responds with an appraising glance and a grin. "Why not?"[55]

I still have many of these photos, hidden away on a hard drive. The last image, La Descuartizada, haunts me the most, and it is the one I know least about. The image's atrocious intimacy and the total lack of information provoke endless questions. Who did this, and why? Was it personal? Did she suffer long before she died? Her hair has been clumsily shorn away, suggesting defile-ment before death. There are no visible wounds besides her missing limbs. There is hardly any blood. Did the killer or killers do this to her as a means of making someone who loved her suffer? Or was she chosen at random to become the bearer of some message to some third party in a contest of wills that had nothing to do with her? Or was she involved in some bad business, did she cross the wrong ally or enemy, and was in some sense an agent of her own disaster?

My questions and my curiosity are accompanied by a surge of fascinated horror and a quickening of the pulse. The image of La Descuartizada, this anonymous unfortunate, has made me an erstwhile witness to a crime the details of which I will never know, and now she is victim to my unkempt imagination. I am, like all witnesses distant and near, sucked into the vortex of the crime. Her image draws me in, and I cannot help but become party to her violation.

———

This is where I had once thought to place the image of La Descuartizada, but for better or for worse, the book's publishers will not allow it. Such images are, however, found easily enough on the internet, accessible to all at the click of a button. And like La Descuartizada, their immediate impact is to paralyze, to undermine the capacity for language and even thought. The visceral and psychological shock of witnessing such an image is beneath and beyond words, and saying anything risks saying the "wrong thing" and deepening the subject's denigration and one's own complicity. But letting La Descuartizada's victimizers simply speak for themselves is also a form of complicity and would make me no better than a voyeur. Worse, it would be giving in to the power of violence and pain to silence and steal our voices. Through voice we have language, and through language, the power to describe and gain some control over what counts as reality.[56] Like legions of others whose violated bodies are forced before the public eye, La Descuartizada is a window into a world in which mere words spoken by mere people have lost their meaning. I *have* to make her mean something or forfeit meaning making altogether. But is it possible to do this without foisting upon her my own need for a sense of safety and certainty, participating once again in the alienating violence of our constant ordering of the world?

Her absolute anonymity layers her image into the endless mosaic of nameless dead floating about the internet and infesting collective consciousness. Her violation represents an endgame of human callousness; the image of her ruined body captures hell incarnate, but the details of her story remain out of reach. This photograph flattens the particularities of her life and her death into the vague and overwhelming horror of the world. Like so many others, she emerges before our eyes shorn of history and of place.

In the erasure of her stories, dreams, hopes, and fears, perhaps she can be translated into a means of connection beyond the intellect and beneath the categories of difference that so deeply divide humans from one another. Can she remind us that no matter how diverse the human species may be, no matter how distinct and untranslatable our experiences on this earth may seem from those of distant others, we remain irrevocably linked through the undeniable fact of our bodies? This would be kinship through awareness of carnality. As Kanan Makiya wrote of other crimes in other places, "The violation of the human body . . . has a visceral, irrational, and irrevocable quality about it. It is the bedrock under all the layers of horrible things that human beings do to one another."[57]

But in the end, I do not know how to bridge the yawning abyss that La Descuartizada exposes, that undermines any attempt to draw some kind of universal truth out of such horror. Even my own attempt to do so ends up signaling my remarkable privilege, reifying an irrevocable distance and disjuncture. I am a white, educated, comfortably middle-class male citizen of the United States whose power and freedom emerge out of the self-same histories that make La Descuartizada's suffering possible in the first place. Her image makes me face myself. To honestly face La Descuartizada means to come up against the very limits of our fears and desires about our own vulnerability, personal and bodily dignity, and mortality.[58] The degrees of separation between her and me are vast and innumerable, and yet I can find no reason or argument that justifies her infinite violation and my safe, secure well-being. It is by pure chance that I was born into a place from which I may witness her destruction and not the other way around, and it is precisely this irrevocable distance that makes my speech possible and her violation so absolute. She cannot speak. They have stolen what words she might have spoken. Who can give them back? Across an arbitrary and absolute divide, her image screams. It is deafening and encased in silence.

Farewell, Guatemala City

In my last days living in Guatemala City, I threw myself a going-away party on the roof garden of my apartment building. This place had always been my sanctuary. It had brick benches, barbecue grills, neat carpets of manicured grass, and a polished concrete patio. The building's elevator gleamed, brushed steel interior burnished mirrorlike, and the buttons glowed a phosphorescent blue.

The day of the party, with help from Calavera and Irineo, the building's custodian, I swept out the patio, prepared the grill, and set up a small stereo on the rooftop garden. I checked over my cache of fireworks, bought especially for this occasion: mortars of various sizes and "butterflies," small blobs of magnesium and phosphorus that explode in red and blue and yellow a few seconds after their fuses are lit. When all was ready, Irineo went back to his post guarding the entrance, Calavera went to fetch Eddy, his adopted brother, and I stood smoking a cigarette, watching the sun set over the city. To the south, I could see the glittering high-rises of the zona viva, with its malls and hotels and nightclubs, and the hazy blue outline of the Volcano of Fire smoking on the distant horizon; to the north, the Tower of Tribunals and the historic zone; and in the east, the dense green slopes where the rich build their enclaves rising above the city. I watched the underbellies of passenger planes against the sky above, arriving from and bound for far-flung cities.

As dusk descended, my guests began to trickle in. Guided by a half-baked notion of conducting a haphazard social experiment, I had invited practically everyone I knew: social workers, journalists and government functionaries, scholars and taxi drivers, gangsters and ex-cons and police. Elizabet and Elena, gang rehabilitation social workers who had given me passage into the prisons, were the first to arrive, followed shortly by Calavera and Eddy. My *kakero* friends—as the relatively rich are called here—showed up in force. Most of them were upper-middle-class professionals—doctors and businessmen and bureaucrats—with whom I played rugby a couple of times a week on the military grounds a few blocks from my apartment. Journalists from Reuters and a few stringers for Associated Press also came, as well as some local crime-beat reporters I had met in court. There was also a smattering of government functionaries: Federico (the investigator in Andy's case) and some lawyers from the prosecutor's office, but no police. Scholars from local research institutes came, but the evangelical pastors I had invited did not. Neither did Gato. Throughout the evening, I called him a few times, and each time he said he was about to get a taxi and come over, but somehow I knew he would not. At the last minute Cheeky decided to come, after I told him I would pay for the taxi. Several young men from Villa Nueva and zone 18—whom I had met and befriended through my work with Gato's antiviolence outreach programs—also made it. Smiley and Silence, ex-mareros struggling to maintain peaceful lives, came early but left almost immediately. Neither felt safe outside his home at night. "You know what could happen," Silence muttered apologetically as he said good-bye. Tommy came, but thankfully, without his band of solvent-sniffing extortionists.

As the evening lurched into the night, my guests clustered on the roof garden in awkward, isolated circles, drinking my beer and whiskey. I stuck to cheap red wine, my grin a deepening purple through the evening. Around 10 p.m., Elena handed me her cell phone. It was Juande calling from Pavón prison, sending me the well wishes of Mo, Shaggy, Ervin, and the rest of the boys. Earlier that week I had caught the bus up the Carretera El Salvador to see them, trudging one last time down the rutted, muddy road to the prison gate. The fog was thick, and I could see perhaps thirty yards ahead. I walked past the army base, where soldiers leaned against an armored vehicle and smoked one cigarette after another. I passed the women's prison, silent except for guards in gray uniforms conversing quietly as they queued up to buy hot breakfast from an old woman with a woven basket. I passed the squat, brooding presence of maximum security facilities housing gang and cartel leaders. Perhaps Pavón has disappeared altogether, I thought, not without a guilty sense of hope, swallowed by the rain, sunk into the earth. I might walk a repeating loop forever, passing the same men in uniform coalescing and dissolving in the fog.

On this last visit I took no notes, smuggled in no camera, recorded no dialogue. I just wanted to say good-bye. Without the distraction of trying to collect information, the boredom, the tension, and the immense sadness of the place bore into me more deeply than ever before. All those lives wasted in that limbo, and I had milked their desperation all this time. After a last lunch at a restaurant run by two gay men who had once posed for pictures before their floral still life, hands on chubby hips, Juande and I took a stroll along the perimeter fence. The sun had burned away the last of the fog, and men gathered in small groups, talking and looking up into the blue, blue sky.

Standing on my rooftop terrace talking to Juande, city lights glowing yellow on every horizon, I felt again the terrible expectation of purgatory, waiting for that freedom that might one day come. Or never.

"I'm going to see you get out of that place," was all I could say. "I'm gonna see you on the outside."

"If God wills it," he replied. Then we said good-bye.

Below me, dispersed throughout the city, were spaces that are prisons in all but name: ad hoc detention centers in police stations where the arrested might spend weeks without regular food or water awaiting a hearing before a judge; abandoned middle-class homes renovated by evangelical churches into privately run drug rehabilitation centers. They hold drunks, drug addicts, and clinically insane inmates, remanded there by exasperated families or else caught by the "hunting parties" sent out by the pastors to pick up homeless derelicts. Some stay for years at a time, giving and hearing endless testimonials of sin and redemption in six-hour stretches, day in and day out.

There were also the innumerable abandoned lots where street children lock themselves away for protection from these hunting parties and from vigilantes and off-duty policemen, huffing gasoline and taking comfort from those stained concrete walls. Years before, Gato had taken me to visit one of these lots for the first time in the company of a born-again Christian official from the first lady's office. He promised the street urchins a rehab clinic in the walled-off trash heap where they hid each night. Of course it would never materialize. The holy bureaucrat had icy blue eyes and chain-smoked cigarettes lit by a paunchy assistant. "I will save them!" he bellowed at the steering wheel of his late-model Mercedes sedan as we left the petrol and feces stench in a cloud of nicotine. Months later I ran into him at a government gala and he remembered nothing, flashing an amiable grin as he gave me his business card again and rushed off to hobnob with US embassy officials.

Standing on my rooftop, I found myself avoiding the awkward party I had contrived. The little circles had hardened, each defined by class, profession, familiarity. No alchemical magic of connecting people from different walks of life here. I hadn't expected anything revolutionary, but still . . . . To each their prison, I thought, trapped by the conditions of life we are born into, by our bodies, our desires, our fears. Like the street children huffing away their fear in the abandoned lot, the most privileged do their best to push away the unwelcome realities of the world, and with far more success. I was reminded of an evening spent with a couple from New England in their twelfth-story condominium in zone 14 of Guatemala City. She worked with the World Heritage Foundation, and he was the media spokesperson for the US embassy. She bubbled with enthusiasm over indigenous artisans she employed to make perfect replicas of Crate and Barrel furniture. "And for a fraction of the price!" she kept saying. Later, he took me up to the palatial rooftop terrace—a lap pool, open bar, sauna—where we sipped single malt whiskey and smoked Cubans. It was a foggy night, and the city was reduced to a collection of high-rises floating like pleasure vessels above a vague luminescence far, far below. "The embassy treats us well," he remarked. "This is a good life." I couldn't disagree.

Toward 11 p.m., the storm that had been gathering all evening finally broke. Cold gusts of rain drove my party off the roof and into my polished concrete apartment, austere to the point of emptiness. I only had two chairs, a table, and a few handcrafted rugs and wall hangings, prompting a kakero friend to joke, "Gringo does Guatemala!"

Calavera had gotten more drunk than I had ever seen him, but still managed to rescue the stereo from the rain. I plugged it in, and reggaeton beats caromed about the echo chamber of an apartment. The cacophony was comforting, because things seemed to be falling apart. Elizabet and Elena had disappeared into my bedroom, trying to comfort Eddy, who was having some kind of hysterical episode. Cheeky and the young men from Villa Nueva were the only ones dancing. The kakeros gathered in the margins, talking to one another.

Here in the dim lamplight, cigarette haze wafting out the balcony window, Tommy emerged from a shadowed corner to greet me. He was dressed in a cream cashmere sweater. A year had passed since I took part in his extortions.

Months before, I had returned with him to zone 8, careening around in his car to visit dance clubs where a few of his lovers worked. They were dim, noisy places where Tommy greeted the bouncers by name and harassed other patrons. "Do you know Tommy?" he kept shouting at apparent strangers. "Do you?" We ended up at a brothel he owned, staffed by veteran prostitutes. Business was slow. The women sat in plastic chairs and beat-up couches against the wall, a few swaying to lugubrious love songs. Tommy proceeded to entertain everyone by lofting liter beer bottles across the room toward a small metal wastebasket, laughing uproariously each time they shattered on the ragged linoleum.

The last time I had seen Tommy, he was whiskey drunk in a 1960s-themed karaoke bar with a sixteen-year-old—his steady girl—and her friend in tow. But there in my apartment, he was sober and thinner, with dark circles around his eyes. He had become somehow more reptilian, if that is the right word. We stood together, and I watched him watch the kakeros laughing at some inside joke.

"You know fine people," he said, an unexpected awe in his voice. He seemed unsure of how to conduct himself with such a crowd.

Then he leaned in close, his lips almost brushing against my ear. "I am having troubles," he said in a stage whisper and glanced quickly over his shoulder. "They put four bullets into one of my women. Sandra. Do you remember her? She was so beautiful. And they put five in one of my little girls. All because some business went bad, very bad, and I had to kill somebody. And since then they have been after me." He paused for a moment and scrutinized me, as if to measure the effect of his words.

Before I could reply, he went on, "You should have asked me more questions. So I could tell you more things for your book. Tommy knows so many things! We should have spent more time together. Gato and all these others you interview," he snorted, "they live everything in their imagination. But I, I live in reality. I have been involved in some serious shit. Look up the *Tikal Futura* shooting. I organized that. That was I. Look it up on YouTube and you will see how I am."

I told him I was sorry for his loss.

He shrugged, flashing a ghostly smile. "We should have spent more time together."

I told him I agreed, but suddenly someone was tapping me on the shoulder. I turned to find Cheeky looking apprehensive. "Anthony!" he said. "There is no beer. We've run out."

Grateful for the intervention, I apologized to Tommy. "We'll have to finish our conversation later." He nodded and turned away. I have not seen him since.

Once again, I played the conscientious host. No party of mine was going to go without alcohol. I told my guests I would be back shortly and enlisted Cheeky and a few of the guys from Villa Nueva. They followed me out the door, piling into the gleaming elevator, and descended to the ground floor. Irineo was sitting at the receptionist desk, his eyes red with fatigue, hunched over a tiny radio. The rain had stopped and the air outside was cool and still. The street was very quiet. I led my little hunting party to a store a few blocks down the street. The sign, which sported a black rooster head and "*Tienda Magali*" in block letters, was illuminated in faint halogen light. Inside, a few middle-aged men sat in plastic chairs around a scratched metal table, sipping rum and coke from little plastic cups. I had seen them all before, though I knew none of them by name. They watched my companions, who had gathered shyly at the entrance, with open suspicion. I asked for a dozen liters of Gallo beer from the storekeeper, a weary, middle-aged woman sitting behind a counter girded with steel bars mounted to the floor and the ceiling. She handed me the bottles in plastic bags, and I passed them to Cheeky and the others. I paid and nodded good night to the other patrons, and we hurried back into the night.

I could hear the music thumping when we emerged from the elevator onto my floor. But when I walked back into my apartment, the living room was empty save for Calavera, shoeless in white socks, standing forlorn in front of my open balcony window, and two other young men—one from Villa Nueva, the other from el Limon in zone 18.

"*Todos se volaron,*" Calavera said. "They all flew away." He was contrite, as if he were somehow to blame. Swearing under my breath, I checked the bedroom. Elizabet and Elena had left as well. Only Eddy was there, curled up in my bed, moaning softly in a nightmare.

I wondered to myself if I should feel betrayed. Whatever, I thought. Fuck it.

"Alright *muchachos*. We're all that's left. Let's light some fireworks."

And so we gathered the beer, the stereo, and a backpack full of pyrotechnics and headed back up to the roof garden. Thunderheads flashed in the distance, and the city lit up the warship clouds in stunning detail. I set up the firing tubes, and we launched round after round of rockets into the sky, shouting and exultant with each Technicolor explosion. But then we launched a faulty one. Instead of exploding in the sky, the mortar started falling back toward the rooftop. "*Ojo!*" I shouted. "Look out!" I hit the deck as it detonated, shoot-ing streams of heat and light across the terrace. When I got to my feet again, all I could see were hazy figures coughing and groping through a thick cloud of acrid smoke.

I had to catch my breath. "Is everyone okay?" I called out.

Like a seasoned mariachi, Cheeky let out a high-pitched cry, and everyone else joined in.

We went on like that, deep into the night. Sometime later, Calavera was stumbling so badly in his now sopping wet socks that I took him back down to the apartment in the hopes he would join Eddy. As I emerged again onto the terrace, Cheeky, confusing a mortar for a firecracker, lit one and tossed it off the roof, where it detonated in the street, cracking a warehouse window and setting off car alarms. Later, when he passed out slumped in a corner, we lit all the remaining butterflies and tossed them at him until he leapt up hol-lering and slapping at himself. On and on, until there were no more fireworks and the beer was once again and finally finished. I gave Cheeky and the boys headed for Villa Nueva and zone 18 taxi money, and we said good-bye. Dawn was approaching. When I walked back into the living room, Eddy was curled up on the floor, sobbing, as Calavera stood over him, a swaying silhouette against the faint outlines of the city. "God sees all things, brother," he whis-pered, over and over again. "God sees all things, and forgives."

———————

Once again I am alone on my rooftop. I am exhausted, sad in a soft sort of way, and relieved. The clouds have moved off to the east, and I can see the last stars glimmering. Only passenger planes flying low over the city disturb the stillness of the hour. A few days hence, I will give away my furniture and kitchenware to Irineo and the other guards, pack up the few objects worth keeping, and board one of those planes bound for California. Rising up, up, and away from the runway, I will press my face against a cabin window. There are the high-rises of the zona viva, the Palace of Culture, the Tower of Tribu-nals, the bustling markets. There is the cemetery, an uneven swath of green on the edge of the ravine of trash, and the ravines cutting jaggedly through the city. There is the boulevard where they killed Andy. There is my apartment building and my roof garden. A minute later, the plane flies so high and so far that the city and its sprawling suburbs give way to mountains and valleys of dense jungle. And then I rise up through a ceiling of clouds.

CHAPTER 6

Liminal Redemption

Our image of happiness is indissolubly bound up with the image of redemption.

—Walter Benjamin, *Reflections*[1]

One night in 2011, around 8:00 p.m., Mario Flores, aka Joker, a former clique leader of Barrio18, was shot six times—once in the back and five times in the head—in the crowded zone 12 market of Guatemala City. He was twenty-five years old. Joker's killers also gunned down his seventeen-year-old brother-in-law as he tried to flee. His body lay ten meters away. Cecilia, Joker's wife, arrived fifteen minutes later to find her husband and brother sprawled among spent 9mm casings and a milling crowd of policemen and civilians. She screamed and flung herself across Joker's body while the crowd looked on and newspaper photographers snapped pictures.

Forty days later, sitting across from me at a Formica table in a Wendy's, Cecilia tried to smile. Her eyes were bloodshot. She clutched a rag soaked with paint thinner, brought it to her nose, and inhaled. "He always told me, 'One of these days they're going to kill me,'" she said. "He told me when they did, I must collect his things. He did not want anything to fall into the pigs' hands." Before the police could stop her, she had lifted his wallet, cell phone, and jewelry from his body.

"Who is the 'they' he knew would come after him?" I asked.

She shrugged and looked down at the table. "Who knows?"

Joker's body bore dozens of tattoos, the most prominent an "18" in black ink across his chest. This was enough for the police to pigeonhole him and his brother-in-law as Barrio18 extortionists and to write off the double murder as a settling of accounts between him and his would-be victims. The newspapers followed suit. *Nuestro Diario's* nota roja proclaimed: "Gangster extortionists paid back with the same coin."[2] Their murders, like so many Guatemala City murders, were written off as brutal street justice and quickly washed away in the tide of bodies that flood the headlines each day.

But scratch the surface of this story, and the official narrative becomes immediately suspect. Cecilia insisted that Joker had left the gang two years before and dedicated himself to honest work, an argument corroborated by officials who worked with Joker at CONJUVE, a government office involved in antiviolence youth intervention. Cecilia also claimed Joker distanced himself from his clique to stop her brother Cesar from joining Barrio18. "They fought and fought. Joker never wanted Cesar to be in the gang and he made him leave." Joker extended this message to other youngsters as well. Every few weeks he would go before schoolchildren and give his testimony, taking his shirt off to show the tattoos and scars, souvenirs of the violence he had survived.

However, he had to maintain a double life. Cecilia wanted him out of the gang permanently. But, she said, he kept in regular contact with gang members as a means of protection. He also tried to intervene against what he saw as his gang's growing brutality against enemies and extortion victims. His advocacy put him in direct conflict with his gang's interests. "Joker is dead because he tried to keep his clique from threatening women and children," claimed another former gang leader, "not just in the other gang, but the families of extortion victims too. He wanted to stop them from hurting innocent people. And now that he is dead I fear what will happen in his Barrio." Cecilia would not accuse her husband's homies of betraying him, but neither would she accept their offer to care for her. Huffing away her sorrow and carefully sidestepping his former homies, Cecilia wanted to leave it all behind. "It is better to be ignorant," she said.

Were Joker and his brother-in-law killed by vigilantes in revenge for extorting shopkeepers in zone 12, as the newspapers and police claimed? Or was he recognized by a rival gang and killed in a gang war from which he had tried to extricate himself and his family? Or could it be that Joker was killed by his homies because he advocated for peace, or simply because he betrayed them with his absence? As for so many boys and young men caught up in gang life, the possibility of escape was always thin and fading. And now the "truth" of his fate is buried amid the explanations that pretend to neatly tie up all loose ends.

———

Musing on a Parisian café garcon's subtle deviations from how such a person ought to comport himself, Sartre wrote, "There are indeed many precautions to imprison a man in what he is, as if we lived in perpetual fear that he might escape from it. That he might break away and elude his condition."[3] The gaze of another fixes a person in his or her skin and position in society, and in the dominant ideological and symbolic order.[4] We are all bound, trapped by the expectations of others, by the ways we have learned we must be. From the ways we talk to the contours of the futures we conceive for ourselves, the space of possibility in which we each live and die allows for infinite variation, but only within certain boundaries, and these boundaries are strictly policed.[5] Violating the expectations imposed by these lines of differentiation and hierarchy inevitably presents some kind of danger: a risk to the violator and to others invested in safeguarding the status quo. But this risk is not apportioned equally. As I have shown, the marero forms a particularly dense, packed subjectivity embodying the very worst ills of postwar society. This, of course, has consequences for the young men seeking to leave the gangs. The suspicion, rage, and fear moored in the mareros make their "condition" difficult indeed to elude.

Joker's escape was transitory and quickly reversed. He died like so many others have and will, their deaths foretold, written into their lives and their skins. Sucked into the media stream, his story was forced into the stark narrative of brutal street justice and deserved death. In the concatenation of contradictory loyalties, his efforts to change, or seem to change, into something other than what was expected were erased. I have met many men struggling to carve out a place of safety against Joker's all-too-common fate. Some were able to narrate their experiences with excruciating detail and apparent honesty. Others were so eager to distance themselves from what they once were that their stories appeared flimsy and false. A few became, and still are, my friends. All of them struggle within the severely delimited space of possibility in which the radical transformation from a marero into something else might take place. Those who have survived continue to search for some kind of redemption: to make amends to God, society, and themselves.

But the redemption these men seek is ever incomplete because the world they live in does not allow for its possibility. Even as they become evangelical converts, protected witnesses, drug addicts, and so on, the past they try to abandon never seems far enough away. Whatever internal transformation a former gang member may have undergone, the evidence of gang belonging remains in myriad signs that are not so easily erased. For some, their history is written in the tattoos and scars staining their bodies like the mark of Cain.

For others, it remains in their physical and social habits. But most important, the violence they claim is behind them continues to invade and shape their communities, homes, and daily lives.

To *redeem* means to ransom, free, or rescue by paying a price. It also means to free from the consequences of sin and to make good on a promise by performing it. Payment, purification, and performance. Essentially, "redemption" is a radical reformation of one's relationship to one's past and a reinvention of one's self in the present. While *liminal* most often describes a transient, shifting moment between two states, by *liminal redemption* I mean a permanent state of becoming, or failing to become, or seeming to become a new person freed from the debts of the past.[6]

When a marero seeks to be something other than a marero, what scripts can possibly make this transformation legible—to himself, to his gang, and to his community—and what routes can lead away from a violent death so certain that it seems like fate? It is the struggle to find a way out where apparently none exists that I wish to chronicle. I want to rescue Joker's and others' efforts to make themselves anew away from the gangs, to pull away from implacable gravity even if they so often fail. I want to make them "grievable."[7] The dystopian future that gangs have come to represent for so many often seems intransigent, omnipresent, and without recourse other than more violence. Ex-mareros' stories destabilize this fatalistic perspective, even if the cracks and fissures they escape into are transient, fading, or false.

CERTAIN DEATH

I met Travieso in Pavón prison a month after he had been transferred there from sector II of the Preventivo, home to active Barrio18 members. He was bone thin, had "18" tattooed on each eyelid, and stuttered painfully when he got stirred up. For years, he said, he had led a Barrio18 clique in a Pacific coast port city before getting arrested for homicide. Once in prison among his Guatemala City brethren, Travieso found himself isolated and picked on. Other members beat him because he could not or would not participate in extortion rackets organized from inside the prison. I suspect he simply could not maintain leadership and organization housed so far from his hometown. To pressure him to cooperate, he said, they killed his pregnant girlfriend, who had moved to Guatemala City to be near him, and chopped her into pieces. Shortly afterward he made his second desperate run for the guards' office, and prison authorities finally agreed to transfer him to a different facility. If they had not, Travieso claimed, his so-called homies would have killed him. Like other gang-involved men I interviewed, he evinced a deep paranoia. As we spoke, he would glance about nervously as if hidden assailants lurked around every corner.

"They kill everyone," he said of his gang. "One has to be in their game, you have to be in their periphery, at the edge of the game they are playing. It is a hard game, a game of death. Everything is death death death!" His voice cracked, and he paused to collect himself. "Death of drivers, death of women, death of children, death of gangsters, death of family, all the way to death of government officials. . . . They are willing to kill anyone. They are prepared. . . . When I belonged to the gang we were men of death . . . suicidal men, like terrorists."

Ex-mareros' struggle to carve out a precarious peace between their violent past and unforgiving present is a fight for life itself. Success is contingent upon myriad factors far beyond their control, and failure can mean death, or worse. Constructed as thoroughly killable killers in the social imaginary, emissaries of the worst failures of postwar progress, and marked for execution by their old homies, they have little room to maneuver.

Their former homies refer to them as "Gayboy Gangsters" and *pesetas* (pennies), because they aren't worth a damn. In conversation with me, former mareros usually referred to themselves simply as "ex," a deceivingly simple term conjuring up the nonspace, the identity-as-nothing in which former gang members find themselves.[8] Many are left with only the stains of the violence— on their bodies and in their psyches—that was once their claim to power. As one incarcerated ex-MS member said, "If I spent time thinking about all those I have hurt, I would die crying."

Guatemalan society is in general no more forgiving of ex-gang members than of active ones.[9] "You cannot change once you are in. You cannot find another road," said a public relations officer for a transnational anti-gang task force, summing up popular sentiments toward mareros. "Really, I have not met a single person who has successfully abandoned his gang."[10] With so little public sympathy for mareros and so little faith in their capacity to leave la vida loca behind, former gangsters struggle to find shelter and support. Going straight may in fact make their already tenuous chances at survival thinner. Still caught in the crosshairs of rival gangs and law enforcement, fleeing mareros must also face the wrath of their former comrades in arms;

today, both MS and Barrio18 prohibit most members from ever leaving, and they kill those who seek to escape without permission.

The avenues to escape were not always so narrow. A decade ago, it was possible to honorably exit the gang through negotiation with the gang leader and a promise to go straight. Tired of gang life, a homie could decide to leave, settle down, go to church, get married, have kids, and get a job. The gang would honor this decision, as Andy claimed, as long as "the vato didn't start screwing around again, using the lessons [like robbing, intimidating, extorting] the gang taught him to enrich himself." If an ex-gang member could stick to the straight and narrow, his former gang would look upon him kindly, as if "maybe the vato has changed. As long as he didn't get into any shit. If he goes and fucks up one time, the beast will take him. If you screw up *one time*," Andy held a finger in the air, "the beast will take you. Do not screw up. We've got our eye on you. And since the Barrio has so many people watching, you will always be watched."

The gang acted like an archangel of order, protecting its monopoly over illicit activities in its territory. But over time, what passed as the maras' permissive generosity and goodwill toward former colleagues gone straight has worn away. Today, the maras are far more likely to hunt down and kill anyone who tries to leave, no matter the reason. "The sucker who runs gets a green light"—meaning a death sentence—was a refrain I heard over and over again from active and retired gang members alike.[11]

The reasons given me for the loss of all viable escape routes are contradictory and ambiguous. Some mareros connect the change to heightening police pressure and the maras' need to become more professional and more hermetic. "In the early 2000s, the police started to take a much deeper interest in how the maras worked," Juande recollected, "and the vatos began to understand that all these guys that left by becoming Christians, a lot of them talked to the police. . . . The logic now is 'they must be killed, they know too much.'" Juande claimed it was the MS leader El Diabólico who first pushed for a harsher policy. "While he was imprisoned in Pavoncito, he gave the order to other members of the Coronados Locos Salvatrucha to start killing anyone who left. The clique grew, and the others followed their example."

Some say the order to close down exit routes came from El Salvador, where in the late 1990s and early 2000s draconian mano dura policing drove many members to jump ship and hide in neighboring Guatemala. Around 2006, to enforce loyalty and survival under heightened state pressure, Salvadoran gang leaders imposed harsher policies for those who might want to escape. "An order was sent out to every clique: 'You will enter, but you will never leave,'" Andy said. "It came from El Salvador. Many from there came fleeing here, and so we found them, and were like 'What's this dude doing here?' And they were like 'I left, but I'm a Christian.'"

Gang leaders in Guatemala would call their Salvadoran counterparts to find out what was going on. "'For sure bro,' they would answer, 'the guy went running and here we're getting fucked.'" Andy shrugged. "It was lost, you understand. With all of the pressure, we had to just kill those who fled."[12]

Finally, there is widespread consensus—among both gangsters and security experts—that too many homies claiming to go straight instead went into business for themselves, becoming freelance hitmen, joining local drug cartels, or starting up their own extortion networks. The maras, caught up in a constant feud against each other and reeling from heightened police pressure, could not abide these interlopers.

Whatever the combination of causes closing down previously available exits from the gangs, today the bottom line is clear: ex-mareros, already hunted by police, vigilantes, and rival gangs, must survive the wrath of their former homies as well. The vast majority do not survive.

THE PROBLEM OF ATTRIBUTION

What drives a gang member to give up la vida loca and pursue a peaceful existence? What kinds of policies and programs, if any, can draw mareros out of the gang and help them survive? For government ministries, NGOs, and funding institutions involved in antiviolence work, the problem of helping boys and young men leave gang life begins with a basic conundrum of cause and effect. This conundrum, in policy speak, is known as "the problem of attribution."[13]

As the director of a Guatemalan antiviolence NGO lamented, "Any number of events, experiences, or influences can lead a gangster to say 'no more.' Maybe his brother gets killed, and he doesn't want to die too and leave his mother alone. Maybe he has a child and decides he wants to be there for his kid. Maybe the gang betrays him and he's disgusted and wants something different."[14]

The motives and conditions pushing gang members out of violence are multifarious and contingent. This is a problem for antiviolence groups because most funders, especially large state donors like USAID, the biggest single source of money for Central American security and antiviolence programs, are not interested in such nuanced entanglements.[15] To get support from these agencies, projects that promise to rehabilitate ex-mareros must demonstrate in no uncertain terms that their strategies will have concrete benefits: a direct and verifiable reduction of violence, measured by a drop in homicides, stolen cell phones, femicides, and so on. As Mark Lopes, a USAID official in charge of overseeing projects in Central America, said, "I want my staff to connect the programs we fund with a murder that hasn't happened yet."[16]

Then there is the problem of scale. Most gang rehabilitation projects that have even a modicum of success work on a local basis, dependent upon a single social worker, priest, or official who has enough cachet with his or her community to make a difference. But this approach flies in the face of what most international donors want to support. "Don't talk to me about one priest, or one nun, and how charismatic they are," Lopes exclaimed. "I want to deal with hundreds of thousands of lives. How can I make my money work for that many people? If a project rests on the goodwill of one nun or one priest, how can it be sustainable?"

Growing gang intervention projects beyond the local—a single neighbor-hood, or a single church parish—can be quite difficult. One widely celebrated success story comes from Ciudad Peronia, a peri-urban community of Guatemala City where for years war between the rival gangs Los Metales and Los Caballos had terrorized the community.[17] In 2009 Pastor Mardoqueo, an evangelical minister who lives in Peronia directing a church, school, and community center, brokered an unprecedented peace between the two gangs. I spoke with him in a KFC in Guatemala City in 2011. He was open, articulate, and tired of being interviewed. He only agreed to talk to me after I convinced him I was not a journalist. In his experience, all journalists do "is ask questions, treat everyone like a circus animal, use our stories like vultures, and then leave."

"There are 65,000 people in Peronia," he said. "And in 2009 there were 220 gang members. The gangs were responsible for 75 percent of the violence—and I thought to myself, 'How is it possible that 200 people determine the fate of 65,000, make 65,000 live in fear?' There were five shootings a week, many of them in public spaces."

Leaders of both gangs sought him out to help them make peace. On July 1, 2009, Los Metales and Los Caballos made a formal truce. They invited the media, who made it a spectacle.[18] Mardoqueo then offered to go to other churches, leaders of the local business community, and municipal and national governments to gather funds and support, and to try to expand the project to other communities. But he discovered that no one would help. Other church leaders, Mardoqueo said, were jealous of the fame he had garnered and protective of their positions in their communities. The national finance minister offered to lend him $50,000 of international donor money if he could guarantee the investment with matching funds. "I told him, 'If I had that kind of money I wouldn't be here asking for more. And if the mareros knew I had $50,000 they would kill me!" The business sector and local representatives of government proved more fractious and difficult to deal with than the mareros had been. "Some of them threatened to show up at meetings armed with pistols, and often refused to sit at the same table as their rivals."

Officials from USAID approached him with an offer of $30,000. But they would give him the money only *if* he changed his project from one of "reinsertion"—helping former gang members find jobs and reintegrate into society—to "prevention," stopping kids from joining gangs. As a general policy, the US government does not offer support to criminals, even reformed ones. "'We have no funds for what you are doing,'" USAID officials told him. Mardoqueo's reply: "But we don't need prevention."

In the end, Mardoqueo gave up on trying to gather support from outsiders or go beyond his community. He claimed that of the two hundred-odd mareros in Ciudad Peronia, thirty had established stable lives. The others still struggled with drug addiction, deep poverty, or crime. "The problem mareros face is something on the inside," he said in parting. "But it goes deep, and the church cannot help them with all that they need. The church can only help with spiritual problems, but the rest? Who will assist with their poverty, the educational training they need, and the issues with justice and security that they face every day?"

However, the majority of Guatemalans seem to share the sentiments directing US funding policies: no succor of any kind for criminals, period. Amid the overwhelming poverty and inequality defining Guatemalan society today, paying special attention to mareros' lives and livelihoods strikes many as wrongheaded, naive, and deeply unfair.

Mareros deserve no help not only because they have caused such pain to others, goes the argument, but also because they will twist any material aid to evil ends. I heard many tales of mareros turning gifts of goodwill to their own devices. It is difficult to tell what is true and what is urban myth. Take, for example, the story of the church group that provided incarcerated MS members with a clutch of rabbits so they could establish a prison rabbit farm. The gangsters' rabbits quickly multiplied, and all seemed to be going to plan,— that is, until guards discovered that the rabbits had been put to work burrowing an escape tunnel beneath the prison walls.

A public prosecutor related a slightly more plausible account of a project in 2008 to give ex-mareros honest work. Using international and local funding, an NGO employed them in a metalworking shop, where they could learn how to make fences, balcony railings, and the like. The Guatemalan government matched funds for materials and workspace. "Perfect," the prosecutor said,

> and they went through the process. . . . They bought the welding equipment, and they gave them the iron, and the metal sheeting for doors, and some model frames to make pretty designs. . . . It worked for a few days. Then, they made homemade guns (*armas hechizas*). They didn't make any balcony railings, or doors, or window-frames. Nothing. They were like, "Why should we make doors, why should we make windows? Anyway, one has to work to make them, and they're difficult to sell. Better to make guns." They circulated dozens of homemade guns in Villa Nueva, and the NGO was shut down.

The moral of the story is clear; any tool, any favor offered the gangs will be turned against society for the mareros' benefit, often in the most violent way possible.

BODY AND SOUL

Once a marero, always a marero, as the saying goes. "That's why," Andy said, "when you enter now they tell you that there will be no turning over another leaf, your soul already belongs to the barrio, to the devil (bestia)." To deprive the devil of his due, many mareros try to escape the gang by finding sanctuary with God, particularly an evangelical God, who intervenes on their behalf.

Being born again as a good evangelical Christian has become the most popular "peaceful" answer to and exit from maras in Guatemala, Central America, and indeed, throughout the Americas.[19] Ex-marero converts are part of an evangelical Christian phenomenon sweeping through large swaths of post–Cold War Latin America. Today, nearly half of Guatemala's population has become either charismatic or Pentecostal Christian.[20] Evangelical Christian "gang ministries" have grown in number and reach throughout the postwar period. With North American evangelical groups flush with cash and eager to extend their goodwill into the blighted corners of Central America, today they support Guatemala's (and Central America's) most popular and well-funded violence prevention initiatives.[21] In effect, rampant gang violence has been made "into a Christian problem with a Christian solution" attractive beyond the circles of the faithful themselves.[22] Today, even for liberal and ostensibly secular security officials throughout the Americas, gang ministries appear as the best, if not the only, viable peaceful solution to the problem of gangs.[23]

Becoming a good Christian no longer guarantees an ex-marero's survival. But perhaps unsurprisingly, it is the single most convincing transformation through which a former gangster can show the world, and himself, that he is redeemed. Ex-gangsters-cum-good-Christians' narratives tend to follow a particular, and familiar, script: conversion to faith provoked by great trial and suffering—physical and/or psychological—and a transformation of soul and body through which they try to keep the past firmly in the past.

David

David is a former member of Los Cyclones Salvatrucha, a now defunct MS clique that once operated in zone 18 of Guatemala City. He was thirty-three when we met at the Gloria de Dios (Glory of God) Ministry in the neighborhood where he grew up. He was a born-again Christian and gave regular testimonies in praise of God and conversion away from gang life. When he was a twenty-three-year old marero, members of a rival gang shot him three times in the head. "The first thing I thought of was of my family," his voice was high-pitched and strained, as if speaking took great effort.

> It is a kind of terror that I cannot explain in words. When I was in the street, they came with scissors and cut off my clothes. I put my arm to one side and there were pools of blood. In the middle of a situation like that. . . really it's terrible, and there are no words. The loss of blood. . . you have an incredible thirst. . . . "Water, I was saying, "Water." I wanted to go to sleep, the body was giving up. But I fought, because I knew if I went to sleep I wouldn't wake up. . . . I didn't think about God, but I wondered if there was a heaven or hell. If I die, I thought, I won't have done anything good. . . . I'd seen many of my companions hit the ground and never get up again. Just the yellow tape. I awoke in another place, all hooked up, a bullet lodged in my jaw. . . . [A] doctor told me that I was part of God's plan, because it was a miracle I was still alive.

The bullets did irreparable harm to his optical nerve, leaving him permanently blind, and damaged his motor skills. He did not immediately give up membership in the MS. But after a few months, he told them that as a marero, he could do nothing and give nothing. They agreed, released him of any further obligation, and left him to his own devices. He spent the next couple of years relearning how to do the simplest tasks.

Having lost his capacity to be a worthwhile soldier for MS, and abandoned by those for whom he had been willing to kill and be killed, David was lost. He wanted a new life away from the drugs and the violence, but, he said, man's will is weak. Left to his own devices, he was unable to turn away from the constant temptation of ephemeral pleasures and swollen pride gang life had given him. But, he said, God was not done with him. God sent two men, catechists from a local church, to bring him into the flock. For months David refused their offers. He even drew a gun at one point, threatening to shoot them through his front door. But they kept coming, and David started going to church. Then a dramatic transformation took place:

> Look, my flesh, my ego, my pride as a marero, all of it began to break down. God began to break me, to put me to pieces. . . . The most beautiful thing is that he himself came to put the pieces back together again, he reformed me after breaking me down. He put me back together, but in a distinct form, in a different way, with a different heart. Because as a marero, one has no feelings. There is no love for fellow man, there is NOTHING, there exists no God, no love. Love does not exist . . . except for love of the drugs. . . . But love for God, love toward children, to show love to children, all of that does not exist. But God put all of this anew into my heart. So it was an impressive thing because what I could not do with my effort, my will, God was able to do. God did it. . . . Many times I had tried to leave by myself, by my will, but man's will breaks too easily.

David has since transformed his broken body into a living message against violence. Unlike others who hide or burn away their gang tattoos, he would not give them up. He bore an M and an S tattooed on each of his elbows, among many others, which he refused to even cover with a long-sleeved shirt. They became part of his message of peace and redemption. As he made the rounds at several evangelical churches, some in rival gang territory, his scarred and tattooed body was a packed message and warning for children who might want to join up with the gangs.

"If I had not been blinded," he said, "I would still be with the gang, and I would probably be dead." The only other surviving members of his gang—he counted off three—were incarcerated for life.

> So, it's like when you eat cake, I chose the best slice, right, because I am outside and I can enjoy my liberty. . . and I'm not talking about enjoying life on the street.

No. I'm talking about the liberty that God has given me to speak of him, of having gotten to know him. . . . Many have died that don't have tattoos. And I, who is so stained, I go about with just a T-shirt. Through all this no one has come up and said, "Look, remember what you did to me that one time," or, "You are from MS," and shot me. Never. I have confidence that He who goes with me is more powerful than any weapon.

He has faced death threats. Once after he gave a sermon in Barrio18 territory, two boys attacked him outside the church. After forcing him to his knees, they demanded he explain the tattoos on his arms. "'Whatsup? You're of the Letters.' And I said to them, 'I was of the Two Letters. Now I serve God.' I begged their forgiveness for the hurt my gang might have done them." They did not kill him. Instead, they tried to cut away the tattoos by slashing his elbows with broken glass, then left him bleeding on the sidewalk.

David said it was God who kept him alive. It was God who was helping him, protecting him, because he was engaged in God's work. This belief has given him the strength to face incalculable dangers as he walks sightless through the territories of his former enemies. His faith is his shield that protects him from his past sins and the lens through which he interprets all the death he has witnessed while, against all odds, he has survived.

Silence

As usual, I met Silence in a Wendy's on the corner of Guatemala City's central park. The bells of the national cathedral chimed the hour, mixing with reggaeton music pumping from the storefronts. Seventeen years had passed since he joined the Barrio18, and a decade since he had left the gang for good. Silence was wearing a long-sleeved rugby jersey to hide the gang tattoos on his arms. He had already removed the most visible ones on his neck and wrists. To lose these vestigial markings of gang membership, Silence was going once a month to Alianza Jovenes, an antiviolence NGO. A trained nurse, who doubled as the receptionist, would don UV glasses and go to work on him with a laser gun. The machine, bought with USAID dollars, emits rapid-fire pulses of heat and light. Tattoo ink is embedded in several epidermal layers. The laser heats the skin cells until the ink boils, bursts the cell walls, and dissipates into the blood. Depending on the color of the ink and the location and age of the tattoo, the experience can range from mildly uncomfortable to extremely painful. Elbows and knees are particularly tender, and yellow ink is the most excruciating to remove.[24]

Sitting across from Silence at Wendy's, I asked again to see his tattoos. He looked over his shoulder, then rolled up his sleeve. He had a blue compression wrap on his right forearm and up past the elbow, faded and frayed, covering some of his partially erased tattoos. Again, he scanned the other patrons. There were few, and none were paying any attention to us, so he gingerly peeled back the compression wrap. There were a blotched demon's hand throwing a gang sign, a roughly drawn skyscraper, and an eight ball etched into his forearm and bicep. The lines of the hand and skyscraper had begun to blur, like the images of a dream upon waking, and the eight ball had faded to an ugly, uncertain smudge. Silence was waiting for these images to be erased completely, when he would have only the mottled scars of their exorcism, discolored patches of skin that would make his adolescent past with Barrio18 irretrievable to all but the keenest observer. But he could only visit the free clinic once a month, so his immaculate body was still years away.

An integral part of gangs' mystique and their visual circulation, mara tattoos are hieroglyphs communicating mareros' loyalty, history of violent deeds and incarceration, eulogies to slain comrades and loved ones, and so on. Depending on the audience, they inspire respect, fear, disgust, or wonder. Silence recalled the fear that showing his tattoos to robbery victims inspired. "We could rob a gasoline station with just a water pistol because of our tattoos," he laughed. Over the last two decades, however, gang tattoos have become the easiest way for law enforcement and vigilante groups to identify gang members, literally trapping tattooed mareros in their skins. These days, most mareros still on the street don't even get gang tattoos, and many only start etching their allegiance on their bodies in prison while serving life sentences. It still works to advertise the mara brand. Images of mareros' leering tattooed faces, long-nailed fingers curled into gang signs, gesticulating into the camera from packed prison cells, have become iconic worldwide.[25]

For his part, Silence wants his body to be immaculate to escape the image of what he was and now must convince the world he is not.

The Dream of Redemption

Before Silence could begin to transform his body, he said, he had to transform his soul. He claimed his spiritual redemption arrived unbidden one night in Pavoncito prison on the eve of the sureño riot to kill El Negro Beteta (see chapter 3). He had promised to throw himself into the front lines, and he expected to die. At the time, he was caught up in his violent destiny, convinced there was no other future. "The point is I had zero probability of being able to go straight (*cuadrarme*) successfully because I didn't have the will to do it. I had no hope of being able to do it. For me it was preferable to die, maybe in a prison riot. . . . I was going to die like a hero."

The night before the riot, he said, he had a dream of biblical proportions. In the many interviews I conducted with Silence, he often stumbled over his words, got stuck on minor tangents, or spoke so vaguely that we had to backtrack. He would apologize for his lack of eloquence, lamenting his adolescent addictions to crack, glue, and other substances that had addled his brain. But each time he recounted this vision of God and of his redeemed self, he spoke articulately and without hesitation, as if he had practiced the telling many times.

And then I had a dream that changed my life. I dreamed I was walking in another country, and I was listening to a young man who was telling me he had lived the same as I had lived, the same that I had suffered, and that he had changed. In my dream I was under the impression that someone had told him my experience and that this dude was making stuff up so that I would believe in his change and then believe that I myself could do it. "But," I said to myself, "he's not going to convert me like that."

. . . For all that I had lived, I came to the conclusion that God did not exist, the devil did not exist, and hell did not exist. I became a total atheist. The only thing I carried was that I could create life, and I could also take it away. This and nothing more. But then this young man tells me to look into his eyes. He said, "What you are seeing in me is what God has in store for you." When he says this to me it hit me. To believe that I could do something better than what I was doing. This was something, well, appealing. Truly, I wanted to be someone different. I never wanted to be a delinquent. A criminal. Psychological studies and the experts say a psychopath, a criminal, or a sociopath isn't born, he's formed (*no nace, se hace*). I am formed. So I can be reformed. You understand?

So I'm listening to my history, and this young man says. "Look at me, you know me." But I had never seen him. And my answer was, "No, I don't know you."

"Look closely. This is what God will do with you." When I looked closely, and my vision cleared, he was myself. The only reason I didn't recognize him was because I had changed. It was no longer the face of that marero, of that demon that I saw in the mirror every morning when I got out of bed. Or of that drug addict. I was totally changed. Different. After that dream and through to today, my life was never the same. My heart was changed. I could never again go back to being a criminal.

Early the following morning, mere hours before the riot was to begin, Silence said, the authorities transferred him without explanation out of Pavoncito prison. A few months later, he was released.

Rarely are dreams easy to recount in full, dancing away like a will-o'-the-wisp upon waking. Silence must have worked hard to accentuate and draw more clearly in his mind's eye the vision of God and of his changed self, dependent as he was upon this evidence of divine intervention to convince his gang, and perhaps himself, that real change was possible, that he had jumped tracks and could no longer follow the gangs' edicts.

Silence was clear that it was not desire to change that was lacking, but will and fortitude against temptation. The will and fortitude could not be found in his tattered self, but had to be a gift of divine deliverance that transformed him from the inside out. He held up his dream as evidence of his change. I can see him practicing its telling, getting it just right. When Silence returned to his homies on the street, he told them of his dream and that he was transformed. But they did not believe. "The last thing they made me do was that I had to keep a bible with me like a shadow to show them that I really had changed," he said, "because they said, 'You can't change. You will not change. Know what, we'll give you like a vacation. Go, enjoy yourself, relax. But in three months you're going to come back and ask us for one more opportunity.'"

Defying his homies' expectations, Silence did not return to the fold. He ended up alone on the street. He couldn't go to his family because he did not want to put them in danger, and anyway he had little connection with them. He went deep into drugs, huffing solvent, smoking crack, sleeping on scraps of cardboard in the street, and sometimes begging for food. But he stayed away from his gang and, for a time, they left him alone.[26]

Then, in September 2005, weeks after MS broke the SUR, Silence got word that he and all other former gang members had to report back to the gang. Their retirement was cut short. If they did not respond within a few weeks, the gang would hunt them down. Silence refused to return, and he learned later that his gang had indeed put out the order for his death. To this day, he lives in fear that he might be recognized—on the buses and in the transit centers where he works selling cookies as an ambulant vendor, or simply walking in the street. Several times, on my way through El Trebol market on the south side of the city, I have seen him skulking around the bus depot. He said he must remain constantly vigilant for surviving members of his gang who might recognize him and carry through with the punishment reserved for all deserters.

A decade ago, Silence's performance of his conversion—the clarity of his dream, his determination to follow it—was sufficient to convince his gang to let him leave and to lend him enough courage to radically change his life. But the shrinking space of possibility for ex-mareros has cast his survival deeper into doubt. Nevertheless, he is still pursuing that vision of himself he saw in his dream, burning away the last physical vestiges of his gang past so that his body will resemble what he says his soul has become.

The Evangelical Answer?

The spectacular failures of harsh, punitive law-and-order strategies to repress gangs and reduce out-of-control crime have pushed Central American governments and international donors to stress more "integrated" approaches to insecurity, combining intensified policing with "soft" reintegration and rehabilitation efforts.[27] Supporters of the evangelical approach tout it as the best nonviolent means of curtailing gang membership, pairing spiritual discourse with modern-day self-help and confidence-building rhetoric to transform mareros from the inside out.[28]

Silence, David, and other ex-mareros who seek refuge in the church find a place to belong. The simplified, starkly drawn dichotomies and choices the church offers resonate deeply and provide an alternative community that in many ways mirrors the maras themselves. "Mareros often find themselves already inside the discourse of sin and guilt, and the great pain of spiritual loss," said Isabel Aguilar of Interpeace, an antiviolence NGO. "Great pain is part of their lives. They usually join gangs because they're running from some pain. And to get in they must undergo a gauntlet of giving and receiving pain. So pain is normalized, and evangelical organizations use fear of pain as encouragement to avoid sin."[29]

However, mano dura and evangelical interventions are, in a sense, flip sides of the same coin. Mano dura's populist rhetoric promises to eliminate urban violence by incarcerating (or executing) mareros and other criminals. For proponents of such punitive measures, urban crime will be eradicated through the elimination of gang members—and the "criminal element" in general—often by any means necessary.

Likewise, the evangelical answer roots urban violence within the marero himself. "Only by cleansing his stained soul," it proclaims, "can peace be attained." Like mano dura, the evangelical approach shoves the structural origins of gang violence—severe poverty and inequality, the failing shell of democracy, weak security forces and corrupt legal institutions, and so on—into the background, shifting attention from economic and political conditions and the historical roots of postwar disorder to the interior domain of the individual.

By removing criminal bodies from the street, mano dura promises to excise the cancer of crime. The evangelical approach shifts security concerns from the bodies in the street to the state of the soul. Accordingly, maras, as social issue and security problem, begin "*within* each person (with one's thoughts, attitudes, habits, and sense of self) and can be rectified only though a concerted Christian effort to adjust one's relations to one's own self."[30] Such talk plays easily into the hands of those who would make gangs a singular cause of criminal violence rather than an expression of far deeper problems rooted in postwar society and beyond. Seen in this light, evangelical Christianity's popularity as an anti-gang strategy demonstrates a widespread refusal to understand or accept the complexity of the problem.

Then again, given the abject failure of every policy initiative to reduce urban violence and the rising death tolls in poor urban communities, a retreat to the immaterial and otherworldly could be understood as a collective act of desperation. Even if the bodies of children and young adults must die, their souls can survive. Violent death has become so common and hopes of saving lives have been dashed so continuously that targeting the soul becomes a matter of pragmatic choice.

"When you are facing death you must ask for forgiveness from Christ," said a woman who volunteered with the Gloria de Dios ministry where David preached. "We must be ready for when death surprises us," she continued. "One day I was in my house and I heard a shoot-out. People were gathered around a boy who had been shot. And I lifted him up and told him to start praying. And we prayed together until his lips got pale and voice quiet and then he died in my arms. I left and went back to my house because my job was done."

Despite its widespread failure to save their lives, evangelical Christianity remains a favored script through which ex-mareros can convince the society they live in that they have truly changed. It is still the best, and perhaps the only, way of making their transformation out of gang life intelligible to others as well as to themselves. The stark dichotomies of Christian faith—heaven and hell, God and devil, damnation and redemption—provide a clear road map to salvation for men ready to leave gang life behind. In this sense, written out of every other script, mareros must follow the same route to enlightenment Western societies have forced upon "barbarous savages" since the conquest of the Americas, when embracing the Christian faith and performing its rites was the only means by which conquered natives could hope to survive colonial conquest.[31]

But what if the subject seeking to change does not buy into the script and will not let himself be drawn into the simple archetypes it permits? As Calavera said, repeating an old Spanish proverb, *"mas sabe el diablo por viejo que por diablo,"* which translates, roughly, into, "The devil knows more from being old than being the devil."[32] I take this to mean that the master of evil is not evil because he was born so, but because he has lived long enough to know that being evil is quite practical. Likewise, the maras were forged in the crucible of extreme peacetime violence and have developed a modus vivendi to fit their environs. Whatever desire a person may have to change, the world does not change with him, and he must find ways to survive in it.

Calavera

"So much has changed," Calavera said two weeks after he left prison, "so much that sometimes I'm like, 'What's happening to me? Who am I?' One is accustomed to the easy way, and suddenly, boom, to stop oneself and try to follow a straight path. It costs me. It's not just saying, 'Yes I can do it. . . .' Well, he who has always walked straight, it doesn't cost him so much maybe. But he who hasn't been that way, . . . Oh god, it costs a ton. . . . It is a great fight with myself."

Calavera's struggle with redemption is, for me, the most confusing to grapple with, because he refuses an easy out from his violent past. Having grown up a gang member and served six years behind bars for drug trafficking, Calavera returned to the street stained by his former life and with few viable options for honest work. The course he has charted since gaining his freedom captures the essence of liminal redemption. He knew he never wanted to work with the MS again, but temptations to return to "the easy way" and real or imagined threats connected to his past have consistently troubled his resolve. Some are ghostly reminders provoking long-buried memories to rise again. Others are terribly clear and present poltergeists haunting his neighborhood, his home, and his family. Unwilling or unable to perform what he calls the "charade" of the born-again Christian converts, Calavera has carved his own path: a narrow, treacherous route between specters of violence both old and new. What follows is a chronicle of Calavera's experiences, in which I linger on the moments of choice and decision, chance and contingency, temptation and resolution he and his family have lived as they have tried to keep alive hopes for a better future.

November 2013

Finally, two years after I met him in prison, eighteen months after his release and six months since I moved back to California, Calavera has invited me to his family's home. He has told me of this place many times but has never extended an invitation because it was not safe even for him. I returned to Guatemala a week earlier and am sick with fever. Before catching a taxi to get here, I had spent two hours in a mall waiting for a public ministry official who never showed up and never returned my calls.

Calavera meets me on the steps before the door, mumbling, "Remember, this is a humble home." It was right here, exactly in this place, that narco-traffickers had shot his brother. Long ago somebody plastered and painted over the bullet holes scattered about the front entrance. Calavera maps them for me, tracing his fingers across the constellation engraved into his memory. Inside, in the dim light of a bare bulb hung from the ceiling, I look upon his lineage. There are photographs of his great-grandparents, who bought this house in the 1920s when General Jorge Ubico ruled the banana republic. There is Calavera's grandfather, wearing a soccer uniform sometime in the 1960s. He would play for a few quetzales or simply room and board. His father appears as a chubby adolescent, before he became a drug dealer and an addict. He spent most of Calavera's childhood in and out of prison. They were estranged for years, finally making amends while both were serving time in Pavón. There are many other images: faded pictures of weddings and baptisms, the people tinged with that grim, austere quality old photographs can imbue in their subjects. A portrait of Giovanni, Calavera's brother, hangs prominently among the family memorabilia. It was taken before he got tattoos. There he is, a serious fifteen-year-old, with Calavera's same eyes and nose. His is the most recent photograph, and the color is still vibrant, as if the family stopped recording their lives after he died.

I have brought the fixings for a barbecue to thank Calavera and his family for their friendship, celebrate Calavera's homecoming, and bid a proper fare-well. I know I will not be returning to Guatemala for a long while. Calavera guides me through two dark rooms cluttered with old tables and bookshelves, into an inner courtyard. The courtyard was once protected from the elements, but part of the roof has caved in, leaving the back third open to the sun and the rain. Beneath the crumbling brickwork are rotting beams and tangled wire. The intact walls are painted turquoise, and Calavera's grandfather has hung up dozens of dolls, puppets, and plastic figurines. "He's a creative man," Calavera says, smiling ruefully, "and a bit crazy." C3PO huddles with several Ewoks above the bathroom. A dusty teddy bear with angel wings hangs above the entrance to the grandfather's room, and here and there bald baby dolls smile vacuously into the courtyard.

Rain from a morning storm has gathered in shimmering pools at the far end of the courtyard, behind where Calavera's sister Sandra is preparing the barbecue. She greets me warmly, her four daughters lined up by age beside her, each of them hugging me and kissing me on the cheek.

I slump into a broken-down chair against the wall, and Calavera brings me a Coca Cola. I watch the children play. A tiny sprite of a girl pushes a baby in a crib across the floor, giggling and making faces. A little boy, the skin on one side of his face cracked and scaly, sits down on the floor before me and asks me questions about my country. Tinkling laughter fills the space as sunshine filters through the broken roof.

Sandra orders me to the table and portions out lunch to me, Calavera, and his grandfather. Calavera talks about volunteering with a gang rehabilitation NGO that works inside Pavón prison, the same one I have worked with for the past few years. He accompanies Elena and Elizabet a few times a week and assists with carpentry and painting classes, helping out Juande and the rest of his old buddies still stuck inside. The NGO pays him a stipend of Q800/ month ($100) and promises to hire him full time once the funding comes through (which will never happen). He also brings in a little money painting portraits in a little kiosk along 6th Avenue in zone 1. It's not much money, but it's a start. Getting regular employment has been impossible because of his record. By his last count, he had filled out more than forty job applications, mostly with private security companies, knowing full well he would be rejected by each one. Nevertheless, he seems happy and calmer than I've seen him since he got out of prison. I think about how Calavera has maybe, just maybe, finally arrived in a place of safety and peace. It has been a long road.

April 2001

My brother got up to go to the door and there outside was a chick they called La Shadow. She was of my brother's clique but she was signaling to like seven guys, all with AK-47s and M16s. They start firing in the front of the house. A comrade who was named Vaquero, who is still alive in Boquerón [prison], was the first to start firing back. . . . Others too. Casper had a gun, but he just hid under a table. They were trying to come in, but when they saw people were firing back they ran. They hit my brother with one bullet, one and no more, in the leg. But in the hospital they didn't want to attend to him, since like he was so tattooed. . . . We were really angry, and they nearly threw us out. But we were able to talk with my brother, and he told us who it was and everything and we tried to find a way to calm him down. We thought he was going to survive because it wasn't a mortal wound or anything. In the hospital they gave him anesthesia, and he never woke up.

After Giovanni died, Casper started trying to recruit Calavera to join his Northside Salvatrucha clique. Sandra wanted to keep him from joining up with the Mara. But then another MS clique killed her ex-sureño husband for his desertion, and fourteen-year-old Calavera joined up with Casper to get some income to help his family and to avenge his brother's death.

They made him do things that they could not. He could move through spaces prohibited to known members of the gang, many with tattoos betraying their allegiance. He committed many murders on their behalf, he said, and served a short stint as a contract killer with narco-traffickers, before moving up to running extortion rackets and eventually selling and transporting crack and cocaine.

January 2006

As he drove his motorcycle across the bridge from Guatemala City to Villa Nueva, the police caught Calavera with several thousand quetzales' worth of crack cocaine. The guy riding point on another motorcycle panicked when he saw the police checkpoint, failed to warn Calavera, and sped away. Calavera tried to ditch the backpack with the drugs by a telephone pole, but an old woman picked it up and brought it to the cops. The police already had his picture and knew him as an MS gang member. So upon arresting him, they brought him directly to Boquerón, a prison reserved for active members of the MS. But Calavera did not want to go in there. He knew that a lot of guys ended up dismembered or disappeared when leaving Boquerón on transfers. "The police wait for you to leave and then nab you." So he insisted that he was an ex-marero, that he didn't have anything to do with the Mara anymore, and that if they put him in Boquerón he would get killed and human rights organizations would be breathing down their necks. Apparently they believed him, because he ended up incarcerated in El Preventivo prison with the general population.

He received a six-year sentence. During his incarceration, the stipend the MS promises to every homie never arrived, and Calavera grew disgusted with Casper's hypocrisy and his gang's increasingly uncontrolled brutality toward women and children. After reading in the newspaper about a murder his gang had pulled off against a Barrio18 member in which an infant was killed in the cross fire, he tried to order the perpetrator punished. "An ungrown child has not lived what an adult has, and is not conscious of anything!" But Casper and the others ignored him. After that, he said, he cut off communication with the Mara completely.

Over the years, Casper continued to make frequent visits to Calavera's home, where Sandra lived with her children. Again and again he offered her help if she would work for him. She said she always refused. However, a few months before Calavera completed his sentence, their mother started working for Casper. She would not tell her children how exactly she was involved, but they suspected that she was moving weapons and even murdered bodies for the gang. Sandra begged her not to tell Casper that Calavera would soon be free.

February 2012

Calavera finished his six-year sentence and walked free. His sister and Eddy, his adopted brother from the orphanage where they both had lived as children, came to pick him up. Both Calavera and Sandra were desperate to live under the same roof again, but with Casper still making regular visits and their mother so deeply involved with the gang, it seemed impossible. Instead, he went to live with Eddy and his wife and children. His mother did not know Eddy's address, and he did not tell her.

Shortly after Calavera's release, I met with his sister Sandra in a fancy zone 1 coffeeshop. When I asked about her relationship with Calavera's old homies, she exclaimed: "El Casper is *bad*, really bad. He only thinks about dismembering people, he doesn't even consider killing someone in a normal way. No! He thinks only of torturing and dismembering them. He's gone bad, that one."

"'I'm gonna turn him into *ceviche*'," she growled in a guttural cartoon villain voice. "That's how he talks. I have seen so many boys (*patojos*) get caught up with Casper and his people—kids who are fourteen or fifteen. Some of them are dead, and others are in Gaviotas [a minors' prison], for double or triple homicide. He would send anyone into the wolf's mouth. He makes a lot of money, but he pays practically nothing. He has the look of a *burguesito* (petit bourgeois or yuppie) rolling around in his brand new Toyota Yaris. He always dresses in the best that there is, and talks about his work as if he were tired of it. But he doesn't do anything. He just gives orders. Casper is thirty, but he looks like a young kid of twenty because . . .," she giggled and lowered her voice, "he injects his face! For vanity. Because, he says, he doesn't want to grow old."

The previous day Casper had walked into Sandra's home without knocking, wearing a spotless Armani T-shirt and Prada shades. His face was red and swollen across the forehead from another Botox session. "He told me again that he would pay my rent, he would pay my children's school fees, plus Q800 weekly, and everything," she said. "Almost Q3,000 a month, if I would work for them. It's a temptation because I have people to look after. My brother, my daughters. . ." She sighed. "But I won't do it. Everything that I have lived and everything my family has suffered in all this time is because of *them*."

"What do they want from you?" I asked.

"They want a drug house (*punto de drogas*). They want me to serve them by selling drugs. They want me to move weapons. . . and all that." She shook her head and sighed again. "Casper asked after my daughters' well-being, like a well-mannered person. 'Ah, look how big they are. If they are wanting for something, you could give it to them.' And I laugh. 'I give them what I can,' I say. 'And you all? What do you give them? Death, prison, and the hospital. That's the reality.' It's true that they pull in the boys with money. They pass them cash, they buy them things, and the poverty here is so very hard."

"How does he react when you say this to his face?"

"He says that I am the one who loses and my children too because I don't want to work to get out of my situation."

Before Casper left, he asked Sandra about Calavera. "Is he out, where is he? Have you talked to him?"

"Who knows?" she said. "Who knows when he's getting out because he has twelve years on his head."

"Poor kid!" Casper replied.

But both Calavera and Sandra wondered, why were they looking for him? Did they suspect? They did not trust their mother—not that she would give him away on purpose, but she might slip up.

A few days after Calavera left prison, his mother called him on the phone from an MS safe house with a homegirl. "Here, this is my son," she said, and handed the phone to the girl. Calavera was quick enough to say he was Eddy, his adopted brother. The girl talked about how hard it is to leave and to change, and he freaked out, because why would she be talking about that?

Several weeks later, Calavera told me, "Now I understand things, why my mom never came to the prison. It's because she's working with *them*. She is doing the things that are impossible for men to do. They know that with a woman as old as she is, it is unlikely that the police will stop her. They take advantage. Even I have done it. Take advantage of children, grown women, tell them to take *this* to such and such a place. Now, when I see a kid on the street I pay more attention than I do with someone older. I know that kids. . . shit. . . . They're toys or puppets for the people of the underworld."

Calavera was happy to be free, but the dangers of the street made it treacherous terrain to navigate. And how is one to discern between real threats and figments of the overwrought imagination? No stranger can be trusted, not even, as Calavera said over and over again, the most innocent seeming. On the few days he risked venturing into zone 3 for a quick visit to his old home, his paranoid fantasies would put demons in children's smiles and a predator around every corner.

March 2012

Calavera and I met at a hole-in-the-wall cantina in zone 1. I bought beers, and he eventually got uncharacteristically drunk. He told me of a dream that has woken him several nights running now, feeding his creeping insomnia.

> I'm out looking for work and I see Juande, and we go together. He says, "We'll use this!" and takes out a giant iguana that seems to be growing out of his arm. I ask him what we're going to use it for and he says you'll see.[33] So then we get to the courthouse, the tower of judgment, and all my old homeboys are there, climbing the walls and standing on top of pillars, waving guns at me and laughing and saying they're going to kill me. The street is flooded, it is a river, a moat around the courthouse, and inside that body of water are reptiles of every description, diamond headed lizards and snakes I've never seen before. Snakes that probably don't exist. And I have to wade through that water to get to the other side. The homies are all threatening me, waving guns at me. Then they fall, one by one, into the water, and the snakes eat them.

Waking life also offered invitations to violence. Living off the charity of others, even his loved ones, was hard on Calavera's pride. Opportunities to slide back into a life of crime—a self-reliant life—arose again and again. One afternoon while walking through zone 1 on his way to meet with me, he came

234 SPECTACLE, STRUCTURE, AND AGENCY

face to face with an old extortion "client." Upon recognizing him, the man offered Calavera money to kill members of a gang that was levying la renta from him.

"'Look,' the guy says. 'I'm gonna give you my number. The truth is I have some businesses here. And I want to see if you'll do me a favor. We'll pay you, there are several of us, and the truth is these others are fucking up our business.'" Calavera responded to the request as if he were still an active gang member, even pretending that he had an SUV parked around the corner to hide the fact he was traveling on foot, something he never would have done as a bona fide homie.

I asked him why he hadn't come clean.

"I feel like it would be a mistake to tell them," he said. "They're going to say, 'Well, what's up with this dude? He's fleeing or something. Maybe I can tell his gang what's up, maybe he owes something to them.' He'll tell them in the hopes I'll make better business for him. So I say, 'Okay then, I'll call you.' But I don't call, and I don't give them my number."

To protect his flank, to cover up the fact of his desertion and consequent vulnerability, he acted the part.

"I haven't told anyone this, not even my brother Eddy," Calavera said, glancing quickly around the bar. "But there have been mornings when I wake up and I have to fight a battle with myself to not go out and do the things I know how to do to make easy money. It's like I have a little devil sitting on my shoulder, and he tells me things. He tells me just go do it, you know how, you'll have enough money to get all the things you need. Just like that. In two days I could have enough for a computer. In one day I could get enough to pay my own rent."

The urge to return to a life of crime, he told me, was always only a voice in his head, an internal struggle never manifested. The temptation arose, he examined it, and he pushed it down with the memory of prison, the lost, useless years rotting in damp cells, the numerous times he almost died in riots he knew almost nothing about. That is how he had explained his struggle to me. But several months after gaining his freedom, he confessed that he had come much, much closer to falling into the bad old ways than he had let on. "We're men, we're humans, right?" Calavera said to me. "I think that at any moment we're capable of anything. So the thing about temptations is that they come to one right at the moment when one is thinking 'I've changed,' right, and they're like tests. That's how life is."

Two weeks after leaving Pavón prison, he returned to pick up some papers from the administration office. He had a shouted conversation with some of the boys in the isolation block (*el modulo*) a stone's throw from the perimeter fence. El Chaparro, in for narco-trafficking and, ironically, stuck in the isolation block for defrauding fellow prisoners by packaging and selling oregano as Zacatecas weed, shouted through a square peephole in the black metal door:

"There's a job in zone 3. You interested?"

"Give me the number anyway," I said.

So later, the dude calls me, well, not him, but Elias, who was with me in Pavoncito [prison] when they wanted to kill us. So he calls me.

"Whatsup brother?"

"What's up?"

"The deal is that there's a job with La Navaja (The Knife)." She's a woman who runs drug-trafficking in zone 3.

"That's great," I say.

"Yeah, the truth (*la neta*) is that they're paying 30," he says.

"Fuck! Why?"

"You have to kill a dude," he says, "and pick up the money and valuables he's holding."

I asked him, "Will they give me a pistol? A car?"

"Absolutely."

"Okay then, pass me to the chick whose gonna do business."

"Who are you?" she asks.

"I am so and so," I say, "so what's up?"

"There's a job. . . . Are you gonna take it?"

"Yeah," I say, "when can I come for everything?"

"Right on. Tomorrow, at 9 in the morning. Come by the Texaco in Barrio Gallito."

"Good," I say.

I went early the next morning and I brought my brother Eddy.

[I interrupted, laughing. "What?"]

Yeah, the dumbass didn't have a clue. I was like, "The deal is I think I might have a painting job over there. If it comes through, I can help you out."

"Right on," he says to me.

I dropped my brother off near the meeting place with La Navaja. "Wait here, okay. . . . If the job comes through I'll come to get you in a taxi and we'll go from here together.". . .

"That's great," he says, totally fooled.

So I went with the girl.

"You're La Navaja?"

"Yes," she says, "who are you?"

"I'm the one that's gonna do the job. Give me the stuff. If I came it's cuz I came to do it."

"Alright." She gives me the keys to a car with polarized windows.

"Here," she gives me a 9mm.

"Good." To the belt.

I went for a ride in the car. Coming back, the girl got in.

"I'm going to show you where the house is."

"Ok."

"Here," she says. "Knock there, and there's where the bullet is served. The guy will come out and there he stays."

So I dropped her off. And it's cool, right. I'm gonna do the job. Alright, I tell myself, come what may. Decided.

Popopop, the door. [Calavera mimes waiting.] Ding-dong the doorbell. [More waiting.] And PA PA PA, hard kicks, and buddy, I am ready to break in, believe me. I was jonesin for those bills! And look, I was there for like twenty minutes. My brother, he calls me in that moment.

"Whatsup, what happened?"

"Look, I'm doing the job. Wait," I tell him. "I'll come to pick you up." And I don't know what all. I'm acting like a jackass, going from here to there, seeing how I can break into the house. And after a while a patrol comes by. And I see the patrol. . . . I'm looking here, but seeing over there. And I tell myself that if I take off in a flash, those dudes are going to stop me, they'll take the gun off me and it's back to prison for possession. So, I just stand at the door, knocking like it's nothing. Popopo. And nothing. I stay another few minutes and the police go on farther down. And I'm acting respectable, right.

"Good," I say to myself. Then—nothing. I got the keys, I got in the car, and I left. I didn't have a desire to do anything. My plane had landed. I'd left my brother there waiting a long time. The girl calls me, "Look, the job is good now."

But I say, "You know what, with people like you it's not worth doing things. Do what you're gonna do. Don't be giving me so much bullshit. I am gonna leave your stuff in such and such a place." And I went to leave the car in the cemetery. . . . I left the pistol under the gearshift, and I returned to get my brother.

"Let's go, carnal. The neta is that nothing came of it." I say. "Let's go." And he still doesn't know, has no idea.

La Navaja and El Chaparro, her contact in the prison, pursued Calavera, calling him several dozen times over the next few days. Calavera cut off all communication.

"And if the man had been in the house when you knocked?" I asked Calavera.

"I'd already be enrolled, man. We wouldn't be talking today. I would have seen the easy money, buddy. And I'd say, okay, here we go again. I'd arm my band. Pull in kids from the street, or purse-snatchers who go around stealing wallets and robbing old ladies, and I'd raise it."

"Under the Mara Salvatrucha flag?"

"Hell no. Outside the gangs. For ourselves. Anti-cholos, we'd be killing ourselves against the gangs. I think a lot about this, you understand. They are things that take away my . . . hell, my peace. Because I tell myself, the moment I do that . . . sonofabitch. I start to analyze what it would have started."

In the months following this incident, he spoke more and more of a dawning clarity, a sense that he could really make it in the world without having to take "the easy way." The nightmares of his old homies and bloody battle occurred less frequently, replaced with quieter, sadder visions of his former life. "I have walked down some of my old streets and I remember many things, bad things, things I did thinking I was the best. Sonofabitch, I remember so much. So much. And so many buddies to remember. When I walk into the 3 [zone 3] I see my dead brother, my dead buddies . . . and I also try to see a way to take this in an optimistic way, a second chance, a chance to move on."

August 2012

Calavera called me on my cell phone in the United States. He was distraught. Three men had raped his girlfriend, he said. They lived in her neighborhood, and she had to pass them on the street every day on her way to work. There was no question of going to the police. He said he woke shouting in the night with rage and impotence. If he were still connected with the gang, resolving this problem would be quite simple. But since he was not, he obsessed over how to kill the men who had done this thing. He asked me for advice. What could I say? What would you have told him?

May 2013

The police finally caught up with Casper. In the months preceding his capture, his behavior had grown increasingly erratic. According to Sandra, who got regular reports from her mother, Casper was high all the time and was becoming more and more paranoid. After fifteen years of killing and evading death, feeding underlings and rivals to the wolves, threatening and extorting transportation companies, drug traffickers, and prostitutes, he was finally done. His threats against enemies and allies alike became more and more histrionic; the cold pragmatism that had kept him alive and free for so long was gone.

Abusing his own people did him in. An old man who for years had moved weapons, drugs, and bodies on Casper's behalf made the fateful call to the anonymous tip hotline "Cuéntaselo a Wáldemar" (Tell it to Waldemar) and gave the police the location of Casper's safehouse. Police detectives caught up with him before he could get into his car, and there was a shoot-out. Pinned against his Toyota Yaris, Casper took a bullet in the foot and took off limping down a side street. The police followed the trail of bloody sneaker prints and found him sprawled on the steps of an apartment building.

Casper's sudden departure from the neighborhood made it possible for Calavera to move in once again with his sister. It was a good thing, too, because the situation at Eddy's place had become impossible. Initially filled with goodwill, Eddy turned on Calavera and became deeply suspicious of his every move. Perhaps he knew more than Calavera gave him credit for about his flirtations with the old life in those first few months of freedom.

November 2013 Again

Calavera, his grandfather, and I finish our lunch, and it is nearly time for me to leave. I don't want to go out into these harsh city streets again. It all seems too much to bear. But I have several interviews to complete before I return to California two days hence. What I wouldn't give to just sit in a chair in the last of the daylight streaming into the courtyard and watch the kids play.

But I tell Calavera I have to go, and he quickly ushers me into his bedroom. There are bottles of paint and half-finished canvases stacked in a corner beside a single bed with a thin mattress. He turns to me, and speaking quickly, tells me how I more than anyone have made him want to change. Not directly, not with advice or by pushing or chiding him, but simply by listening and encouraging him to paint, by being a safe place to speak his mind on events and thoughts that he can confess to no one else. He is smiling, but somehow, it hurts to look into his eyes.

Then he reaches up and takes a tennis racket bag down from the top of a dark wooden dresser. Unzipping it, he draws out an object wrapped in an old sweatshirt. As he unwraps it I catch a dull gleam of metal. He tosses the sweatshirt onto the bed and holds out an AR-15 fully automatic assault rifle. The barrel has been expertly shortened, and the grip and body are smooth with use.

"What the hell. . . ?" I exclaim.

He tells me a man named Santos, a veteran of his old clique, passed him the gun a few days after Casper was arrested. I ask him why.

"In case of trouble," he says, his eyes darting from mine.

"What kind of trouble?"

"Once word of Casper's capture goes out, other cliques might want to move in on his territory." Then he shrugs. "Anyway, Santos just wants me to hold it for him." I know there is something, something important, he isn't telling me. But I can't make myself probe further. The moment doesn't seem right, or I'm too tired. Perhaps I don't want to know. He offers me the gun, and I take it. The metal is cool in my hands, the weight of the thing somehow comforting and also terrifying.

"Is it in working order?"

Calavera snorts. "Ha! Of course it is."

I hold the AR-15 fully automatic assault rifle and hear in my head Calavera saying again and again, like a mantra, "I don't want trouble, but if it comes my way, I will be ready." I hand the weapon back to him and watch him wrap it carefully. I can hear the children laughing in the courtyard.

"I just wanted you to know what's really going on," Calavera says. We walk back into the sunlight to say good-bye.

Epilogue

Of Violent Others and Orders of Violence

This book begins and ends with Guatemala's maras and the children, youth, families, and communities who, day in and day out, cannot escape the reality the maras represent. But as I said at the start, the maras are not the problem, and the problem does not begin or end with them. Through histories of war and uncertain peace out of which the maras emerge, into the prisons and illicit businesses binding state and society firmly to the underworld upon which they rest, and out through the bloody spectacles drawing gangs into the global imagination, the maras provide a means of mapping cycles of violence that refuse to be fixed in time and space. They form a climactic link between flesh and blood brutality and incessant efforts to impose a sense of order and certainty on rampant insecurity. Such efforts warp maras and "their" violence beyond the murdered bodies, the crime scenes, and gang territories into every realm of social, political, and economic life. Today the maras loom larger than life, and their image grows, mutates, and takes on new meaning with every murder and massacre. For the people whose stories make up this book, the consequences of this deadly play between order and uncertainty are never far away. And though we who reside in safer and more secure environs might imagine ourselves protected in some way from these consequences, it seems to me such assurances are wearing thin. We all live in a world that seems to be moving faster than ever before into uncharted and very possibly catastrophic territory, a world "characterized by an increasing instability of time and the fracturing of lived space."[1] In this sense, the dilemmas facing Calavera, Juande, Andy, Byron Lima, and the rest of those whose lives (and deaths) make up the stories in this book are a result of collective forces driving human development and degradation on a far larger scale.

———

Over the years of writing and rewriting this book, I have traveled to Guatemala City several times a year and kept in touch as best I could with my friends and contacts. After I saw him in 2013, Calavera's struggle on the street intensified. In late 2014, after learning that Gloria, his girlfriend, was pregnant with a boy, he called me, overjoyed, and told me that they would name the child after me. He also asked me to be his son's godfather. Perhaps he knew that trouble was brewing. Four months before the child was born and less than three years after Calavera was released from Pavón, police arrested him for illegally transporting a firearm. This was a violation of his parole, so he expected to receive a sentence of eight years, the legal maximum. But this was not the worst of it. While he was awaiting trial for the weapons charge, anti-gang police raided his house and arrested him for involvement in an extortion and kidnapping ring. El Lobo and other Barrio18 leaders incarcerated in sector 11 of the Preventivo prison organized and directed the network. The police had tapped their phones and the phones of those they communicated with on the outside. When they came for Calavera, the police tore apart his grandfather's house. He was one of forty-odd people swept up in the operation and charged with conspiracy to commit kidnapping and extortion.

Calavera flat out denied the conspiracy charges. The police claimed to have recorded his conversations with one of El Lobo's contacts on the outside. Calavera claimed, and he still claims, that he was merely making arrangements for a painting he was going to do for a friend of a friend. He also said that the recorded conversations linking him to the kidnapping ring—conversations that were played in court to demonstrate his alleged guilt—were cut and clipped so as to falsely convey active involvement in the criminal network.

In late 2015, after being sentenced on the weapons charge, Calavera asked to be transferred to Pavón while the kidnapping and extortion case ground toward its conclusion. El Preventivo, the pretrial prison where he spent the first several months after his arrest, was packed to more than 500 percent capacity. When I visited him in Preventivo, several times with a very pregnant Gloria, we sat crowded elbow to elbow among other prisoners and their visitors with hardly room to turn around. In Pavón, Calavera hoped, at least he could get some privacy with Gloria and their infant.

However, in Pavón he also had to contend with a new neighbor. When I returned to Pavón to see Calavera, I encountered none other than El Buffón (of the Canada prison isolation block), crouched on the terrace of the sector next to Calavera's. He got up and approached us, nodding at Calavera, and grinned at me. He had lost his paunch, in fact had withered to skin and bones, as if from sickness or too much crack.

"Ah, Gringo, remember me?"

"Of course, Buffón."

"I skewered this Gringo with a snake," he sniggered.

"That's right."

I asked him what had happened to him and the other guys in the isolation block after the gang-rape incident three years earlier. "Ah, that bullshit." he shrugged. "The chick just disappeared. She never showed up to give evidence to the MP, so they had no case."

I wanted to ask him more questions, but his eyes flicked away and he muttered something and walked back into his sector. Later, I saw him palming baggies of crack into customers' hands from his station on the terrace.

———

Meanwhile, in a historic corruption case in 2015, Guatemalan president Otto Perez Molina and much of his cabinet were ousted from office and arrested. Working with a vast network of government officials, they had stolen millions of dollars of taxpayers' money through embezzlement schemes, skimming off national health care and import taxes.[2] The ensuing legal investigation exposed a degree of fraud and corruption never before made public and inspired a wave of national protests that helped bring down the administration. One accidental victim of this sea change in national politics was Captain Byron Lima. Shortly after Calavera arrived in Pavón, Lima joined him there, transferred from the Matamoros Air Force Base, where space was needed for the recently arrested former president and members of his administration.

Lima quickly took control in Pavón, in much the same way he had in every other prison. On a visit I made in March 2016, he once again gave me a tour of his "prison public works" projects: a high school degree program, a new church, a new health services office, and other improvements. Clearly he was drawing on his old tried and true playbook. Calavera and other old friends in Pavón, along with prison guards I interviewed in secret, however, spoke in hushed tones of a new reign of terror. Lima had the prison director in his pocket, and any guards who refused to do his bidding got transferred to work in far-flung provinces far from their families. He was methodically taking over or taxing the most lucrative licit and illicit businesses while punishing any who dared defy him. When I spoke with Lima, he acted as calm and cool as ever, but beneath his self-assurance, I learned later, there were serious doubts. In retrospect, he was not rising again like a phoenix, but flailing for survival.[3]

On July 18, 2016, a team of nine well-armed and highly organized prisoners assassinated Lima as he walked down Pavón's central shop-lined boulevard with an Argentine woman named Joanna Birriel, who worked as a model in Guatemala City, on his arm. She was caught and killed in the cross fire, along with several of Lima's bodyguards.[4] Calavera was nearby when the shooting began, and when it was over he checked the scene. "I saw the girl, with her brains on the floor and the Cappy had two bullets in the back of his head. He had a gold-plated gun, a .45 I think, that he never had a chance to draw. I could also see his wallet. 'How many thousands of quetzals in that wallet!' I thought to myself. And I wanted to take it," Calavera shrugged, "but I didn't. There could be trouble." I asked him if he or others he knew had said anything to the authorities. "They say that the [prison] director left with a backpack full of guns, and they never found any of the guns that were actually used to kill Lima and his crew." Then he shook his head vehemently. "But I'd never talk to the cops. Whoever did it would disappear my whole family."

Authorities quickly accused a prisoner named El Taquero—a prison drug-trafficker—of organizing and carrying out the hit in a dispute over Lima's effort to shut down prison crack sales. But the theories swirling about Lima's murder—as well as a lot of credible evidence—point to the involvement of the highest echelons of Guatemalan government.[5] To this day, no clear explanation for his murder has surfaced. In all likelihood, none will. But even now, more than a year after his death, Lima lives on as a damning link between the elite networks that dominate Guatemalan society and the murky underworlds through which power and profit flow. Recent revelations have exposed Lima's underhanded dealings with Alvaro Arzú, former president and longtime mayor of Guatemala City, putting yet another elite politician in the hot seat for robbing taxpayer money to shore up his hold on power.[6]

When all this went down, Juande was already out of prison. In late 2015, after fifteen years behind bars, he finally got his parole and walked free. Like Calavera and so many other ex-cons, Juande returned to the world of the free haunted by his past and facing an uncertain future. Finding work was very difficult. The first thing potential employers do is check for gang tattoos and check police records, and Juande was unemployed for the first year out. Frustrated and confused, he fell back into drinking for a spell but soon became terribly sick. Prison is a dirty place, and the years on the inside without access to proper medical care had left his body weak. He learned that he had severe kidney damage. On one of several emergency trips to the hospital, he had to be hooked up to a dialysis machine, and he overheard doctors discussing his MS tattoos and arguing whether or not to treat him or to "send him with Pancho," the old death squad euphemism for execution. With desperate eloquence, he convinced them he was reformed, and they decided to help him live.

When I saw Juande in September 2016, he had been transformed. Sickness had robbed him of his intimidating bulk, and his flesh hung loosely from the bones. But he was still strong enough to be working for his brother, who ran a construction crew and had gotten him a temporary gig as a foreman. He was helping to build new additions to the Cayalá complex, the shining white sanctuary of the Guatemala City elite. Perched in the hills above the city, Cayalá is a sprawling enclave community where the rich can live, work, eat, shop, and party without ever having to leave the whitewashed, Mediterranean-style complex. We talked during one of Juande's breaks. He was dressed in a hard hat and neon yellow vest and chain-smoked as he reflected on his new lot in life. He worked twelve-hour days, six days a week, and earned about Q3,000 ($275) a month. The work he did was "the same as on the inside," working with his hands, but much of it, since he was a foreman, was ordering guys about and organizing them. With pride he told me that he was one of the few foremen who actually joined in the work themselves. He was also able to reach out and get friends recently released from Pavón jobs as construction assistants. He just had to make sure they were able to sneak past the inspector, because most of them didn't have the proper boots for such work.

That ex-con, ex-gangster bodies were literally constructing a fortified living space for the rich struck me as entirely appropriate. The situation leapfrogged more rarefied connections between the symbolic and the material to proclaim an undeniable symbiosis between elite efforts to create security and the criminalized populations they hope to keep out. The irony of Juande and his ex-con compatriots building Cayalá was not lost on him. During his off-hours he would wander along the cobblestone streets of this playground for the rich. "You know, all these rich people are doing drugs and drinking the same as the rest of us. Just in prison it was pot and crack and moonshine. Here at Cayalá they have their crystal and ecstasy pills and champagne. But they're still trying to get fucked up." He laughed in wonder. "They even have an indoor contraption for surfing!"

He was living in a cramped apartment with his baby mama and their two children (conceived and born while he was in prison), as well as his father-in-law, in a rundown neighborhood on the opposite end of town. It took three hours on several buses to get to work. When he came and went from his home, he always took a circuitous back way to avoid young toughs who knew about his past and might start something to get some street rep.

Late one afternoon, as I walked home with him along the winding dirt trail, he said, "Don't get me wrong, Anthony, I'm glad to be out and with my family. But in some ways, life was easier inside. I knew the rules of the game. Here on the street, just feeding my family seems impossible. I'm thinking about trying to go to the US so I can at least earn some money, but I don't know. Do you think that's possible?"

I told him it was possible, but very, very difficult. The routes by which Central Americans migrate to the United States have become far more treacherous in the last few years. In 2014 more than ninety thousand unaccompanied minors from Guatemala, El Salvador, and Honduras were caught attempting to cross from Mexico into the United States. Protests—both in favor of and against allowing these children entry—erupted along the US southern border.[7] Amid images of detention centers packed with Central American children and border patrol guards changing diapers, the Obama administration moved quietly to prevent such media spectacles in the future. In the following years the US government has pushed and paid the Mexican immigration authorities to ramp up efforts to hunt, detain, and deport undocumented Central Americans migrating through Mexican territory.[8] This has made the trip through Mexico—already treacherous with kidnapping rings and marauding gangs—riskier still.

And as this book goes to press, the Trump administration continues to push for a "big beautiful wall" to be built along the US-Mexican border to keep out the "drug dealers, criminals and rapists" threatening peaceful American communities and the poor and hungry masses taking American jobs.[9] In spectacular fashion, the 2016 presidential campaign and election of Donald Trump exposed just how shaky US society's sense of order has become (and ought to be). Tapping into seething anxieties over the national political, economic, and racial order, Trump rode a tide of fear, rage, and indifference into the White House. As president, he has continued to draw on the same playbook. Like so many right-wing politicians in the United States and elsewhere, he gathers strength and support by invoking images of violent Others upon which he heaps blame for the loss of US citizens' quality of life. During his first year in office, this list of enemies evolved to include radical Muslim terrorists, the liberal media, and, it should come as no surprise, the Mara Salvatrucha. As part and parcel of the administration's campaign to reform the US immigration system, it has thrust the MS before the national public to feed the fantasy that savage foreigners are turning US cities into "bloodstained killing fields."[10] In a disastrous show of force, the US government even resorted to ripping immigrant children from their parents and keeping them in cages, leveraging their suffering for political gain.[11] Such Machiavellian calculation and savage disregard for its consequences are all too familiar. Ironically, in the name of keeping the violence and chaos of Central American societies at bay, the US government is employing scripts and symbols drawn directly from Central American politics that have been integral to the rise of the maras and extreme peacetime violence.

And for Juande, who still has MS tattoos emblazoned across his chest, such developments put dreams of finding safety and prosperity in el Norte permanently out of reach.

————

In September 2016, on the day after Calavera was sentenced for kidnapping and extortion, Juande and I went to visit him in Pavón prison. It was a Saturday, an official visiting day, and when we arrived hundreds of women were already waiting in a muddled line stretched out beneath the burning sun. A gaggle of discomfited guards tried to keep order as the women jockeyed for position and shouted for things to move more quickly. Juande and I hunkered down in the men's line, which consisted of a few evangelical pastors and a prisoner's grandfather. I hadn't brought a camera or a voice recorder. I wasn't sure what kind of security would be operating after Lima's spectacular assassination. Nothing had changed, however. If anything, the guards appeared even more lax and inattentive, barely patting me down before we entered. Inside, prisoners immediately caught sight of Juande and called out to him. We lingered by the metal door of an isolation block, a windowless concrete hut with a sheet metal door. Scrawled on the door was a biblical proverb, John

8:32: "Conocereis la verdad y la verdad os hara libres" ("You will know the truth and the truth will set you free"). Eyes shone through ragged two-inch holes, and fingers clutched at the light. A voice inside said he was Juande's friend and welcomed him back. Juande greeted the voice warmly, but gestured to me that he had no idea to whom he was speaking.

When I saw Calavera I hugged him tight against my chest. He and I separated from the boisterous crowd gathering around Juande and slowly walked toward Calavera's quarters. "They sentenced me to thirty-three years," he blurted out. The color drained from his face, and for the first and only time he cried in front of me. "Thirty-three years," he kept saying, "thirty-three years. I'm going to be an old man when I get out." After a few harsh, dry sobs, he wiped the tears away and set his shoulders back. He was still in shock, it seemed to me, with a vacant look in his eyes I had not seen before. "Man, on the bus home, after the sentencing," he said, "I wanted to jump off. Or take a gun and just start shooting. Just end it." We arrived at his sector, a squat, ramshackle sheet metal structure with a single window. Inside, sheets hung from the ceiling divided a dozen prisoners from one another, and Calavera had constructed plywood walls to mark off a rectangle of space about four by six feet. These were his quarters. "I spent last night crying here in my room, thinking about killing myself. I saw my child and I saw Gloria and I couldn't stop crying." He shook his head. "Now, I'm of two minds," he said. "Part of me wants to just start doing drugs. Just become a drug addict and fuck it all. The other part wants to keep walking, to keep moving, keep painting, keep doing projects. I want to do it for my child. When I close my eyes, there is a blackness, but in the blackness my child is there before me."

"For now," he continued, staring at the wall as if talking to himself, "I just don't want to be a weight." The stress and uncertainty of the court proceedings had strained his relationship with Gloria. "It's been *my* bad decisions, *my* choices that got me here. I'm the one who decided to bring that gun for sale." He was referring to the arms-trafficking charge. "But this other case is garbage, it was always garbage. From the very beginning."

I asked him again, point blank, if he had had anything to do with the kidnapping ring. As he had done each time previously, he denied everything. "They had me on a phone call with a guy I know named El Huicho, and there is a Huicho involved in this ring. But it was a different Huicho!" He shook his head. "Anyway, I would *never* work with Barrio18. They cut up the audio recordings to make me sound involved, and then there is my record of course."

He told me prosecutors had given him the opportunity to save himself. "They offered me the chance to be a protected witness. . . . But how could I do that? I didn't even know the other guys involved in this. And it would be a risk to my family along with myself."

I nodded at his denials. I had been out of the country during the court proceedings and unable to obtain the records. Calavera and I discussed ways to reopen the case once he could get the money together for a decent lawyer. I promised to help in the legal battle. But there would be time for this. He still has to serve out at least four years of his weapons charge before he can apply for parole. I still do not know the whole truth of the matter, but I do not believe that Calavera spending the rest of his life in prison will do anyone any good. For the time being, Calavera will make do in Pavón. "At least now I have open air," he said as we left his quarters. "I can walk beneath the sky and even see stars, and have my own little space."

As Calavera takes cold comfort in these things and struggles for his family's survival, Guatemala's disordered order lurches on, and around the world, in rich and poor nations, among world powers and former colonies, specters of profound social and political chaos continue to grow and take on new urgency. In desperation, unprecedented portions of humanity are fleeing their homes and homelands in search of safety and the thin chance to prosper.[12] In reaction, European nations, the United States, and other imagined sanctuaries are finding new ways to bar and eject poor foreigners, forcing the vast majority to wait for salvation that might never come. Just as Trump relies on the MS to anchor the imagined ills of immigration in the United States, politicians and publics across the globe are (re)turning to fascist visions of order. Such visions rely on precisely the same kind of Othering discourses, authoritarian instincts, and fearful ferment integral to the making of the maras and so many other vehicles of violence.

The targets of these revanchist political projects are legion. Those who would rule draw on their images to carve out the battle lines of twenty-first-century survival and pull the ties that bind human society into an unruly whole. The sense of collective certainty they strive to instill must necessarily be short-lived, relying as it does on the specter of barbarous Others perpetually threatening to tear it asunder. There is no outside to these conflicts, and there are no outsiders. As both producers and consumers of the world we live in, we cannot stop our conscription into the struggle for order. We are all the terrain upon which these struggles take place and must make the choice to act consciously or remain mere mindless fodder. This means wrestling with the intense discomfort—if not the outright horror—that comes with facing up to such existential and ethical confusion. It means acknowledging that all of us—victims and perpetrators, experts and laypeople, witnesses both distant and near—are also ensnared in the tangled skein out of which the maras emerge.

───────

After spending the day with Calavera, Juande and I left Pavón. We navigated the gauntlet of prisoners—some familiar, most not—asking for handouts or favors, until we reached the prison gate. The midafternoon sun was still high in the sky, and there was still a crowd of women queued up outside. A middle-aged woman who had come to visit her husband, tired of the guards' clumsy efforts at order, had taken it upon herself to help direct the slow-moving line. She talked and joked with the guards and other visitors. Children played in the rutted dirt road. Several boys, none of them older than ten, threw dirt clods and garbage at a stray dog. Then they chased after another group of kids running alongside Pavón's outer fence. Wielding sticks as mock guns, the two groups shouted at one another in pitched battle.

"I have an AK-47, yours is a 9mm!"

"No, it's a 45!"

"I shot you! Barrio18 wins!"

"No! Mara Salvatrucha wins!"

"I shot you and you didn't die!"

ACKNOWLEDGMENTS

This book would not exist without the trust, insights, and openness of all the people who allowed me into their lives and told me their stories. Most of all I want to thank the man I call Calavera and his family for your help and support all these years. I have been humbled again and again by your generosity, your fortitude, and your art. I know your trials and tribulations are not over, and I will be there for you, your child, and your family in whatever capacity I am able.

Special thanks go to the incredible crowd of remarkable individuals I met conducting fieldwork in and around Guatemala City over the last four years, most of whom I cannot even name for their own protection. I owe more than I can say to the men and women who have lived through so much suffering and guided me through the spaces of violence they still struggle to survive. Thank you Elu, Brenda, Juande, David, and Juan Carlos for your trust, your guidance in and out of prison, and your stories. And thank you Gato and family for welcoming me into your home. And of course, thank you Andy. May you rest in peace. Thank you Shaggy, Ervin, Mo, Vago, Cholo, Merida, Pablo, Hugo Escobar, Ericson, Rana, Manitas, Payaso, Mouse, El Gato Amaya, Nica, Triste, Chooky, Shadow, El Skorpion, La Negra Tomasa, Estuardo, Erick Alvarez, Chino, Claudia, Cheeky, DJ Fender, Tommy, and many others surviving on the street or still stuck in prison.

Throughout my fieldwork, I depended on a coterie of Central America–based journalists and researchers whose generosity and insights were absolutely invaluable. Thank you Peter Marchetti and Jennifer Casolo, who caught me when I landed in Guatemala City and never let me go. Mike McDonald, you are the best journalist I've ever met and a fine companion to get in trouble with. Thank-you Sofia Menchu as well as Carlos Martinez and Jose Luis Sanz of *el Faro* for trusting a crazy gringo. Thank you Marcelo Colussi, Rodolfo Kepfer, Megan Thomas, and Daniel Barczay for your depth of knowledge in all manner of historical and contemporary arenas.

Numerous government officials working on the front lines of peacetime violence and insecurity provided me with invaluable help and advice. Your rigor and courage before often daunting institutional corruption is truly amazing. Thank you Claudia Paz y Paz and Arturo Aguilar for helping me in the midst of far more important responsibilities. Thank you to all the judicial officials who shared their stories and insights: Edwin Marroquin, Eluvia Lima, Aldrin, Walter Villatoro, Walter Pineda, Rodolfo Flores, and Rodrigo in the Ministerio Publico. I would also like to thank Hugo, Chino, and others working with the Ministry of Sports and Culture, Edwin Ortega of the PNC, and Pastor Mardoqueo.

Special thanks are owed to all those working at AVANCSO, to Mario Polanco and his Grupo de Apoyo Mutuo, to Jose Suasnavar of FAFG, to Emilio Goubaud and APREDE, to Isabel Aguilar and Francisco Irungaray of InterPeace, and to Mark Lopes of USAID.

And of course, I would not have lasted in Guatemala without the companionship of many others who never made it into these pages. Thank-you Ivahn Aguilar—my neighbor, my friend, my brother in arms—and the rest of the Guatemala Rugby Club for giving me so much to laugh about.

My home in Guatemala was always in zone 4, in my industrial chique apartment, and I am so grateful to Chuy, Fernando, El Bailarín, and Irineo for guarding my apartment building night and day. You work so hard and such long hours for so little, and you deserve more.

Thank you Mike Capriel de Leon for the strange and wonderful conversations in cantinas and our wanderings through the city on the back of your motorcycle. You showed me parts of Guatemala City I never would have known otherwise, and all that laughter did my body and soul so much good. Eres mi hermano por siempre.

I am deeply grateful to the Drugs, Security and Democracy Program and all those in the Social Science Research Council and Open Society Foundations (OSF) who created it. The DSD program provided me with the funds to make fieldwork possible in the moment I needed them most. Even more important, the network created through this program linked me with kindred spirits who have become the most important intellectual community of my career. Thank you David Holiday, Cleia Noia, and everyone else at the SSRC and OSF who believed in my project. Special thanks also go to Dennis Rodgers, Vanda Felbab-Brown, Falko Ernst, Katherine Saunders Hastings, and Alex Fattal, as well as the entirety of the Drugs, Security, and Democracy network, for your advice, feedback, and fellowship.

Thank you Graham Denyer-Willis and Kimberly Theidon for reviewing and editing my manuscript and for seeing its potential. Your insights made it shine. I would also like to thank Elizabeth Woodward and Scott Straus for your key advice and feedback on early versions of these chapters.

Kevin O'Neill, my longtime friend and mentor, and editor of the Atelier book series, you have been a font of wisdom and clear-sighted guidance for almost a decade now, and I am so very grateful for the support and feedback you have given me over the years. You are also a ninja.

Books take a long time to write. It's humbling to realize just how many institutions stepped in to support me on this long, strange trip. I must thank the HF Guggenheim Foundation and the Institute on Global Conflict and Cooperation for stepping in to support me when I needed it most.

The UC Berkeley Geography Department is a rare and wonderful place to carry out scholarly research. I owe a depth of gratitude to Michael Watts, Beatriz Manz, and Wendy Brown, for the insights, guidance, and freedom granted me in writing the dissertation that became this book. I owe more than I know how to repay to Jake Kosek, a brilliant scholar and the busiest man alive, for your valuable time and insights, and for putting me to work on your farm when I needed the money (and for the worst case of poison oak I ever had). Thank you Julie Klinger and Shannon Cram. Our exchanges gave me more eye-opening epiphanies than I know how to express. Erik Jønsen, Penelope Anthias, and Meleiza Flores, your help in editing the dissertation before it was a book was absolutely invaluable.

In 2015, for reasons I still cannot fathom, the University of Wisconsin's Geography Department and Center for Humanities offered me a Mellon Post-Doctoral Fellowship, a gift that made my dreams come true. I want to thank my colleagues there for welcoming me with more warmth and support than I ever could have expected. Thank you Keith Woodward for your selfless and rigorous mentoring, and thank you Elsa Noterman, Charles Carlin, Nick Lally, Douglas Adams, and Jessi Lehman for reading so many strange stories before I knew what they were for. At the Center for Humanities, Megan Massino and Marrion Ladd make it all happen. Thank you for your support and friendship. And special thanks also to Stephen Young and Kris Olds of UW Madison Geography for making this dude from California feel so very much at home.

I am so very privileged to be a faculty member in the School of International Service at American University. Thank you to the faculty and staff of this uniquely diverse and dynamic institution for believing in me. Thank you for opening up an entirely new world of insights and possibilities and for giving me crucial support to finish this book and get it out into the world.

Nathan Groth, Thomas Jack Waldo Allen, John Elrick, Ramon Quintero, and PJ Johnson, your friendship enriches my life and your insights on life and death, art, morality, politics, and the Absurdity of It All are, for me, essential knowledge. I miss you all very much and keen for the all the trouble, crazy spaces, and conversations I have only ever been able to find with you.

I owe the deepest depth of gratitude to my family. Gwendolyn and Norah, thank you for loving and supporting me through all these years of trial and separation. Audrey Alabama, your daddy loves you more than you will ever know, and this book, as is everything I do from here on out, is for you. The three of you are the lights of my life by which I find my way out of the darkness again and again. Thank you Mama and my dads Tony and Georges for teaching me about dreams and how to follow them. Marc and Paul, my brothers, you have always been and always will be my greatest companions of the soul. Grandma Priscilla, your support throughout my career has been key to any success I can claim. Thank you Grandma Audrey for your never-ending curiosity. You taught me how to ask questions and how to listen and made me who I am. Of all the people in my life, you would have enjoyed reading this book more than anyone else.

APPENDIX

Notes on Methodology

.

The logistics, dynamics, and politics of ethnographic research in and on violent contexts are deeply fraught and complicated. As I noted in the introduction, questions of access, security (for myself and my contacts), representation, and responsibility haunted both the research and the writing of this book. In each chapter and story I have highlighted the ethical and epistemic conundrums that were present throughout my fieldwork and from time to time would sharpen into stark focus. In this appendix I describe in a more systematic fashion the strategies and tactics I employed to access, grow, maintain, and protect the network of contacts, informants, and friends whose experiences and perspectives fill these pages.

Ethnographic research for this book began in the summer of 2010, when I visited Guatemala City for the first time and made contact with several government and nongovernment gang rehabilitation organizations. That summer I lived in Guatemala City for two months, returning again for a month from December 2010 to January 2011. Six months later, in July 2011, I moved to Guatemala City to live there on a permanent basis until September 2012. During this period I carried out the bulk of the ethnographic research for this book and established the networks that I continue to draw from today. Since September 2012, I have returned to Guatemala City three or four times a year for two to four weeks at a time and have maintained regular contact with my network of friends and contacts via cell phone, Skype, email, and WhatsApp.

INTRODUCTIONS

My first contact with gang-involved individuals came through gang rehabilitation organizations. Two in particular—one run under the auspices of the Guatemalan government, the other an NGO funded mostly by Scandinavian donors—became my primary means of getting into prisons and gang-affected neighborhoods. Upon making contact with these organizations in June 2010, I informed them that I was a US doctoral researcher conducting a study of Guatemala's maras, their history and modus operandi, the forces that drive criminal violence in post–Cold War Guatemala City, and efforts to bring peace to the streets. After I had a few initial meetings with the directors of these organizations, they invited me to accompany and participate in their projects on the street and in prisons.

In my conversations with the administrators and social workers who ran these organizations, I expressed an open (and honest) sympathy for their efforts. After studying the consequences of the harsh, draconian law-and-order responses to gangs exported from the United States and embraced across Central America's Northern Triangle, I believed (and still believe) that these organizations' peaceful, rehabilitation-oriented interventions offered a badly needed alternative. In the midst of public outrage against anyone or anything affiliated with Central American gangs and widespread support for violent extrajudicial anti-gang strategies, organizations practicing nonviolent intervention methods are increasingly rare. A severe lack of funding, institutional support, and trained personnel ensure their efforts have little measurable impact. Still, their very existence, to my mind, speaks against the harsh politics determining government and societal responses to gangs and crime in general.

Both organizations operated on shoestring budgets, but the NGO was in a particularly precarious financial position. After years of barely getting by, in fact, it folded in 2013 amid accusations of embezzlement against top administrators.

In practice, my inclusion and participation in the organizations' activities depended entirely on the generosity and goodwill of the social workers who ran their day-to-day operations. During my initial visits and in my first months of living in Guatemala City, these men and women were essential in helping me gain the trust of the gang-involved men with whom they worked. They introduced me to community members and prisoners as someone who could be trusted, a "North American doctoral student writing a book on the struggle to survive in Guatemala." For various reasons, I suspected that having a foreign observer along may have helped the social workers boost their own legitimacy in the eyes of prisoners, community members, and prison authorities. In several workshops in Pavón prison, for example, the social worker in charge would reference my presence as evidence that people outside of prison do in fact care about the welfare of prisoners. My presence also seemed to pique the interest of the social workers' higher ups; for example, in late 2012 the minister in charge of the department that housed the government gang rehabilitation project I volunteered with asked me into his office for a staged interview. With cameras rolling, he pushed me to assess the department's peaceful intervention program. I lauded the social workers' efforts with all the enthusiasm I could muster.

TELLING STORIES

Establishing rapport with gang-involved individuals took time. For the first few months of ethnographic research—both in prison and on the street—I conducted very few in-depth interviews. In fact, at first I spent most of my time in prison simply assisting the social workers and participating in organized activities. I helped in any way I could: by transporting materials, keeping notes during meetings, organizing meals, and becoming the organizations' unofficial photographer. I also helped set up and run icebreakers and arts and crafts activities; played basketball, volleyball, and *futbol* with inmates; shared meals in prison restaurants or communal barbecues; and engaged in what anthropologists call "deep hanging out"—that altogether informal but nonetheless rigorous approach to developing understanding and rapport through engagement with the world of one's research subjects.[1] Many of the conversations from this period began (and ended) with prisoners questioning me about my background, where I came from, why I was in Guatemala, and so forth.

With every person I spoke with, I had to establish who I was and what I wanted. How I established my identity would dictate how they responded to me. This meant weaving my way among the stereotypes they expected of a foreigner in Guatemala asking questions about crime and violence. Many of the men I spoke with wanted to know why I cared so much about the maras of Guatemala that I would leave my country, my home, and my family to live in a foreign country, with all the difficulties and deprivations such a move entails. A common assumption, unsurprisingly, was that I was somehow connected to US law enforcement. Many gang-involved men I spoke with joked (or half-joked) about me working for the FBI, the CIA, or the Los Angeles police department (there were many inmates in Pavón prison who had been deported from Los Angeles). Such suspicions were logical in light of the intense scrutiny US law enforcement has focused on Central America's maras and their transnational reach.

I did my best to mitigate such suspicions. At the beginning, I asked very few direct questions about specific criminal activities, or about gang structures, chains of command, or modus operandi. Instead, I confined conversations to personal histories and perspectives about how and why the interviewee became involved in gang life, his experience in the gang, and his perspective on his own life and involvement in violence. Over time, as I became a familiar face in the prisons, the suspicions seemed to fade, but as the Interpol accusation I shared in the introduction demonstrates, they never disappeared completely.

All social science research is entangled with the problem of power, and ethnographic research, especially in and on vulnerable populations, is especially so.[2] In most cases the magnitude and asymmetry of the power imbalance between myself and my imprisoned and/or impoverished interlocutors was extreme. And, as I conveyed in the stories that directly precede chapters 3 and 4, desperate prison conditions and my comparative wealth and freedom of movement meant that I had to navigate treacherous ethical terrain each time I went to the prisons.

After establishing a degree of trust with people in prison and in some gang-affected neighborhoods, I began to initiate more in-depth interviews with those who were willing to talk to me. As other ethnographers have noted, the problem of gaining informed consent across an extreme power divide from vulnerable subjects begins with the ambiguities of what "informed consent" means in the particular research context. No matter how exhaustively one might explain research protocols, research subjects will often still have their own ideas about why they choose to participate and what they might receive in exchange. For example, in her research on South African black child development under apartheid, Ivy Goduka pointed out that, because of how vulnerable and impoverished her research subjects were, they may have consented to take part in her research out of fear that they or their families might suffer if they did not.[3] To avoid such misunderstandings, I was careful to telegraph the fact that, beyond the gang rehabilitation programs I was working with, I had absolutely no connections to any authority that could help or hurt my interview subjects in any way.

Given such suspicions, I worked to avoid the obvious risk of leaving a paper trail that could expose my interview subjects to investigations by Guatemalan authorities or, indeed, by criminal organizations. I eschewed written consent forms in favor of oral consent. In every case, I informed interviewees about the nature and purpose of my project and the steps I would take to protect their identities. After hearing my spiel, most of my interview subjects readily consented to being recorded. At first I was surprised that some men were so open and even eager to talk about their experiences as perpetrators (and victims) of violence. Over time I came to realize that, for some of these men anyway, having a chance to tell their stories to a willing and apparently neutral listener was in itself a kind of luxury. Trapped behind bars or struggling to survive on the street, they knew, and sometimes openly expressed, that they were probably doomed to live and die in anonymity. In their eyes, I provided a slim hope that their stories would reach beyond their environs. I also believe that at least for some of them, the chance to have their stories in a book published in the United States appeared very attractive. As you have read, the lives (and deaths) of poor young men in Guatemala (as elsewhere) are in many respects invisible and ignored by mainstream society. For these young men who have seen so many like them die, and for gang-involved men facing decades or even lifetimes behind bars, having their stories recorded in a book may have seemed like a chance to escape the sense of anonymous futility that haunted them. Such expectations, of course, can influence how personal stories are recited and recorded, a conundrum of ethnographic fieldwork I explored in chapter 1.

It should be added that throughout my research I have maintained several cautionary practices to safeguard my notes and recorded conversations in order to protect those who shared their stories with me. I used pseudonyms in all written notes so that, for example, should prison authorities confiscate a notebook, nothing incriminating could be directly connected with any specific interview subject. At the end of each day of fieldwork I transcribed my written notes onto my computer and saved them, along with recorded audio of interviews, in a password-protected cloud account. Afterward, I erased the audio files on the voice recorder so that, again, should it fall into the hands of law enforcement or other prisoners, it would contain nothing that could cause problems for my interviewees.

OUTSIDER STATUS

My subjects' faith that I could "tell their side of the story" truthfully was based, at least in part, on my obvious outsider status. My complexion, height, and accented Spanish immediately marked me as a "gringo" in Guatemala. At first this irked me. However, it may in fact have been a blessing (albeit mixed). On the one hand, at first I had a difficult time keeping up with the flow of slang-filled conversation of my interlocutors and sometimes missed the finer nuances of conversations unless someone was willing to explain things to me. On the other hand, the fact that I was not of the same society or background as my interlocutors may have made some of them more willing to engage honestly with my questions. Class and ethnic prejudices in Guatemala are extremely powerful and virulent. As an obvious outsider, I did not have to navigate the inborn suspicions and strictly enforced social barriers that exist between people of different class and ethnic backgrounds in Guatemala. It is a sad fact that the extremely polarized nature of Guatemalan society means that a foreigner may be able to cross social, economic, and ethnic divides with far more ease than native Guatemalans.

The privileges I enjoyed as an outsider were intimately linked to my gender, income, and nationality. As a male prison visitor, for example, I received a mere surface inspection from prison guards, while female visitors underwent cavity searches (see chapter 3 and the stories before and after it). On the inside, I fended off prisoners begging for money or pushing goods to sell. Occasionally I would buy prison-made wares, but as a rule, I never gave money in exchange for a conversation or information. But it felt deeply callous to simply shrug off the fact of my incredible wealth in comparison with the prisoners' incredible poverty, especially that of those who shared their lives with me. I found other means of giving back: buying and sharing meals with prisoners, liaising with lawyers to help push release papers through, arranging for appointments with prison social workers, and so on.

One important (and surprising) means of exchange with the imprisoned men I worked with was my camera. Taking pictures of imprisoned men became not only a way of documenting prison life, but also a mode of giving back. Most of the prisoners I met were not only happy, but incredibly eager, to have their pictures taken. After taking the photos, I would process and print them in Guatemala City and return to prison to hand them out. The men used these photos in a variety of ways; some kept them in their cells, others gave them to their families, and others circulated them to women on the outside in their efforts to woo new visitors.

Over time I shifted more and more to working inside prisons. As I mentioned in the introduction, in the first couple of months living and working in Guatemala City, I found I could not gain the regular access to gang-affected communities that I could to prisons. Whereas I could visit the same prisons two to four days a week, visits to gang-affected neighborhoods occurred on a far more sporadic schedule, depending on numerous factors beyond my control. For example, for weeks on end, according to my social worker companions, a particular neighborhood might be too "hot" to enter. Or shifts in local gang leadership—or recent raids by police—might suddenly make us unwelcome. Ultimately, as time went on, I found I did not have the tools to overcome the obstacles blocking my access to gang networks on the street.

At the same time, even when I did find individuals involved in illicit networks on the street who were willing to let me accompany them in their daily lives, the potential risks, or the chances of being dragged into harmful illegal activities, made me wary of such opportunities. What Lee Ann Fujii calls the "dilemma of proximity" is particularly salient in ethnographic work in and on criminal networks.[4] My "outsider" status could not buffer me from the very real suffering some of the illicit actors I came to know were inflicting on others, and the fact that my mere presence could make me an accomplice to such crimes was ethically untenable. As I related at the end of chapter 4, spending time with extortionists means that one might inadvertently become one. After several experiences witnessing innocent people being victimized by Tommy and others of his ilk, I ceased regular contact with such people and focused my efforts in other areas. As a result, I found myself spending more and more time and attention on my networks in prison.

The relationships of trust and affinity I was able to establish among my networks in prison drove my research in new directions. But my reliance on these networks also dictated whom I could access on the outside. This is one reason, for example, that the book contains so few conversations with women. Since so many of my most important contacts were men trapped behind bars, I depended on them for growing my network of interview subjects and contacts beyond the space of the prison. But given the sexual politics of male prisons (see chapter 3) and how fetishized light skin and a foreign passport can be in Guatemalan society, I was reticent to pursue interviews with my prisoner contacts' female companions too avidly. In no way did I want to risk bringing further tension into already fraught relationships between prisoners and their families on the outside. The unfortunate result is that for most of my time conducting ethnographic research for this book, my male prisoner contacts mediated my relationships with the women in their lives. I have since tried to correct this deep imbalance. In subsequent research, I have delved deeper into the roles and experiences of the female prison visitors who, as I argue in chapter 3, effectively triage Guatemala's failing prison system.[5]

BEYOND THE UNDERWORLD

After several months of building my network of gang-involved individuals, I began pursuing interviews with Guatemalan law enforcement. I had my first contact with law enforcement officials while attending court hearings in Guatemala City's Tower of Tribunals. As I developed networks of contacts and interview subjects among police, prosecutors, and criminal circuit judges, I had to contend with a very obvious dilemma: how to avoid awkward and very possibly dangerous questions about my knowledge and contact with gang-involved individuals. I was always wary of exposing myself and my contacts to law enforcement scrutiny. But to my surprise, the police, prosecutors, and other officials I spoke with never attempted to interrogate me, and I did not have to proactively protect my sources. Perhaps they thought I could have little to tell them, and I was careful to encourage this opinion. In retrospect, I'm not sure why officials tended to take this "hands-off" approach, but I suspect it had something to do with my being a gringo. Upon learning I was from the United States, many of the government officials I came into contact with tended to treat me with a deference that made me uncomfortable. But acting the part of the incredulous, naive gringo appeared the best strategy to avoid betraying the confidences of my friends and contacts involved in the gangs.

Over time my networks on both sides of the law grew, and I ceased to rely so deeply on the gang rehabilitation organizations that had provided initial access to prisons and gang-affected neighborhoods. In addition to gang-involved prisoners and their families, I developed working relationships with evangelical church pastors, taxi drivers, scholars, prosecutors, journalists, police chiefs, prison officials, street children, public defenders, bartenders, street artists, narco-traffickers, and a myriad of others. My days were spent shuttling back and forth among prisons, gang-affected neighborhoods, the cemetery, government offices, courts, police stations, evangelical churches, and the downtown cafés and restaurants where my better-heeled interlocutors preferred to meet. On a typical day of research, I might eat breakfast with Juande and other former MS members in Pavón prison, interviewing them about their trials and tribulations. In the afternoon I might visit a police precinct to interview a police chief who was involved in torturing and disappearing suspected gang members. And that evening I might have a drink with a high-level official from the attorney general's office. And so on. My kaleidoscopic understanding and rendering of the marero as symbolic figure in Guatemalan society arose out of myriad conversations about crime and violence with this diverse range of subjects.

NOTES

1. Neighboring Honduras, Belize, and El Salvador have, respectively, the first-, third-, and fourth-highest national murder rates in the world. As Rodgers and Jones. (2009) note, "Central America features amongst the highest rates of reported homicidal and criminal violence in Latin America and indeed the world. The annual global homicide rate was approximately 7 per 100,000 in 2004, while in South America it was 25 per 100,000 and in Central America it soared above 29 per 100,000. . . . In contrast to virtually every other region, South and Central America feature the fastest and most dramatic temporal escalation of (homicidal) armed violence since 1999." For official regional homicide counts and analysis, see also World Bank LAC, "Crime and Violence in Central America."

2. This book draws on fieldwork completed in Guatemala City between 2010 and 2016 in the following months: December 2010 through January 2011, July 2011 through September 2012 and December 2012; March, June through August, and December 2013; May through July 2014; January, March, and June–July 2015; and March and September 2016. Those interviewed remain anonymous or are cited by pseudonym. In some cases, certain details (insignificant to the analysis) have been changed to protect the identities of particular people. This includes the use of composite scenes that contain elements from more than one situation. These scenes accurately reflect actual events but have been rearranged to preserve anonymity. Direct quotations, edited for length and style, are from recorded interviews or from detailed notes. All translations are my own. All images, also edited to preserve anonymity, are published here with the subjects' oral consent. Unless otherwise noted in the caption, all pictures were taken by the author.

3. While post–Cold War violence has been mostly concentrated in cities, it is most extreme among marginalized urban populations/spaces. For Latin American–wide treatment of urban violence, see Auyero, Bourgois, and Scheper-Hughes, *Violence at the Urban Margins*.

4. Such trends extend beyond Central America. In many Latin American societies, the end of the Cold War and the growth of democracy have been accompanied by the rise of criminal violence. For regional analyses, see Arias and Goldstein, *Violent Democracies in Latin America*, as well as Arias, *Criminal Enterprise and Governance*.

5. Guatemala's National Civil Police reported there were 4,520 homicides in 2016, 258 fewer than in 2015. The country's murder rate fell from 29.5 per 100,000 to 27.3, continuing a trend seen in recent years following a high of 46.5 per 100,000 in 2009 (Gagne, "InSight Crime's 2016 Homicide Round-up"). See also UNODC, "International Homicide Count and Rate per 100,000 Population."

6. "Guatemala is a good place to commit a murder, because you will almost certainly get away with it" (Alston, "Report of the Special Rapporteur," 17). For most of the postwar era, the prosecution rate lingered at 5 percent, and it was as low as 2 percent for violent crimes targeting women. The increase to 10 percent represents a marked improvement, engineered by former attorney general Claudia Paz y Paz before she was ejected from office in 2013 for pursuing high-profile war crimes cases.

7. For a seminal study of how deeply the Guatemalan state and organized criminal groups interpenetrate one another, see Peacock and Beltran, *Poderes Ocultos*.

8. For example, in a recent analysis of homicides in a gang-dominated area, Steven Dudley found that in more than 40 percent of murders the police were unable to verify whether the crime was related in any way to gangs or organized crime ("Homicides in Guatemala").

9. I borrow this term from Zilberg's account of postwar San Salvador, El Salvador ("Gangster in Guerilla Face," 39).

10. Widespread anxiety over insecurity has proven a useful tool for Latin American politicians across the region. See, for example, Chevigny, "The Populism of Fear," and Pearce, "Perverse State Formation."

11. I draw from Laclau and Mouffe's characterization of "nodal points" in discursive formations that stabilize, at least in part, the otherwise ongoing flux of discourse and contestation (*Hegemony and Socialist Strategy*, 112–113).

12. Maras, then, are key figures in what Laclau and Mouffe call the "structuring of a discursive field" (*Hegemony and Socialist Strategy*). That is, they are nodal points in how Guatemalan society makes meaning out of criminal violence. This has great import for how people both make sense of and react to violent events. As Laclau and Mouffe note, "An earthquake or the falling of a brick is an event that certainly exists, in the sense that it occurs here and now, independently of my will. But whether their specificity as objects is constructed in terms of 'natural phenomena' or 'expressions of the wrath of god' depends upon the structuring of a discursive field" (*Hegemony and Socialist Strategy*, 108).

13. For the theoretical underpinnings of the concept of the social imaginary, see Castoriadis, *Imaginary Institution of Society*.

14. The Cold War played a pivotal role in Guatemalan history, and Guatemala occupied an important place in the Cold War struggle to determine the political order of the world. As historian Greg Grandin argues, "In [the] 1980s it seemed like something

NOTES TO PAGES 4–7 ✦ 265

new and vital was taking place, in terms of the political alliances being formed between urban workers and peasants, the fusion of radical Christianity and socialism, and in Guatemala, the incorporation of indigenous communities as such into the struggle. Yet in retrospect, the killing unleashed to contain the threat turned the region into one of the cold war's endgames, and the place where Latin America's revolutionary century broke and rolled back" ("Living in Revolutionary Time," 31–32).

15. See the Commission for Historical Clarification, *Guatemala: Memory of Silence*.

16. For a definitive accounting of civil war era atrocities, see Archbishop's Office of Human Rights (ODHA), *Guatemala: Nunca Más*.

17. On history and mechanisms of massacre, see Manz, *Paradise in Ashes*. For background on ongoing efforts to find justice for wartime atrocities, see Oglesby and Ross, "Guatemala's Genocide Determination and the Spatial Politics of Justice." For the global importance of this case in international efforts to prosecute genocide and other war crimes, see Ross, "The Rios Montt Case and Universal Jurisdiction."

18. Memories of the disappeared are still in the process of disinterment. In 2015, for example, a warehouse's worth of decayed and rat-eaten police files documenting the capture, torture, and execution of the disappeared was discovered in a Guatemala City government building. In most cases, such documentation is all that remains of the disappeared (see Weld, *Paper Cadavers*).

19. See Manz, *Paradise in Ashes*.

20. This story was related to me by Mario Polanco, whose Grupo de Apoyo Mutuo (GAM) was the first organization in Guatemala to help survivors' efforts to locate the disappeared.

21. For more on ongoing struggles over wartime atrocities and the politics of memory, see Sieder, "War, Peace, and the Politics of Memory in Guatemala."

22. For the history of secrecy enshrouding victims of military war crimes, see Sanford, *Buried Secrets*; and Figueroa Ibarra, "Guatemala: El recurso del miedo."

23. Translated and quoted in Franco, *Cruel Modernity*, 193.

24. Suarez-Orozco, "The Treatment of Children," 238.

25. For the processes of polarization and organization that pushed poor Central Americans into armed insurgent action in Guatemala, see Manz, *Paradise in Ashes*; and in El Salvador, see Wood, *Insurgent Collective Action*. For a seminal discussion of how and why civil war violence unfolds in particular ways, see Kalyvas, *The Logic of Violence in Civil War*.

26. See Grandin, *Last Colonial Massacre* and "Living in Revolutionary Time."

27. For example, see, among many others, Biden, "Joe Biden: A Plan for Central America"; Shifter, *Countering Criminal Violence in Central America*; Renwick, *Central America's Violent Northern Triangle*; UNDP, *Understanding Social Conflict in Latin America*; and UNDP, *Decade of Work on Citizen Security and Conflict Prevention*.

28. Mario Polanco (executive director of GAM), interview with author, Guatemala City, March 9, 2012.

29. For parallel nostalgia in neighboring El Salvador, see Zilberg, "Gangster in Guerilla Face," 40.

30. Here I draw from Walter Benjamin's observation of how, in interwar Europe, particular subjugated bodies became emissaries for a brutal sovereign order. The first was the sandwich-board man walking the streets of Paris. Typically drawn from the city's homeless laborers, for a few pennies he would make himself a walking advertisement for commodities he could not himself afford. The second figure was a naked Jewish man in Berlin, flanked on each side by SS men, a sign hanging from his neck proclaiming support for Hitler. In each of these cases, a body has been "subjectivated," transformed into a courier of political messages askew from the individual's will. The purity of the message in both of these cases is striking; the indigent advertising capitalism's commodities and the soon-to-be-extinguished racial other forced to celebrate his executioner's power both evoke the total domination of the economic or political order (see Buck-Morss, *Hegel, Haiti*).

31. Zilberg, "Gangster in Guerilla Face." In postwar El Salvador, Zilberg explores the murkiness and "double faced" (*doble cara*) nature of these connections by showing how the language of violence and the figure of the gang member are used by all political sides, reinvoking images and nightmares from the past in new forms that are misrecognized even as they take on the identities imputed to them. She calls the double face the "dialectical image" through which one can begin to understand the historical connections and misrecognitions that divide our understanding of how violence occurs and "the Real."

32. Goldman, *Art of Political Murder*.

33. See Girard, *Violence and the Sacred* for how the socially constructed figure of the scapegoat becomes a means of mediating cultural struggle and violence by focusing it on a single individual or group. The scapegoat is, to quote Begoña Aretxaga, "a ritual repository of the jarring violence inhabiting the national community" ("Maddening States," 397).

34. Manwaring, *Street Gangs*.

35. Rodgers, "Slum Wars of the 21st Century," 2. For language and analyses that reproduce the image of war in post–Cold War Central America, see also Arana, "New Battle for Central America"; and Farah, *Transformation of El Salvador's Gangs*.

36. Here and elsewhere I draw on the notion formulated by Benjamin and made explicit by Derrida (in "Spectres of Marx") that the past "haunts" the present as a specter arising again and again unbidden to intrude upon world history. Drawing on Benjamin, Harvey (*Spaces of Global Capitalism*) references 9/11 and the US move to make war as an example of such haunting in the contemporary United States, as soldier allies (the Taliban) of past wars became new enemies. In my case, the gangs of Central America represent defunct ideological warriors of the past. In the hands of political actors, this past can also be "conjured" into the present, called upon to push forward political projects, as is the case with *mano dura* law-and-order initiatives as well as left-wing efforts for justice (see chapter 5). For scholarly analysis that questions the same ideological comparison, see Rocha, "Mareros y pandilleros."

37. Zilberg, "Gangster in Guerilla Face."

38. See, for example, Arana, "New Battle for Central America"; ERIC et al., *Maras y Pandillas en Centroamerica*; and Hagedorn, *World of Gangs*. Hagedorn roots the

"institutionalization" of gangs across the world in a wide array of localized factors, including ethnic identity, urban conditions, and local drug markets.

39. Baird, "Negotiating Pathways to Manhood." Meanwhile, media scapegoating of youths from poor urban neighborhoods has made it even more difficult for them to find jobs and vulnerable to targeting by police and vigilantes and so has driven more kids into the maras. See Huhn et al., "Exploding Crime?"

40. For comparable observations by scholars of Guatemalan gangs, see Brenneman, *Homies and Hermanos*. For gangs in Colombia and other Latin American countries, see Baird, "Negotiating Pathways." And for seminal studies of marginalized youth struggling for a sense of dignity through involvement in illicit activities, see Jankowski, *Islands in the Street*; Bourgois, *In Search of Respect*; Contreras, *Stickup Kids*; and Goffman, *On the Run*.

41. DeCesare, "Children of War," 25.

42. For background on Kaibiles, see Guatemala Human Rights Commission, "Guatemala's Elite Special Forces Unit."

43. The breadth and variety of security solutions targeting gang youth is astounding. The following is an incomplete list of public policy interventions from across the political spectrum: WOLA, *Youth Gangs in Central America*; Eguizábal et al., *Crime and Violence in Central America's Northern Triangle*; ERIC et al., *Maras y Pandillas en Centroamerica*; Farah, *Transformation of El Salvador's Gangs into Political Actors*; Moser and Winton, "Violence in the Central American Region"; UNODC, *Crime and Development in Central America*; and USAID, *Central America and Mexico Gang Assessment*.

44. Here I parallel Fanon's characterization of how colonial rule leads to "internecine violence" among colonized populations. When a colonized population cannot rise up to throw off the yolk of colonial rule, Fanon argues, the inherently violent nature of colonial society infiltrates everyday social relations, "poisoning the blood" (Fanon, *Wretched of the Earth*).

45. For the most insightful deconstruction of evangelical Christian discourses of the maras' association with the devil, see Brenneman, *Homies and Hermanos*; and O'Neill, *Secure the Soul*.

46. Emilio Goubaud (youth advocate), interview with author, Villa Nueva, Guatemala, September 10, 2011.

47. Walter Villatoro (criminal circuit court judge), interview with author, Guatemala City, August 5, 2012.

48. For theories of the Other and encountering the Other, see Lévinas, *Totality and Infinity*; Said, *Orientalism*; and Rorty, "Human Rights, Rationality and Sentimentality."

49. That this image is so gendered speaks to how the mara phenomenon in particular and criminal violence in general are deeply associated with poor young males in the collective imagination. There have been few in-depth examinations of the role of "home girls" (female gang members) in Central American gangs, and those that exist speak of considerable misogyny and mistreatment (see Interpeace, *Violentas y violentadas*). Clearly, more research is needed.

50. 1 Corinthians 13:12.

51. Arendt, *On Violence*, 5.

52. See, for example, Hansen, Blom, and Stepputat, *Sovereign Bodies*, for a seminal discussion of state sovereignty (and lack thereof) in the postcolonial era.

53. Comaroff and Comaroff, *Law and Disorder in the Postcolony*, 5.

54. Post–Cold War Latin America has experienced a "democratization" of brutality such that violence is no longer "the resource of only the traditionally powerful or of the grim uniformed guardians of the nation . . . [and] increasingly appears as an option for a multitude of actors in pursuit of all kinds of goals" (Koonings and Krujit, *Societies of Fear*, 11). For regional assessments of this phenomenon, see Davis, "Urban Violence, Quality of Life and the Future of Latin American Cities"; Briceño-Leon and Zubillaga, "Violence and Globalization in Latin America"; and Adams, *Chronic Violence and Its Reproduction*.

55. For in-depth analysis of how deeply linked agents of the Guatemalan state are to illicit actors, see Peacock and Beltran, *Poderes Ocultos*.

56. Jütersonke, Muggah, and Rodgers, "Gangs, Urban Violence, and Security Interventions," 375–376.

57. Other factors include inequality; globalization; violent masculinity; civil war legacies; corrupt law enforcement; transnational drug markets; US domestic and foreign policy; failed families; authoritarian sociocultural structures; personal desperation; the weak, troubled shell of democratic government; social prejudice; and hyperaggressive capitalism.

58. Moodie, *El Salvador in the Aftermath of Peace*, 207.

59. Carter, "Gothic Sovereignty."

60. Green, *Fear as a Way of Life*.

61. Nelson, *Reckoning*.

62. Taussig, "Culture of Terror," 492–493.

63. Precarity is "a condition of vulnerability relative to contingency and the inability to predict" (Ettlinger, "Precarity Unbound," 320).

64. Williams, *Marxism and Literature*.

65. For theoretical discussions on false consciousness, see Althusser, *Lenin and philosophy*; Gramsci, *Selections from the Prison Notebooks*; Lukács, *History and Class Consciousness*; Mannheim, *Ideology and Utopia*; Marx, *Capital*; and Marx and Engels, *German Ideology*.

66. For in-depth treatment of how structural violence shapes contemporary life in the Americas, see, for example, Farmer, *Aids and Accusation*; and Vogt, "Crossing Mexico."

67. The breadth and diversity of the maras' multiple associations with specters of violence both past and present ensure that their image infiltrates collective consciousness in ways that violate any clear boundaries between the local and the global, the past and the present, reason and unreason. To study and capture this state of affairs, I follow Derrida's provocation to allow the "paradoxical state of specters" to shine through by refusing to categorize them and thereby fix their meaning in a static state (see Derrida, "Spectres of Marx").

68. My decision to use ethnographic encounters to reach beyond intellectual decon-struction and convey carnal knowledge is in part a response to Loïc Wacquant's invo-cation to "expand textual genres and styles so as to better capture the taste and ache of social action" ("Body, the Ghetto, and the Penal State," 101).

69. Like many ethnographers before me, I was seduced by the idea of talking to perpetrators of violence. In response, I explore what Antonius Robben would call the "seduction" of conducting ethnography with and on gang members and other violent actors in my appendix on methodology ("Ethnographic Seduction, Transference, and Resistance").

70. See, for example, Rodgers, "'We Live in a State of Siege'" and "Living in the Shadow of Death."

71. Carroll, "Killers of Filmmaker . . . Jailed."

72. For an in-depth examination of how homicide counts obfuscate the dynamics of urban violence, see Denyer-Willis, "Before the Body Count."

73. As Cruz and Durán-Martinez show ("Hiding Violence to Deal with the State"), state ignorance about the "truth" of criminal violence is widespread across Latin America, and criminal organizations often labor (with complicity from state agents) to keep the state security forces officially in the dark.

74. Dudley, "Homicides in Guatemala."

75. Feldman, "Ethnographic States of Emergency," 231.

76. Ibid., 231.

77. Ibid., 234.

78. For more on gender issues in this research, see the appendix.

CHAPTER I. PORTRAIT OF A "REAL" MARERO

1. All names besides Andy's have been changed to protect the subjects' security. I have kept Andy's identity intact because he is dead and because he wanted me to use his real name. A note on translation. The Central American gang vernacular is laced with English and Spanglish terms imported with the Los Angeles gang symbols and structure by deported US gang members, gang films, and other conduits of cultural transfusion. When possible, I have tried to retain some of Andy's and others' original language, which includes both terms such as *watchear* (to watch or look) and Spanish slang like *paro*, *carnal*, and *la onda*, which have no direct English translation.

2. Taussig, *Law in a Lawless Land*, 112.

3. Portelli, *The Death of Luigi Trastulli*, 1.

4. Reconstructing life histories through interviews with gang-involved youth and other young people surviving in violent environments is a complex ordeal, and many researchers have explored its limits. For example, see Levenson, *Adiós Niño*; Ward, *Gangsters Without Borders*; and Zubillaga, "Un testimonio reflexivo."

5. Even under the safest and most secure circumstances, acts of representation always entail a threading together of truth and fantasy. The inborn ambiguities that arise are essential to individual notions of self as well as collective imaginaries.

6. Vargas Llosa, *Making Waves*, 330.

7. See Zilberg, "Fools Banished from the Kingdom," and Kurtenbach, "Youth Violence as a Scapegoat" for police profiling of gang-involved youth in the Northern Triangle of Central America.

8. The maras incorporate (and are incorporated into) a wide variety of illicit structures across the region. See Rodgers, "Living in the Shadow of Death," for comparable dynamics in Nicaragua; Pine, *Working Hard, Drinking Hard*, and Gutierrez Rivera, *Territories of Violence*, for Honduran gangs and organized crime; D'Aubuisson, *En las profundidades de una pandilla salvadoreña*, for El Salvador; and Rodgers and Jones, *Youth Violence in Latin America*, for Latin America more generally.

9. For another perspective on this phenomenon, see Grassi, "Territorial Conflicts and Gangs in Guatemala."

10. See Levenson, *Adiós Niño*.

11. Andy's being a member of both gangs was something of a rarity. It is extremely unusual for a gang member to switch allegiances between the two major gang franchises. However, it is not uncommon for gang members to have siblings and other family members in rival gangs. Certain poor, urban neighborhoods are so completely carved up among competing gangs that immediate neighbors and even members of the same household can join up with gangs at war with one another. Such intimate relations between mortal enemies is part of what makes gang warfare so deadly.

12. Herrera, "Identifican a testigo."

13. The word *carnal* means "brother" or "comrade," but with a deeply visceral connotation. "Blood brother" is probably the most literal translation, but the expression lacks the sense of casual friendship that *carnal* can also imply.

14. Federico related his last conversation with Andy to me that same evening.

15. See Skarbek, *Social Order of the Underworld*. *Sureño* is the catchall term for Latino gangs in Southern California united under the Mexican Mafia (La Eme), a powerful Latino prison gang operating throughout the American Southwest. Both the MS and Barrio18 originated as sureño gangs in Los Angeles and abided by the sureño's codes of Latino solidarity, known as the SUR (Southern United Raza) until La Mara Salvatrucha broke the pact in August 2005.

16. *Vato* is common slang meaning guy, dude, or fellow; *a la gran* is a contraction of "*a la gran puta*" or "to the great whore," an expression of dismay; and *hacer paro* means to help, to do favors for. *Paro* is also the term for a "gang associate," a person who does favors for the gang.

17. *La onda* means the vibe. The term can have spiritual connotations, such as "the way" or "the feeling."

18. Zepeda, "El Salvador de Guatemala" and "Fue un lujo conocer al 'Soldado' y sus 'hommies'."

19. *Barrio* in general terms means "neighborhood" or "neighborhood community," but in mara vernacular it refers to the gang itself. In some sense it is an atavistic term that recalls when gangs proactively protected the neighborhood communities from which they sprang instead of preying upon them.

20. *Ramflero* is the leader of a gang clique. It is a transnationally constructed word that literally means the pilot (*flero*) of the Dodge Ram.

21. *Chante* is slang for "house" or "pad," and *huario*, pronounced "wario," is a bastardization of the English word *war*.

22. All gang *apodos* (nicknames), also known as *takazos*, have been left in their original language.

23. Andy uses the term *bestia*, which means both beast (brutal animal) and the devil. The spiritual stakes of gang belonging are often translated entirely through an Evangelical Christian lens. See O'Neill, "The Reckless Will" and *Secure the Soul*.

24. Andy's refrain echoes what Levenson has called the gangs' proclivity for "necro-living" (*Adiós Niño*, 6).

25. Andy's parroting of the mara motto exemplifies the gangs' self-conscious embrace of their own carefully cultivated alterity—what Jon Horne Carter in his work on Honduran maras has called an "anti-idealist epistemology" ("Gothic Sovereignty," 492): the maras' self-mutilation and satanic iconography in their tattoos, their brash celebration of death and violence, and their triumphant mimicking of societal discourses that label them fit only for extermination.

26. Biehl, *Vita*, 40.

27. For analysis of the meaning of horror in the modern age, see Kristeva, *Pouvoirs de l'horreur*.

28. In *structural violence* some social structure or social institutions may harm people by preventing them from meeting their basic needs (see Galtung, "Violence, Peace, and Peace Research"). For in-depth analyses of the consequences of structural violence in postcolonial societies, see Farmer, *AIDS and Accusation* and "On Suffering and Structural Violence."

29. See Freud, *Civilization and Its Discontents*.

30. Found in a wide variety of ancient mythologies, the Ouroborous (Greek for "tail-devouring serpent") motif represents self-perpetuating cyclical forces without any clear beginning or end.

31. See also Baird, "Negotiating Pathways to Manhood."

32. Feldman, *Formations of Violence*.

33. Hoffman, "West-African Warscapes," 336.

34. I was trying to catch Andy in a lie with this question, to make him contradict himself, because the story sounded so fantastic.

35. Hackford, *Blood In, Blood Out*.

36. The phenomenon of criminals copycatting their Hollywood doppelgangers is not unique to Central American maras. The Sicilian Mafia never left decapitated horse heads in victims' beds before they saw *The Godfather*, and members of the contemporary mafia often take their stylistic cues from *The Sopranos* (see Gambetta, *Codes of the Underworld*). Similarly, Indonesia's 1960s paramilitary henchmen would often watch Hollywood Westerns—the genocidal genre par excellence—before executing suspected Communist sympathizers (see Oppenheimer and Cynn, *The Act of Killing*).

CHAPTER 2. EMISSARIES OF THE VIOLENT PEACE

1. I gleaned the meanings of the tres puntos tattoo through conversations with gang members deported from the United States. For obvious reasons, US law enforcement also tracks the presence of tattoos associated with sureño gangs, often (mistakenly) using tattoos as prima facie evidence of gang membership. For the consequences of such unsound strategies, see Joyce, "Stars, Dragons, and the Letter M."

2. Dudley, "Homicides in Guatemala: Analyzing the Data." Recent in-depth investigations to understand what proportion of daily homicides can reasonably be connected to gangs indicate that maras seem to be involved in about 40 percent of urban murders. However, the same study showed that authorities are unable to identify likely perpetrators in nearly 35 percent of all homicides.

3. UNODC, *Crime and Development in Central America*; and USAID, *Central America and Mexico Gang Assessment*, 45.

4. Harvey, drawing on Benjamin, makes a clear distinction between "historicizing" past events and "memorializing" them. This distinction pivots on the difference between history, which he calls "a relative temporal concept," and memory, "a relational temporal concept." Referencing the struggle over what to build upon the site of 9/11, he writes:

> We have a choice of whether to historicize the events of 9/11 at the site or to seek to memorialize them. If the site is merely historicized in relative space (by a certain sort of monumentality) then this imposes a fixed narrative on the space. The effect will be to foreclose on future possibilities and interpretations and through that closure constrict the generative power with which to build a different future. Memory, on the other hand, is, according to Benjamin, a potentiality that can at times 'flash up' uncontrollably to reveal new possibilities. The way the site might be lived by those who encounter it then becomes unpredictable and uncertain. Collective memory, a diffuse but nevertheless powerful sense that pervades many an urban scene, can play a significant role in animating political and social movements. ("Space as Keyword," 285–286)

5. Malkki, *Purity and Exile*; and Pred, *The Past Is Not Dead*.

6. See Kosek, *Understories*, 34; and Boyarin, *Remapping Memory*.

7. Aretxaga, "Maddening States."

8. "The 'worlds made' through narrations of the past are always historically situated and culturally constructed," writes Liisa Malkki, "And it is these that people act upon and riddle with meaning" (*Purity and Exile*, 104). The history I strive to recount is that which makes the maras' world and that makes the maras so essential to ordering contemporary society. Tracing this history's dystopian trajectory means traveling back and forth along decaying temporal circuits through which the past gives rise to the present and the interests of the present illuminate—but also eclipse—the dreams and nightmares of the past.

9. Across Central America, the transition from Cold War–era authoritarianism to peacetime democracy has not been easy and has involved a considerable "reimagining"

of how democracy is supposed to function. See Burrell and Moodie, *Central America in the New Millennium*.

10. See Casa Alianza, *Torture of Guatemalan Street Children*.

11. Such mourning for a lost past does not, of course, belong solely to former members of the maras disgusted with and fearful of the gangs' present form. Rich or poor, leftist or conservative, urban Guatemalans from across the political and economic spectrums lament the loss of a certain sense of security that made life feel less precarious than it does today. Residents of gang-dominated communities lament the loss of "los codigos de antes" (the codes of before), which limited the scope and trajectory of gang violence (Saunders-Hastings, "'Los Códigos de Antes'"). Many urbanites rage at the government's present weakness, longing for the days when, backed by martial law, police could "disappear" anyone who looked like a marero. Others bitterly recall the loss of a collective political consciousness that made effective political action from below seem like a real possibility, whereas today the poor spend more time tearing at each other than working together to overcome their shared squalor. And so it seems the ideal future has been lost along the way, buried somewhere in the irrecoverable and irrevocable past.

12. Levenson, "Por sí mismos."

13. Levenson, *Adiós Niño*, 46.

14. A no less haunting refiguring of civil war atrocities is still taking place through educational programs sponsored by the Guatemalan government and the US government, which actively erases the political agency of the massacred and disappeared, posing them as mere "victims" of an ugly war rather than political subjects fighting for their rights (Oglesby, "Educating Citizens in Postwar Guatemala").

15. For more background on the long civil war and the transition to peace in Guatemalan history, see Sieder, "War, Peace, and the Politics of Memory in Guatemala"; Sanford, *Buried Secrets*; Levenson, *Trade Unionists Against Terror*; Figueroa Ibarra, "Guatemala: El recurso del miedo"; and Manz, *Paradise in Ashes*.

16. The general consensus on the etymology of this term links it to a 1970s Brazilian film popular in many parts of Latin America that featured a destructive species of ant called "marabunta" (see Merino, "Las maras en Guatemala").

17. Levenson, *Adiós Niño*, 64.

18. Ibid., 75.

19. See Sieder, "War, Peace, and the Politics of Memory in Guatemala"; and Nelson, *Finger in the Wound*.

20. Asturias, *El Señor Presidente*.

21. Arthur and Carroll, "El Salvador Holds Its Breath after Day without Murders."

22. Martinez and Sanz, "El dia de la traicion."

23. *Morro* means darkie, moor, or Arab.

24. *Patojo* is slang for youth, that is, "youngster."

25. *La neta* is slang for the truth, the reality, the "real deal."

26. *Simón* indicates emphatic assent.

27. Cruz, "Central American *Maras*."

28. Cf. ibid.; Manwaring, *Street Gangs*. The Federal Bureau of Investigation still maintains offices in Central American countries to monitor gangs that pose a "threat to the United States," and the present administration (2018) is considering putting the MS on the US list of designated terrorist organizations.

29. Cruz, "Central American *Maras*," 387.

30. This history has been exhaustively documented. For clear explanations of US Cold War interventions in Guatemala, see Rabe, *Killing Zone*; and Kinzer, *Brothers*.

31. See, for example, Adam Curtis's documentary *Century of Self*, which chronicles the role of renowned publicist Edward Bernays (Sigmund Freud's nephew) in the 1954 coup.

32. Kinzer, *Overthrow*.

33. For a general analysis of the American dream among migrant communities, see, for example, Clark, *Immigrants and the American Dream*.

34. See O'Neill, *Secure the Soul*.

35. Héctor Aguilar Camín, quoted in Radden Keefe, "Cocaine Incorporated."

36. See Dudley, "How Drug Trafficking Operates."

37. Fogelbach, "Gangs, Violence, and Victims."

38. Sanz and Martinez, "Los Maras de Centro America."

39. Ibid.

40. Nietzsche, *Genealogy of Morals*; Foucault, *History of Sexuality*; and Brown, *Politics Out of History*.

41. O'Neill, "Reckless Will."

42. UNODC, *Transnational Organized Crime*.

43. For a historical and theoretical approach to identity-making processes, see Hacking, "Making Up People."

44. Gregory, *Colonial Present*.

45. See Skarbek, *Social Order of the Underworld*, for deep background on the Mexican Mafia's birth and evolution.

46. Ibid.

47. Ibid. See also Rafael, *Mexican Mafia*.

48. In opposition to La Eme's heavy-handed control of imprisoned Latinos, other Latino prison gangs, most notably Nuestra Familia, have risen up to challenge La Eme's dominance. In California, Nuestra Familia comprises mainly Latino gangs based in Northern California, who have become known as Norteños, affiliated gangs utilizing "14" to show their allegiance. The geographical dividing line is said to be in Soledad Prison, near Salinas in central California. Other racially organized prisoner associations/gangs rose up in the California prison system in the 1960s and 1970s and still operate today. The Black Guerrilla Family (BGF) began in San Quentin Prison, founded by George Jackson and W. L. Nolen and inspired by the teachings of Marcus Garvey. The Aryan Brotherhood formed around the same time (late 1960s and early 1970s) espousing an (obviously) white supremacist ideology and often aligning with

the Mexican Mafia against the BGF in fights over control of prison black markets (see Skarbek, *The Social Order of the Underworld*).

49. Skarbek, *Social Order of the Underworld*.

50. For an in-depth look at clecha among US-based gangs, see Cruz, "Letting Go of Clecha, While Holding Corazón."

51. See chapter 3, "Porous Prisons," for more on mara-led riots and the united sureños in prison.

52. The same process of imported rivalry occurred across the Northern Triangle of Central America, and with similar results (cf. Zilberg, *Space of Detention*; and Pine, *Working Hard, Drinking Hard*). In an interview with Zilberg, a deported gangster in El Salvador complained, "Whoever brought my neighborhood back here in the 90s, they fucked up, really fucked up my country. Because man, you really see the writing on the walls in the streets. It's like you're seeing the freeways from L.A., and they don't even know how to write on the walls. They write real stupid, you know. They put 'Westside 18th Street' or 'Northside MS,' and we're not really on the Northside or Westside here. We're in South Central. Or they put area '213.' Man, that's a telephone call from downtown California, ... or put '818.' That's El Monte, you know. They get me real mad because they don't even know about the Southside thing, or the Northside thing. They just know enemy 18th Street, or enemy MS" (*Spaces of Detention*, 133–134).

53. Arana, "The New Battle for Central America"; Cruz, "Central American *Maras*"; Levenson, *Adiós Niño*; and Huhn et al., "Exploding Crime?"

54. Martinez and Sanz, "El dia de la traicion."

55. In interviews with former gang members in Los Angeles and El Salvador, Martinez and Sanz found similar sentiments regarding the failures of gang peace pacts ("El origen del odio").

56. Martinez and Sanz, "El origen del odio."

57. Ibid.

CHAPTER 3. POROUS PRISONS

1. McDonald, "Caging in Central America." For an in-depth analysis of life in Comaygua Prison before the blaze, see Carter, "Tears of the Damned."

2. Wacquant calls this unprecedented growth the "irruption of the penal state" (Wacquant, *Punishing the Poor*, xiii). This has not quelled crime or made life more secure for anyone (see Gilmore, *Golden Gulag*; Wacquant, *Punishing the Poor*; and Simon, "'The 'Society of Captives'"). Only in the last five years have industrialized countries, the United States included, begun to change course and reduce incarceration rates and prison populations.

3. See Foucault, *Discipline and Punish*; Goffman, *Asylums*; Bauman, *Social Issues of Law and Order*; and Irwin, *Prisons in Turmoil*.

4. Fleisher, *Warehousing Violence*. For the history that led to such unprecedented levels of mass incarceration, see Simon, "The 'Society of Captives'."

5. See Foucault, *Discipline and Punish* for how the prison as an institution and mode of punishment reveals logics of power and governance that reach far beyond the prison itself.

6. For a seminal study of how political economic contingencies, racism, and institutional logics create the conditions of mass incarceration in the United States, see Gilmore, *Golden Gulag*.

7. In the United States, long histories of racial discrimination have found brutal expression in the mass incarceration of African Americans. See, for example, Alexander, *The New Jim Crow*; Gilmore, *Golden Gulag*; and Wacquant, "From Slavery to Mass Incarceration"

8. Prisons are one of those "heterotopias of deviation," sites separated from society in which, nonetheless, the realities of social life are "simultaneously represented, contested, and inverted" (see Foucault, "Of Other Spaces").

9. This has *not* been the driving factor behind the overall decline in violent crime over the last two decades. Prisons, according to many experts, *never* do what they in theory are supposed to. For example, Bauman argues, "No evidence of any sort has been thus far found and collected to support, let alone to prove, the assumption s that prisons performs the roles ascribed to them in theory, and that they achieve any degree of success if they try to perform them—while the assumed justice of most specific measures which such theories propose or imply fails the simplest test of ethical soundness and propriety" ("Social Uses of Law and Order," 208).

10. For analysis of mass incarceration in Latin America, see, for example, Müller, "Rise of the Penal State in Latin America"; Ungar, "Prisons and Politics in Contemporary Latin America"; and Salvatore and Aguirre, *Birth of the Penitentiary in Latin America*.

11. Similar trends mark other Latin American countries. See Müller, "Punitive Entanglements."

12. Cruz, "Central American *Maras*." Researchers have documented the failures of prisons and punitive justice to quell criminal violence across Latin America and increasingly in the United States. For empirical research on the power of prison gangs in Latin America, see Denyer-Willis, "Deadly Symbiosis?" on Brazil; Martinez and Sanz, "El día de la traición" on El Salvador; Cruz, "Central American *Maras*" for the Central American region; and Lessing, "Hole at the Center of the State" for a general overview of various Latin American countries.

13. See Cruz, "Central American *Maras*"; and Huhn et al., "Exploding Crime?"

14. See chapter 2.

15. Martinez and Sanz, "El día de la traición."

16. See, for example, Müller, "Punitive Entanglements."

17. Prisons rarely live up to their ideal function. By and large, they cannot be considered "total institutions" (Goffman, *Asylums*) in the sense of keeping the incarcerated population completely isolated from the free world (Berg and DeLisi, "Correctional Melting Pot"). In many Latin American countries, the contradictions between the prisons' "ideal" function—to isolate prisoners completely from society—and the real-

ity of the situation on the ground are particularly glaring. Prisons have come to represent "a hole at the center of the state" (Lessing, "Hole at the Center of the State"), as imprisoned gang members and organized criminal groups make them staging grounds for projecting their influence and authority beyond prison walls.

18. Many of Guatemala's prison structures are aging and deteriorated, but Guatemala's penitentiary system—as a "system"—is very young. The penitentiary system administration did not come back under civilian authority until 1985. In 1996, at the end of the civil war, no systematized set of rules governing the administration of prisons existed. It took ten more years, under sustained pressure from civil society groups and international watchdog organizations, to pass the 2006 Ley de Regimen Penitenciario, which was meant to strategically organize the administration of prisons in accordance with internationally recognized human rights laws. More than ten years later, extensive revisions to this law are still being debated. The system finds itself, architecturally and bureaucratically speaking, making do.

19. The way that prison visitors link prison life and the outside—and sustain imprisoned populations—has been extensively explored by US- and UK-based scholars. Megan Comfort, for example, has conducted fieldwork with women visiting men at San Quentin State Prison in the United States and demonstrated how the presumed boundary between home and prison dissolves in ways that turn these visitors into what Comfort calls "quasi inmates" (*Doing Time Together*, 15–16). There is far less written on such dynamics in the context of Latin America, though the literature is growing. Some notable extant scholarship is Wacquant, "Militarization of Urban Marginality"; Ross, *Globalization of Supermax Prisons*; and Garces, Martin, and Darke, "Informal Prison Dynamics in Africa and Latin America."

20. Comfort, "Papa's House."

21. These statistics were provided by the Guatemalan director of prison administration during a 2014 investigation of drug use in prisons, carried out by the author and Kevin O'Neill under the auspices of a presidential commission. It should be noted that Guatemala's prison system is not as desperately underfunded and overcrowded as are those of its immediate neighbors, Honduras and El Salvador. But obtaining an accurate prison population count is quite difficult. Mike McDonald of *Global Post* put the total population at around 13,200 in 2012, 160 percent over the prison system's planned capacity. President Perez Molina (2015–present) vowed to build seven new prisons and raise total official capacity from 7,000 to 10,000 (McDonald, "Caging in Central America").

22. Prison riots in response to the state taking away conjugal visits happen often. For example, see Martinez and Sanz, "El día de la traición" and chapter 5 of this book.

23. In Pavón, there was a minor scandal when a government inspection found that a DVD-burning computer was housed directly next door to the guards' barracks.

24. In the Guatemalan penal code, homicide is equivalent to what the US system recognizes as first-degree murder, that is, murder with premeditation and intent.

25. Indeed, Disney characters are particularly common among prisoner-made artifacts. During a visit to Pavón prison, an ex-sureño thrust a panel of plastic Disney princess refrigerator magnets at me. Ariel in her Prince's arms, Jasmine and Aladdin on a flying carpet, Sleeping Beauty gazing into Prince Charming's eyes—five *quetzales* for the lot of them. I bought them for my stepdaughter in the United States.

26. Fontes and O'Neill, "*La Visita.*"

27. For an analysis of surveillance of visitors' bodies at the prison gate in Latin America, see Garces, "Denuding Surveillance."

28. See Fontes and O'Neill, "*La Visita,*" for and in-depth exploration of prison drug trafficking.

29. Prices for these sorts of goods in the prison market can fluctuate drastically, depending on visiting day schedule, charitable donations, and the vendor's desperation.

30. In urban Guatemala and throughout the region, extortion rackets originating in prisons have become the most feared and despised criminal activity, fueling popular support for the extrajudicial murder of prisoners and suspected criminals. The most well-organized extortion rackets depend on street operatives to carry out threats against recalcitrant victims. Transnational gangs (maras) are the most accomplished at these sorts of operations. But most prison-run extortion rackets are simply "cold-call" schemes: prisoners riffling randomly through telephone directories and demanding deposits into anonymous bank accounts from their victims without the capacity to carry out the threatened violence (see chapter 4).

31. Fraijanes I, Fraijanes II, El Infiernito, and others.

32. The term *wirla* is slang originating from US-based Latino prison gangs.

33. For analysis of how carceral spaces shift the experience of time passing, see Moran, *Carceral Geography.*

34. For in-depth accounts of evangelical Christian interventions in the name of security, see, for example, O'Neill, *Secure the Soul*; and Brenneman, *Homies and Hermanos.*

35. Criminal organization behind bars can, however, lead to greater stability in poor urban spaces. The PCC, Brazil's most powerful prison gang, has arguably helped reduce homicidal violence by monopolizing and organizing a wide variety of illicit markets both in prison and on the street. See, for example, Denyer-Willis, "Deadly Symbiosis?"

36. For analysis of gender, race, and body politics in Guatemala, see Nelson, *A Finger in the Wound*; and Hale, *Más que un Indio.*

37. The literature on machismo is substantial. See generally Gutmann, *Meanings of Macho*; Lancaster, *Life Is Hard*; de La Cruz, "On Men's Hypocrisy"; and Archetti, "Soccer and Masculinity."

38. While no official etymology of this term exists, it seems to bear the traces of civil war history, when Cold War polarization made any connection to communism dangerous.

39. Foucault, *Discipline and Punish.*

40. For analyses of the unfortunate consequences of mass incarceration in the United States, see, among many others, Garland, *Culture of Control.* For mass incarceration's

built-in racism, see Alexander, *New Jim Crow*. In the United States, the carceral state par excellence, state and federal governments have built more prisons and incarcerated more bodies than any other nation on earth, with little effect on overall crime rates; it seems the illusion of security and the brutal satisfaction of punitive justice (and punitive injustice, too) have appeared more convincing than prisons' "real" effects on society.

41. In Guatemala, where historically indigenous communities have meted out their own justice (see Sieder, "Contested Sovereignties") and the state was more concerned with disappearing and murdering political opponents than in dealing with crime (see, e.g., Manz, *Paradise in Ashes*), the prison system was never a significant state concern until the end of civil war became the beginning of unprecedented waves of violence (see O'Neill and Fontes, "Making Do").

42. See, for example, Skarbek, *Social Order of the Underworld*. Throughout the world, state authorities "outsource" various functions of prison governance to privileged inmates. The situation in Guatemalan prisons is distinct from, say, that in US prisons, only by an order of intensity.

43. Foucault, *Discipline and Punish*; and see, for example, Goffman, *Asylums*.

44. Los Zetas is one of the major Mexican drug-trafficking cartels competing for dominance in Mexico and, increasingly, in Central America. For analysis of the Zetas' rise and the new model of organized crime that they represent, see Correa-Cabrera, *Los Zetas, Inc.*

45. Ellingwood and Renderos, "Massacre Leaves 27 Dead."

46. A little history is in order. Pavón was designed as an agricultural rehabilitative center with enough land and space for prisoners to grow their own food and thus become productive, self-sustaining citizens. When construction was completed in 1976, reformers cited Pavón as a victory for progressive liberalism during a time of increasing social instability and reactionary politics. Distracted by civil war and the long peace-making process, however, state authorities largely abandoned everyday operations and upkeep). In 1996, the same year the nation's peace accords were signed, President Alvaro Arzú made official what had long been accepted: a Committee of Order and Discipline (Comité de Orden y Disciplina) would run the prison. The COD, as it is known, would be staffed by Pavón inmates, while prison guards would maintain the perimeter (Ordoñez, "Planificación de una granja modelo de rehabilitación penal"). The COD largely ignored state authorities and frequently used violence to enforce discipline. By dominating all forms of business in a cash-strapped prison economy, the COD accrued considerable wealth and privileges. By the mid-2000s the Guatemalan government had lost even the facade of control over Pavón. Well-to-do prisoners linked to the COD used the prison's ample terrain to build comfortable residences. One such residence even had a hot tub. The prisoners also built a night club and a mechanics' shop that refurbished stolen vehicles. In 2006 the Guatemalan government decided to finally take back Pavón. Five thousand heavily armed soldiers and policemen stormed the prison, ultimately executing seven prisoners (WOLA, *International Commission Against Impunity in Guatemala*, 11). The military and police demolished the residences and other prisoner-built structures and reestablished nominal government control.

47. Facing death threats and criminal charges in Guatemala, Viellman fled to Austria, where he had dual citizenship. Human rights organizations carried the case against him into Austrian courts.

48. Talacha collection inside Preventivo prison—where Calavera found himself—was perhaps less strict than in other prisons because of the abundance of newly arrested men flowing into the prison. Preventivo is the holding facility for all new arrests and for those awaiting trial—a period that can last as long as three years. Newly arrived inmates are often scared, their families shocked and deeply concerned about their loved ones' welfare, and squeezing talacha money is generally easier than in other facilities.

49. The modus operandi of the talacha—the intel and guesses at available resources, the expectation that kin groups will pool collective resources toward payment, the ability to negotiate the demand—replicates the system of extortion rackets that gangs direct beyond the prisons as well.

50. *El Enano* means "the Dwarf."

51. See Girard, *Violence and the Sacred*.

52. Such dynamics are by no means isolated to prison space. In *Global Outlaws*, Carolyn Nordstrom highlights how licit and illicit economic activities are entangled with one another on a world scale.

53. UNDP, *Guatemala: ¿Un país de oportunidades para la juventud?*

54. According to Foucault, such similarities between military and prison life should not be surprising. Alongside the factory, the school, and the reformatory, these spaces are part of what he called a "carceral archipelago," spaces ordered and defined by penitentiary techniques of spatial and bodily control (*Discipline and Punish*, 298).

55. Peacock and Beltran, *Poderes Ocultos*. See also Sanford, *Buried Secrets*.

56. For background on the kaibiles' training, links to US Cold War politics, and activities during Guatemala's civil war, see Green, *Fear as a Way of Life*; Manz, *Paradise in Ashes*; and Oglesby and Ross, "Guatemala's Genocide Determination."

57. Campbell, "Los Zetas: operational assessment."

58. See Goldman, *Art of Political Murder*, for the many competing theories regarding Archbishop Gerardi's murder.

59. D'Aubuisson and Dudley, "Reign of the Kaibil."

60. This was before the maras had been isolated into their own prison blocks, and sector II, where active 18th Street members are incarcerated together, had been built.

61. Goldman, *Art of Political Murder*.

62. "In the prison," recalled a former prisoner incarcerated in the early years of the maras' rise to prison power, "I saw that up through 2004 how Plan Escoba captured many for having tattoos and for dressing like gangsters. . . . And they did manage to arrest a high percentage of real gangsters. There were already lots of imprisoned *paisas* from organized criminal groups. Los Pasacos, los AR15s, La Banda de Kangooroo, Agosto Negro. They were powerful criminal organizations. . . . They formed structures in the prisons so that the homies couldn't cross a certain line. In Pavoncito [Prison], for example, not a single gangster—no matter how intelligent, cooperative, or powerful—could become leader of a sector. They maintained this until the uprising (*levan-*

tamiento) of the united sureños. After that, it was like 3 gangsters could assault 50 *paisas*. They had a great power, a power made by fear."

63. El Negro Beteta was the nephew of Sergeant Manuel Beteta, the man imprisoned for the political assassination of Myrna Mack. I interviewed Sergeant Beteta in Pavón Prison, where he has a private residence. He refused to answer any questions about his nephew's death.

64. Sanz and Martinez, "Los Maras de Centro America."

65. See chapter 5 for exploration of decapitations, dismemberment, and other forms of spectacular brutality.

66. Much has been written on how and why prison riots happen from a criminological perspective. See, for example, Useem and Kimball, *States of Siege*.

67. Prison riots can also have significant social impact on the outside world, though only if they are particularly violent or otherwise unique. The most famous prison riot in US history, for example, was the 1971 uprising in Attica Prison in upstate New York. This riot became symbolic of a panoply of political struggles against racism, the Vietnam War, and other issues. See, for example, Thompson, *Blood in the Water*; and Davis, *Are Prisons Obsolete?*

68. The organizations were the Guatemalan Human Rights Ombudsman (Procurador de Derechos Humanos) and the ODHAG (Archbishop's Office for Human Rights of Guatemala), which each spent years putting together the case against Lima and his coconspirators. See Goldman, *Art of Political Murder*, for a detailed account of this historic case.

69. Since La Mara Salvatrucha broke the prison peace accord in 2005 by attacking Barrio18 leaders in nine prisons, most—but certainly not all—active mareros from the two major maras have been kept in separate facilities dedicated to one gang or the other. After the Preventivo riot, authorities transferred Psycho and Spyder to Canada Prison. They were eventually separated and were killed soon after the breaking of the SUR in 2005. El Diabolico is now in F-2 (a maximum security facility) with other gang leaders. Over the last two years the state has attempted to isolate those it identifies as leaders in maximum security facilities, where la visita is officially limited to once every three months. In 2015, when I interviewed prison administrators regarding these arrangements, no prison officials had been killed in retaliation; so, a prison security adviser told me, they thought it was going well.

70. Pollo Campero is Guatemala's most popular fast-food chain, owned by one of its richest families.

71. See Cawley, "Bishop's Killer Ran Prison Bribery Ring in Guatemala."

CHAPTER 4. EXTORTED LIFE

1. Much of this material was previously published in Fontes, "Extorted Life."

2. Tilly, "War Making and State Making," 69. I follow J. M. Cruz's assertion that "organized crime would be understood as any group with the capability to develop an illegal system in which the members of the group demand money from someone to

provide protection against any threat or to avoid any harm perpetrated by the same members of the group" (Cruz, "Central American *Maras*," 381–382).

3. Tilly, *Politics of Collective Violence*, 172.

4. For the problem of shaky state sovereignty in postcolonial societies, see Hansen and Stepputat, *Sovereign Bodies*. In Guatemala since the end of the civil war, criminality has steadily escalated. The state has continually failed to adequately respond, but not for lack of some officials trying. Under the direction of Attorney General Claudia Paz y Paz (2010–2014), the prosecution rate of reported violent crimes has more than doubled, from 5 to 10 percent (McDonald, "Caging in Central America"). In 2014, however, she was dismissed from the Guatemalan government because of her support for the prosecution of former president Efrain Rios Montt for genocide.

5. Arnson and Olson, *Organized Crime in Central America*; and Farah, *The Transformation of El Salvador's Gangs into Political Actors*.

6. Ministerio Publico, "La Extorsion."

7. See, for example, Manz, *Paradise in Ashes*.

8. Gambetta, *Sicilian Mafia*.

9. Saunders Hastings, "'Los Codigos de Antes'."

10. For a regional study of the effects of massive incarceration on gang networks, see Cruz, "Central American *Maras*"; and Lessing, "Hole at the Center of the State."

11. In chapter 5 I explore the rise of spectacular violence as a means of political discourse.

12. For an exploration of territorial disputes, criminal insurgencies, and state sovereignty, see Ballvé, "Everyday State Formation." See also Schmitt, *Nomos of the Earth*.

13. Literally, the plebians, the common people, a term for fellow gang members of the same rank.

14. Saunders-Hastings, "'Los Codigos de Antes'."

15. Ibid.

16. In 2007 the national civil police received nearly six hundred reports of homes abandoned to the threat of extortion across Guatemala City. Given the uncounted threats that victims never report for fear of retaliation from the perpetrator(s), it is likely that the actual number is far higher.

17. Comaroff and Comaroff, *Law and Disorder in the Postcolony*, 8.

18. As Saunders-Hastings has shown, government and vigilante efforts to police against extortion have had mixed results. In May 2012, for example, the Guatemalan military conducted a widely publicized invasion of the mara-dominated neighborhood El Limon. A week earlier a fifteen-year-old had shot and killed a respected community police officer. For seven years the officer had maintained a kind of détente with Solo Raperos of Barrio18, managing after-school soccer tournaments and other programs. Suspecting local police of collaborating with the gang, the army never consulted them about the raid. With media cameras in tow, they rounded up several dozen low-level gang associates—no one with any real power—and "occupied" the neighborhood with round-the-clock patrols. While the gang made efforts to keep its operations less conspicuous, six months later its extortion rackets continued unhindered. Residents

continued to pay la renta—and refused to report the extortionists—because they knew that the army must eventually withdraw, and the media cycle would spin on. But no matter what, the gang would still be there, eager to punish even the slightest betrayal.

19. The incarcerated chief of a major Barrio18 clique is said to receive more than Q50,000 ($7,500) a week from extortion tithes (Saunders-Hastings, "'Los Códigos de Antes'").

20. Arturo Aguilar, interview with author, Guatemala City, July 7, 2013.

21. The most powerful of these organizations is CACIF, Comité Coordinador de Asociaciones Agrícolas, Comerciales, Industriales y Financieras (Coordinating Committee for Agricultural, Commercial, Industrial, and Financial Associations).

22. Argueta, "Private Security in Guatemala."

23. Yagoub, "Just One Percent of Guatemala Private Security Guards Operate Legally."

24. For similar processes in Brazil, see Huggins, "Urban Violence and Police Privatization,"

25. See Caldeira, City of Walls, for a transnational analysis of fortified enclaves.

26. The meteoric rise of both extortion rackets and private security corporations exposes the ironies of the tax debate in Guatemala. To provide a little background, the 1996 peace accords mandated a progressive tax scheme meant to help the struggling Guatemalan economy rebound from thirty-six years of civil war. This never happened. (Sridhar, "Tax Reform"). Guatemala continues to vie with Haiti for the lowest tax revenues in the Americas, suggesting that many Guatemalans do not pay their taxes. Indeed, elite arguments against raising tax rates hinge on the claim that the poor simply will not pay. Clearly, however, large portions of the urban poor make regular payments for their own survival and security—just not to the state.

27. Isabel Aguilar, interview with author, Guatemala City, September 12, 2011.

28. Alaniz, "Death Porn."

29. As a security analyst for the Guatemalan prison system stated in an interview, "[T]he police and the media are too quick to connect every new murder, decapitation, and quartering to extortion when there is often no evidence whatsoever" (Guatemala City, May 23, 2013).

30. See Bayart, Ellis, and Hibou, Criminalization of the State; and Comaroff and Comaroff, Law and Disorder in the Postcolony, for the wide variety of counterfeit crimes committed throughout the postcolonial world. As the Comaroffs note, "Revenues are . . . routinely raised by impersonating the state: by putting on counterfeit uniforms, bearing phony identity documents, and deploying other fake accouterments of authority" (17).

31. This is not the same "El Nica" as the character in the story that precedes this chapter, "The Prisoners and the Cascabel." Many nicknames are linked to nationality.

32. Dudley, "Inside: The Most Dangerous Job in the World."

33. Ibid. Rumors and more rumors. Many leftist Guatemalans suspect that actors connected to the military and loyal to current president Perez Molina orchestrated bus attacks to undermine his predecessor's administration.

34. Even so, extortion has also become a useful tactic for union busting, threatening human rights activists, and stymieing political organization from below. Maras are inevitably implicated—but whether they act at the behest of, say, *maquila* owners intent on taking out union leadership; are part of some other masquerade; or are wholly uninvolved, is never certain. In these situations, the blurred lines among personal survival, political violence, and criminal acts often disappear. For example, maquila bosses sometimes gather employees suspected of having ties to maras and threaten to fire them if any unions are formed. Then, as one activist told *Americas Quarterly*, "[I]t's up to (the mareros) to see what they have to do (to keep their jobs)" (Delpech, "Guate-Mara").

35. The flip side of all this fear is clumsy, reactive violence, which can have tragic consequences. For example, in La Terminal, a transport and wholesale market hub in the heart of Guatemala City, the vigilante group *Los Angeles de Justicia* (The Angels of Justice), employed by merchants to maintain security, executed a deaf woman accused of extortion. A local merchant told me that while extortion was a big problem, he wasn't sure if justice had been served. The deaf often communicate using handwritten messages, the same means by which extortionists often deliver demands to their victims. "Perhaps the Angels got confused," he said, laughing.

36. For an insightful mapping of the connections between generalized violence and perceptions of personal security, see Adams, *Chronic Violence and Its Reproduction*.

37. Narco-corridos memorialize the lifestyle and exploits of the Mexican narcotics trade.

CHAPTER 5. MADE-FOR-MEDIA MURDER

1. Gadda, *That Awful Mess on the Via Merulana*.

2. Nordstrom, *Global Outlaws*, 53.

3. In *Formations of Violence*, Feldman analyzes how IRA political prisoners made their bodies into sites and surfaces for the transcription of political discourses of protest. Here, I follow his analysis and extend it to the confused modes of meaning making that take place upon and through the bodies of both victims and perpetrators of criminal violence.

4. I echo Guy Debord's definition of spectacle: "The spectacle is not a collection of images; it is a social relation between people that is mediated by images" (*Society of the Spectacle*, 1).

5. Benson, Fischer, and Thomas, "Resocializing Suffering."

6. See Laclau and Mouffe's *Hegemony and Socialist Strategy* for a seminal discussion of how discursive meaning is made and becomes hegemonic (or not) in the public sphere.

7. As Linda Green writes, "Terror is the taproot of Guatemala's past and stalks its present" (*Fear as a Way of Life*, 65).

8. Cf Taussig, "Terror as Usual." Taussig writes how the "talk of terror" has a way of "undermining meaning while dependent on it, stringing out the nervous system one

way towards hysteria, the other way towards numbing and apparent acceptance, both ways flip-sides of terror, the political Art of the Arbitrary, as usual."

9. Eliot, "The Love Song of J. Alfred Prufrock," in *Waste Land and Other Poems*, 7.

10. Francisco Jimenez Irungaray (former public security minister), interview with author, Guatemala City, November 12, 2011.

11. See, for example, Moser and Winton, "Violence in the Central American Region." One often-cited example of such ingrown violence is lynchings in rural Guatemala. These are often misunderstood and misrepresented in the mainstream press, but nevertheless speak of a deep distrust in official institutions of justice. See Godoy, "Lynchings and the Democratization of Terror in Postwar Guatemala" and "When 'Justice' Is Criminal."

12. Struggles over collective memories of atrocities take place in every society. For discussions of the politics, ethics, and poetics of these struggles in postcolonial societies, see Soyinka, *Burden of Memory*.

13. Cf. Myrna Mack Foundation, *La discriminacion*.

14. Nietzsche, *Geneaology of Morals*, 68. For more in-depth discussion of who decides which pain makes sense and which is senseless in Guatemala, which pain is legitimate and which unjust, see, for example, Sanford, "From Genocide to Feminicide"; and Nelson, *Reckoning*.

15. Cf. Nelson, *Finger in the Wound*.

16. For analysis of the rise of peacetime death squads in El Salvador, see Hume, *Politics of Violence*; for Honduras, see Gutierrez Rivera, *Territories of Violence*. For comparable dynamics in other Latin American countries, see, for example, Jütersonke, Muggah, and Rodgers, "Gangs, Urban Violence, and Security Interventions in Central America."

17. In *In Search of Respect*, Bourgois captures a comparable dynamic among Puerto Rican men involved in the drug trade who self-consciously take on the identities thrust upon them by their interactions with mainstream society.

18. For accounts of kaibil violence during the civil war, see Manz, *Paradise in Ashes*. For the links between kaibiles and other Latin American counterinsurgencies and the US School of the Americas, see GHRC, "Guatemala's Elite Special Forces Unit"; Doyle, "Atrocity Files"; and Rabe, *Killing Zone*.

19. It is an open question whether this puppy-killing business has actually taken place or is an urban legend. Accusations of such training methods have previously been leveled at the Third Reich's SS, Israel's Mossad, and Saddam Hussein's private guard force, among others.

20. Stone and Wells, "Zetas to Face Trial for 2011 Farm Massacre in Guatemala."

21. See Saunders-Hastings, "'Los Códigos de Antes'."

22. Notice the very extreme extent to which this rigid form of governmentality (not on behalf of the state in this case, but on behalf of the authority structure of the gang) is played out at the individual level. It becomes so central to the (re)making of self that individuals become integrated into the structure of governance; they perform it, make it their own, and try to outdo each other in proving that they have wholly become the beast.

23. See Levi-Strauss, "Introduction à l'oeuvre de Marcel Mauss." A floating signifier "represents an undetermined quantity of signification, in itself void of meaning and thus apt to receive any meaning."

24. Sontag, *Regarding the Pain of Others*, 43.

25. See Debord's *Society of the Spectacle* for a deeper assessment of the role of spectacle in modern life. For the role of global media in forming perceptions about distant terror, see Lewis, *Language Wars*. For deconstruction of the use of violent spectacle in power struggles between the state and criminal actors in Mexico, see Carlin, "Guns, Gold and Corporeal Inscriptions."

26. Alaniz, "Death Porn," quoted in Pine, *Working Hard, Drinking Hard*.

27. Linfield, *Cruel Radiance*, 22.

28. Today, with an average print run of 230,000 copies, the paper has 75 percent of the market of newspaper readership at the national level, with two million Guatemalans reading it daily. In the capital these readers account for 55 percent of the reading population, while in the interior of the country 82 percent of people who see a newspaper every morning read *Nuestro Diario*. Collussi, "Análisis del recorrido hemerográfico."

29. Collussi, "Análisis del recorrido hemerográfico."

30. In 1860s Europe, Charles Baudelaire observed, "It is impossible to glance through any newspaper, no matter what the day, the month, or the year, without finding on every page the most frightful traces of human perversity, together with the most astonishing boasts of probity, charity, and benevolence, and the most brazen statements regarding the progress of civilization. . . . And it is with this loathsome appetizer that civilized man washes down his morning repast. . . . I am unable to comprehend how a man of honor could take a newspaper in his hands without a shudder of disgust" (Baudelaire, *Intimate Journals*, 91). Collussi, "Análisis del recorrido hemerográfico," 4.

31. For in-depth discussions of the politics of mourning, see, for example, Eng and Kazanjian, *Loss*.

32. Butler, *Precarious Life*.

33. Muñoz, "Asesinan a Marero."

34. Caldeira, *City of Walls*, 38. Caldeira calls this work to distance oneself from the image of the criminal a form of "symbolic labor." For comparable discursive efforts to put distance between the spectacle of suicide bombing and oneself, see Asad, *On Suicide Bombing*.

35. The Guatemalan government has purposefully misconstrued the civil war's lines of opposition in state-issued history books as a tale of "two demons": the Guatemalan military facing off against leftist guerrillas, with the civilian population caught up in the cross fire. The result has been that even the small percentage of the Guatemalan populace who possess a high school education have little knowledge of the military's targeting innocent civilians for massacre and genocide. See Oglesby, "Educating Citizens in Postwar Guatemala."

36. Though beyond the scope of this chapter, human rights discourse has become the language of resistance and protest for the fragmented remains of the political Left. War crimes cases against Guatemalan military officials; protests against rural land

displacements; and everyday struggles over property rights, employee salaries, and taxation are fought out using human rights frameworks. For the multiple uses and abuses of human rights discourses in Guatemala, see, for example, Sieder, "Contested Sovereignties" and "Building Mayan Authority and Autonomy."

37. The version of justice at stake in human rights struggles is quite thin, however. Because the discourse and legal structures through which human rights claims gain traction have no space for redistributive justice (and often only work to establish symbolic methods of reconciliation), some scholars argue that the human rights framework is in fact the inheritance of Cold War counterinsurgencies through less violent means. See Meister, *After Evil*.

38. See Malkin, "Ex-Dictator Is Ordered to Trial in Guatemalan War Crimes Case"; and Laplante, "Memory Battles."

39. See, for example, ICTJ, "Conviction of Ríos Montt on Genocide."

40. For abuse of human rights discourse in South Africa, see Wilson, *Politics of Truth and Reconciliation in South Africa*. For parallel trends in Brazil, see Caldeira, *City of Walls*.

41. See, for example, Nelson, *Who Counts?*

42. Their appearance, too, would have counted against their murders mattering. The victim shown here had a patterned buzz cut, evidence that for many Guatemalans could be a sign of his potential guilt.

43. The literature on femicide is growing. For a review see Carey and Torres, "Precursors to Femicide." For legal discussions of this category, see Musalo, Pellegrin, and Roberts, "Crimes without Punishment." For Latin American–wide trends, see Fregoso and Berajano, *Terrorizing Women*.

44. GHRC, "Guatemala's Femicide Law."

45. Sanford, "From Genocide to Feminicide," 107.

46. Musalo, Pellegrin, and Roberts, "Crimes without Punishment," 188.

47. Franco, "Killing Priests, Nuns, Women, Children."

48. Ibid.

49. See Carlin, "Guns, Gold and Corporeal Inscriptions" for analysis of violent drug war iconography in Mexico.

50. For example, the 2015 film *Sicario*, starring Emily Blunt and Benicio del Toro, utilized macabre images drawn directly from ongoing Mexican drug war violence.

51. See Friis, "'Beyond Anything We Have Ever Seen'." Analyzing an ISIS video of a decapitation of an American journalist, she writes, "the videos have played an important role in the reframing of ISIS from a 'regional', 'humanitarian' problem to a 'direct', 'imminent threat', and a 'cancer' that 'risks spreading to other parts of the international community and affecting us all directly'. In the words of the Republicans John McCain and Lindsey Graham, 'in this cowardly and gruesome murder of an innocent man, we see the true nature of the evil that confronts us. . . . It is an enemy of humanity, a darkness that will spread as far as it can, unless it is stopped'" (736).

52. Concern over whose lives and deaths can "count" and whose cannot is a theme taken up by legions of scholars. Judith Butler captures the central conundrum when

she writes, "[W]hose life, if extinguished, would be publicly grievable and whose life would leave either no public trace to grieve, or only a partial, mangled, and enigmatic trace[?]" (*Frames of War*, 73).

53. For insight into the crucial role of the media in spreading terror, see Lewis, *Language Wars*.

54. The buffers and bulwarks we construct to keep terror at bay are multifarious, called upon constantly to establish the appropriate "distance" between oneself and inscrutable fear. Ultimately, establishing the appropriate distance between oneself and, to quote Taussig, "An-Other Place" where the world's order always breaks down, becomes another means of holding the reality they signal at bay. "But perhaps such an elsewhere should make us suspicious about the deeply rooted sense of order here," Taussig writes, "as if their dark wildness exists so as to silhouette our light" ("Terror as Usual," 3).

55. Most of these were images he and his staff had captured at Guatemalan crime scenes. Others he received from fellow police commanders in Central America and Mexico with whom he coordinated via FBI and Drug Enforcement Agency security workshops.

56. See Scarry, *Body in Pain*. Power is found in the voice, while the body is the locus of pain. Thus, the greater distance from the body, the more power is to be had. The less voice one has, the less power. Pain destroys language, as language makes the building blocks of consciousness. In Scarry's account, she shows how seasoned torturers increase the destruction of language by giving the victim, the torture chamber, everything, absurd names—nullifying the victim's reality and distancing themselves from the pain they inflict. For this reason, Scarry argues that *objectifying pain*, giving voice to it, letting victims speak their experiences, name what happened to them, can in some way diminish both their pain and the torturer's power.

57. Quoted in Linfield, *Cruel Radiance*, 39.

58. "The body implies mortality, vulnerability, agency: the skin and the flesh expose us to the gaze of others, but also to touch, and to violence, and bodies put us at risk of becoming the agency and instrument of all these as well" (Butler, *Precarious Life*, 26).

CHAPTER 6. LIMINAL REDEMPTION

1. Benjamin, *Reflections*, 254.
2. Muñoz, "Asesinan a Marero," 1.
3. Sartre, *Being and Nothingness*, 59.
4. Althusser defines the concept of being "fixed" by the attention of another in his famous formulation of "hailing." That is, the moment a police officer calls out, "Hey, you there," and a person turns in response, he or she has become, or enacts the role as, a "subject" in an ideological and symbolic order. Althusser, "Ideology and Ideological State Apparatuses."
5. See Hacking, "Making Up People."

6. For illuminating analysis of the importance of the liminal in human life (marked by rituals of transition—i.e., coming-of-age ceremonies, marriages, births, deaths, etc.) see Turner, "Betwixt and Between."

7. Butler, *Precarious Life*, 32.

8. According to the Oxford English Dictionary, the adjective "ex" means "former, outdated"; the preposition "ex" is used to mean "out of" in reference to goods; and the noun "ex" refers to "one who formerly occupied the position or office denoted by the context," such as a former husband or wife. "Ex" also means "to cross out, to delete with an x" and stands for the unknown. Being an "ex" is to inhabit an identity without a home, an emptiness that must be transformed by will or by happenstance into something else. Cf. Biehl, *Vita*, 90–91.

9. See chapter 5 for more in-depth analysis of the marero's role in public discourse.

10. Cf. Brenneman, *Homies and Hermanos*, 8. "When I asked a Guatemalan psychiatrist who treats incarcerated gang youth what can be done to help a gang member leave his gang and reintegrate into society, he shook his head in silence for several moments and finally offered a suggestion: 'Take them to another planet.'"

11. *Green light (luz verde)* is taken from US gang slang. To be "green-lighted" means to carry a death sentence. Every member of your gang has the duty to kill you on sight.

12. Other informants attribute the trend to close down exit routes to the breaking of the SUR in Guatemala—the intergang agreement that prohibited violence inside the prisons—in August 2005.

13. For in-depth analysis of the attribution problem in international funding regimes, see Leeuw and Vaessen, "Address the Attribution Problem."

14. Isabel Aguilar (director of Interpeace), interview with author, Guatemala City, October 14, 2011.

15. USAID, the United Nations Development Programme (UNDP), the Organization of American States (OAS), and a vast panoply of international organizations offer up analyses of how and why gangs and violent criminality have risen so powerfully in Guatemala and its neighboring countries. See, for example, Manz, "Central American (Guatemala, Honduras, El Salvador, Nicaragua): Patterns of Human Rights Violations"; UNDP, *Informe sobre desarrollo humano para América Central 2009–2010*; USAID, *Central America and Mexico Gang Assessment*; UNODC, *Crime and Development in Central America*; UNODC, *Transnational Organized Crime in the Caribbean and the Americas*; WOLA, *Youth Gangs in Central America*; World Bank, *Urban Crime and Violence in LAC*; and Pan American Health Organization, *Interpersonal Youth Violence in Latin America and the English-Speaking Caribbean*.

16. Mark Lopes (USAID), interview with author, Washington, DC, June 4, 2013.

17. For background on the truce between Los Metales and Los Caballos, see Cardona Montenegro, "El proceso estrategico de la reinsercion social."

18. The media returned three months later to mark the anniversary of the peace. Footage can be found at "La Paz en Peronia noticia en (noti7)," published October 4, 2009, https://www.youtube.com/watch?v=YNITQ8pn3ag.

19. Evangelical churches have been pivotal in efforts to intervene "peacefully" against gangs in the United States as well. For example, the first official "gang czar" of Los Angeles was Pastor Jeff Car, a minister with a liberal evangelical church called Sojourners/Call for Renewal (Helfand, "Anti-gang Czar"). See O'Neill, *Secure the Soul*, for the most insightful analysis of transnational evangelical security initiatives.

20. Pew Research Center, "Historical Overview of Pentecostalism in Guatemala."

21. O'Neill, "Reckless Will."

22. Ibid., 64.

23. O'Neill, *Secure the Soul*.

24. The organization asks no questions of its clients. They might be ex-mareros on the lam or simply poor urbanites who want to get rid of tattoos that provoke so much suspicion.

25. See, for example, Discovery Channel's "World's Most Dangerous Gang," http://channel.nationalgeographic.com/explorer/episodes/worlds-most-dangerous-gang/.

26. He was lucky. Barrio18 is not as puritanical regarding serious drug use as MS is known to be. The latter gang has executed current and former members who become obviously and abjectly addicted to drugs, which besmirches MS's reputation for hardline discipline.

27. For analyses of nonviolent gang intervention strategies in the United States and Central America, see O'Neill, *Secure the Soul*; Aguilar and Miranda, "Entre la articulacion y la competencia"; Brenneman, *Homies and Hermanos*; and Cruz, "Letting Go of Clecha."

28. See O'Neill, *Secure the Soul*.

29. Isabel Aguilar (director of Interpeace), interview with author, Guatemala City, October 5, 2011.

30. O'Neill, *Secure the Soul*, 70.

31. See, for example, Todorov, *Conquest of America*.

32. The more common form of this saying is, *Mas sabe el Diablo por viejo que por diablo* (The devil knows more from being old than from being cunning/clever).

33. Chucho was another ex-marero released from Pavón shortly before Calavera. They spoke on the phone often and helped each other through the transition back into society.

EPILOGUE

1. Gregory, *Colonial Present*, 11.

2. BBC News, "Former Guatemala Leader Otto Pérez Molina to Face Trial."

3. For a detailed account of Lima's prison power and the theories swirling around his death, see Dudley, "Who Killed Guatemala's Prison 'King' Byron Lima?"

4. Ibid.

5. Dudley, "Murder of Guatemala's Prison 'King' Byron Lima: A 'Self-Coup d'etat'?"

6. Associated Press, "Ex-Guatemalan President Accused of Campaign Corruption."

7. Markon and Partlow, "Unaccompanied Children Crossing Southern Border in Greater Numbers Again."

8. Tourliere, "La migración no para: Encuentra nuevas rutas."

9. Sacchetti and Miroff, "How Trump Is Building a Border Wall That No One Can See"; and BBC News, "'Drug Dealers, Criminals, and Rapists'."

10. Woody, "Trump: The MS-13 Gang."

11. New York Times Editorial Board, "When Did Caging Kids Become the Art of the Deal?"

12. Today there are more people displaced by violent conflict than at any other time in human history (McKirdy, "UNHCR Report: More Displaced Now Than after WWII").

APPENDIX

1. Geertz, "Deep Hanging Out," 1.

2. Ethnographers who work in war, postwar, or violent peacetime contexts must be especially wary of such power differentials. For deeper analysis of this point, see, for example, Fujii, "Research Ethics 101"; and Gusterson, "Ethnographic Research."

3. Goduka, "Ethics and Politics of Field Research in South Africa"

4. Fujii, "Research Ethics 101," 720.

5. See Fontes and O'Neill, "La Visita."

BIBLIOGRAPHY

Adams, Tani Marilena. *Chronic Violence and Its Reproduction: Perverse Trends in Social Relations, Citizenship and Democracy in Latin America*. Washington, DC: Woodrow Wilson International Center for Scholars, 2011.

Agamben, Giorgio. *State of Exception*. Chicago: University of Chicago Press, 2005.

Aguilar, Jeanette, and Lisette Miranda. "Entre la articulación y la competencia: Las respuestas de la sociedad civil organizada a las pandillas en El Salvador [Between articulation and competence: Civil society responses to gangs in El Salvador]." In *Maras y pandillas en Centroamérica: Las respuestas de la sociedad civil organizada* [Gangs in Central America: Civil society responses], edited by José Miguel Cruz, 37–144. San Salvador: UCA Editores, 2006.

Alaniz, Jose. "Death Porn: Modes of Mortality in Post-Soviet Russian Cinema." In *Interpretation of Culture Codes: Madness and Death*, edited by Vadim Mikhailin, 185–211. Saratov, Russia: Saratov State University Laboratory of Historical, Social, and Cultural Anthropology, 2005).

Alexander, Michelle. *The New Jim Crow: Mass Incarceration in the Age of Colorblindness*. New York: New Press, 2010.

Alston, Philip. "Report of the Special Rapporteur on Extrajudicial, Summary or Arbitrary Executions, Philip Alston: Addendum." United Nations General Assembly, Human Rights Council, A/HRC/4/20/Add.2, 2007.

Althusser, Louis. *Lenin and Philosophy, and Other Essays*. London: New Left Books, 1971.

———. "Ideology and Ideological State Apparatuses (Notes Towards an Investigation)." In *The Anthropology of the State: A Reader*, edited by Aradhana Sharma and Akhil Gupta, 86–98. Malden, MA: Blackwell Publishing, 2006.

Álvaro López, Juan Alberto. "Realidad del Sistema penitenciario guatemalteco en el Departamento de Guatemala y la falta de atencion especial en los centros penitenciarios." Tesis de Licenciatura, Facultad de Ciencas Juridicas y Sociales, Universidad Rafael Landívar, Guatemala, 2001.

Anderson, Benedict. *Imagined Communities.* New York: Verso, 2007.

Appadurai, Arjun. *Dead Certainty: Ethnic Violence in the Era of Globalization.* Colombo, Sri Lanka: SLFI, 1998.

Arana, Ana. "The New Battle for Central America." *Foreign Affairs* 80, no. 6 (November–December 2001): 88–101.

Arendt, Hannah. *On Violence.* New York: Harcourt Brace & Company, 1969.

———. *Eichmann in Jerusalem: A Study of the Banality of Evil.* New York: Penguin Books, 1976.

———. *The Origins of Totalitarianism.* New York and London: Harcourt Brace and Company, 1976.

———. *The Human Condition.* Chicago: University of Chicago Press, 1998.

Aretxaga, Begoña. "Maddening States." *Annual Review of Anthropology* 32 (2003): 393–410.

Arce, Manuel Valenzuela, Alfredo Nateras Domínguez, and Rossana Reguillo Cruz, eds. *Las Maras: Identidades juveniles al límite.* Mexico City: Universidad Autonoma Metropolitana, 2007.

Archbishop's Office of Human Rights (ODHA). *Guatemala: Nunca Más; Report of the Project for the Recuperation of Historical Memory (REMHI).* Vols I–IV. Guatemala City: ODHA, 1998.

Archetti, Eduardo. "Soccer and Masculinity." In *The Argentina Reader: History, Culture, Politics,* edited by Gabriela Nouzeilles and Graciela Montaldo, 519–524. Durham, NC: Duke University Press, 2002.

Argueta, Otto. "Private Security in Guatemala: Pathway to Its Proliferation." *Bulletin of Latin American Research* 31, no. 3 (2012): 320–335.

Arias, Enrique Desmond. *Criminal Enterprise and Governance in Latin America and the Caribbean.* New York: Cambridge University Press, 2017.

Arias, Enrique Desmond, and Daniel M. Goldstein. *Violent Democracies in Latin America.* Durham, NC: Duke University Press, 2010.

Arnson, Cynthia J., and Eric L. Olson, eds. *Organized Crime in Central America: The Northern Triangle.* Washington, DC: Woodrow Wilson International Center for Scholars, 2011. www.wilsoncenter.org/sites/default/files/LAP_single_page.pdf.

Arthur, Wayne, and Rory Carroll. "El Salvador Holds Its Breath after Day without Murders." *Guardian,* May 1, 2012. www.theguardian.com/world/2012/may/01/el -salvador-murders-gang-truce.

Asad, Talal. *On Suicide Bombing.* New York: Columbia University Press, 2007.

Asociacion para la Avance de las Ciencias Sociales en Guatemala (AVANCSO). *Más allá de la sobrevivencia: La lucha por una vida digna.* Guatemala City: AVANCSO, 2006.

Associated Press. "Ex-Guatemalan President Accused of Campaign Corruption." *Washington Times,* October 5, 2017. https://www.washingtontimes.com/news/2017 /oct/5/lawyer-for-ex-guatemalan-presidents-arrested/.

Asturias, Miguel A. *El Señor Presidente*. n.p.: Signitario del Acuerdo Archivos, Universidad de Costa Rica, 2000.

Auyero, Javier, Philippe Bourgois, and Nancy Scheper-Hughes, eds. *Violence at the Urban Margins*. New York: Oxford University Press, 2015.

Baird, Adam. "Negotiating Pathways to Manhood: Rejecting Gangs and Violence in Medellín's Periphery." *Journal of Conflictology* 3, no. 1 (2012): 30–41.

———. "The Violent Gang and the Construction of Masculinity amongst Socially Excluded Young Men." *Safer Communities* 11, no. 4 (2012): 179–190.

Balibar, Étienne. "Uprising in the Banlieus." *Constellations* 14, no. 1 (2007): 47–71.

Ballvé, Teo. "Everyday State Formation: Territory, Decentralization, and the Narco Landgrab in Colombia." *Environment and Planning D: Society and Space* 30, no. 4 (2012): 603–622.

Baudelaire, Charles. *Intimate Journals*. Translated by Ch. Isherwood. San Francisco, CA: City Lights Books, 1983.

Bauman, Zygmunt. "Social Uses of Law and Order." *British Journal of Criminology* 40, no. 2 (Spring 2000): 205–221.

Bayart, Jean-François, Stephen Ellis, and Béatrice Hibou. *The Criminalization of the State in Africa*. Translated by Stephen Ellis. Bloomington: Indiana University Press, 1999.

BBC News. "'Drug Dealers, Criminals, and Rapists': What Trump Thinks of Mexicans." BBC, August 31, 2016. www.bbc.com/news/av/world-us-canada-37230916 /drug-dealers-criminals-rapists-what-trump-thinks-of-mexicans.

———. "Former Guatemala Leader Otto Pérez Molina to Face Trial." BBC, October 28, 2017. www.bbc.com/news/world-latin-america-41786239.

Benjamin, Walter. *Illuminations*. Edited by Hannah Arendt. Translated by Harry Zohn. New York: Harcourt Brace Jovanovich Press, 1969. First published 1940.

———. *Reflections: Essays, Aphorisms, and Autobiographical Writings*. Translated by Edmund Jephcott. New York: Harcourt Brace Jovanovich, 1978.

Benson, Peter, Edward F. Fischer, and Kedron Thomas. "Resocializing Suffering: Neoliberalism, Accusation, and the Sociopolitical Context of Guatemala's New Violence." *Latin American Perspectives* 35, no. 5 (2008): 38–58.

Berg, Mark T., and Matt DeLisi. "The Correctional Melting Pot: Race, Ethnicity, Citizenship, and Prison Violence." *Journal of Criminal Justice* 34, no. 6 (2006): 631–642.

Biden, Joe. "Joe Biden: A Plan for Central America." *New York Times*, January 29, 2015. www.nytimes.com/2015/01/30/opinion/joe-biden-a-plan-for-central-america. html.

Biehl, João G. *Vita: Life in a Zone of Abandonment*. Berkeley: University of California Press, 2005.

Blok, Anton. *The Mafia of a Sicilian Village, 1860–1960: A Study of Violent Peasant Entrepreneurs*. New York: Harper & Row, 1975.

Bourdieu, Pierre, and Jean-Claude Passeron. *Reproduction in Education, Society and Culture*. London: Sage, 1990.

———. *Language and Symbolic Power*. Cambridge, MA: Harvard University Press, 1991.

Bourgois, Philippe. *In Search of Respect: Selling Crack in El Barrio*. New York: Cambridge University Press, 1995.

———. "The Power of Violence in War and Peace: Post-Cold War Lessons from El Salvador." *Ethnography* 2, no. 1 (2001): 5–34.

Boyarin, Jonathan, ed. *Remapping Memory: The Politics of Timespace*. Minneapolis: University of Minnesota Press, 1994.

Brenneman, Robert. *Homies and Hermanos: God and Gangs in Central America*. New York: Oxford University Press, 2012.

Briceño-León, Roberto. "Violencia y desesperanza: La otra crisis social de América Latina." *Nueva Sociedad* 164 (1999): 122–132.

Briceño-León, Roberto, and Verónica Zubillaga. "Violence and Globalization in Latin America." *Current Sociology* 50, no. 1 (2002): 19–37.

Brown, Wendy. *Politics Out of History*. Princeton, NJ: Princeton University Press, 2001.

Buck-Morss, Susan. *Hegel, Haiti, and Universal History*. Pittsburgh, PA: University of Pittsburgh Press, 2009.

Burrell, Jennifer. "In and Out of Rights: Security, Migration, and Human Rights Talk in Postwar Guatemala." *Journal of Latin American and Caribbean Anthropology* 15, no. 1 (2008): 90–115.

Burrell, Jennifer L., and Ellen Moodie, eds. *Central America in the New Millennium: Living Transition and Reimaging Democracy*. New York: Berghahn Books, 2013.

Butler, Judith. *Precarious Life: The Powers of Mourning and Violence*. New York: Verso, 2004.

———. *Frames of War: When is Life Grievable?* New York: Verso, 2009.

Caldeira, Teresa P. R. *City of Walls: Crime, Segregation, and Citizenship in São Paulo*. Berkeley: University of California Press, 2000.

Campbell, Lisa J. "Los Zetas: Operational Assessment." *Small Wars and Insurgencies* 21, no. 1 (2010): 55–80.

Cardona Montenegro, Hector Alberto. "El proceso estrategico de la reinsercion social de los jóvenes provenientes de las pandillas Los Caballos y Los Metales de Ciudad Peronia, Villa Nueva." Master's thesis, Universidad de San Carlos de Guatemala, 2016. http://biblioteca.usac.edu.gt/tesis/28/28_0932.pdf.

Carey, David, Jr., and M. Gabriela Torres. "Precursors to Femicide: Guatemalan Women in a Vortex of Violence." *Latin American Research Review* 45, no. 3 (2010): 142–164.

Carlin, Matthew. "Guns, Gold and Corporeal Inscriptions: The Image of State Violence in Mexico." *Third Text* 26, no. 5 (2012): 503–514.

Carroll, Rory. "Killers of filmmaker Christian Poveda jailed." *Guardian*, March 11, 2011. https://www.theguardian.com/world/2011/mar/11/christian-poveda-murders-jailed.

Carter, Jon Horne. "Tears of the Damned: On the Prison Fire in Comayagua, Honduras." *Anthropology News*, March 24, 2012, "Media Notes." www.academia

.edu/34170743/Tears_of_the_Damned_On_the_Prison_Fire_in_Comayagua_ Honduras.

———. "Gothic Sovereignty: Gangs and Criminal Community in a Honduran Prison." *South Atlantic Quarterly* 113, no. 3 (2014): 475–502.

Casa Alianza. *Torture of Guatemalan Street Children: Report to the United Nations Committee Against Torture.* Guatemala City: Casa Alianza, 1995.

Castoriadis, Cornelius. *The Imaginary Institution of Society.* Translated by Kathleen Blamey. Cambridge, MA: MIT Press, 1987.

Cawley, Marguerite. "Bishop's Killer Ran Prison Bribery Ring in Guatemala." InSight Crime, September 4, 2014. www.insightcrime.org/news/brief/bishops-killer-rain -prison-crime-ring-in-guatemala/.

Chevigny, Paul. "The Populism of Fear: Politics of Crime in the Americas." *Punishment and Society* 5, no. 1 (2003): 77–96.

Clark, William A. V. *Immigrants and the American Dream: Remaking the Middle Class.* New York: Guilford Press, 2003.

Cohen, Stanley. *Folk Devils and Moral Panics: The Creation of Mods and Rockers.* London: Macgibbon and Kee Ltd., 1972.

Collussi, Marcelo. "Análisis del recorrido hemerográfico de 'Nuestro Diario'." Unpublished manuscript, 2004.

Comaroff, Jean, and John Comaroff. *Law and Disorder in the Postcolony.* Chicago: University of Chicago Press, 2006.

Comfort, Megan L. "Papa's House: The Prison as Domestic and Social Satellite." *Ethnography* 3, no. 4 (2002): 467–499.

———. *Doing Time Together: Love and Family in the Shadow of the Prison.* Chicago: University of Chicago Press, 2008.

Commission for Historical Clarification. *Guatemala: Memory of Silence.* Report of the Commission for Historical Clarification: Conclusions and Recommendations. Guatemala City, 2000.

Conrad, Joseph. *Heart of Darkness.* 1902. Reprint. New York: Penguin Books, 1999.

Contreras, Randol. *The Stickup Kids: Race, Drugs, Violence, and the American Dream.* Berkeley: University of California Press, 2012.

Correa-Cabrera, Guadalupe. *Los Zetas, Inc.: Criminal Corporations, Energy, and Civil War in Mexico.* Austin: University of Texas Press, 2017.

Cruz, Cesar A. "Letting Go of Clecha, While Holding Corazón: Developing a New Approach to Empowering Youth in Gangs the Homeboy Industries Way." PhD diss., Harvard Graduate School of Education, 2016.

Cruz, José Miguel. "Central American *Maras*: From Youth Street Gangs to Transnational Protection Rackets." *Global Crime* 11, no. 4 (2010): 379–398.

———. "Criminal Violence and Democratization in Central America: The Survival of the Violent State." *Latin American Politics and Society* 53, no. 4 (2011): 1–33.

Cruz, José Miguel and Angélica Durán-Martínez. "Hiding Violence to Deal with the State: Criminal Pacts in El Salvador and Medellin." *Journal of Peace Research* 53, no. 2 (2016): 197–210.

Curtis, Adam. *Century of Self*. London: BBC, 2002.

Darke, Sacha. "Managing without Guards in a Brazilian Police Lockup." *Focaal* 68 (2014): 55–67.

Das, Veena, ed. "The Act of Witnessing: Violence, Poisonous Knowledge, and Subjectivity." In *Violence and Subjectivity*, edited by Veena Das, Arthur Kleinman, Mamphela Ramphele, and Pamela Reynolds, 205–225. Berkeley: University of California Press, 2000.

———. "Violence and Translation." *Anthropological Quarterly* 75, no. 1 (2002): 105–112.

D'Aubuisson, Juan Josó Martínez. *En las profundidades de una pandilla salvadoreña*. San Salvador, El Salvador: AURA Ediciones, 2013.

D'Aubuisson, Juan Josó Martínez, and Steven Dudley. "Reign of the Kaibil: Guatemala's Prisons Under Byron Lima." InSight Crime, January 26, 2017. www.insight-crime.org/investigations/reign-of-kaibil-guatemala-prisons-under-byron-lima.

Davis, Angela Y. *Are Prisons Obsolete?* New York: Seven Stories Press, 2011.

Davis, Diane E. "Urban Violence, Quality of Life, and the Future of Latin American Cities: The Dismal Record So Far, and the Search for New Analytical Frameworks to Sustain a Bias towards Hope." In *Approaches to Global Urban Poverty: Setting the Research Agenda*, edited by Allison Garland, 57–88. Washington, DC: Woodrow Wilson Center Press, 2008.

Davis, Mike. "Planet of Slums: Urban Involution and the Informal Proletariat." *New Left Review* 26 (2004): 5–24.

de La Cruz, Sor Juana Inés. "On Men's Hypocrisy." In *The Mexico Reader: History, Culture, Politics*, edited by Gilbert Joseph and Timothy Henderson, 156–159. Durham, NC: Duke University Press, 2002.

Debord, Guy. *The Society of the Spectacle*. Canberra, Australia: Hobgoblin Press, 2002.

DeCesare, Donna. "The Children of War." *NACLA Report on the Americas* 32, no. 1 (1998): 21–42.

Delpech, Quentin. "Guate-Mara: The Extortion Economy in Guatemala." *Americas Quarterly* 7, no. 2 (Spring 2013): 94–97. www.americasquarterly.org/content/guate-mara-extortion-economy-guatemala.

Denyer-Willis, Graham. "Deadly Symbiosis? The PCC, the State, and the Institutionalization of Violence in São Paulo, Brazil." In *Youth Violence in Latin America: Gangs and Juvenile Justice in Perspective*, edited by Dennis Rodgers and Gareth Jones, 167–182. New York: Palgrave Macmillan, 2009.

———. *The Killing Consensus: Police, Organized Crime, and the Regulation of Life and Death in Urban Brazil*. Oakland: University of California Press, 2015.

———. "Before the Body Count: Homicide Statistics and Everyday Governance in Latin America." *Journal of Latin American Studies* 49, no. 1 (2016): 29–54.

Derrida, Jacques. "Force De Loi: Le Fondement Mystique De L'Autorité [The force of law]." *Cardozo Law Review* 11, nos. 5–6 (1990): 920–1045.

———. "Spectres of Marx." *New Left Review* 205 (1994): 31.

Doyle, Kate. "The Atrocity Files: Deciphering the Archives of Guatemala's Dirty War." *Harper's Magazine*, December 2007.

Dudley, Steven. "InSide: The Most Dangerous Job in the World." InSight Crime, March 8, 2011. www.insightcrime.org/investigations/inside-the-most-dangerous-job-in-the-world/.

———. "Homicides in Guatemala: The Challenge and Lessons of Disaggregating Gang-Related and Drug Trafficking-Related Murders." InSight Crime, 2016. http://www.insightcrime.org/investigations/homicides-in-guatemala.

———. "How Drug Trafficking Operates, Corrupts in Central America." InSight Crime, July 2016. www.insightcrime.org/news/analysis/how-drug-trafficking-operates-corrupts-in-central-america/.

———. "The Murder of Guatemala's Prison 'King' Byron Lima: A 'Self-Coup d'etat'? (Part III)." InSight Crime, July 2016. www.insightcrime.org/news/analysis/the-murder-of-guatemala-s-prison-king-byron-lima-a-self-coup-d-etat-part-iii/.

———. "Who Killed Guatemala's Prison 'King' Byron Lima? (Part I)." InSight Crime, July 2016. www.insightcrime.org/news/analysis/who-killed-guatemala-s-prison-king-byron-lima-part-i/.

Eguizábal, Cristina, Matthew C. Ingram, Karise M. Curtis, Aaron Korthuis, Eric L. Olson, and Nicholas Phillips. *Crime and Violence in Central America's Northern Triangle: How U.S. Policy Responses Are Helping, Hurting, and Can Be Improved.* Washington, DC: Wilson Center Latin America Program, 2015. www.wilsoncenter.org/sites/default/files/FINAL%20PDF_CARSI%20REPORT_0.pdf.

Elden, Stuart. "Missing the Point: Globalization, Deterritorialization and the Space of the World." *Transactions of the Institute of British Geographers* 30, no. 1 (2005): 8–19.

Eliot, T. S. *The Waste Land and Other Poems.* New York: Harcourt Brace and Company, 1934.

Ellingwood, Ken, and Alex Renderos, "Massacre Leaves 27 Dead in Northern Guatemala." *Los Angeles Times,* May 15, 2011. http://articles.latimes.com/2011/may/15/world/la-fg-guatemala-massacre-20110516.

Eng, David L., and David Kazanjian, eds. *Loss: The Politics of Mourning.* Berkeley: University of California Press, 2003.

Equipo de Reflexion, Investigacion y Comunicación (ERIC), Instituto de Encuestos y Sondeo de Comunicacion (IDESCO), Instituto de Investigaciones Economicas y Sociales (IDIES), and Instituto Universitario de Opinion Publica (IUDOP). *Maras y Pandillas en Centroamerica.* Vols. 1 and 4. Managua, Nicaragua: UCA Publicaciones, 2001.

Ettlinger, Nancy. "Precarity Unbound." *Alternatives* 32 (2007): 319–340.

Fanon, Frantz. *Black Skin, White masks.* Translated by Richard Philcox. New York: Grove Press, 1952.

———. *The Wretched of the Earth.* Translated by Richard Philcox. New York: Grove Press, 1963.

Farah, Douglas. *The Transformation of El Salvador's Gangs into Political Actors.* Washington, DC: Center for Strategic and International Studies, 2012. https://csis-prod.s3.amazonaws.com/s3fs-public/legacy_files/files/publication/120621_Farah_Gangs_HemFocus.pdf.

Farmer, Paul. *AIDS and Accusation: Haiti and the Geography of Blame*. Berkeley: University of California Press, 1992.

————. "On Suffering and Structural Violence: A View from Below." *Daedalus* 125, no. 1 (1996): 261–283.

Feldman, Allen. *Formations of Violence: The Narrative of the Body and Political Terror in Northern Ireland*. Chicago: University of Chicago Press, 1991.

————. "Ethnographic States of Emergency." In *Fieldwork Under Fire: Contemporary Studies of Violence and Survival*, edited by Carolyn Nordstrom and Antonius C. G. M. Robben, 224–252. Berkeley: University of California Press, 1995.

Figueroa Ibarra, Carlos. "Guatemala: El recurso del miedo." *Nueva Sociedad* 105 (1990): 108–117.

Fleisher, Mark S. *Warehousing Violence*. Newbury Park, CA: Sage Publications, 1989.

Fogelbach, Juan J. "Gangs, Violence, and Victims in El Salvador, Guatemala, and Honduras." *San Diego International Law Journal* 12, no. 2 (2010): 417–462.

Fontes, Anthony W. "Extorted Life: Protection Rackets in Guatemala City." *Public Culture* 28, no. 3 (2016): 593–616.

Fontes, Anthony W., and K. O'Neill. "*La Visita*: Prisons and Survival in Guatemala. *Journal of Latin American Studies* (forthcoming).

Foucault, Michel. *Discipline and Punish: The Birth of the Prison*. Translated by Alan Sheridan. New York: Vintage Books, 1977.

————. *The History of Sexuality*. Translated by Robert Hurley. New York: Pantheon Books, 1978.

————. "Of Other Spaces." Translated by Jay Miskowiec. *Diacritics* 16, no. 1 (Spring 1986): 22–27.

————. *Society Must Be Defended: Lectures at the Collège de France 1975–76*. Edited by Mauro Bertani and Alessandro Fontana. Translated by David Macey. New York: Picador, 2003.

————. *Security, Territory, Population: Lectures at the Collège de France, 1977–1978*. Edited by Michel Senellart. Translated by Graham Burchell. New York: Palgrave Macmillan, 2007.

Franco, Jean. "Killing Priests, Nuns, Women, Children." In *Violence in War and Peace: An Anthology*. Edited by Nancy Scheper-Hughes and Philippe Bourgois, 196–199. Oxford: Blackwell Publishing, 2004.

————. *Cruel Modernity*. Durham, NC: Duke University Press, 2013.

Fregoso, Rosa-Linda, and Cynthia Berajano, eds. *Terrorizing Women: Feminicide in the Americas*. Durham, NC: Duke University Press, 2010.

Freud, Sigmund. "Instincts and Their Vicissitudes." In *The Standard Edition of the Complete Psychological Works of Sigmund Freud*, translated by James Strachey, 117–130. London: Hogarth Press and the Institute of Psycho-Analysis, 1953.

————. *Civilization and Its Discontents*. Translated by James Strachey. New York: W. W. Norton & Company, 1961.

————. *Group Psychology*. Translated by James Strachey. New York: W. W. Norton & Company, 1961.

Friis, Simone Molin. "'Beyond Anything We Have Ever Seen': Beheading Videos and the Visibility of Violence in the War against ISIS." *International Affairs* 91, no. 4 (2015): 725–746.

Fujii, Lee Ann. "Research Ethics 101: Dilemmas and Responsibilities." *PS: Political Science and Politics* 45, no. 4 (2012): 717–723.

Gadda, Carlo Emilio. *That Awful Mess on the Via Merulana*. Translated by William Weaver. New York: New York Review Books Classics, 2007.

Gagne, David. "InSight Crime's 2016 Homicide Round-up." InSight Crime, January 16, 2017. www.insightcrime.org/news-analysis/insight-crime-2016-homicide-round-up.

Galtung, Johan. "Violence, Peace, and Peace Research." *Journal of Peace Research* 6, no. 3 (1969): 167–191.

Gambetta, Diego. *The Sicilian Mafia: the Business of Private Protection*. Cambridge, MA: Harvard University Press: 1996.

———. *Codes of the Underworld: How Criminals Communicate*. Princeton, NJ: Princeton University Press, 2011.

Garces, Chris. "Denuding Surveillance at the Carceral Boundary." *South Atlantic Quarterly* 113, no. 3 (2014): 447–473.

Garces, Chris, Tomas Martin, and Sacha Darke, "Informal Prison Dynamics in Africa and Latin America." *Criminal Justice Matters* 91, no. 1 (2013): 26–27.

Garland, David. *The Culture of Control: Crime and Social Order in Contemporary Society*. Chicago: Chicago University Press, 2001.

Geertz, C. "Deep Hanging Out." *New York Review of Books* 45, no. 16 (1998): 69–72.

Gilmore, Ruth. *Golden Gulag: Prisons, Surplus, Crisis, and Opposition in Globalizing California*. Berkeley: University of California Press, 2007.

Girard, René. *Violence and the Sacred*. Translated by Patrick Gregory. Baltimore, MD: Johns Hopkins University Press, 1977.

Godoy, Angelina Snodgrass. "Lynchings and the Democratization of Terror in Postwar Guatemala: Implications for Human Rights." *Human Rights Quarterly* 24, no. 3 (2002): 640–661.

———. "When 'Justice' Is Criminal: Lynchings in Contemporary Latin America." *Theory and Society* 33, no. 6 (2004): 621–651.

Goduka, Ivy N. "Ethics and Politics of Field Research in South Africa." *Social Problems* 37, no. 3 (1990): 329–340.

Goffman, Alice. *On the Run: Fugitive Life in an American City*. London: University of Chicago Press, 2014.

Goffman, Erwin. *Asylums: Essays on the Social Situation of Mental Patients and Other Inmates*. Garden City, NY: Anchor Books, 1961.

Goldman, Francisco. *The Art of Political Murder: Who Killed the Bishop?* New York: Grove Press, 2007.

Goldstein, Daniel M. *Outlawed: Between Security and Rights in a Bolivian City*. Durham, NC: Duke University Press, 2012.

Gramsci, Antonio. *Selections from the Prison Notebooks of Antonio Gramsci*. Translated by Q. Hoare and G. Nowell-Smith. New York: International, 1971.

Grandin, Greg. *The Last Colonial Massacre: Latin America in the Cold War*. Chicago: University of Chicago Press, 2004.

⸻. "Living in Revolutionary Time: Coming to Terms with the Violence of Latin America's Long Cold War." In *A Century of Revolution: Insurgent and Counterinsurgent Violence during Latin America's Long Cold War*, edited by Greg Grandin and Gilbert M. Joseph, 1–44. Durham, NC: Duke University Press, 2010.

Grandin, Greg, Deborah T. Levenson, and Elizabeth Oglesby, eds. *The Guatemala Reader*. Durham, NC: Duke University Press, 2011.

Grassi, Paolo. "Territorial Conflicts and Gangs in Guatemala." *Etnografia e ricerca qualitative* 7, no. 3 (2014): 445–462.

Green, Linda. *Living in a State of Fear*. New York: Columbia University Press, 1998.

⸻. *Fear as a Way of Life: Mayan Widows in Rural Guatemala*. New York: Columbia University Press, 2010.

Gregory, Derek. *The Colonial Present*. New York: Blackwell, 2006.

Guatemala Human Rights Commission (GHRC). "Guatemala's Elite Special Forces Unit: The Kaibiles." Fact Sheet. GHRC-USA. Accessed May 18, 2018. http://ghrc-usa.org/Publications/factsheet_kaibiles.pdf.

⸻. "Guatemala's Femicide Law: Progress Against Impunity?" GHRC-USA, 2009. www.ghrc-usa.org/wp-content/uploads/2012/01/Guatemalas-Femicide-Law-Progress-Against-Impunity.pdf.

Gupta, Akhil, and James Ferguson. "Beyond 'Culture': Space, Identity, and the Politics of Difference." *Cultural Anthropology* 7, no. 1 (1992): 6–23.

Gusterson, H. "Ethnographic Research." In *Qualitative Methods in International Relations*, 93–113. London: Palgrave Macmillan, 2008.

Gutiérrez, Édgar. "Guatemala fuera de control: La Cicig y la lucha contra la impunidad." *Nueva Sociedad* 263 (2016): 81–95.

Gutierrez Rivera, Lirio. *Territories of Violence: State, Marginal Youth, and Public Security in Honduras*. New York: Palgrave Macmillan, 2013.

Gutmann, Matthew C. *The Meanings of Macho: Being a Man in Mexico City*. 10th anniv. ed. Berkeley: University of California Press, 2007.

Hackford, Taylor, dir. *Blood in, Blood Out*. Hollywood Pictures, Touchwood Pacific Partners, Vato De Atole Productions, 1993.

Hacking, Ian, and S. Morton. "Making Up People." In *Reconstructing Individualism: Autonomy, Individuality, and the Self in Western Thought*, edited by T.C. Heller, M. Sosna, D.E. Wellbery, A.I. Davidson, A. Swidler, and I. Watt, 222–236. Stanford, CA: Stanford University Press, 1986.

Hagedorn, John M. "Globalization, Gangs, and Collaborative Research." In *The Eurogang Paradox: Street Gangs and Youth Groups in the U.S. and Europe*, edited by Malcolm W. Klein, Hans-Jürgen Kerner, Cheryl L. Maxson, and Elmar G.M. Weitekamp, 41–58. Norwell, MA: Kluwer Academic, 2001.

———. *A World of Gangs: Armed Young Men and Gangsta Culture*. Minneapolis: University of Minnesota Press, 2008.

———. "Making sense of Central America Maras." *Gang Research*. Accessed September 2, 2010. www.gangresearch.net/Archives/hagedorn/mara.pdf.

Hale, Charles R. "Does Multiculturalism Menace? Governance, Cultural Rights, and the Politics of Identity in Guatemala." *Journal of Latin American Studies* 34, no. 3 (2002): 485–524.

———. *Más que un Indio = More Than an Indian: Racial Ambivalence and Neoliberal Multiculturalism in Guatemala*. Santa Fe, NM: School of American Research Press, 2006.

Hansen, Thomas Blom, and Finn Stepputat, eds. *Sovereign Bodies: Citizens, Migrants, and States in the Postcolonial World*. Princeton, NJ: Princeton University Press, 2009.

Harvey, David. *A Brief History of Neoliberalism*. New York: Oxford University Press, 2005.

———. *Spaces of Global Capitalism*. New York: Verso, 2006.

———. "Space as Keyword." In *David Harvey: A Critical Reader*, edited by Noel Castree and Derek Gregory, 270–293. Malden, MA: Blackwell, 2006.

Helfand, Duke. "Anti-gang Czar for L.A. Is Chosen." *Los Angeles Times*, June 20, 2007. . http://articles.latimes.com/2007/jun/20/local/me-gang20.

Herrera, Paola. "Identifican a testigo." *Prensa Libre*, June 30, 2017, 4.

Hobbes, Thomas. *Leviathan*. 1651. Reprint. New York: Penguin Classics, 1985.

Hoffman, D. (2005). "West-African Warscapes: Violent Events as Narrative Blocs; the Disarmament at Bo, Sierra Leone." *Anthropological Quarterly* 78, no. 2 (2005): 329–353.

Huggins, Martha K. "Urban Violence and Police Privatisation in Brazil: Blended Invisibility." *Social Justice* 27, no. 2 (2000): 113–134.

Huhn, Sebastian, Anika Oettler, and Peter Peetz. "Exploding Crime? Topic Management in Central American Newspapers." GIGA Working Paper no. 33, 2006.

Hume, Mo. 2009. *The Politics of Violence: Gender, Conflict, and Community in El Salvador*. Malden, MA: Wiley, 2009.

International Center for Transnational Justice (ICTJ). "ICTJ: Conviction of Ríos Montt on Genocide a Victory for Justice in Guatemala, and Everywhere." ICTJ, April 18, 2013. www.ictj.org/news/ictj-conviction-rios-montt-genocide-victory-justice-guatemala-and-everywhere.

Interpeace. *Violentas y violentadas: Relaciones de gónero en las maras Salvatrucha y Barrio 18 del triángulo norte de Centroamórica*. Guatemala City: Interpeace, 2013. www .interpeace.org/resource/violentas-y-violentadas/.

Irwin, John. *The Felon*. Englewood Cliffs, NJ: Prentice Hall, 1970.

———. *Prisons in Turmoil*. Boston: Little Brown, 1980.

———. *The Jail*. Berkeley: University of California Press, 1985.

———. *The Warehouse Prison: Disposal of the New Dangerous Class*. Los Angeles: Roxbury Publishing, 2005.

Jankowski, Martín Sánchez. *Islands in the Street: Gangs and American Urban Society.* Berkley: University of California Press, 1991.

Joyce, Katie L. "Stars, Dragons, and the Letter M: Consequential Symbols in California Prison Gang Policy." *California Law Review* 104, no. 3 (2016): 733.

Jütersonke, Oliver, Robert Muggah, and Dennis Rodgers. "Gangs, Urban Violence, and Security Interventions in Central America." *Security Dialogue* 40, nos. 4–5 (2009): 373–397.

Kalyvas, Stathis N. *The Logic of Violence in Civil War.* New York: Cambridge University Press, 2006.

Kalyvas, Stathis N., Ian Shapiro, and Tarek Masoud, eds. *Order, Conflict, and Violence.* New York: Cambridge University Press, 2008.

Kinzer, Stephen. *Overthrow: America's Century of Regime Change from Hawaii to Iraq.* New York: Henry Holt and Company, 2006.

———. *The Brothers: John Foster Dulles, Allen Dulles, and Their Secret World War.* New York: Time Books/Henry Holt and Company, 2013.

Kleinman, Arthur, Veena Das, and Margaret Lock, eds. *Social Suffering.* Berkeley: University of California Press, 1997.

Koonings, Kees, and Dirk Kruijit, eds. *Societies of Fear: The Legacy of Civil War, Violence, and Terror in Latin America.* London: Zed Books, 1999.

Kosek, Jake. *Understories: The Political Life of Forests in Northern New Mexico.* Durham, NC: Duke University Press, 2006.

Kristeva, Julia. *Pouvoirs de l'horreur: Essai sur l'abjection.* New York: Columbia University Press, 1982.

Kurtenbach, Sabine. "Youth Violence as a Scapegoat: Youth in Post-War Guatemala." Social and Political Fractures after Wars: Youth Violence in Cambodia and Guatemala Project Working Paper no. 5, Institute for Development and Peace, University of Duisberg-Essen, Diusberg, 2008.

Laclau, Ernesto, and Chantal Mouffe. *Hegemony and Socialist Strategy: Towards a Radical Democratic Politics.* Translated by Winston Moore and Paul Cammack. London: Verso, 1985.

Lancaster, Roger N. *Life is Hard: Machismo, Danger, and the Intimacy of Power in Nicaragua.* Berkeley: University of California Press, 1992.

Laplante, Lisa J. "Memory Battles: Guatemala's Public Debates and the Genocide Trial of Jose Efrain Rios Montt." *Quinnipiac Law Review* 32, no. 3 (2013): 621–673.

Leeuw, Frans, and Jos Vaessen. "Address the Attribution Problem." In *Impact Evaluations and Development: NONIE Guidance on Impact Evaluation,* by Frans Leeuw and Jos Vaessen, 21–34. Washington, DC: The Network of Networks on Impact Evaluation (NONIE), 2009. http://siteresources.worldbank.org/EXTOED /Resources/chap4.pdf.

Lefebvre, Henri. *The Production of Space.* 1974. Reprint. Cambridge, MA: Blackwell, 1991.

———. *The Urban Revolution.* Translated by Robert Bononno. Minneapolis: University of Minnesota Press, 2003. First published 1970.

Lessing, Benjamin. "A Hole at the Center of the State: Prison Gangs and the Limits of Punitive Power." CDDRL Working Papers no. 143, Stanford University, Stanford, CA, 2013.

Levenson, Deborah. "Por sí mismos: Un estudio preliminar des las 'maras' en la ciudad de Guatemala." Cuaderno de Investigación no. 4. Guatemala: Asociación para el Avance de las Ciencias Sociales en Guatemala (AVANCSO), 1990.

———. *Trade Unionists against Terror: Guatemala City, 1954–1985*. Chapel Hill: University of North Carolina Press, 1994.

———. *Adiós Niño: The Gangs of Guatemala City and the Politics of Death*. Durham, NC: Duke University Press, 2013.

Levi, Primo. *The Drowned and the Saved*. Translated by Raymond Rosenthal. New York: Simon & Schuster, 1988.

Lévinas, Emmanuel. *Totality and Infinity: An Essay on Exteriority*. Translated by Alphonso Lingis. Pittsburgh, PA: Duquesne University Press, 1969.

Levi-Strauss, Claude. "Introduction à l'oeuvre de Marcel Mauss." In *Sociologie et anthropologie*, by Marcel Mauss, IX–LII. Paris: Presses universitó de France, 1950.

Lewis, Jeff. *Language Wars: The Role of Media and Culture in Global Terror and Political Violence*. London: Pluto Press, 2005.

Linfield, Susie. *The Cruel Radiance: Photography and Political Violence*. Chicago: University of Chicago Press, 2010.

Lukács, György. *History and Class Consciousness: Studies in Marxist Dialectics*. Cambridge, MA: MIT Press, 1971. First published 1920.

Lutz, Catherine A., and Lila Abu-Lughod. *Language and the Politics of Emotion*. New York: Cambridge University Press, 1990.

Macaulay, Fiona. "Knowledge Production, Framing and Criminal Justice Reform in Latin America." *Journal of Latin American Studies* 39, no. 3 (2007): 627–651.

Malkin, Elisabeth. "Ex-Dictator Is Ordered to Trial in Guatemalan War Crimes Case." *New York Times*, January 29, 2013.

Malkki, Liisa H. *Purity and Exile: Violence, Memory, and National Cosmology among Hutu Refugees in Tanzania*. Chicago: University of Chicago Press, 1995.

Mannheim, Karl. *Ideology and Utopia*. Translated from the German by Louis Wirth and Edward Shils. New York: Harcourt, Brace and Company, 1936.

Manwaring, Max G. *Street Gangs: The New Urban Insurgency*. Carlisle Barracks, PA: Strategic Studies Institute, US Army War College, 2005.

Manz, Beatriz. *Paradise in Ashes: A Guatemalan Journey of Courage, Terror, and Hope*. Berkeley: University of California Press, 2004.

———. "Central American (Guatemala, Honduras, El Salvador, Nicaragua): Patterns of Human Rights Violations." United Nations High Commissioner for Refugees, Status Determination and Protection Information Section (DIPS), 2008.

———. "The Continuum of Violence in Post-war Guatemala." *Social Analysis: the International Journal of Social and Cultural Practice* 52, no. 2 (2008): 151–164.

Markon, Jerry, and Joshua Partlow. "Unaccompanied Children Crossing Southern Border in Greater Numbers Again, Raising Fears of New Migrant Crisis." *Wash-*

ington Post, December 16, 2015. www.washingtonpost.com/news/federal-eye
/wp/2015/12/16/unaccompanied-children-crossing-southern-border-in-greater
-numbers-again-raising-fears-of-new-migrant-crisis/?utm_term=.40ee7179a685.

Martinez, Carlos, and José Luis Sanz. "El origen del odio." *El Faro*, August 6, 2012. www.salanegra.elfaro.net/es/201208/cronicas/9301/.

———. "El día de la traición." *El Faro*, November 11, 2012. www.salanegra.elfaro.net
/es/201211/cronicas/10145/.

Marx, Karl. *Capital: A Critique of Political Economy.* Vol. 1. 1867. Reprinted with translation by Ben Fowkes and introduction by Ernest Mandel. Harmondsworth, UK: Penguin Books, 1976.

Marx, Karl, and Friedrich Engels. *The German Ideology.* 3rd rev. ed. Moscow: Progress Publishers, 1970. Originally published 1845–1849.

Mbembe, Achille. "Necropolitics." *Public Culture* 15 (Winter 2003): 110–140.

McDonald, Mike. "Caging in Central America." *Global Post*, May 14, 2012. www.global post.com/dispatch/news/regions/americas/120513/honduras-prison-fire-central -america-jail-crisis.

McKirdy, Euan. "UNHCR Report: More Displaced Now Than after WWII." CNN, June 20, 2016. www.cnn.com/2016/06/20/world/unhcr-displaced-peoples-report /index.html.

Medina, Juanjo, Pedro Mateu-Gelabert, and Demoscopía. *Maras y pandillas, comunidad y policía en Centroamérica: Hallazgos de un estudio integral* [Gangs, community and police in Central America]. San José, Costa Rica: Demoscopía, 2007.

Meister, Robert. *After Evil: A Politics of Human Rights.* New York: Columbia University Press, 2011.

Merino, Juan. "Las maras en Guatemala." In *Maras y Pandillas en Centroamerica*, edited by ERIC, IDESO, IDIES, and IUDOP, 1:109–118. Managua, Nicaragua: UCA Publicaciones, 2001.

Ministerio Publico de Guatemala. "La Extorsion." n.d.

Moodie, Ellen. *El Salvador in the Aftermath of Peace: Crime, Uncertainty, and the Transition to Democracy.* Philadelphia: University of Pennsylvania Press, 2010.

Moran, Dominique. "Carceral Geography and the Spatialities of Prison Visiting: Visitation, Recidivism, and Hyperincarceration." *Environment and Planning D: Society and Space* 31, no. 1 (2013): 174–190.

———. *Carceral Geography: Spaces and Practices of Incarceration.* Surrey, UK: Ashgate Publishing, 2015.

Moser, Caroline, and Ailsa Winton. "Violence in the Central American Region: Towards an Integrated Framework for Violence Reduction." Overseas Development Institute Working Paper no. 171, London, 2002.

Moser, Caroline O. N., and Cathy McIlwaine. *Encounters with Violence in Latin America: Urban Poor Perceptions from Colombia and Guatemala.* New York: Routledge, 2004.

Müller, Markus-Michael. "The Rise of the Penal State in Latin America." *Contemporary Justice Review* 15, no. 1 (2012): 57–76.

————. "Punitive Entanglements: The "War on Gangs" and the Making of a Transnational Penal Apparatus in the Americas." *Geopolitics* 20, no. 3 (2015): 696–727.

Muñoz, Marta. "Asesinan a Marero." *Nuestro Diario*, September 19, 2011, 2.

Musalo, Karen, Elisabeth Pellegrin, and S. Shawn Roberts. "Crimes without Punishment: Violence against Women in Guatemala." *Hastings Women's Law Journal* 21, no. 2 (2010): 161–221.

Myrna Mack Foundation. *La discriminación de la inefable realidad a su punibilidad en Guatemala*. Guatemala: Myrna Mack Foundation, 2006.

Nelson, Diane M. *A Finger in the Wound: Body Politics in Quincentennial Guatemala*. Berkeley: University of California Press, 1999.

————. *Reckoning: the Ends of War in Guatemala*. Durham, NC: Duke University Press, 2009.

————. *Who Counts? The Mathematics of Death and Life after Genocide*. Durham, NC: Duke University Press, 2015.

New York Times Editorial Board. "When Did Caging Kids Become the Art of the Deal?" *New York Times*, June 18, 2018. https://www.nytimes.com/2018/06/18/opinion/trump-children-border-immigration-nielsen.html.

Nietzsche, Friedrich. *Thus Spake Zarathustra*. Translated by R. J. Hollingdale. London: Penguin Classics, 1969.

————. *Beyond Good and Evil*. Translated by Walter Kauffman. New York: Vintage Books, 1989.

————. *Genealogy of Morals*. Translated by Walter Kauffman. New York: Vintage Books, 1989.

Nordstrom, Carolyn. *A Different Kind of War Story*. Philadelphia: University of Pennsylvania Press, 1997.

————. *Global Outlaws: Crime, Money, and Power in the Contemporary World*. Berkeley: University of California Press, 2007.

Oglesby, Elizabeth. "Educating Citizens in Postwar Guatemala: Historical Memory, Genocide, and the Culture of Peace." *Radical History Review* no. 97 (2007): 77–98.

Oglesby, Elizabeth, and Amy Ross. "Guatemala's Genocide Determination and the Spatial Politics of Justice." *Space and Polity* 13, no. 1 (April 2009): 21–39.

O'Neill, Kevin Lewis. "The Reckless Will: Prison Chaplaincy and the Problem of Mara Salvatrucha." *Public Culture* 22, no. 1 (2010): 67–88.

————. *Secure the Soul: Christian Piety and Gang Prevention in Guatemala*. Oakland: University of California Press, 2015.

O'Neill, Kevin Lewis, and Anthony W. Fontes. "Making Do: The Practice of Imprisonment in Postwar Guatemala." *Journal of Latin American Geography* 16, no. 2 (2017): 31–48.

O'Neill, Kevin Lewis, and Kedron Thomas, eds. *Securing the City: Neoliberalism, Space, and Insecurity in Postwar Guatemala*. Durham, NC: Duke University Press, 2011.

Oppenheimer, Joshua, and Christine Cynn, dirs. *The Act of Killing*. Final Cut for Real, Docwest, 2012.

Ordoñez, Edison Roderico Tello. "Planificación de una granja modelo de rehabilitación penal: la rehabilitación en el sistema penitenciario." PhD diss., Universidad de San Carlos de Guatemala, 2007.

Organization of American States. *OAS Peace Security Democracy Development*. Washington, DC: OAS, 2012. www.oas.org/docs/publications/OAS-Peace-Security -Democracy-Development.pdf.

Pan American Health Organization. *Interpersonal Youth Violence in Latin America and the English-Speaking Caribbean*. Washington, DC: World Health Organization, 2015. iris.paho.org/xmlui/handle/123456789/10018.

Peacock, Susan, and Andrea Beltran. *Poderes Ocultos: Grupos ilegales armados en la Guatemala post conflicto y las fuerzas detrás de ellos*. Washington, DC: Washington Office on Latin America (WOLA), 2004.

Pearce, Jenny. "Perverse State Formation and Securitized Democracy in Latin America." *Democratization* 17, no. 2 (2010): 286–386.

Pew Research Center. "Historical Overview of Pentecostalism in Guatemala." Pew Research Center, Religion & Public Life, October 5, 2006. www.pewforum .org/2006/10/05/historical-overview-of-pentecostalism-in-guatemala/.

Pine, Adrienne. *Working Hard, Drinking Hard: On Violence and Survival in Honduras*. Berkeley: University of California Press, 2008.

Portelli, Alessandro. *The Death of Luigi Trastulli, and Other Stories: Form and Meaning in Oral History*. Albany: State University of New York Press, 1991.

Pred, Allen. *The Past Is Not Dead: Facts, Fictions, and Enduring Racial Stereotypes*. Minneapolis, MN: University of Minnesota Press, 2004.

————. "Situated Ignorance and State Terrorism: Silences, WMD, Collective Amnesia, and the Manufacture of Fear." In *Violent Geographies: Fear, Terror, and Political Violence*, edited by Derek Gregory and Allen Pred, 363–384. New York: Routledge, 2007.

Rabe, Stephen. *The Killing Zone: The United State Wages Cold War in Latin America*. London: Oxford University Press, 2012.

Radden Keefe, Patrick. "Cocaine Incorporated." *New York Times Magazine*, June 2012. www.nytimes.com/2012/06/17/magazine/how-a-mexican-drug-cartel-makes-its -billions.html.

Rafael, Tony. *The Mexican Mafia*. New York: Encounter Books, 2007.

Renwick, Danielle. *Central America's Violent Northern Triangle*. Washington, DC: Council on Foreign Relations, 2016. www.cfr.org/backgrounder/central-americas -violent-northern-triangle.

Ribando Seelke, Clare. *Gangs in Central America*. Washington DC: Congressional Research Service, 2016.

Robben, Antonius C. G. M. "Ethnographic Seduction, Transference, and Resistance in Dialogues about Terror and Violence in Argentina." *Ethos* 24, no. 1 (1996): 71–106.

Rocha, José Luis. "Mareros y pandilleros: ¿Nuevos insurgentes, criminales?" *Envío*, no. 293 (2006): 39–51.

Rodgers, Dennis. "'We Live in a State of Siege': Violence, Crime, and Gangs in Post-Conflict Urban Nicaragua." Development Studies Institute (DESTIN) Working

Paper Series no. 02-36, London School of Economics and Political Science, London, 2002.

———. "'Disembedding' the City: Crime, Insecurity, and Spatial Organization in Managua, Nicaragua." *Environment and Urbanization* 16, no. 2 (2004): 113–123.

———. "Living in the Shadow of Death: Gangs, Violence and Social Order in Urban Nicaragua, 1996–2002." *Journal of Latin American Studies* 38, no. 2 (2006): 267–292.

———. "Slum Wars of the 21st Century: Gangs, Mano Dura and the New Urban Geography of Conflict in Central America." *Development and Change* 40, no. 5 (2009): 949–976.

Rodgers, Dennis, and Gareth Jones, eds. *Youth Violence in Latin America: Gangs and Juvenile Justice in Perspective*. New York: Palgrave Macmillan, 2009.

Rorty, Richard. "Human Rights, Rationality and Sentimentality." In *On Human Rights*, edited by Stephen Shute and Susan Hurley, 112–134. New York: Basic Books, 1993.

Ross, Amy. "The Ríos Montt Case and Universal Jurisdiction." *Journal of Genocide Research* 18, nos. 2–3 (2016): 361–376.

Ross, Jeffrey Ian, ed. *The Globalization of Supermax Prisons*. New Brunswick, NJ: Rutgers University Press, 2013.

Sacchetti, Maria, and Nick Miroff. "How Trump Is Building a Border Wall That No One Can See: While the White House Fights Court Orders Seeking to Halt the President's Agenda, Key Advisers Are Finding Ways to Shrink Immigration." *Washington Post*, November 21, 2017. www.washingtonpost.com/local/immigra-tion/how-trump-is-building-a-border-wall-no-one-can-see/2017/11/21/83d3b746 -cba0-11e7-b0cf-7689a9f2d84e_story.html?utm_term=.3c8ca73a17d3.

Said, Edward W. *Orientalism*. Harmondsworth, UK: Penguin Books, 1985.

Salvatore, Ricardo D., and Carlos Aguirre. *The Birth of the Penitentiary in Latin America: Essays on Criminology, Prison Reform and Social Control, 1830–1940*. Austin: University of Texas Press, 1996.

Sanford, Victoria. "The 'Grey Zone' of Justice: NGOs and Rule of Law in Postwar Guatemala." *Journal of Human Rights* 2, no. 3 (September 2003): 393–-405.

———. *Buried Secrets: Truth and Human Rights in Guatemala*. New York: Palgrave Macmillan, 2003.

———. "From Genocide to Feminicide: Impunity and Human Rights in Twenty-First Century Guatemala." *Journal of Human Rights* 7, no. 2 (June 2008): 104–122.

Sanz, Jose Luis, and Carlos Martinez. "Los Maras de Centro America." Foro del Periodismo, May 2012, El Marte, San Salvador.

Sartre, Jean-Paul. *Being and Nothingness: A Phenomenological Essay on Ontology*. New York: Washington Square Press, 1956.

Saunders-Hastings, Katherine. "'Los Códigos de Antes': Insecurity, Nostalgia, and Community Experience in Mara Territory." Paper presented at Latin American Studies Association Annual Conference, Chicago, IL, June 2014.

Scarry, Elaine. *The Body in Pain: the Making and Unmaking of the World*. New York: Oxford University Press, 1985.

Scheper-Hughes, Nancy. *Death Without Weeping: The Violence of Everyday Life in Brazil*. Berkeley: University of California Press, 1992.

———. "Who's the Killer? Popular Justice and Human Rights in a South African Squatter Camp." *Social Justice* 22, no. 3 (1995): 143–164.

Scheper-Hughes, Nancy, and Philippe Bourgois, eds. *Violence in War and Peace, an Anthology*. Malden, MA: Blackwell Publishing, 2004.

Schmitt, Carl. *Nomos of the Earth in International Law and Jus Publicum Europaeum*. New York: Telos Press, 2006.

Scott, James C. *Weapons of the Weak: Everyday Forms of Peasant Resistance*. New Haven, CT: Yale University Press, 1985.

———. *Seeing Like a State*. New Haven, CT: Yale University Press, 1998.

Shifter, Michael. *Countering Criminal Violence in Central America*. Washington, DC: Council on Foreign Relations, 2012. www.cfr.org/sites/default/files/pdf/2012/03/Criminal_Violence_CSR64.pdf.

Sieder, Rachel. "War, Peace, and the Politics of Memory in Guatemala." In *Burying the Past: Making Peace and Doing Justice after Civil Conflict*, edited by Nigel Biggar, 209–234. Washington, DC: Georgetown University Press, 2003.

———. "Contested Sovereignties: Indigenous Law, Violence and State Effects in Postwar Guatemala." *Critique of Anthropology* 31, no. 3 (2011): 161–184.

———. "Building Mayan Authority and Autonomy: The 'Recovery' of Indigenous Law in Post-peace Guatemala." In *Studies in Law, Politics, and Society*, 43–75. Bingley, UK: Emerald Group Publishing Limited, 2011.

Simon, Jonathan. "The 'Society of Captives' in the Era of Hyper-incarceration." *Theoretical Criminology* 4, no. 3 (2000): 285–308.

Skarbek, David. *The Social Order of the Underworld: How Prison Gangs Govern the American Penal System*. New York: Oxford University Press, 2014.

Sontag, Susan. *Regarding the Pain of Others*. New York: Farrar, Straus and Giroux, 2003.

Sorel, Georges. *Reflections on Violence*. Edited by Jeremy Jennings. New York: Cambridge University Press, 1999.

Soyinka, Wole. *The Burden of Memory, the Muse of Forgiveness*. New York: Oxford University Press, 1999.

Sparke, Matthew B. "A Neoliberal Nexus: Economy, Security and the Biopolitics of Citizenship on the Border." *Political Geography* 25, no. 2 (2006): 151–180.

Spivak, Gayatri Chakravorty. "'Can the Subaltern Speak?': Revised Edition, from the 'History' Chapter of *Critique of Postcolonial Reason*." In *Can the Subaltern Speak? Reflections on the History of an Idea*, edited by Rosalind C. Morris, 21–78. New York: Columbia University Press, 2010.

Sridhar, Archana. "Tax Reform and Promoting a Culture of Philanthropy: Guatemala's 'Third Sector' in an Era of Peace." *Fordham International Law Journal* 31, no. 1 (2007): 186–229.

Stoler, Ann Laura. *Carnal Knowledge and Imperial Power: Gender, Race, and Morality in Colonial Asia*. Oxford: Oxford University Press, 2002.

Stone, Hannah, and Miriam Wells. "Zetas to Face Trial for 2011 Farm Massacre in Guatemala." InSight Crime, March 1, 2013. www.insightcrime.org/news/brief /zetas-to-face-trial-for-2011-farm-massacre-in-guatemala/.

Strauss, Scott. *The Order of Genocide: Race, Power, and War in Rwanda.* Ithaca, NY: Cornell University Press, 2006.

Suarez-Orozco, Marcelo M. "The Treatment of Children in the 'Dirty War': Ideology, State Terrorism and the Abuse of Children in Argentina." In *Child Survival. Culture, Illness and Healing,* edited by Nancy Scheper-Hughes, 11:227–246. Dordrecht, Netherlands: Springer, Kluwer, 1987.

Sullivan, John P. "Third Generation Street Gangs: Turf, Cartels, and Net Warriors." *Transnational Organized Crime* 3, no. 3 (1997): 95–108.

Taussig, Michael. "Culture of Terror-Space of Death: Roger Casement's Putumayo Report and the Explanation of Torture." *Comparative Studies in Society and History* 26, no. 3 (1984): 467–497.

———. "Terror as Usual: Walter Benjamin's Theory of History as a State of Siege." *Social Text* 23 (1989): 3–20.

———. *The Nervous System.* New York: Routledge, 1992.

———. *Law in a Lawless Land: Diary of a Limpieza in Colombia.* Chicago: University of Chicago Press, 2003.

Thompson, Heather Ann. *Blood in the Water: The Attica Prison Uprising of 1971 and Its Legacy.* New York: Pantheon Books, 2016.

Thrasher, Frederic M. *The Gang: A Study of 1313 Gangs in Chicago.* Chicago: University of Chicago Press, 1927.

Thrift, Nigel. "Immaculate Warfare? The Spatial Politics of Extreme Violence." In *Violent Geographies: Fear, Terror, and Political Violence,* edited by Derek Gregory and Allan Pred, 273–294. New York: Routledge, 2007.

Tilly, Charles. "War Making and State Making as Organized Crime." In *Violence: A Reader,* edited by Catherine Besteman, 35–60. New York: Palgrave Macmillan, 2002.

———. *The Politics of Collective Violence.* Cambridge, UK: Cambridge University Press, 2003.

Todorov, Tzvetan. *The Conquest of America: The Question of the Other.* Translated by Richard Howard. New York: Harper & Row, 1984.

Tourliere, Mathieu. "La migración no para: Encuentra nuevas rutas." Proceso, December 30, 2016. www.proceso.com.mx/467787/la-migracion-encuentra-nuevas-rutas.

Turner, Victor. "Betwixt and Between: The Liminal Period in Rites of Passage." In *Betwixt and Between: Patterns of Masculine and Feminine Initiation,* edited by Louise Carus Mahdi, Steve Foster, and Meredith Little, 3–19. La Salle, IL: Open Court, 1987.

Ungar, Mark. "Prisons and Politics in Contemporary Latin America." *Human Rights Quarterly* 25, no. 4 (2003): 909–934.

United Nations Development Program (UNPD). *Informe sobre desarollo humano para América Central 2009–2010: Abrir espacios a la seguridad ciudadana y el desarollo humano*. New York: UNDP. Accessed May 15, 2017. www.latinamerica.undp.org /content/dam/rblac/docs/Research%20and%20Publications/Central_America _RHDR_2009-10_ES.pdf.

————. *A Decade of Work on Citizen Security and Conflict Prevention in Latin America and the Caribbean 2001–2010*. Panama City: UNDP Regional Service Centre for Latin America and the Caribbean, 2012. www.undp.org/content/undp/en/home /librarypage/ crisis-prevention-and-recovery/a-decade-of-work-on-citizen-security-and-conflict -prevention-in-.html.

————. *Guatemala: ¿Un país de oportunidades para la juventud?, Informe Nacional de Desarrollo Humano 2011–2012*. Guatemala City, Guatemala: UNDP, 2012. www .gt.undp.org/content/dam/guatemala/docs/publications/UNDP_gt_INDH2011 _2012.pdf.

————. *Understanding Social Conflict in Latin America*. New York: UNDP, 2013. www .undp.org/content/undp/en/home/librarypage/crisis-prevention-and-recovery /Understanding-Social-Conflict-in-Latin-America.html.

United Nations Office on Drugs and Crime (UNODC). *Crime and Development in Central America. Caught in the Crossfire*. New York: United Nations Publications, 2007.

————. *Transnational Organized Crime in the Caribbean and the Americas: a Threat Assessment*. Vienna: UNODC, 2012. www.unodc.org/documents/toc/Reports /TOCTASouthAmerica/English/TOCTA_CACaribb_cocaine_SAmerica_ US.pdf

————. "International Homicide, Count and Rate per 100,000 population (1995– 2011)." 2013. www.unodc.org/documents/data-and-analysis/statistics/crime /Homicide_statistics2013.xls.

————. "International Homicide Count and Rate per 100,000 Population, by Coun-try/Territory (2000–2012)." 2014. www.insightcrime.org/images/PDFs/UNOD Chomicides.pdf.

United States Agency for International Development (USAID). *Central America and Mexico Gang Assessment*. Washington, DC: USAID Bureau for Latin American and Caribbean Affairs, 2006.

Useem, Bert, and Peter Kimball. *States of Siege: U.S. Prison Riots, 1971–1986*. New York: Oxford University Press, 1991.

Vargas Llosa, Mario. *Making Waves*. New York: Farrar, Straus, and Giroux, 1996.

Venkatesh, Sudhir Alladi. *Off the Books: The Underground Economy of the Urban Poor*. Cambridge, MA: Harvard University Press, 2006.

Vogt, W.A. "Crossing Mexico: Structural Violence and the Commodification of Undocumented Central American Migrants." *American Ethnologist* 40, no. 4 (2013): 764–780.

Wacquant, Loïc. 2001. "Deadly Symbiosis: When Ghetto and Prison Meet and Mesh." *Punishment and Society* 3, no. 1 (2001): 95–133.

————. "From Slavery to Mass Incarceration." *New Left Review* 13 (2002): 41–60.

————. "The Militarization of Urban Marginality: Lessons from the Brazilian Metropolis." *International Political Sociology* 2, no. 1 (2008): 56–74.

————. *Punishing the Poor: The Neoliberal Government of Social Insecurity.* Durham, NC: Duke University Press, 2009.

————. "The Body, the Ghetto and the Penal State." *Qualitative Sociology* 32, no. 1 (2009): 101–129.

Ward, Thomas W. *Gangsters Without Borders: An Ethnography of a Salvadoran Street Gang.* New York: Oxford University Press, 2013.

Washington Office on Latin America (WOLA). *Youth Gangs in Central America: Issues in Human Rights, Effective Policing, and Prevention.* Washington, DC: WOLA, 2006. www.wola.org/publications/youth_gangs_in_central_america.

————. *The International Commission Against Impunity in Guatemala: A WOLA Report on the CICIG Experience.* Washington, DC: WOLA, 2015. www.wola.org /analysis/wola-report-on-the-international-commission-against-impunity-in-guat emala-cicig/.

Watts, Michael. "Geographies of Violence and the Narcissism of Minor Differences." In *Struggles Over Geography: Violence, Freedom, and Development at the Millennium,* 7–34. Hettner-Lectures 3. Heidelberg, Germany: Department of Geography, University of Heidelberg, 2000.

Weld, Kirsten. *Paper Cadavers: the Archives of Dictatorship in Guatemala.* Durham, NC: Duke University Press, 2014.

Williams, Raymond. *Marxism and Literature.* Vol. 1. New York: Oxford University Press, 1977.

Wilson, Richard A. *The Politics of Truth and Reconciliation in South Africa: Legitimizing the Post-Apartheid State.* New York: Cambridge University Press, 2001.

Wood, Elisabeth Jean. *Insurgent Collective Action and Civil War in El Salvador.* New York: Cambridge University Press, 2003.

————. "The Social Processes of Civil War: The Wartime Transformation of Social Networks." *Annual Review of Political Science* 11, no. 1 (2008): 539–561.

Woody, Christopher. "Trump: The MS-13 Gang Has Turned 'Peaceful Parks' and 'Quiet Neighborhoods' in the US into 'Blood-stained Killing Fields'." *Business Insider,* July 28, 2017. www.businessinsider.com/trump-ms-13-has-turned-us-into -blood-stained-killing-fields-2017-7.

Wolf, Sonja. "*Maras transnacionales*: Origin and Transformations of Central American Street Gangs." *Latin American Research Review* 45, no. 1 (2010): 256–266.

World Bank Sustainable Development Department, Latin America and Caribbean Region. *Urban Crime and Violence in LAC: Status Report on Activities.* Washington, DC: World Bank, 2008. http://siteresources.worldbank.org/EXTLACREGTO-PURBDEV/Resources/ViolencebrochureFINAL.pdf.

World Bank Sustainable Development Department and Poverty Reduction and Economic Management Unit, Latin America and the Caribbean Region. *Crime and*

Violence in Central America: A Development Challenge. Washington, DC: World Bank, 2011. https://siteresources.worldbank.org/INTLAC/Resources/FINAL _VOLUME_I_ENGLISH_CrimeAndViolence.pdf.

Yagoub, Mimi. "Just One Percent of Guatemala Private Security Guards Operate Legally." InSight Crime, July 14, 2014. www.insightcrime.org/news-briefs/just-one -percent-of-guatemala-private-security-guards-operate-legally.

Zepeda, Andres. "El Salvador de Guatemala." *El periodico,* March 9, 2004. www .elperiodico.com.gt/es/20040903/12/6598/.

———. "Fue un lujo conocer al 'Soldado' y sus 'hommies'." *Albedrío,* September 9, 2004. www.albedrio.org/htm/articulos/a/azepeda-002.htm.

Zilberg, Elana. "Fools Banished from the Kingdom: Remapping Geographies of Gang Violence between the Americas (Los Angeles and San Salvador)." In "Los Angeles and the Future of Urban Cultures," special issue, *American Quarterly* 56, no. 3 (2004): 759–779.

———. "Gangster in Guerilla Face: A Transnational Mirror of Production between the USA and El Salvador." *Anthropological Theory* 7, no. 1 (2007): 37–57.

———. *Space of Detention: The Making of a Transnational Gang Crisis Between Los Angeles and San Salvador.* Durham, NC: Duke University Press, 2011.

Zubillaga, Verónica. "Un testimonio reflexivo sobre la experiencia de construir histo-rias de vida con jóvenes de vida violenta" [A reflexive testimony on the experience of constructing the life histories of youths with violent lifestyles]." *Revista Mexicana de Sociología* 65, no. 2 (2003): 305–338.

INDEX

Figures are indicated by page numbers followed by *fig.* and notes are indicated by page numbers followed by n.